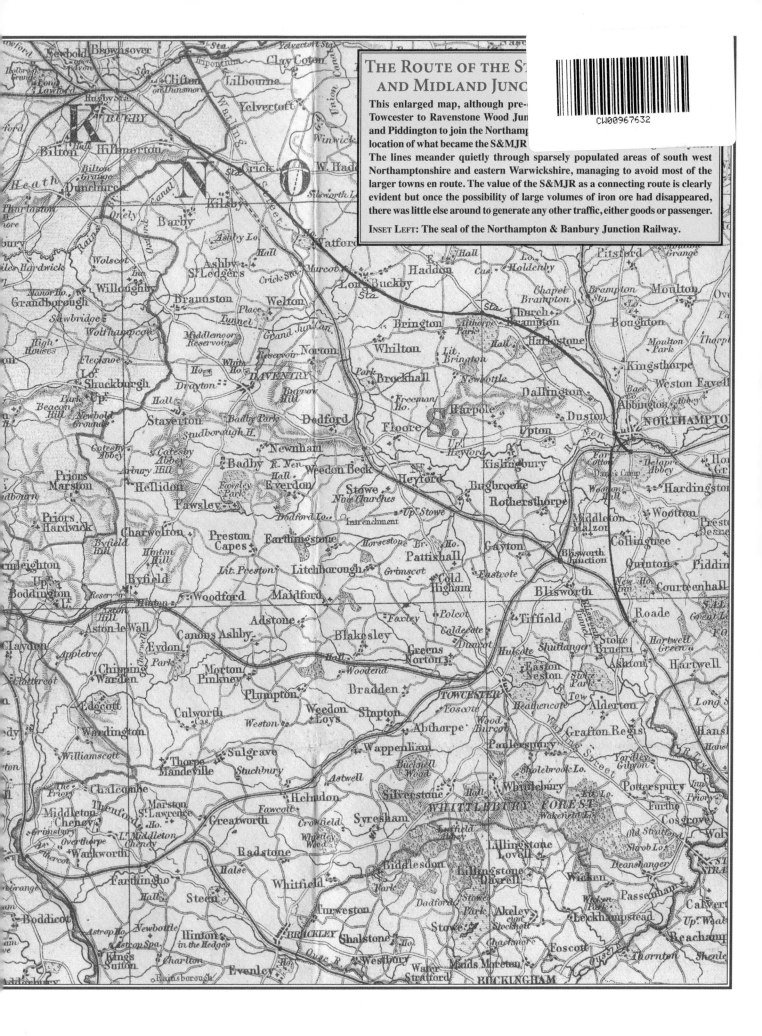

CW00967632

THE ROUTE OF THE S~~...~~
AND MIDLAND JUNC~~...~~

This enlarged map, although pre-~~...~~
Towcester to Ravenstone Wood Jun~~...~~
and Piddington to join the Northamp~~...~~
location of what became the S&MJR ~~...~~
The lines meander quietly through sparsely populated areas of south west
Northamptonshire and eastern Warwickshire, managing to avoid most of the
larger towns en route. The value of the S&MJR as a connecting route is clearly
evident but once the possibility of large volumes of iron ore had disappeared,
there was little else around to generate any other traffic, either goods or passenger.

INSET LEFT: The seal of the Northampton & Banbury Junction Railway.

THE
STRATFORD-UPON-AVON
& MIDLAND JUNCTION
RAILWAY

VOLUME 1
The years before the S&MJR – 1866 to 1909:
The constituent companies

Stratford-on-Avon station from the eastern end of the platform, showing the three-doll signal gantry controlling access to the west. The dominant centre arm was for the Evesham, Stratford & Redditch Junction Railway's line onwards to Binton, Bidford and Broom Junction, whilst the left and right subsidiary arms denoted the routes to the engine shed yard and the siding connection to the Great Western Railway respectively. The new signal box of 1919 is evident at the platform end, whilst the superseded old East & West Junction Railway cabin is obscured by the station building. The unusually wide space between the two platforms is accounted for by the existence of a siding between the running lines during the very earliest years of the line. The small engine shed was located immediately beyond the platform wall on the left of the picture. Finally, note that whilst the official name of the owning company was the Stratford-upon-Avon & Midland Junction Railway, the nameboard called the station Stratford-on-Avon – a legacy presumably, of the E&WJR era – and this distinction will be maintained throughout this history. *Author's collection*

Lightmoor Press

THE STRATFORD-UPON-AVON & MIDLAND JUNCTION RAILWAY

VOLUME 1
The years before the S&MJR – 1866 to 1909:
The constituent companies

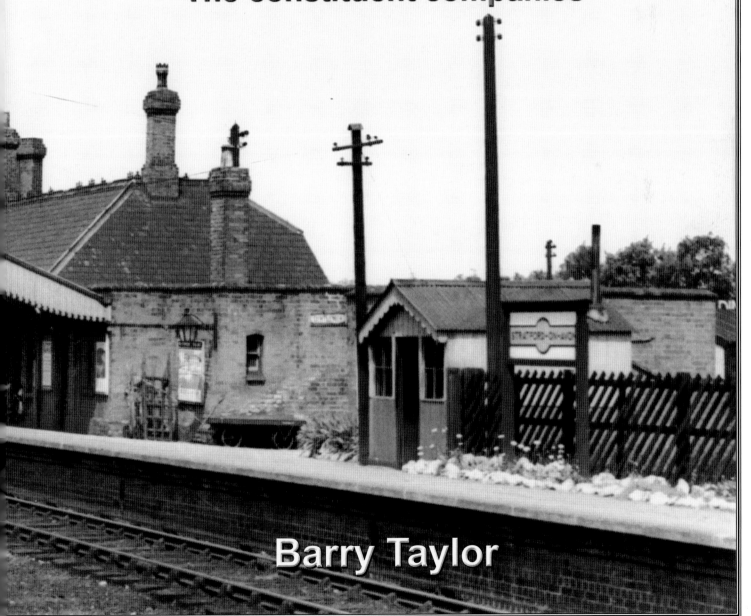

Barry Taylor

S. & M. Junction Rly. Station.

Byfield station building, festooned with ivy and with a couple of members of staff in front, possibly the station master and the signalman, posing for the camera. The picture is not dated but the poster on the left has a July 1909 event advertised on it and is also headed 'Stratford-upon-Avon & Midland Junction Railway'; the two noticeboards on the front of the building have also been fitted with name plaques for the S&MJR. The photograph was thus taken around six months after this East & West Junction Railway station and its owning company had amalgamated with the Stratford, Towcester & Midland Junction Railway to form the Stratford-upon-Avon & Midland Junction Railway, on 1st January 1909; the new ownership is also indicated by the inked notation at the top of this locally produced picture postcard. The final piece of the S&MJR jigsaw, the absorption of the Northampton & Banbury Junction Railway, was completed eighteen months later, on 1st July 1910. *John Alsop collection*

ABBREVIATIONS USED IN THIS VOLUME

E&WJR...........................East & West Junction Railway
ENM&TR&OJR............Easton Neston Mineral & Towcester, Roade & Olney Junction Railway
ER&SJR.........................Evesham, Redditch & Stratford-upon-Avon Junction Railway
GCR..............................Great Central Railway
GWR.............................Great Western Railway
IMCA............................Imperial Mercantile Credit Association
L&NWR........................London & North Western Railway
LD&ECR.......................Lancashire, Derbyshire & East Coast Railway
LYR...............................Lancashire & Yorkshire Railway
MP.................................Member of Parliament
MS&LR.........................Manchester, Sheffield & Lincolnshire Railway
MC&SWJR....................Midland Counties & South Wales Junction Railway
MR................................Midland Railway
N&BJR..........................Northampton & Banbury Junction Railway
NLR...............................North London Railway
NRO...............................Northamptonshire Record Office
PS&NWR.......................Potteries, Shrewsbury & North Wales Railway
R&G...............................Railway & General Company
S&MJR...........................Stratford-upon-Avon & Midland Junction Railway
SDJR...............................Somerset & Dorset Joint Railway
SM&AR............................Swindon, Marlborough & Andover Railway
SSR...................................South Staffordshire Railway
ST&MJR...........................Stratford, Towcester & Midland Junction Railway
TNA..................................The National Archives Kew

Published by LIGHTMOOR PRESS
© Lightmoor Press & Barry Taylor 2017
Designed by Neil Parkhouse

British Library Cataloguing-in-Publication Data. A catalogue record for this book is available from the British Library

ISBN: 9781911038 25 2

All rights reserved. No part of this publication may be reproduced, stored in a retrieval system or transmitted in any form or by any means, electronic, mechanical, photocopying, recording or otherwise, without the written permission of the publisher.

LIGHTMOOR PRESS
Unit 144B,
Harbour Road Trading Estate,
Lydney, Gloucestershire
GL15 5EJ
www.lightmoor.co.uk
info@lightmoor.co.uk
Lightmoor Press is an imprint of Black Dwarf Lightmoor Publications Ltd

Printed in Poland
www.lfbookservices.co.uk

CONTENTS
VOLUME 1: THE CONSTITUENT COMPANIES 1866-1909

INTRODUCTION

A journey along the minor roads and country lanes of south-west Northamptonshire and the eastern part of the adjoining county of Warwickshire, will often reveal unmistakeable traces of long abandoned railway lines. There is a strong possibility that these now overgrown cuttings, embankments and occasional bridges will be on the route of the erstwhile Stratford-upon-Avon & Midland Junction Railway. This railway, popularly remembered as the 'SMJ', once meandered its way from the fringes of Buckinghamshire, in the east, to Shakespeare's Avon, in the west, and also threw off tentacles towards Northampton and Banbury along the way.

The 'SMJ' had been formed by the amalgamation of four even smaller railway companies, the earliest of which was the Northampton & Banbury Junction Railway (N&BJR), opened in 1866 with the expectation of eventually carrying huge volumes of Northamptonshire iron ore to supply the South Wales furnaces. The anticipated volumes did not materialise and financial disaster quickly followed; the N&BJR, having abandoned its grand plans at an early stage, then eked out a spartan existence for the next forty-four years as a much reduced secondary route, almost – but not quite – linking the two towns in its corporate title.

of the Joint Committee into a new company. Old practices, and in many cases personnel, were quickly swept away, operating costs were reduced and waste eliminated, and a new air of efficiency replaced the old habits of the Joint Committee years.

The Stratford-upon-Avon & Midland Junction Railway (S&MJR) came into being on the 1st January 1909 and eighteen months later, the transformation was completed when the N&BJR, having ploughed its lonely, neighbourly furrow since 1866, fell rather resignedly into the arms of the new company. This was a long overdue development, which could probably have occurred many years earlier were it not for the internal wranglings of the Joint Committee.

The inclusion of the N&BJR finally brought the Blisworth to Green's Norton section under a single ownership and thus allowed the rationalisation of facilities around Towcester. However, the already under-used branch line thence to Cockley Brake and Banbury, a route that once had pretentions of being a main line to South Wales, became even further diminished in importance. Nevertheless, the first day of 1909 was a turning point in the fortunes of the collection of railways that formed the S&MJR.

On a personal level, my first encounter with the 'SMJ' was in the

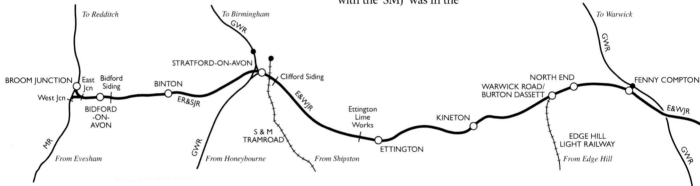

The similarly ambitious East & West Junction Railway (E&WJR) finally opened as a through route from Towcester to Stratford-upon-Avon in 1873 but financial pressures and continued hostile action by larger railway concerns combined to restrict the success of the company. A low point was reached in 1877, when passenger services were suspended and the line struggled on for another eight years carrying only a meagre amount of goods traffic, operated by a succession of hired or borrowed locomotives. Despite being in receivership at the time, the E&WJR somehow managed to encourage nominally independent extensions at either end of its route which, by 1891 at least, produced a through route, usefully linking two branches of the much larger Midland Railway.

The 1883 Act of Parliament which authorised the second of these extensions also allowed the E&WJR and its two scions to operate as a Joint Committee but this seemingly logical step was a long time coming and once formed was operated in a rather less than efficient manner. Several attempts were made to sell the ramshackle concern to other railway companies but apart from a brief flirtation with the nascent Great Central Railway, little interest was forthcoming.

However, the arrival of new management in 1908 prepared the way for a much needed restructuring of the disparate components

1950s, when my railway signalman father pointed out 'the line that goes to Towcester' as we rattled past the lonely signal box at Ravenstone Wood Junction on a Northampton to Bedford branch line train. As my horizons expanded, I again encountered the 'SMJ' at Roade Junction and Blisworth but at the latter my eyes were more interested in the expresses on the main line from Euston to the north than the occasional, and largely invisible, trains that wheezed away behind the hedge on their way to Towcester and beyond.

Gradually my curiosity grew, however, and a cycle ride on a hot Sunday afternoon gave me a first sight of a deserted and silent Towcester station. This was quickly followed by excursions to other locations within the reach of pedal-power.

These were the catalysts of my subsequent interest in the 'SMJ' and I have to thank the Oakwood Press for providing the next impetus, when a visit to the Ian Allan Book Counter in Conduit Street London, provided a copy of J.M. Dunn's excellent potted history of the line. It is interesting to compare those days of the late 1950s, when railway literature was a rarity, to today's era of plenty, when details of any particular line can be easily found in either the printed word or on a computer screen. Max Dunn's history enabled me to appreciate the full extent of the 'SMJ' for the first time and my explorations widened, fortunately just in time to see much of the infrastructure before the lines were closed and abandoned.

Since then, there have been many pilgrimages to the sites of old stations, junctions, cuttings and latterly, in some cases, just ploughed fields, to witness the gradual disappearance from the landscape of a favourite railway line.

My incentive to write this history of the S&MJR was two-fold. Firstly, I had collected so much information on the line over the years that it somehow seemed appropriate to make some use of it all. Secondly, as my knowledge grew of, in particular, the earliest years of the line, I began to realise that the full story had not yet been told.

This is not to decry any of the books and articles that have been published by other authors subsequent to Max Dunn's little history, as they have all progressively added to the knowledge and profile of the 'SMJ'. However, as I was able to delve deeper into the files held by the National Archives at Kew, and more recently into the fascinating resource of on-line historical newspaper archives, I began to realise that there were significant gaps in the recorded history of, in particular, the constituent companies of the S&MJR. Along the way, I have also been able to question the authenticity of one or two of the old myths and legends that have so far been handed down

1982) which is required reading for any serious student of the line.

The signalling has been covered in detail by Mike Christensen (in fact I rather surprisingly contributed to this in a very small way back in the 1970s) and R.A. Cooke's track diagrams are a further invaluable resource. I have appended a list of other articles and publications which will repay further reading.

I would also like to acknowledge a number of individuals and organisations that have assisted me, in various ways, in the compilation of this book. The staff of the vast National Archives at Kew and the Northamptonshire Record Office at Wootton Hall have all provided great assistance when requested, and the many members of Andy Thompson's excellent on-line 'Unofficial SMJ Society' have entered into the spirit of a good many discussions and arguments over the minutiae of the S&MJR, and continue to reveal many hidden aspects of the line through anecdote and personal experiences.

On an individual level, I would also like to thank, in no particular order, Mike Mitchell, Graham Onley, Peter Butler, John Downing, Peter Trenchard, Ian Lyman, David Scudamore, Keith Fenwick, Tommy Tomalin, Robin Cullup, Dick Bodily, Mike Christensen, Roger West, Robin Waywell, Mike Musson, David Geldard, John Alsop, Tony Marsh and Harry Jack for support, encouragement and all sorts of bits and pieces over the years.

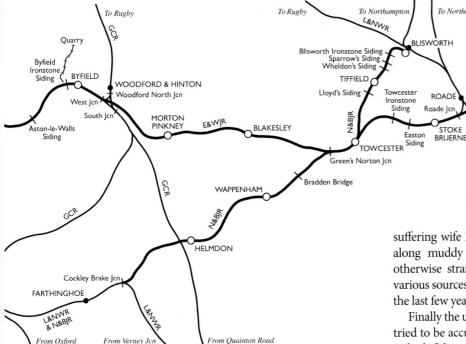

Last but of course not least, I must acknowledge the contribution of my long-suffering wife Elizabeth, who has cheerfully endured many walks along muddy remains of the line, unexplained detours from otherwise straight-forward journeys and my many visits to the various sources of information that have monopolised my time over the last few years.

Finally the usual, and very necessary, disclaimer; although I have tried to be accurate and non controversial, if there is anything that is doubtful or incorrect it is entirely of my doing. I would, however, be very pleased to receive, via the publishers, corrections and any further information that might add to our collective knowledge of the S&MJR. As I have been reminded on many occasions, as soon as anything is published, a previously unobtainable photograph or other piece of essential information will then reveal itself; I therefore look forward to the almost inevitable appearance of a photograph of either Warwick Road or North End stations, or failing that rather unlikely occurrence, perhaps just one of Aston-le-Walls siding with the track actually in place.

Barry Taylor
Loddington, 2017

unchallenged over the years.

I therefore hope that this attempt at a fuller history of the Stratford-upon-Avon & Midland Junction Railway and its constituent companies fills some of the gaps in the already published information. It is, however, intended to complement and not necessarily replace the previous works, and I have tried to not stray too far into some of the areas that have already been expertly covered. In this context, I would particularly mention Arthur Jordan's masterly coverage of the human and social side of the S&MJR in his *Shakespeare Route* (Oxford Publishing Company

The Route of the Stratford-upon-Avon and Midland Junction Railway c1880

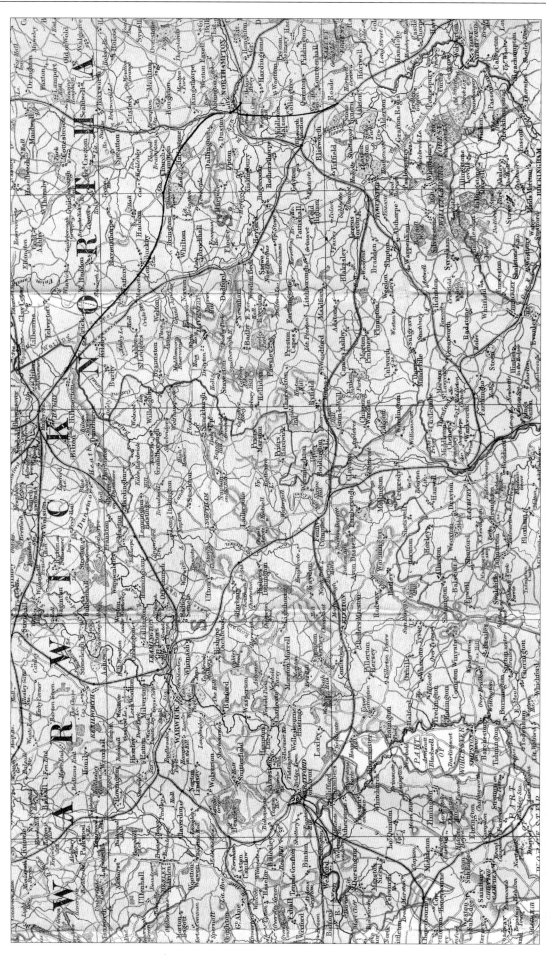

This map, although pre-dating the construction of the line from Towcester to Ravenstone Wood Junction (running via Stoke Bruerne, Roade and Piddington to join the Northampton to Bedford line) does show the general location of the S&MJR system within its surrounding countryside. The lines meander quietly through sparsely populated areas of south west Northamptonshire and eastern Warwickshire, managing to avoid most of the larger towns en route. The value of the S&MJR as a connecting route is clearly evident but once the possibility of large volumes of iron ore had disappeared, there was little else around to generate any other traffic, either goods or passenger.

Chapter 1.1
THE NORTHAMPTON & BANBURY JUNCTION RAILWAY

'A line of railway which has been the subject of more litigation than any little line in the Kingdom'

The logical starting point in the story of what would eventually become the Stratford-upon-Avon & Midland Junction Railway (S&MJR) is the opening of the first part of the Northampton & Banbury Junction Railway (N&BJR), in 1866. A small company with impressive but ultimately unfulfilled ideas of expansion to the west, the N&BJR would endure another six difficult years before its trains could reach Banbury. Even then, this was only achieved by the use of a running powers agreement with the London & North Western Railway (L&NWR), who also provided similar access to Northampton at the other end of the N&BJR system, although this facility was never used.

The official corporate seal of the Northampton & Banbury Junction Railway company. *Author's collection*

Although never really profitable, the N&BJR at least managed to remain nominally independent through to amalgamation with the S&MJR in 1910, whilst the other constituents of the latter had been indulging themselves in a succession of receiverships, reinventions and mergers.

That is not to suggest that the N&BJR was a successful and trouble-free enterprise; in fact as the story unfolds, it will be seen that life was to be a constant struggle almost from the outset. The early years were particularly difficult and it was not until an agreement was made for the L&NWR to provide locomotives and rolling stock in 1875 that any degree of stability was achieved. Thereafter, the N&BJR whiled away its time as a small but independent backwater, regarded in many circles as almost a branch of its larger neighbour. The invitation to join the newly created S&MJR in 1910 was an opportunity not to be missed.

Before The Railways

In the 1840s, Northampton and Banbury were important south Midlands market towns of somewhat different character, separated by around twenty-five miles of rolling, sparsely populated agricultural countryside.

Northampton was leaving behind its rural roots and was fast becoming a significant manufacturing town. It had already become the nation's leading producer of boots and shoes, an industry that would see further rapid expansion throughout the remainder of the 19th century, with the town's population also set to rise significantly; the thirty years from 1831 to 1861 would see almost a doubling in size to 33,000.

Banbury, by contrast, was still largely an agricultural centre, with a population in 1841 of some 6,700 souls. The local economy was based mainly on corn and cattle, with

a large weekly market for the latter, whilst a variety of small manufacturing industries included *'plushes, girth, and other webbing'* and of course the renowned 'Banbury cakes', which were produced in great quantities and distributed nationally, and even worldwide. The population had struggled to reach 7,000 by the beginning of the 1860s and had seen little expansion since.

In between the two market towns lay little of consequence, save for the locally important centre of Towcester, set at the crossroads of the Northampton to Oxford turnpike and the ancient route of the Watling Street, which connected London with the West Midlands and North Wales.

In terms of communication, the larger towns and villages had been well served by coaching services utilising the major roads, whilst access to the growing network of canals had opened up still further horizons for both Northampton and Banbury. The two towns had been linked since ancient times by the long established east to west drove route known as 'Banbury Lane' and more recently by various local carriers, who plied their traditional horse-drawn commercial services throughout the area, several connecting Northampton and Banbury on their respective traditional market days.

Thoughts of any faster form of communication across the area had yet to emerge but all of this would soon change with the coming of their own Railway Age.

The Railway Arrives

In an editorial published on Saturday 15th November 1845, the redoubtable *Northampton Mercury* weekly newspaper was forced to apologise to its public for the *'utter swamping'* of its advertisement columns, which precluded the inclusion of the usual announcements intended *'for the entertainment and information of general readers.'* The reason for the apology was the requirement to publish notices of applications to Parliament for no less than thirty-nine new local railway schemes. This resulted from the Parliamentary announcement that plans for any proposed new railways must be deposited with them by midnight on 30th November 1845 at the latest.

'Railway Mania' was at its height and, nationally, almost seven hundred schemes were eventually deposited for inclusion in the next session of Parliament.

Local schemes varied from a rather unlikely London & Northampton Direct Atmospheric Railway, a Midland Grand Junction Railway which would have joined Northampton with

Reading, the South Midland & Southampton Railway linking Northampton with Towcester and beyond, and a perhaps much more practical branch line connecting Northampton with Bedford. Amongst the plethora of other proposals, the Northampton & Banbury Railway, the Northampton, Banbury & Cheltenham Railway, and the East & West of England Junction Railway seemed most likely to provide a useful direct connection between Northampton and Banbury.

The vast majority of these schemes would never come to fruition but the tide of new proposals did not slacken and even in November of the following year, the *Mercury* was forced to append two supplements to a normal weekly issue, to cover another sixty-two notices for yet more speculative schemes relevant to the local area.

Meanwhile, the London & Birmingham Railway (L&BR), which had opened in 1838 bypassing the town of Northampton, was busily engaged in throwing off branches on both sides of its main line. The result was that, in 1845, Northampton was itself provided with a railway but only a straggling cross-country branch to Peterborough from a junction with the main line at Blisworth.

The inhabitants of Banbury were also anxious to have a railway connection, although opinion in the town was divided over whether to support a broad or narrow (standard) gauge proposal. The *Banbury Guardian* of 23rd May 1844 published a petition advocating a narrow gauge approach but a meeting in the town in July was in favour of broad gauge. In August of the following year, the Great Western Railway (GWR) was indeed successful in obtaining an Act for their broad gauge Oxford & Rugby Railway proposal, serving Banbury. This would later be superseded by the Birmingham & Oxford Junction Railway but it was then stipulated that a line of narrow gauge rails must also be added to the route.

Meanwhile, the L&BR, having merged in 1846 with the Grand Junction Railway to form the London & North Western Railway Company (L&NWR), harboured thoughts of outflanking the rival GWR for the potential West Midlands traffic. As a result, the already established and L&NWR-operated Buckinghamshire Railway was extended westwards to reach Banbury in September 1850, just four months before the arrival of the GWR from the south.

Thus, both Northampton and Banbury had benefited independently from the arrival of the railway age by the mid 19th century and, somewhat inevitably, proposals for establishing this new and faster form of communication between the two market towns were soon to emerge.

Schemes and Dreams

Of the earlier mentioned proposals, the broad gauge East & West of England Junction Railway, which would have passed through Banbury on a cross-country meander from Northampton to Cheltenham, was not successful in an attempt to obtain an Act for its line and the company was dissolved during 1846.

However, the directors of the L&BR had already given instructions for a survey to be made of the country between Blisworth and Banbury, with a view to applying for powers to construct their '*Northampton and Banbury branch railway*'.

This was effectively a western extension of their existing branch from Blisworth, which passed through Northampton on its way to Peterborough. In due course, in November 1845, it was announced that an application to Parliament would be made for a line commencing in the parish of Gayton, near Blisworth, and terminating '*at or near the town of Banbury*' but, by January, this had been modified into a proposal for a line through to Cheltenham.

Also under consideration during 1845 was another line linking the same three towns; the Northampton, Banbury & Cheltenham Railway would make a junction with the Buckinghamshire Railway at Farthingho (*sic*) and, having accessed a joint station at Banbury, then continue to a junction with the Birmingham & Gloucester Railway and a proposed Ashchurch and Hampden line. The Bill was presented in early 1846 and received some opposition, although the objections were largely dismissed as being of a frivolous nature. Nevertheless, all was not well with the application, which apparently did not comply with Parliamentary Standing Orders and this resulted in it being thrown out. However, by September of that year, the chairman had announced that '*in conjunction with the spirited liberality of the Directors of the London & North Western company*', a line from Northampton to Banbury only was to be applied for in the ensuing session of Parliament.

In due course, the *Mercury* carried an announcement, in its issue of 26th September 1846, to the effect that the '*London & North Western Railway have agreed to subscribe one-third of the capital, and to take a lease on the line in perpetuity, with a guarantee of £4 per cent per annum, and half the surplus profits.*'

Notice was duly given in November of the intention to apply to Parliament for this railway, '*commencing by a junction with the Northampton & Peterborough branch of the L&NWR, at or near the Gayton Wharf on the Grand Junction canal, terminating near the town of Banbury, in or near the southern side of the highway from Warkworth to Banbury ... also to form a junction in Warkworth parish with the Oxford & Rugby line of the Great Western Railway.*'

A subsequent editorial in the *Northampton Mercury* ventured that they were not aware that any opposition to the scheme was contemplated and they had every reason to believe that the next session of Parliament would '*secure to our town this important line of communication with our neighbours*'. Although the Act was obtained on 9th July 1849, owing to the prevailing economic situation capital could not be raised and the scheme was allowed to lapse, with the company eventually being wound up in 1852.

A Different Emphasis

Until this point in time, these various proposals had been promoted mainly as improvements to local communication but this approach was quickly changed by the realisation that large deposits of iron ore existed in Northamptonshire.

Colonel Arbuthnot, who owned land at Woodford near Kettering, provided samples of recently discovered Northamptonshire ore for the Great Exhibition of 1851 and this was further promoted by S.H. Blackwell, a Northampton ironmaster and mine engineer. Although the ore was of relatively low grade, producing between 20% and 35% of iron per ton and of high phosphor content, it was nevertheless attractive to the ironmasters of South Wales, with other potential markets being the ironworks of Staffordshire and Derbyshire.

The early 1850s saw trial pits opened at Blisworth and, in January 1853, the Dowlais Iron Company contracted for a supply of 20,000 tons of Northamptonshire ore at 9s 6d per ton delivered by rail to Gloucester, for onward transportation by water to Cardiff. Northamptonshire ore production then grew rapidly; annual output reached 74,000 tons in 1855 and, ten years later, had increased five-fold to a total of 364,000 tons.

The ironworks of South Wales quickly became the new focus of attention and, before long, thought was again being given to a line heading west from Northamptonshire. The *Northampton Herald* reported on 5th November 1853 that '*A fresh line of narrow gauge railway is contemplated from the L&NWR near Blisworth, to the Oxford Worcester and Wolverhampton, near Campden. The scheme is looked on as being favourable for the transmission of iron stone from Northamptonshire to the furnaces, and providing desirable communication for a large district which is at present unprovided. A preliminary meeting has been held at Worcester.*'

Once again, the scheme did not come to fruition but the lure of the South Wales ironworks ensured that it was not too long before the main provisions of the earlier 1849 scheme were revived.

The Beginnings of the N&BJR

On 21st November 1862, the *London Gazette* carried an announcement of the intention to apply to Parliament for powers to incorporate the Northampton & Banbury Junction Railway Company. The objective of the new company was to '*construct and maintain a railway, with stations, approaches and other necessary works and conveniences in connexion therewith, commencing in the parish of Blisworth, by a junction with a siding on the west side of the London & North Western Railway, at or near the Blisworth station of that railway, thence passing from, through, or into all or some of the several parishes or places of Blisworth, Gayton, Tiffield, Caldecote otherwise Caldecot, Towcester, Wood Burcote, Easton Neston, Bradden, Green's Norton, Handley, Abthorpe, Slapton, Wappenham, Weedon Lois otherwise Loys Weedon, Helmedon otherwise Helmdon, Fawcott otherwise Falcott, Astwell, Stuchbury, Gretworth otherwise Greatworth, and Farthinghoe all in the County of Northampton; and terminating in the said parish of Gretworth by a junction with the Banbury extension of the Buckinghamshire Railway about forty yards eastwards of the bridge which carries the public road leading from Marston St. Lawrence to Farthinghoe over the said Banbury Extension, near to a place called Cockley Brake.*'

The promoters of the scheme were Alexander Beattie, Cooke Baines, George James Eady, Robert Stanton Wise and William Gregory. None had apparent local connections; Cooke Baines was a London merchant and Beattie a doctor, with Eady and Gregory both being London solicitors and acting in that capacity for the new venture. Beattie also had interests in several other railway projects, including the Caernarvon & Llanberis Railway in North Wales, where Eady also acted as company secretary.

Despite the various alternative schemes and proposals, this line was destined to be the one that would actually be constructed.

On 6th February 1863, the promoters petitioned Parliament for leave to bring forward their Bill, which was sent up to the Lords in the summer and, after minor amendments, finally received Royal Assent on 23rd July 1863.

Under the powers provided by *26 & 27 Vic.Cap.220*, capital of £140,000 was to be raised from the issue of 14,000 shares of £10 each and further borrowing of up to £46,000 would be available when the whole of the share capital had been subscribed. A time limit of five years was specified for the construction of the line, with compulsory purchase of the necessary lands to take place within three years.

One essential variation from the earlier unfulfilled proposal was for the line to commence at Blisworth, with an indirect junction to the western side of the L&NWR main line, instead of linking with the Blisworth to Northampton branch line near Gayton Wharf; this would prove to be a regrettable omission.

The Act also elaborated all of the usual details of charges to be levied for the carriage of various categories of goods and mineral traffic, and specified the rates per mile for passengers as three pence (3d) for First Class, 2d for Second Class, and 1^{1}/$_2$d for Third Class; interestingly, this latter rate was in excess of the statutory minimum Parliamentary rate of one penny per mile.

The first half-yearly meeting of the new company was held in April 1864 in Westminster, the Board members by then being the above mentioned promoters, plus Jaspar W. Johns, C.J. Tahourdin, and William Cousens.

Johns was an interesting addition, being a civil engineer and promoter or director of several lines in Wales, including the Bedgellert, Brecon & Merthyr, Cambrian, Carmarthenshire, Denbigh, Ruthin & Corwen and Swansea & Aberystwyth railways. In addition, Johns was a financial man, involved with the Albert Life Assurance Company and two banks, and also had an interest in a colliery in Merthyr Tydfil and connections with the Ebbw Vale Company.

J. Wilson Theobald acted as company secretary and John Collister was named as the engineer.

The subsequent report of the meeting reflected the ambition of the railway to evolve into a main line connecting the east of England with South Wales. Northamptonshire iron ore would form a significant part of the traffic, it being estimated that upwards of 400,000 tons would be carried annually. It was also considered that the reduction in mileage offered by the new route would result in significant cost savings in the transportation of the ore, with the competing railway rates per ton/mile then being negotiated as finely as fractions of one penny.

William Menelaus, the manager of the Dowlais Iron Company in South Wales, stated that he had imported between four and six hundred tons of Northamptonshire iron ore a week for the past six years, this being carried by the Great Western and London & North Western railways. In general, the South Wales ironmasters considered railway rates for the carriage of ore to be somewhat on the high side, contributing in the region of 75% to 80% to the final price per ton. They were understandably very keen to see rates reduced by the existing carriers the L&NWR and GWR, or competition provided by the introduction of new railways. Indeed, Menelaus considered that the proposed shorter N&BJR route to South Wales could save a further one shilling, or possibly one shilling and six pence per ton in freight costs.

A healthy return traffic of coal from the Forest of Dean and South Wales was also predicted, so reducing the cost of this essential commodity in the inland areas served by the new line; the future prosperity of the N&BJR seemed assured.

Grand Designs

With construction of the authorised route only just under way, a further announcement for a substantial extension of the N&BJR to Blockley then appeared in the *London Gazette* of 29th November 1864. This new proposal consisted of no less than six interlinking lines of railway, collectively extending from a junction with the Buckinghamshire Railway's line in the parish of Middleton Cheney to join the GWR at Blockley, and also to the south of their Banbury station.

This Act duly received Assent in July 1865, as did another amendment, which varied the authorised route of the 1863 line at either end. Instead of joining the Buckinghamshire Railway line as planned at Cockley Brake, the revised route was to diverge northwards after Wappenham to make a junction with the GWR just to the north of their Banbury station. In addition, at the eastern end of the line, the N&BJR would bridge the L&NWR main line at Gayton Wharf and make direct connection with the Blisworth to Peterborough branch, thus giving the desired through route to Northampton.

In the event, neither of these variations was proceeded with and running powers were instead granted over the L&NWR to allow the N&BJR access to both of the towns in the corporate title, although those to Northampton would never be exercised.

Yet another extension proposal appeared almost exactly one year later, in the *Gazette* of 28th November 1865. The push towards South Wales was to be continued with a scheme for an extension from the already authorised line at Blockley onwards to Ross-on-Wye, with running powers over the variously proposed, authorised or existing lines of the Ashchurch & Evesham; Ashchurch & Tewkesbury; Tewkesbury & Malvern; Worcester, Dean Forest & Monmouth; and Ross & Monmouth railway companies. This proposal also authorised the N&BJR, L&NWR, GWR, Midland and other railways to enter into agreements for the working, management and maintenance of the lines and to enjoy running powers over the extended route. In addition, the N&BJR were to receive powers to purchase the existing Lower Lode ferry, situated on the River Severn close to Tewkesbury and replace it with a bridge of 60ft span, with a 40ft drawbridge opening.

Significantly, the application also sought approval to change the name of the company to the Midland Counties & South Wales Junction Railway, a title that was obviously seen as being far more fitting for a line of railway that was now to extend for almost one hundred miles westwards from Northamptonshire.

Support was soon forthcoming from South Wales. Frederick Finch, a director of the Blaenavon Iron Company, then currently purchasing large quantities of ore from G.E. Bevan at Blisworth, stated that he was *'prepared to offer considerable assistance to secure the line'*. In addition, the Ebbw Vale Company approved a loan of £40,000 to the N&BJR to cover the Parliamentary Deposits required for their Bill; it is probably significant that Alexander Beattie, a director of the N&BJR also held shares in the Ebbw Vale Company.

The three giants of the railway world, the Great Western, Midland and London & North Western railways, were at that time effectively controlling the development of further schemes, having between them, rather restrictively, engaged *'not to promote any new line that all three do not approve of'*. The GWR did initially support the early Northampton & Banbury Junction proposals and were to carry ironstone traffic forward to South Wales on their lines at favourable rates but this was to be in return for an agreement that the new company would not seek to extend any further westwards; understandably, the ever expanding N&BJR did not assent to these proposals and continued with their own plans.

Under Construction

The contract for the construction of the N&BJR line was awarded to one William Shrimpton, who was appointed at a salary of £350 per annum, payable in six monthly instalments. This was inclusive of travel and house rent, initially at a dwelling adjoining the Nelson's Arms in Towcester High Street. Shrimpton was also the first recipient of shares in the new company, which were issued to him on 29th December 1863, as part payment for his work on the line and, by 1866, he owned a large proportion of the issued stock. This approach was quite typical of the time, and such 'contractor's lines' accounted for many small railway schemes which would otherwise never have been completed.

Shrimpton's engagement was for the completion of the entire line from Blisworth to Banbury, or for two years, with an option to terminate at three months notice at any time and it appears that he was also the nominated contractor for the further extensions of the line to Blockley and Chipping Norton. He appointed Thomas Dyson Butler, previously with the Great Northern Railway, as engineer for the new line and George

Weymouth as Assistant of Works. The actual construction of the line was sub-contracted to Charles Noah Foster, of New Wharf, Whitefriars, London.

Shrimpton soon involved himself in the everyday welfare of his workforce, which eventually numbered 850 and he employed a missionary to attend to their spiritual needs. After several successful Sunday meetings had been held in a house at Towcester, this was found to be too small and Shrimpton funded the erection of a 'handsome wooden chapel', with accommodation for two hundred people. An opening tea party was well attended and a speech was given by the notable Reverend Thomas Arnold of Northampton.

Construction of the new line was obviously well under way by the middle part of 1864, as local newspaper reports revealed two cases of fatal accidents on the line, both at Tiffield. The first, on 9th July, was in respect of a 'breakman', who was run over by a wagon carrying spoil after unhooking it from a horse. Then, on 17th September, the Northampton Mercury gave details of another fatal occurrence, at a stone quarry operated by the aforementioned C.N. Foster, who employed between thirty and forty men at Tiffield.

By June 1864, construction had advanced into an area close to Gayton which had for some time been quarried by George Pell, a local ironmaster who, as will be seen later, was also involved with the development of the neighbouring East & West Junction Railway line. An agreement had been made for headways to be provided through the new N&BJR embankment as it progressed through the area, so that Pell could maintain access to his quarries and wagon works whilst the N&BJR contractors undertook the construction of a diversion to his tramway. It was necessary to remove a 500 yard length of the existing tramway and to relocate it on a straighter alignment, after which the headways were to be closed. However, on 19th January 1865, with the necessary diversion almost ready for use, a team of navvies infilled the headways without any prior notice being given. As a result, Pell's operations were immediately disrupted with twenty-three wagons being isolated at the works and he was forced to claim redress from the railway company for loss of trade. The resulting legal action against the N&BJR was heard at the King's Bench in London on 9th March 1865, with Pell claiming further damages in addition to the compensation that had already been agreed.

After a lengthy courtroom discussion, the N&BJR conceded and agreed to an arbitrator being appointed to assess damages, with the Bench ruling that one of the old headways was to be temporarily reopened within a week to allow Pell to clear his works and quarries of equipment. The dispute then rumbled on for some time afterwards, with Pell claiming that the construction of the cutting sides on the diverted section of tramway, and the width of a newly built bridge, were unsatisfactory.

February 1865 brought further reports of the 'works between Blisworth and Towcester being vigorously proceeded with' and the N&BJR engineer, John Collister, also indicated that satisfactory progress was being made with the line for two miles beyond Towcester towards Abthorpe, all of which was already in an advanced state and might be ready for opening by November. The plans for the stations at Blisworth and Towcester were said to already be in the contractor's hands and work was due to commence forthwith.

However, in June 1865, William Shrimpton was obviously in need of additional finance to complete the line, as he approached the International Finance Society for a loan of £90,000. A sum of £88,740, to include interest and commission, was actually advanced on security of Shrimpton's acceptance of the terms, and in return for N&BJR preference shares, debentures, and Lloyd's bonds.

Meanwhile, further evidence of the advanced state of construction was provided by an announcement to 'Quick growers and timber dealers' in the Mercury of 30th September 1865, requiring the supply of '170,000 three year old quick sets, also temporary sleepers 8ft by 8 by 4 inches – further particulars from Thos. D. Butler, Northampton & Banbury Railway Contractors Office Towcester'.

Interesting further details of the construction work were provided in the Northampton Mercury of 30th December 1865 but unfortunately the main focus of the report was an inquest into the death of one Evered Amos, who had been killed on the previous day whilst working on the line a mile from Blisworth.

Giving evidence, Thomas Reeve, a roperunner employed by the railway company to 'uncouple railway trucks', stated that a meeting of company employees had been called at Towcester and an engine with twenty ballast wagons was sent to convey the men to that point. Reeve coupled a further nineteen wagons onto those already provided and another engine assisted in the rear. A total of ninety men boarded the wagons and the train proceeded towards Towcester at the rate of about six miles per hour, with Reeve riding on the rear locomotive. With the train only about one mile from Blisworth, the rear engine was found to be short of water and as soon as 'the carriages were propelled up an incline', that engine was uncoupled with the train apparently still moving. Reeve saw the wagons suddenly jerked, with several employees falling off onto the track. The injured were taken back to Blisworth by the rear engine but Amos was found to be dead.

William Arnold, superintendent of the works, revealed that the occasion at Towcester was actually a 'tea making' for the navvies and their wives, provided by Mr Swainton (sic), the head contractor of the line, with the directors of the company also to be present. The aforementioned arrangements were made to bring all of the workmen to Towcester and William Hornby, an engine driver of the N&BJR, was in charge of the lead engine, with his son John driving the rear locomotive.

Arnold stated that he had examined both engines prior to departure and they both had sufficient water for the journey. However, after the accident, he noticed that on the rear engine 'a piece of rubber out of the suction pipe joint, had got into the bottom clack of the pump, preventing the boiler from being filled and causing the clack joint to blow out'.

The subsequent inquest, held at the Blisworth Hotel, returned a verdict of accidental death due to falling from a ballast wagon onto the track.

The advanced state of construction was confirmed by the sale in Northampton, on 20th January 1866, of 'twelve powerful young and active horses which have been used in the construction of the N&BJR, the heavy portion of the railway now being completed'. This was followed by further sales of cart horses and nags by the sub-contractor Foster at his stables at Tiffield on 5th May and 8th June, 'in consequence of the first section of the railway being completed'.

Where it all began: a view of the former N&BJR terminus at Blisworth from the bridge carrying the minor road to Gayton canal wharf. The N&BJR platforms and station can be seen to the right of the picture, adjacent to the L&NWR facilities on the main line, from where the branch to Northampton runs obliquely away to the east. The small signal box sits snugly behind the single road engine shed and controls the strangely deserted exchange sidings which connected the N&BJR to the outside world. Had early plans come to fruition, a link would have run behind the photographer from the sharply curved N&BJR route and across the main line to the Northampton Branch, to allow direct access to the county town. *Author's collection*

A 1933 view, taken from a slightly different angle to the previous picture, showing the N&BJR engine shed located next to the signal box and turntable. A fast goods headed by an ex-L&NWR 4-6-0 passes on the Down Main line. The engine shed was disused by this time and would soon be relocated to Towcester, where it would act as a storage barn for around thirty years. However, the turntable would continue in use right through to the mid-1950s and a Northampton or Stratford '3F' or '4F' 0-6-0 could sometimes be seen turning before its return working to Towcester and beyond. *Author's collection*

Opening – and a New Title

In due course, the N&BJR was able to inform the relevant authorities of their intention to shortly open the first part of their line and their solicitors, Messrs Gregory, Champion & Eady, submitted a letter to '*The Lords of the Committee of Her Majesty's Privy Council for Trade and Foreign Plantations*' on 4th January 1866.

A second, or 'ten-day notice' of opening was then produced by the company secretary, J. Wilson Theobald, on 5th April, which was this time more appropriately addressed to the '*Secretary of the Railway Department of the Board of Trade*'.

Arrangements were made for the new line to be inspected by Captain Rich on 12th April but two days before this, the N&BJR engineer John Collister indicated that '*the line would not yet be in a fit state*' and the inspection was deferred until 16th April. Captain Rich's eventual report, written on 18th April, nevertheless complimented William Shrimpton on the excellent way in which the works had been completed and approved the line for opening to passenger traffic as far as Towcester from 1st May.

The Captain reported as follows:

'*The new line is about 5 miles long. It commences at the LNW station at Blisworth, and extends to Towcester which is the only station on the line. There is no junction with the LNW railway at Blisworth for passenger traffic, but for minerals a cross-over road from a siding. The line is single throughout with sidings at the terminal stations. Land is enclosed for a double line; over*

bridges and the under bridge just beyond Towcester station are also constructed accordingly. The rail used is double headed and weighs 70lbs per lineal yard. It is laid in 21 and 24 foot lengths and fixed in chairs with wooden keys. The chairs next to the joints weigh 30lbs each and the rest of the chairs weigh 23lbs. They are

The N&BJR route to Tiffield and Towcester curved sharply away from the L&NWR main line and then under this bridge carrying a minor road, from which the picture on the previous page was taken. Up trains were always subject to severe speed restrictions on this difficult section and various *Working Time Tables* and *Appendices* warned engine crews to reduce speed to ensure that they could bring their trains safely to a stand in the station platform, just a few hundred yards behind the camera. *Author's collection*

Looking south-eastwards again in the 1930s but now from track level, the full layout of the N&BJR station at Blisworth is shown, with the brake van to the left standing on the exchange siding separating the minor railway from its larger neighbour. The L&NWR signal box and station can just be made out beyond the brake van, whilst the '4F' 0-6-0 and train in the left background is neatly positioned to illustrate how the Northampton Branch entered the trainshed on the western face of the Up platform. Note the canopy on the N&BJR platform. *Author's collection*

fastened to transverse sleepers with spikes. A fang bolt is inserted in lieu of a spike in each chair near to the joints of the rails and one in the centre of each rail. The sleepers are 10" by 5" and 9" by 4½" - the ballast is gravel. There are eight over bridges, two of which have cast iron girders, and one (carrying a double line of tramway) is of timber, the remainder are built of brick. Four under bridges have cast iron girders, one (the span of which is 39ft on the skew) has wrought iron girders and the sixth is built of brick. All the works appear to be substantially constructed and of sufficient strength. Two over bridges have elliptic brick arches but the work appears sound and strong and I have no reason to anticipate any danger. The under bridge with wrought iron girders is just beyond Towcester station. It was included in the notice for

the present inspection though it should not be included as it is beyond the station. It is not strong enough at present. It appears quite strong enough for the single line of rails now laid on it, but the cross girders are too light to carry two pairs of engine driving wheels, the weight of which will have to be distributed over them, or the girders strengthened when the second line is laid. There is a turntable at Blisworth but none at Towcester, and it will therefore be necessary for the Company to sign an undertaking to work the passenger trains with tank engines only till such time as they provide the means of turning tender engines. An undertaking to work this single line with a train staff will also be required previous to their Lordship's sanction being given for the opening. The line is in good order and there is a signalman's box about 300 yards from

A few steps backwards led into the *'commodious hall'* of the N&BJR station at Blisworth; this may well have been the original structure on the site, to which the later 'joint' booking office shared with the L&NWR was appended in 1871. By the time that this photograph was taken in the 1950s, the platform canopy had been removed but, remarkably, a few years later a new covering was provided to equip the platform for a short career as a temporary parcels sorting centre. *Author's collection*

A view from the deserted N&BJR island platform at Blisworth during the 1930s reveals the line to Towcester passing under the minor road to Gayton, whilst the L&NWR main line has its own bridge to the right of the signal box; between are the exchange sidings which had to be tediously negotiated by all traffic to and from Northampton. In earlier N&BJR days, the water tank was located immediately off the platform end and the signal box was positioned to the left of the line, mid way between the platform end and the roadbridge. *Author's collection*

Blisworth station where the up and down lines to the passenger platforms and the siding communicating to the LNW railway and the company's turntable meet. The points and signals are on the interlocking principle except the points to the turntable which are taken off the siding about 60 yards from the box and are worked from the box. I have recommended that the normal position of these points be reversed so that nothing can come onto the main line without the special permission of the signalman and that a signal to the siding to which they are connected is supplied. The engineer has undertaken to do this at once. The Northampton & Banbury Junction Railway may be opened for passenger traffic as soon as the undertakings are received.'

The N&BJR duly complied with the Colonel's stipulations and, having submitted the required undertakings, were informed on 23rd April of the Board of Trade's approval for the line to be opened for passenger traffic.

The Report of the Minutes of Evidence for the 1866 extension proposals to Ross and Monmouth subsequently indicated that, by July of that year, construction of the line had actually proceeded beyond Towcester and six miles from that point was *'all but completed'*; further on *'there was very little done'*.

Charles Henry Davids, a land agent and surveyor of Tadmarton, stated that he had been employed to arrange valuations and purchase of lands for the new line and this had all been arranged as far as Cockley Bridge (*sic*). However, beyond Banbury the proposed route had only been surveyed and set out, and although no actual purchases had yet been completed, plans had been prepared and some land agreements settled.

All in all, it seemed that good progress was being made and there were few indications of the troubled times that were shortly to descend upon the MC&SWR.

Early Days on the Line

The *Northampton Mercury* duly recorded the opening of the line on Tuesday 1st May 1866, following the successful inspection by Captain Rich. A brief announcement sufficed:

'*Towcester Railway – The section of the Northampton and Banbury Railway from Blisworth to Towcester was opened for passenger traffic on Tuesday last. There are eight trains each way daily.*'

Henry Crabtree, the N&BJR general manager, also announced to the world that:

'*This railway being now open for public traffic between Blisworth and Towcester, goods are booked between Towcester and Northampton, London and other principal stations on the London & North Western Railway. Information as to rates can be obtained on application at the Northampton and Towcester stations.*'

Apparently some goods traffic had already passed over the line during the previous month, a situation not unusual on a new railway which had been completed but was still awaiting official approval to carry passengers.

The initial passenger timetable, published under the heading of the '*Towcester and Northampton Railway*', indeed consisted of eight trains each way from Monday to Saturday, with three return services on Sundays. Weekday departures from Towcester were at 7.30am, 8.35am, 10.25am, 12.45pm, 1.35pm, 3.25pm, 5.05pm and 7.23pm. Trains returned from Blisworth after a short wait and convenient connections were made into services on the L&NWR branch to Northampton.

The three Sunday trains were evenly distributed, beginning with a 10.40am service from Towcester and ending with a late 10.48pm arrival back at that station; in between, the other train was a 3.05pm from Towcester, which arrived back at that station at 3.35pm. All trains provided First and Second Class accommodation, with

TOWCESTER AND NORTHAMPTON RAILWAY.

	WEEK DAYS.									SUNDAYS.		
	1, 2	1, 2.	1, 2, 3.	1, 2.	1, 2.	1, 2.	1, 2.	1, 2.	1, 2.	1, 2, 3.	1, 2.	1, 2.
Leave	a.m.	a.m.	a.m.	p.m.	p.m.	p.m	p.m	p.m.	p.m.	a.m.	p.m.	p.m
TOWCESTER	7 30	8 33	10 25	12 45	1 35	3 25	5	7 23		10 40	3 5	10 18
BLISWORTH (Arrive)	7 40	8 45	10 35	12 55	1 45	3 35	5 15	7 33		10 50	3 15	10 28
NORTHAMPTON (Arr.)	8 5	9 25	10 55	1 15	2 10	3 55	5 35	7 50		11 25	3 35	10 50
Leave												
NORTHAMPTON	7 35	8 40	10 42	12 20	1 30	3 25	5 33	7 50		10 35	5	10 15
BLISWORTH (Arrive)	7 45	8 50	10 57	12 30	1 45	3 35	5 48	8 5		10 50	3 15	10 25
TOWCESTER (Arrive)	8 0	9 20	11 25	1 15	2 10	3 55	6 17	8 15		11 20	3 35	10 48

An N&BJR timetable dated 5th May 1866, four days after the opening of the line to Towcester. The company was never actually known as the Towcester & Northampton Railway, this being just one of various appellations that were used by the local press during the earliest years. Somewhat unusually, trains were provided on Sundays and the single Third Class 'Parliamentary' train in each direction is also of interest. *Author's collection*

just one in each direction also conveying Third Class passenger; journey times were ten minutes in either direction.

Interestingly, the first train of the day originated from Towcester, although it appears that locomotive facilities were only available at Blisworth at that time; possibly a locomotive ran light from Blisworth to work the first train, or perhaps took goods traffic to Towcester.

However, as the *Mercury* wryly noted a few days later:
'*Young railways, like ladies, do not always know their own minds, and it would, we suppose, be unreasonable to complain that the new line of railway from Blisworth to Towcester, which only came out on the first of this month, has manifested some little fickleness and unsteadiness of conduct. From Tuesday, the opening day, to Saturday last, there were eight trains each way. On Monday last they were reduced to six, and the times altered … Return tickets may be taken between Towcester and Blisworth, but not, at present at least, between Towcester and Northampton.*'

These amendments to the initial timetable consisted of the deletion of the first train of the day and an early afternoon service in each direction; in addition, the last train was moved back to 9.40pm. The journey time between Blisworth and Towcester was also extended to fifteen minutes, the ten minute schedule presumably proving too much for the only locomotive; the new engines ordered from Neilson of Glasgow were yet to arrive.

Obviously the new line took a little while to settle into a regular pattern of service but the *Mercury* soon added
'*… the trip by the new line is a pleasant one. At Blisworth and Towcester the arrangements are very comfortable, and have all the charms of newness and perfect cleanliness. The Towcester terminus*

No photographs exist of an N&BJR train at Blisworth but this is a very valuable early view of an East & West Junction Railway train, headed by that railway's Beyer, Peacock 0-6-0 No. 12. This train will use running powers over the N&BJR to Towcester, prior to gaining its own metals at Green's Norton Junction. Also visible is a rather distinctive gas lamp and the canopy that sheltered passengers on what was otherwise a rather exposed platform. The L&NWR station is to the left of the picture, with the signal box in its original location on the Up side of the main line; it was later replaced by a new box in a similar position but on the opposite side of the line. *Author's collection*

Early views of Towcester station are scarce but this photograph does give a flavour of the place in the years before the alterations of 1910, when the platform on the right became an island. The signal arms are rather unusually located on the footbridge, with the left hand doll indicating the route to Blisworth and the other controlling the later Stratford, Towcester & Midland Junction Railway extension to the Midland line at Ravenstone Wood Junction. Towcester East signal cabin is obscured by the footbridge and just beneath the canopy is a glimpse of a carriage in what was once the engine shed siding. *John Alsop collection*

stands in the midst of pretty scenery … We ought to add that the carriages are specially comfortable, light, and convenient, and the railway officials courteous and attentive; new brooms, according to the adage, always sweeping clean. The next section of the line opened will extend, we believe, to Wappenham.'*

Although scenic, the perhaps slightly inconvenient situation of Towcester station, situated about a half mile from the town itself, was alleviated by the fact that Mr Tunnard's omnibus

service to the Pomfret Arms Hotel met every train.

The N&BJR were quick to promote their new line in conjunction with other attractions in the area and with the Whitsuntide holiday approaching on 21st May, an additional special train from Towcester at 7.40am was announced, to connect with an L&NWR excursion from Blisworth to London on that day. In addition, Thomas Shaw quickly publicised the opening of his nearby Blisworth Tea Gardens and Bowling

Looking in the opposite direction, Towcester West signal box can be seen in the left distance. This controlled access over the one mile length of single track to Green's Norton Junction, where N&BJR and E&WJR trains would part company on their respective ways to Banbury and Stratford-upon-Avon. This would all change after 1910, when the junction was abolished and relocated to a point within the station area, with two separate single lines thereafter running westwards as far as Green's Norton. *John Alsop collection*

A view eastwards from between the platforms reveals the junction of the Blisworth, left, and Ravenstone Wood, right, lines beyond the station, controlled by Towcester East box one of the two signal cabins that existed here prior to 1910. In that year, the East and West cabins were replaced by a new larger, taller box located on the Down side just beyond the footbridge. At this time, a goods loop ran behind the Down platform on the right but this would later be upgraded to become a passenger line and the platform widened accordingly. Through the columns supporting the canopy can just be discerned what is thought to be Towcester's wooden engine shed, which was later to be used for carriage storage and eventually as a loading dock. *Author's collection*

Green for the summer season on Whit Monday and Tuesday, and the N&BJR management provided 'cheap special trains' from Towcester at 2.20pm and 4.10pm, returning at 6.00pm and 9.00pm, at a fare of 6d return. The 'excellent brass band' of the Northamptonshire Militia was to perform and admission to the gardens was a further 6d, with a tea available for one shilling.

The railway company then joined forces with Mr Shaw to offer a combined fare for the rail journey and admission to the gardens on 'every Monday from 4th June until further notice'. Tickets were available at Towcester station and included the return rail journey, admission to the gardens and a refreshment voucher to the value of 3d. It seems that passengers were to travel by normal service trains in the afternoon and evening but the departure times had by now been slightly amended by a few minutes from the earlier schedules.

The entertainment continued with another special train, this time at normal fares, on Thursday 5th July. The occasion was a Choral Festival at Peterborough Cathedral and an early departure from Towcester was provided at 6.45am to connect with the L&NWR 'cheap train' at Blisworth. Passengers were to be conveyed back from Blisworth to Towcester 'at night immediately after the arrival of the London & North Western train'.

The timetable of 1st September showed a further reduction in services on the line and some alterations to the departure times. The weekday trains now consisted of six return services, with an additional train in each direction on Saturday mornings. Third Class passengers were now catered for on four of the services but no service was now provided on Sundays.

Nevertheless, trains were provided on Christmas Day 1866, apparently running to a rather unusual timetable. The announcement in the *Northampton Mercury* of 22nd December indicated that trains would run:

'*from Towcester to Blisworth, in the morning, at 10.35 and 10.50 and in the afternoon at 3 and 3.15. From Blisworth to Towcester at, in the morning, 11.10 and 11.25, and in the afternoon at 3.25 and 3.40.*'

However, it seems likely that the newspaper misinterpreted

the information provided by the railway company. The suggested timetable, which does appear rather implausible, could not have been operated by a single locomotive and other reports seem to confirm that this was all that the N&BJR possessed at this date. It therefore seems likely that just one morning train was provided, leaving Towcester at 10.35 and arriving at Blisworth at 10.50am. The return trip from Blisworth then departed at 11.10 and reached Towcester at 11.25am; the afternoon arrangements can be similarly interpreted and all would seem to be confirmed by the standard journey time of fifteen minutes between the two points.

Crisis and Retrenchment

The N&BJR directors, now including newcomers The Rt Hon. Lord Ernest Bruce, H.J. Sheldon and William Banks, were able to report the approval of the Act for the further extension westwards from Blockley, which included running powers through to Ross-on-Wye. This had received Royal Assent on 30th July1866 and extended the authorised length of the N&BJR to a total of just over ninety-six miles. In addition, authorisation was also granted to change the company name to the rather more grandiose title of the Midland Counties & South Wales Junction Railway (MC&SWJR).

However, any optimism that may have resulted from the opening to Towcester and the approval of the extension, was already being undermined by events in the wider world, which were outside of the control of the directors of the newly christened MC&SWJR. The alarming collapse of the financial house of Overend Gurney in early May 1866 had already sent shock waves throughout the nation and many railway schemes, including the MC&SWJR, were destined to be seriously affected by the resultant financial uncertainty.

An early victim was the main contractor William Shrimpton, who was quickly declared bankrupt with debts estimated at over £220,000. Construction was suspended, with the unfinished line petering out in the middle of a field some distance beyond Towcester, intriguingly being caught in time as such on one of the early editions of the One-inch Ordnance Survey.

The International Finance Society, who had earlier provided Shrimpton with a substantial loan, now found themselves with N&BJR securities that were practically worthless and were advised against investing further in any attempt to save the line. However, they do appear to have been quick to reconsider their position and within a year would purchase another 1,600 one pound shares in the N&BJR at a knock-down price of £250. As will be seen later, their successors were to play a significant role in the resurrection of the line.

Another immediate consequence of the collapse was the announcement of a sale, to be conducted by local auctioneers W.J. Peirce '*under an execution from the Sheriff in various parishes between Blisworth and Helmdon*' on 26th and 27th November 1866. The items listed for sale, presumably being the remaining effects of the Shrimpton era, form an almost complete inventory of a railway contracting operation:

'*The valuable and extensive plant, now being on the premises of the Northampton and Banbury Junction Railway Company, in various parishes between Blisworth and Helmdon, in the County of Northampton; comprising a locomotive engine complete, in working order, 358 railway wagons, 30 dobbin ditto, 300 wheelbarrows,*

TOWCESTER AND NORTHAMPTON RAILWAY.

[*In consequence of an oversight on the part of the Railway Authorities, the corrected Time-Table for Towcester did not reach us till late yesterday, when part of our Supplement had been printed. Such of our Subscribers as may receive the uncorrected Supplement will oblige us by cutting out the corrected Time-Table subjoined, and pasting it over the other.*]

			WEEK DAYS.				
	1,2,3	1,2, 3.	Saturday only. 1 & 2.	1, 2.	1, 2.	1,2,3	1,2,3
	a.m.	a.m.	a.m.	p.m.	p.m.	p.m.	p.m.
Leave							
TOWCESTER	8 25	10 15	11 10	12 40	3 18	4 58	7 18
BLISWORTH (Arrive)	8 40	10 30	11 25	12 55	3 33	5 13	7 33
NORTHAMPTON (Ar.) Bridge-st. Station	9 10	10 55	11 40	1 15	3 55	5 35	7 50
Ditto Castle Station...	8 55	...	...	1 15	...	...	7 55
Leave NORTHAMPTON Castle Station	8 18	10 40	..	...	3 42	...	...
Ditto Bridge-st. Station	8 40	10 42	10 15	1 30	4 05	33	7 50
BLISWORTH (Arrive)	8 50	10 55	10 25	1 45	4 10	5 48	8 5
TOWCESTER (Arrive)	9 10	11 45	11 0	2 25	4 35	6 22	8 25

A few months after opening, the N&BJR, still styled in the local press as the Towcester & Northampton Railway, had rearranged its passenger services, no longer providing trains on Sundays. However, connections to and from the Northampton line at Blisworth were now featured; Bridge Street station would be served by trains to Wellingborough and Peterborough, whereas the then smaller Castle station was on the branch line to Market Harborough. *Author's collection*

new wheelbarrow wheels, 33,500 feet of iron rails, 32,700 sleepers, 18,500 keys, joint and intermediate chairs, iron girders for bridge parapet plates, weigh bridge, patent weighing machine, 12 ton crab with 100 yards ³/₈ chain; large quantity of fishfang and other bolts; fish plates, spikes and nails of various descriptions, chains, large quantities of deal battens and planks baulks, elm, ash, and other timber, pumps, with piping, boring tackle, permanent, bridle and other gates, office on wheels, a capital brick yard plant, 100,000 bricks, pantiles, roofing slates, glazed pipes, 600 yards felt covering, centres for bridges and culverts, scaffold poles, ladders, Blacksmiths' portable forge and tools, picks, shovels, hammers, and a great variety of other materials, the whole of which will be set forth in catalogues which will be prepared in due time, and may be had at the Office of the Auctioneer, Derngate, Northampton
Sale to commence each day at Ten o'clock'

Unfortunately, history has not recorded the details of the locomotive involved, which was presumably a contractor's type and owned by Shrimpton rather than the N&BJR. However, the location of the items 'in various parishes between Blisworth and Helmdon' does at least confirm that some preparatory work had been carried out by this date, beyond the end of the permanent way at Bradden.

The remnants were then auctioned again 'between Towcester station and Wappenham' on 27th December, this sale consisting of 'a large quantity of permanent and temporary rails, with points and crossings, permanent and temporary sleepers, chairs, keys, fishplates, switch boxes, five 24in iron girders, with parapet plates, and iron fittings for bridges, two 16ft ditto, with ditto; two 15ft ditto, with ditto; 80 tip wagons, 12 dobbin carts, 60 wheelbarrows, and numerous other effects.'

The infant MC&SWJR was soon in dire financial straits, this being reflected in local newspaper accounts of November 1866 and early 1867, which described how a locomotive named *Vulcan*, actually the property of the sub-contractor Foster, became embroiled in litigation. Foster had owned the engine from new, since delivery from the makers Hunslet in December 1865, and had used it during the construction of the line. The locomotive had then been incorrectly seized by the High Sheriff's officers under a warrant issued against the railway company.

In evidence, Foster stated that the engine, which carried a plate bearing his name and address as proof of ownership, had been in use by him until May 1866, when the first section of the line was opened and his initial contract ended. It was then kept in a shed at the end of the line, around two miles beyond Towcester.

In October 1866, with his contract having then been formally terminated, he agreed to sell the engine to a Mr Ashwell for £1,100. Foster authorised his storekeeper Franklin to release the engine but, on arrival, Ashwell found that the Sheriff's officer had quite incorrectly seized the engine under a writ of *fieri facias* against the railway company, removed it to a siding and secured the wheels to the rails to prevent removal. On hearing this news, Foster went in search of his property and, with the assistance of an L&NWR locomotive, placed it on the L&NWR line at Blisworth for Ashwell to collect.

Proceedings were then instigated against Foster for the supposed unlawful removal of the locomotive and also, in the same action, against Henry Crabtree, the general manager of the railway company, who was also accused of similarly removing some wagons which had also been seized. Local opinion appeared to suggest 'that a great deal of property was seized which did, and a great deal which did not, belong to the railway company'.

The pantomime then moved on to another stage, when Foster himself sued the High Sheriff for the loss of £50 which had resulted from a fall in the price that Ashwell was prepared to pay for the engine by the time that it was eventually made available to him. The ensuing case of 'Foster v Fitzwilliam and another' describes the N&BJR as 'a line of railway which has been the subject of more litigation than any little line in the Kingdom' and which was 'intended to go from Blisworth to Towcester and as much further as the rage for debenture making railways would carry it'. A conference duly took place between the contending parties, during which it was admitted 'that there were many difficulties on both sides'!

Foster continued his disposal of equipment in a sale of 24th and 25th January 1867, conducted by local auctioneers W.J. Peirce, at Blisworth station and Wappenham. 'Contractors and others' were offered a wide selection of timbers, planks, scaffolds, sheds, offices, centres for bridges, slates, tiles, barrels of gunpowder, and carpenter's and blacksmith's equipment. The most surprising item in the sale was however a 'temporary wood station, 38ft. by 12 ft.'. It is interesting to speculate as to the origin of this unusual structure; it may possibly have been a temporary station building from either Blisworth or Towcester but perhaps the more

E&WJR trains also used the N&BJR route to reach Towcester and Blisworth and this undated view shows a typical train of three 6-wheeled coaches, two horseboxes, and a van close to Green's Norton Junction, where the two railways met. The locomotive appears to be E&WJR Beyer, Peacock 2-4-0T No. 5, one of two which were obtained in 1885 for the reintroduction of passenger services on the Stratford route. *Courtesy R. Wharton*

likely explanation is that it was the 'wooden shed' in which Foster's locomotive *Vulcan* was kept at the end of the line at Bradden.

Rather surprisingly, it would not be until August 1868 that Foster would finally sever his connection with the N&BJR. On 27th of that month, auctioneers Beesley & Sons would offer a wide range of wooden and metal items at Wappenham 'in consequence of Mr. C.N. Foster relinquishing his occupation of the premises'.

Further Difficulties

Another serious effect of the sudden financial crisis was that the MC&SWJR was unable to complete the purchase of their new locomotives, which had been ordered from Neilson of Glasgow. The order was cancelled before any engines could be delivered to the line and the makers later sold them to the Caledonian Railway company and not, as recorded elsewhere, to the Solway Junction Railway.

The annual returns to the Board of Trade for the years of 1866 and 1867 do, however, confirm that the MC&SWJR somehow began operations with just a single locomotive and four carriages and mention has also been made of the early use of an engine named *The Owl* but which is otherwise unidentified.

It has also been suggested that the line was operated by the L&NWR after October 1866 and this eventuality had in fact been provided for under the 1863 Act. However, nothing has so far emerged from L&NWR records to substantiate this, or from the annual reports produced by the Board of Trade, wherein such working arrangements were normally recorded. It is perhaps more likely that the L&NWR merely assisted occasionally with the loan of a locomotive, as was certainly to be the case in following years.

It is also significant that a local engineering company, Harrison & Clayton of Northampton, is known to have maintained the 'locomotive operating between Blisworth and Towcester' during those early years, which would seem to provide further confirmation that the railway company did in fact operate their own trains. A local newspaper report, to be more fully mentioned later, also confirms that the railway still only had a single engine in use in 1868.

However, a possible reason for the suggestion of any involvement by the L&NWR may be found in a report in the *Northampton Mercury* of 24th November 1866. Under the heading of '*The Towcester Railway*' it states:

'*We are sorry to say that this railway, which for the short time that it has been opened has been found to be a very great accommodation to Towcester, has come to grief. Under an execution from the Sheriff the locomotive is in the spunging house and the traffic has been suddenly and entirely checked. Surely arrangements might be made with the L&NWR to continue the working pro tem in the interests of Towcestrians, the railway officials, and the general public.*' ('*Spunging house*' is an old term used to denote a place of temporary detention for debtors until the debt has been paid.)

It is likely that this occurrence is the one referred to earlier, involving Foster's locomotive *Vulcan*. If so, this may confirm a suggestion that *Vulcan* had been used to operate the line during this early period but as the engine then appears to have been sold by Foster in late 1866, the N&BJR must have obtained replacement motive power from somewhere to continue the services, and this could indeed have involved the assistance of the L&NWR.

Meanwhile, Business as Usual …

Despite these trials and tribulations, the MC&SWJR had still been able to provide a passenger service and continued to promote itself to the travelling public with trains in connection with Northampton Races on 2nd and 3rd April 1867. Services were advertised for race-goers from Towcester to Northampton at 10.15am, 11.05am and 12.40pm, and for the returning throngs at 5.33pm and 7.50pm. The journey between the two points took between thirty and forty minutes, with a change at Blisworth. A footnote to the advertisement for these trains stated that on and after 1st April, Third Class tickets would be available on all trains between Blisworth and Towcester for 6d.

The Annual Provincial General Meeting of the Province of Northants & Hunts Freemasons then took place at the Pomfret Arms, Towcester on 8th August 1867 and, once again, the MC&SWJR took the opportunity to advertise trains from Blisworth at 10.45am and 1.45pm, with returns at 7.18pm and 8.30pm, the latter service being a 'special'.

M.R. Shaw's Blisworth Pleasure Gardens, a popular local attraction situated adjacent to the Blisworth Hotel, also continued to provide traffic for the new railway, and 'cheap tickets' were again made available from Northampton and Towcester.

However, not all went to plan, and another local newspaper report of 22nd February 1868 relates how '*on Monday last no small inconvenience was felt at Blisworth station (especially to those parties who had taken a return ticket to Towcester) owing to the breaking down of the engine on the Blisworth to Towcester line. As the company have but one engine, parties had the choice of four things; to stay at Blisworth all night, hire a conveyance, walk, or go on the trolley propelled by manual labour, which some of the parties preferred. Happily, the state of things did not last long, as the jibbing engine, as some people called it, was got into good working order on the following day*'.

Unfortunately, the report does not give any details of the engine but significantly it is again stated to be the only one owned by the company, who were obviously running the line on a shoestring but were clearly prepared to resort to any measures to keep their passengers happy and return them to their destination.

Despite these difficulties, the passenger service had been maintained at the same level, with only slight variations in timings, and interestingly connections were now being shown to and from both Bridge Street and Castle stations in Northampton. Bridge Street station, on the original Blisworth to Peterborough Branch, had been open since 1845 but the other station, situated close to the old castle, was a relatively small affair on the 1859 branch to Market Harborough, which was served by Blisworth to Stamford trains.

It is also known from annual Board of Trade statistical returns that all N&BJR services were being run as mixed trains at this time, conveying both passenger and goods traffic. This was doubtless the most economical way of operating the line, with only one locomotive, four passenger vehicles and twenty goods wagons in use.

The MC&SWJR soon had other problems to contend with, as they were summoned to the Court of Chancery in Lincoln's Inn Fields on 1st February 1869, in the matter of Pell versus the Midland Counties & South Wales Junction Railway. It appears that the company (then the N&BJR) had in 1863 agreed with Pell

RIGHT: A major attraction at Blisworth was 'Mr Shaw's Pleasure Gardens', which were handily located for the station and provided many passengers for the N&BJR in the earliest days. The railway companies were quick to take advantage of the potential traffic and this delightful local press advertisement of 1866 is typical of the efforts that were made to promote travel and such attractions by means of a combined fare. *Author's collection*

BELOW: A classic early view of the Blisworth Hotel and associated Pleasure Gardens, ideally located for passengers from both the Northampton & Banbury Junction Railway and the L&NWR. Just off picture to the right is the jointly operated station building of 1871, from which patrons could walk directly onto the N&BJR platforms, or alternatively negotiate the gloom of the subway to reach the L&NWR main line or Northampton Branch trains. *Courtesy T. Marsh*

a payment of £2,000 cash as compensation for lands required for the railway or, at the option of the company, securities bearing 5% interest. Payment in cash was not made but, in 1864, the company gave Pell a bond for £2,000 payable on 16th June 1866 and were then given possession of the land. The MC&SWJR subsequently defaulted in payment of either the bond or the interest and Pell then sought legal recourse by restraining the company from keeping possession of or using the land until payment was made.

The Master of the Rolls ruled that the plaintiff had a *lien* as unpaid vendor of the lands and that, in default of the necessary payment within six months, the lands should be sold. The railway company mounted an appeal but this was dismissed, with costs, by the Lord Chancellor, resulting in the remarkable situation of sections of the railway in the parishes of Tiffield and Gayton actually being sold at auction to a William John Blake, Esquire.

A New Beginning

With the MC&SWJR now technically insolvent, the International Finance Society installed their director Lachlan Mackintosh Rate on to the railway company board to supervise their own considerable interests. They also provided the services of their solicitor W.R. Drake.

In June 1869, Charles Liddell, the MC&SWJR engineer, was then requested to report on the cost of completing the line through to Cockley Brake. On receipt of his estimate of £50,000, Rate indicated that the International Finance Society had decided to promote a Bill to complete the line themselves, this being considered the only way that they could restore any value to the securities that they still held.

Ultimately, on 7th December 1869, the MC&SWJR was forced to file with the Court of Chancery a Scheme of Arrangement with their creditors, under the requirements of the Railway Companies Act 1867. In total, the MC&SWJR owed around £30,000 to landowners, whilst other claims made by creditors amounted to a further £65,000. Various judgments had been made against the company and these, together with the failure of their contractor, meant that the MC&SWJR were unable to '*meet their engagements or proceed with their works*'. The chairman, the Rt Hon. Ernest Augustus Charles Brudenell Bruce, was therefore forced to record the '*general embarrassment of the affairs of the Company*'.

The MC&SWJR board now consisted of the chairman, Lord Bruce, along with Alexander Beattie, Jasper Wilson Johns, Charles Kelson, Lachlan Mackintosh Rate, Walter Amos Michael and Hervey James Sheldon. All stated addresses in London with the exception of Sheldon, who could almost claim to be local to the line, residing at Brailes House, Shipston on Stour. J. Wilson Theobold continued to act as Company Secretary.

It seems clear that the MC&SWJR project had by then evolved far from its beginnings as a purely local scheme and was now viewed very much as a speculative investment. It is also interesting to note that, bearing in mind the serious nature of the company's situation, their chairman had signed the required declaration to the Court of Chancery from a distance, at his address in '*Biarritz in the Empire of France*'.

The rather complex Scheme of Arrangement summarised the MC&SWJR share capital and borrowings for their various authorised lines and extensions, and made provision for defining and settling the rights of shareholders and creditors. As part of this rearrangement, the MC&SWJR Board, in the guise of the International Finance Society, had one month earlier indicated their promotion of a further Bill to complete the line. With the Society covering the necessary Parliamentary Deposit, the Act for the Northampton & Banbury Junction Railway *33 & 34 Vic. Cap.cxxii* was duly passed on 14th July 1870. This was necessary due to the powers from the 1863 Act having expired and allowed for the completion of the line from '*at or near a field in Bradden, in the County of Northampton, numbered 10 in that parish upon the deposited plans*' to join the Buckinghamshire Railway at Cockley Brake.

The new Act included the necessary powers for the compulsory purchase of the lost sections of line in Gayton and Tiffield parishes, and also for the company name to revert back to the original, and seemingly now far more appropriate, Northampton & Banbury Junction Railway. The company was also enabled to create and issue further debenture stock up to a total value of £500,000, subdivided into two classes, with the first £100,000 applying

solely to the Banbury line and the remaining £400,000 being allocated to the Blockley project. Capital thus raised by the issue of the Banbury stock was only to be used to pay off creditors and landowners, and to cover the cost of completing the remainder of the original line; however, a provision was also made for the salaries of the directors and other officers of the company.

Interestingly, the new application was described as '*nearly identical*' to that contained in the original Act of 1863, which suggests that some small changes to the route had occurred. This is possibly borne out by the announcement that '*certain freehold closes of land situate at Abthorpe and Wappenham … in the occupation of Messrs. John and Thomas Parsons … and the Northampton & Banbury Junction Railway*' were to be sold on 5th July 1870 at the Pomfret Arms Inn at Towcester '*pursuant to a decree of the High Court of Chancery*'.

Progress at Last

An equitable settlement having been arranged with the previous incumbent, William Shrimpton, the International Finance Society duly awarded a contract for completion of the route to the experienced engineers John Aird & Son. Aird soon arranged for the purchase of 17,300 sleepers from Gabrial & Sons and 1,080 tons of rails from Bolckow Vaughan, and these were delivered by canal to Blisworth, being paid for by the International Finance Society as each batch arrived.

Construction soon recommenced beyond Bradden and was presaged by a '*welcome sign of progress*' reported in the *Mercury* of 2nd April 1870:

'*The Towcester and Blisworth Railway, as that portion of the*

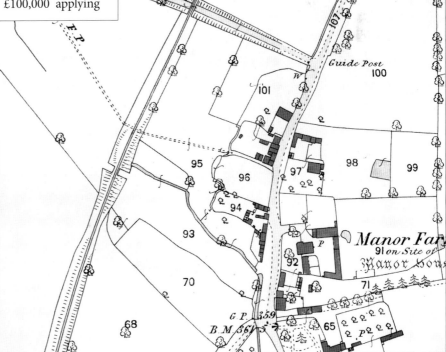

ABOVE LEFT: This wooden staircase, which ascends the eastern side of the embankment adjacent to the village, may be a remnant of the short-lived station at Tiffield, only operational for a few months from late 1869 to early 1871. There is now no trace of the station itself, which was probably only a wooden halt, but local folklore tells of its use for dropping off the occasional package and even unofficial passengers for many years afterwards. *L. Bootman*

ABOVE RIGHT: The probable site of the short-lived station at Tiffield, situated midway between Blisworth and Towcester, may be indicated on this map of 1880 by the curious curved hachures on the western side of the line, immediately adjacent to the point where a footpath crosses the track. Later editions of the Ordnance Survey do not show this feature, which had by then been replaced by normal hatching. *Author's collection*

Northampton and Banbury Railway which is in full working order has come to be designated, appears to be looking up rather more hopefully than formerly. A trivial but significant omen of better days may be found in the increased speed with which the journey between the two places is performed. Instead of occupying some 18 to 20 minutes, as has usually been the case in our experience, the single journey is now performed in nine or ten minutes.'

This significant acceleration, as will be seen later, had resulted from the purchase of a larger engine, which also occasioned the N&BJR to request use of the L&NWR water column at Blisworth, as their own supply was proving insufficient. The L&NWR were, however, unable to accede to their smaller neighbour's request, as they subsequently discovered that, under the terms of their agreement with the nearby canal company, they were prevented from reselling water extracted from that source.

Once again, services were still being maintained under difficult circumstances and a timetable of 1870 reveals that six trains in each direction were being provided daily for First, Second and Third Class passengers, with an additional service on Saturdays. An interesting development was that four trains in each direction would now *'stop by signal at Tiffield'*, where a small halt had been provided, although it is difficult to imagine that very much traffic could have been anticipated from this small village. This service was destined not to last and was only recorded in Bradshaw's timetables from October 1869 to February 1871.

'Cheap trips' to Blisworth Gardens were also still proving popular. In fact, on one Monday afternoon in June 1870, the trains became so overcrowded that *'it became necessary to attach an ordinary wagon to the 3.18 train this having been made convenient for the carriage of passengers, reminding one of times when uncovered carriages were amongst the conveyances provided by the railways – everyone was pleased with the arrangements, and those who were obliged to put up with the apparent inconvenience seemed to enjoy the novelty.'*

It appears that the railway acted quickly to prevent a repetition of this rather unorthodox situation, as when a Volunteer Encampment Week was held at nearby Wakefield Lawn later the same month, special trains were run as required using additional carriages.

The *Mercury* offered further evidence of the progress being made by reporting on July 30th 1870 that the work of completing the line was *'now being carried on with vigour',* adding that *'we need hardly repeat what we have said so many times about the value of this communication between two towns of such importance and activity as Northampton and Banbury'*. A pertinent comment on the troubled times that had recently plagued so many railway undertakings was their closing statement that *'We know of no more promising project and it can hardly have remained so long in abeyance but for the depression and disfavour under which all railway enterprise had been so long lying'.*

October saw the *Mercury* somewhat belatedly confirming the appointment of John Aird as contractor and commenting that it was anticipated that the line would be completed in about twelve

NORTHAMPTON and BANBURY JUNCTION.—4¼ miles.							
Traff. Man., J. B. Crabtree.			Sec. & Gen. Man., J. Wilson Theobald.				
Up.	1,2,3	gov	1,2,3	1,2,3	1,2,3	1,2,3	1,2,3
Towcester .... dep	8 25	1010	11 a10	1 10	3 18	5 30	7 18
Tiffield	....	b	b	b	b	....	....
Blisworth 110, 115	8 37	1025	11 25	1 27	3 33	5 45	7 33
*Frm. London, p.*110.	1,2,3	1,2,3	gov	1,2,3	1,2,3	1,2,3	1,2,3
Blisworth......dep	9 15	10 a45	1130	2 10	4 35	6 7	8 25
Tiffield	b	....	b	b	....	....	....
Towcester .... arr	9 30	11 0	1145	2 25	4 50	6 22	8 40

a Saturdays only.
b Stop to take up by Passengers' own signal, and set down on notice being given at Towcester or Blisworth.

This panoramic view of Towcester from the east on 14th May 1961 shows the full extent of the station area after the alterations of 1910, when the Down platform was converted to an island and a new taller signal box replaced the original east and west cabins. The short spur seen beyond the bracket signal gantry originally lead to the engine shed but was afterwards used for carriage storage and latterly served a loading bay. The Hesketh Hotel, just visible on the right of the picture, shared its approach road with the station. Adjacent to the hotel had been Towcester cattle market, the source of much traffic for the line. *M. Mitchell*

Looking west from Towcester station footbridge during the 1930s. The four signal dolls on the bracket at the end of the Up platform controlled access to the single lines towards Banbury and Stratford-upon-Avon, and the Up yard sidings just beyond the Watling Street road underbridge, the girders of which are just visible between the tracks. The two single lines parted company approximately one mile further on, at the site of the former Green's Norton Junction. Also just visible to the left of the signal is the engine turntable that had been relocated from Stratford in 1910. *Author's collection*

months time and that following the *'undoubted future success'* of the route, the further extension to Ross and South Wales was still being considered. Somewhat strangely, the report also stated that it was expected that there would be three stations between Towcester and Banbury, and that these would *'probably be in the neighbourhood of Wappenham, Helmdon and Farthinghoe, although the exact localities had not yet been fixed'*.

The N&BJR were obviously still entertaining hopes of extending beyond their revised target of Banbury and at the end of November 1870, again with assistance from the International Finance Society, plans were deposited for revisions to their powers gained under the 1865 and 1866 Acts. These indicated

a change to the planned route at Banbury and short deviations at three other locations where the original route was to be abandoned, with an extension of time provided for completion.

However, support was not forthcoming, with the exception of Henry Sheldon, a landowner at Brailes, who had subscribed to an earlier abortive Blockley & Banbury Railway scheme. When that failed, he had transferred his allegiance and support to the N&BJR, eventually joining the Board. Perhaps understandably, these latest proposals were not pursued, and that point effectively marked the end of any prospect of the line ever being extended further west than Cockley Brake.

The *Northampton Mercury* was obviously keeping a close eye

Wappenham was the first station on the new extension of the N&BJR route, opened from Towcester to Cockley Brake Junction in 1872. The modest station building was located adjacent to a minor road and quite some distance from the village after which it was named. The small goods yard, with a grounded coach body used for storage purposes, is just visible beyond the platform end and one of the typical twin-arched N&BJR road bridges can just be discerned in the distance. *Author's collection*

At the somewhat more important village of Helmdon, the N&BJR provided rather more extensive facilities, with a larger goods yard and even a brick built goods shed. At one time there was also a second platform and a passing loop but these were both dispensed with during a reorganisation after the increased traffic brought about by the construction of the Great Central main line in the late 19th century had diminished. This view, taken from the village road bridge during the 1940s, is typical of the sleepy nature of the Banbury Branch, with just a couple of daily passenger services and a few wagons of goods or livestock to disturb the peace; indeed it was often said that the numbers of cattle carried by the line exceeded those of passengers. *Author's collection*

on events, as they indicated on 15th April 1871 that '*the Banbury works are going on, and Towcester station grows livelier … the spoil bank at the western end of the platform has been put in order and prepared for planting, if not planted. At intervals too along the platform trees and shrubs have been planted and it looks as though there was a pleasant intention of making it ornamental as well as useful. One is glad to see that the stationmaster at Towcester adds to his other merits an appreciation of trees and flowers.*'

July 1871 brought further reports that '*the line is rapidly*

emerging from its long season of adversity. For some time past the completed section of line between Blisworth and Towcester has been worked with continually increasing success by Mr J.B. Crabtree, the energetic Traffic Superintendent. The business of the station has been largely augmented of late, more particularly in regards to goods traffic, and the building of a substantial goods shed, with the employment of additional engines on the line, are amongst the evidences of progress.'

The report added that goods traffic would be worked as far

This post-1948 view illustrates well the juxtaposition of the N&BJR and L&NWR premises at Blisworth, with the exchange siding separating the two territories. The joint booking office building of 1871 dominates the view, with the N&BJR platforms visible just beyond but passengers for the L&NWR platforms had to pass beneath the siding in a subway to reach their trains. The yard crane was L&NWR property and formed part of that company's goods yard situated behind the camera. Over to the left, the Blisworth Hotel was looking slightly the worse for wear, whilst the old Pleasure Gardens were long gone. *Author's collection*

The siding leading to the goods yard separating the N&BJR and L&NWR premises at Blisworth was not easy to operate, with any lengthy goods trains between the two systems needing to reverse down its length and then draw forward again. This early British Railways era view shows Class '3F' No. 43698 from Saltley shed shunting a few vans that have probably originated from the N&BJR line, whilst a Class '8F' 2-8-0 lingers in the background awaiting its own turn. *Author's collection*

A view north from the end of the N&BJR platforms at Blisworth, revealing very little activity – just a couple of brake vans standing on the exchange siding. The line to Towcester disappears into the left distance, whilst the L&NWR main line continues straight ahead beneath the road bridge towards Gayton Loops. Water was available for locomotives on both platforms, continuity of supply being ensured by a brazier alongside each column. The water tank itself was of interesting construction and was a replacement for one that stood between the tracks at the platform end. *Author's collection*

as Helmdon from the end of the month and that the line should be fully opened to all traffic through to Banbury by autumn. The '*heavy cutting*' at Greatworth was stated to be the key to the opening of the line but this was now '*more than half excavated*'.

Local traders were also quickly off the mark, with Mr Smith Wickens '*begging to inform his friends that he has taken wharves at Wappenham and Helmdon stations to supply coals on the best terms*'. The stations had by then been confirmed as Wappenham and Helmdon, '*and probably Farthinghoe, but this last mentioned place has not yet been definitely decided upon*'.

As an interesting aside, this apparent indecision over the siting of stations seems to have inadvertently led to the N&BJR featuring in modern day legal case law. It seems that the owner of Manor Farm, Wappenham, a Mr Wilson, initially opposed the building of the railway but later withdrew his objection when it

was agreed that a station would be provided there. However, it appears that the N&BJR, having obtained their Act, must have then built the station in a different place to that indicated to Wilson. If a map of the area is consulted, it will be seen that the railway passes beneath a minor road at a point half way between Manor Farm and Wappenham village, and this would seem to have been a far more logical location for the station. However, it was eventually situated further east alongside a different road far less convenient to both village and farm, and this may well have been the cause of the dispute. The ensuing case of '*Wilson v The Northampton & Banbury Junction Railway Company (1874)*' can now occasionally be found quoted as precedent in modern contractual litigation.

The N&BJR were obviously preparing for the opening of their new section of line, as during 1871 they had been busily engaged

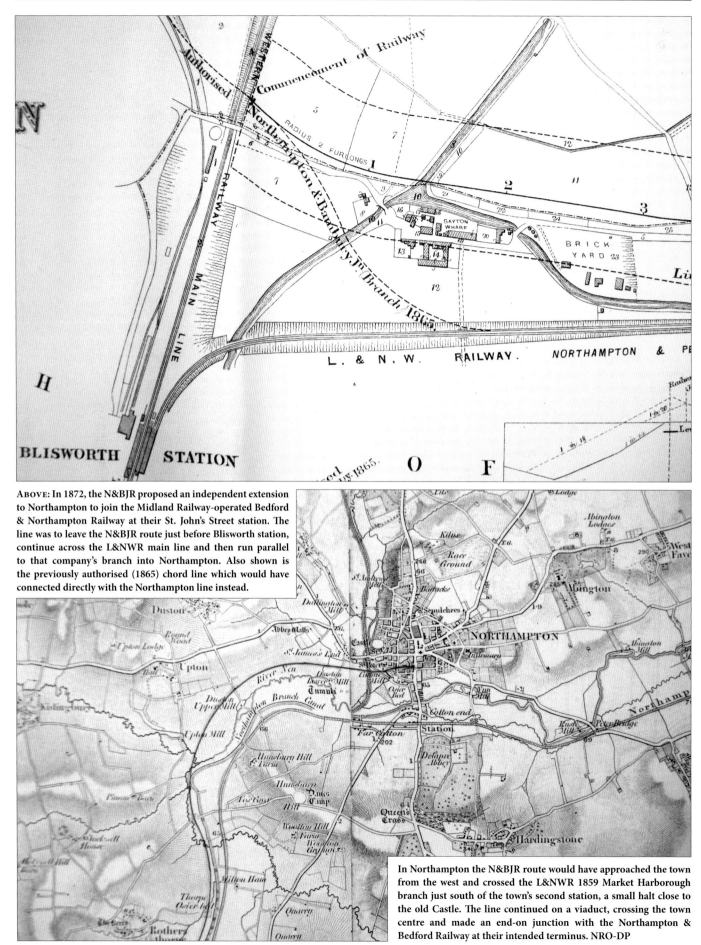

ABOVE: In 1872, the N&BJR proposed an independent extension to Northampton to join the Midland Railway-operated Bedford & Northampton Railway at their St. John's Street station. The line was to leave the N&BJR route just before Blisworth station, continue across the L&NWR main line and then run parallel to that company's branch into Northampton. Also shown is the previously authorised (1865) chord line which would have connected directly with the Northampton line instead.

In Northampton the N&BJR route would have approached the town from the west and crossed the L&NWR 1859 Market Harborough branch just south of the town's second station, a small halt close to the old Castle. The line continued on a viaduct, crossing the town centre and made an end-on junction with the Northampton & Bedford Railway at their intended terminus. NRO-DP

in adding to their rolling stock. As evidenced by the annual Board of Trade return, by the end of the year this had increased to a total of four locomotives and six passenger carriages, plus one further, albeit unspecified, vehicle for use with passenger trains.

In addition, the prospect of increased passenger traffic had lead to the N&BJR and L&NWR agreeing to share a new larger station building at Blisworth, which was completed in early September 1871. However, a report of a concert that took place in the *'spacious hall of the Northampton & Banbury railway'* in April 1870 does suggest that the N&BJR already had a station building on the site, with the original L&NWR facilities provided on their own main line platforms. It therefore seems likely that the new structure was added to the existing N&BJR building and thereafter passengers used the subway to reach the L&NWR trains.

Meanwhile, the dangers of working as a railway navvy were once again vividly illustrated by an inquest held on 21st September 1871, into the death of one Samuel Stanton, employed by Messrs Aird & Son on the N&BJR extension. James Brown, a foreman, described how Stanton was filling wagons at a location rather unfortunately known as Gallows Field, in the parish of Greatworth. Work was being carried on in a cutting about 9ft deep, when part of the face was seen to move. In trying to escape, Stanton instead ran into danger and was hit by the falling earth. Despite the attentions of the local surgeon from nearby Sulgrave, Stanton could not be saved and the inquest once more returned a verdict of accidental death.

The half yearly meeting of the N&BJR directors at the end of 1871 revealed that they considered that *'the traffic on the section from Blisworth to Towcester continued to be satisfactory, having averaged £13 5s per mile per week over the preceding six months'.*

In addition, the directors announced that they would be promoting a Bill for an independent line from Blisworth to Northampton, which they considered would be of great advantage to the Company. This line would bridge the L&NWR main line just north of Blisworth station, under powers already provided by their earlier Act. It would then continue on to enter Northampton from the south-west, along the valley of the River Nene, crossing the L&NWR Market Harborough Branch close to the small halt which would, after 1881, become the site of the

main Northampton Castle station. The proposed line would then have made a junction with the Bedford & Northampton Railway, then under construction (opened in 1872, operated by and later vested in the Midland Railway), close to their St. Johns Street station in the town centre. This line would have provided the N&BJR with their desired route to Northampton but connecting with the then newly arrived Midland Railway rather than directly to their old allies the L&NWR.

In the event, the L&NWR quickly countered this move by instead confirming running powers on their own line through to Northampton, should the N&BJR eventually decide to actually construct their shorter link to a direct junction with the Blisworth & Peterborough Branch at Gayton Wharf. A formal agreement to that effect was signed on 30th April 1872 following pressure from shareholders but it appears that the directors were less than happy with this arrangement, feeling that an independent line of their own would have been in the best interests of the N&BJR.

Through to Banbury

On 31st January 1872 J. Wilson Theobold communicated to the Board of Trade his company's intention to shortly open to passengers their new extension to Cockley Brake. In fact, although the N&BJR line was all but ready at that time, with only

ABOVE: Views of Green's Norton Junction are virtually unknown and even illustrations of the later arrangements are difficult to find, with track in place on both lines. In order to provide even the briefest glimpse of the original junction, which was situated one mile west of Towcester station, it is necessary to resort to this cruel enlargement of an already poor photograph. The last coach of an N&BJR line train has just cleared the points of the junction and is heading away towards Towcester; the Banbury line is visible to the left, whilst the signals and passing loops at the junction itself lead off towards Stratford-upon-Avon in the other direction, with the signal cabin unfortunately just obscured by trees. *Courtesy R. Wharton*

LEFT: Originally, E&WJR and N&BJR trains had shared a single line to Green's Norton Junction but, in 1910, it was abolished and relocated to the environs of Towcester station. The Banbury line of the N&BJR was lifted in the mid-1950s, such that here, on 19th October 1958, just a grassy route to the left of the permanent way cabin remained. The E&WJR line towards Blakesley was still in regular use for goods traffic at this date. *M. Mitchell*

minor items to be completed, the L&NWR had still not started work on the junction at Cockley Brake. It was not until 17th May that a second notice of opening was submitted, which stated that the line should be ready for the required official inspection on or after 27th May.

Colonel Hutchinson duly carried out the formalities on 29th of that month, commenting that the permanent way of the first two miles beyond Towcester was of the same construction as that reported by Captain Rich during his inspection of the Blisworth to Towcester section in 1866; this was of course the part of the line that had already been completed before construction was suspended for the next six years.

The Colonel also recorded that turntables were now available at Blisworth and Banbury, and it must be assumed that, until this point in time, the line had still been worked by tank engines as originally stipulated by Captain Rich in 1866.

There were twelve overbridges and twenty-four underbridges or large culverts on the new line, all of which were '*substantially constructed*'.

The Colonel considered that the signalling and sidings at both of the intermediate stations at Wappenham and Helmdon required attention to the interlocking, with the Wappenham Up Distant signal also needing a white background to aid sighting. Alterations were also required to the fastenings of the track on underbridges, and some additional packing and fencing was still needed in various places.

The N&BJR provided an undertaking that the line would be worked on the train staff system and responded with a letter of compliance on 17th June, requesting a final inspection. Meanwhile, it seems that passenger services had already commenced on 1st June, so presumably the Colonel had been happy to give his approval subject to completion of his stipulations and his further visit on 9th August confirmed that all had been complied with.

It further appears, from the N&BJR report for the half year to 30th June 1872, that the temporary end of the line at Bradden had also acted as a destination for coal traffic for a time, as this revenue was mentioned as being included in the receipts for the period to 30th June 1871; once construction had reached Helmdon, goods traffic was also worked to that point. The directors also commented that additional expenditure had been incurred by the need to engage staff for the anticipated opening, which had then been delayed by the L&NWR's tardiness in completing the junction.

The *Northampton Mercury* conveyed the news of the opening to its readers:

'*At each village are pretty stations, substantial and convenient. Continuing in the direction of Banbury at three miles beyond Helmdon we come to Cockley Brake, where the branch joins the old line between Banbury and Brackley. Here there is no station – although it may hereafter be found desirable to have one – but only an observatory for the policeman and signal keeper in charge of Saxby's costly apparatus. Farthinghoe station is 1¾ miles from*

This 1930s view of the L&NWR owned station at Farthinghoe illustrates the basic nature of the facilities provided there. The simple station building is largely built of wood, with the short, low platform and associated fencing all of similar construction. At the Banbury end, a single siding provided for the small amount of local goods traffic, as typified by the few assorted open wagons on view. The two men unloading one of the wagons have paused to watch the photographer take his picture. N&BJR line trains were not allowed to pick up or set down passengers travelling only between Farthinghoe and Banbury, in order to concentrate local traffic onto the L&NWR trains to and from Bletchley. *Author's collection*

Arrival at the Banbury terminus of the L&NWR was announced by this ancient sign, constructed of wood in keeping with the building itself and quite probably dating back to the very opening of the line in the 1850s; the full-stop after the name is also indicative of an early era. The station, later known as Merton Street, was used by N&BJR trains from Blisworth and Towcester from 1872 through to withdrawal of those services in 1951, although passenger trains from Bletchley continued until the end of December 1960. *Author's collection*

BELOW RIGHT: The outside of the station was no more impressive than the interior, with the basic wooden accommodation set at right angles to the train shed. Seen here in the 1950s, the large wooden bargeboard above the entrance bore a variety of names, 'Banbury Merton Street Station' being the last. The slightly more impressive GWR facilities, which benefited from several extensions and rebuildings over the years, were just a few hundred yards to the right and a little used siding connected the two railways. *Author's collection*

here, and Banbury four miles farther. The whole distance between Northampton and Banbury is 25¼ miles and the entire journey can be performed in little over one hour. Bye-and-bye the power of crossing the main line at Blisworth will be exercised, and the passengers between the two towns will not have to change at Blisworth. We believe that there are to be six trains daily each way.'

The newspaper was not quite correct in its assumptions, as the initial timetable consisted of just three through trains in each direction. The 'Parliamentary' left Blisworth at 8.25am and was followed by services at 11.15am and 5.00pm. Return from Banbury was at 10.05am ('Parliamentary'), 2.35pm and 6.30pm. In addition, however, there were two services each way between Towcester and Blisworth only, leaving the former point at 8.00am and 1.15pm, and returning at 2.25pm and 7.45pm.

In informing its readers of the new service, the newspaper commented that '*notwithstanding that the notice was short the receipt from passenger traffic has been considerable*'.

The use of running powers over the L&NWR line resulted in Banbury bound N&BJR trains only being able to set down passengers at the intermediate station of Farthinghoe, whilst in the Up direction, passengers could only join trains there, in order to maximise local traffic on L&NWR services.

Most trains advertised reasonable connections to and from Northampton at Blisworth, and travel between the two market

towns took around one and a half hours, with the journey on the N&BJR route taking just over two thirds of that total. The importance of market day travel was recognised with the extension to and from Banbury of a Thursday afternoon Blisworth to Towcester service. A later announcement suggested that an improved service would shortly be introduced.

However, within two weeks from the commencement of through services, the N&BJR were faced with further difficulties. The *Northampton Mercury* reported on 15th June how '*on Saturday night last, or early on Sunday morning, an extensive landslip occurred on this line, at the Gayton cutting, about one mile from Blisworth station. A large gang of men was immediately set to work to clear the line, but in spite of the most strenuous exertions, the portions of the line from Tiffield to Blisworth was blocked for several days. The consequent inconvenience to passengers has been lessened as far as possible by the employment of vehicles to run between Tiffield and Blisworth.*'

It is probable that the N&BJR still had their short-lived passenger station *in situ* at Tiffield at this time, although it was no longer being shown in timetables, and it must be assumed that trains from Towcester terminated there for a few days during these difficulties.

The same issue of the *Mercury* also provided more positive news, with details of a forthcoming event from which the newly extended N&BJR would certainly have gained increased patronage. The well established venue of Mr Shaw's Blisworth Gardens was to host an appearance of the famous Blondin, the '*first appearance for ten years of the celebrated and original hero of Niagara … who will give one grand day performance on the high rope, including all his great feats*'. The newspaper announced a '*Grand Fete Champetre*' commencing at half past three on 24th June, when the celebrity performer would present a varied programme including acrobatic feats, standing on a chair, carrying a man, riding a bicycle, and no less than drinking champagne and cooking an omelette – all of which could be seen for the sum of one shilling.

The N&BJR had then to endure yet another appearance in a court of law early in August, when under-sheriff Henry Markham sat with a jury at the Blisworth Hotel to determine damages payable by the railway company to Mrs Frances Sarah Harrison of Towcester, pursuant to the compulsory purchase of land. The jury viewed the property which the N&BJR had taken possession of in April 1865. The first notice had been to purchase just over 3 acres, followed by a further one acre. Mrs Harrison claimed for another 5 poles and also for damage caused to a further acre and 4 poles; the building of the railway had also severed an area of 16 acres from the total holding of 48 acres. Eventually, the jury returned a verdict of £669 compensation for the land and a further £330 for damages, substantial sums which could not have been good news for the N&BJR finances.

The new service to Banbury having settled into place, the close of 1872 then saw the N&BJR reporting to the Board of Trade the ownership of five locomotives, ten carriages and two other vehicles for use with passenger traffic. Strangely, however, the ownership of only one other non-passenger vehicle was indicated, which possibly suggests that the goods stock used by the company was still being hired, as had apparently been the case with all rolling stock for the years of 1869 and 1870.

ABOVE: The N&BJR shared Banbury station with the L&NWR trains from Bletchley. This 1930s view of ex-L&NWR Webb 0-6-0 No. 8336 is thus likely to be awaiting departure on the latter route and will travel via Verney Junction to reach the main line at Bletchley instead of Blisworth. The locomotive was new in November 1882, as L&NWR No. 2466, a member of Webb's famous '18in Goods' Class, popularly known as 'Cauliflowers' due to the resemblance of the company crest carried on the central splasher to the vegetable. Renumbered by the LM&SR in September 1927, it was withdrawn in February 1936 but several classmates survived into the early BR era. *Author's collection*

LEFT: A view from the bufferstops inside Banbury station illustrates the rather flimsy nature of the overall roof, latterly clad with corrugated iron in place of the original glazing. The gloomy interior holds just two non-corridor coaches, one possibly for the N&BJR line service to Towcester and the other probably being a spare for the Bletchley line. *Author's collection*

This plan of 1873 was prepared for the Board of Trade inspection of the connection between the N&BJR and Towcester Ironstone siding, situated just north of Towcester station at 3 miles 37 chains and 70 links from Blisworth. A small signal box, named Lloyd's Sidings, was situated opposite the junction but closed after just a few years use.

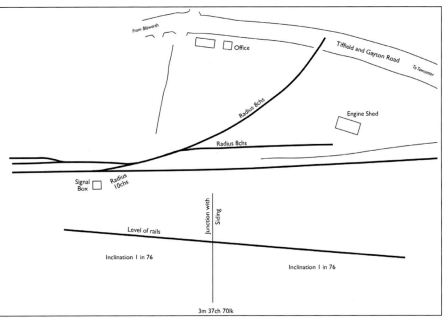

A new connection to the N&BJR was provided in 1873, the company contacting the Board of Trade on 27th May to state that Lloyd's Siding, situated between Blisworth and Towcester, and approximately one mile from the latter station, was almost ready for opening. This siding served iron ore quarries on the nearby Easton Neston Estate, where Samuel Lloyd was also experimenting with the production of iron at the adjacent Towcester Ironworks, using a new design of rotary furnace designed and patented by Dr C.W. Siemens. However, this venture was not successful and the furnaces were certainly disused by around 1878, when they were replaced by conventional blast furnaces. The ownership was then taken over by the Easton Estate & Mining Company Ltd, which was registered on 17th July 1878 to take over the mining activities of Samuel Lloyd and the Towcester Iron Company. However, the concern would be voluntarily wound up on 2nd June 1883, and the lands and effects sold after only a few years of activity; the siding appears to have closed soon afterwards.

A consequence of the completion of construction through to Cockley Brake was reflected in an auction announcement in the *Northampton Mercury* of 8th March 1873:

NORTHAMPTON AND BANBURY JUNCTION RAILWAY
WAPPENHAM STATION

TO CONTRACTORS, BUILDERS AND OTHERS,
SALE OF RAILWAY PLANT AND MATERIALS,
TWO LOCOMOTIVE TANK ENGINES,
80 TONS OF PERMANENT RAILS, FISH PLATES,
BOLTS, SCREWS &c.

W.J. PEIRCE

Has received instructions

TO SELL BY AUCTION,

On Tuesday, March 18th 1873, at the **WAPPENHAM STATION**
of the Northampton and Banbury Junction Railway, in the
County of Northampton,

The following valuable **SURPLUS MATERIALS**, not required
in the construction of the above Line of Railway, comprising
about 40 Tons of Permanent Rails (70lbs.), 20 tons of fish
plates, 2½ tons of Fish plate bolts, 19 tons of fang bolts,
5 tons of screws

Also, **TWO SIX WHEELED** (Four-coupled)
LOCOMOTIVE TANK ENGINES,

with Copper, Fire Boxes, Brass Tubes, &c.

Sale to commence at one o'clock.

The surplus materials are self explanatory but the mention of the two four-coupled tank locomotives is significant, as it presumably marks the end of the requirement to use only tank locomotives on passenger trains on the N&BJR line. This had originally been stipulated by Captain Rich when approving the line for opening in 1866, as there was no means of turning engines at Towcester, the then terminus of the line. However, completion through to the L&NWR station at Banbury meant that the use of a turntable was then available and, as will be seen later, the N&BJR quickly moved to purchase two tender engines from the L&NWR.

Further Changes

The first full year of operation through to Banbury saw the no doubt hoped for increase in the number of passengers carried by the N&BJR, with the 1873 total reported as 62,715, representing an improvement of 50% over previous years. Total receipts from goods traffic also more than doubled to just over £4,700. However, although these figures must have been a welcome improvement over the very sparse years of 1871 and 1872, increased running costs meant that they were still only just sufficient to provide the company with a small annual operating surplus of £188.

The opening of the East & West Junction Railway route to Stratford on 1st July 1873 also brought additional passenger traffic to Blisworth and Towcester stations, by virtue of running powers granted over the N&BJR line from Green's Norton Junction, one mile west of Towcester. The E&WJR trains were interlaced with the existing N&BJR services and for a few years they even included through coaches for London Euston. Initially, the E&WJR services were not allowed to carry local passengers between Blisworth and Towcester; however this restriction would soon become meaningless, with E&WJR passenger services being suspended for eight years from 1877.

These incursions into N&BJR territory by E&WJR and also L&NWR trains will be more fully considered later.

Passenger numbers continued to increase, and the year of 1874 saw a surge to a total of 115,144, a figure that would not

The N&BJR met the L&NWR branch from Bletchley to Banbury at Cockley Brake Junction, situated in the midst of open countryside. A Saxby & Farmer hipped roof signal cabin originally controlled the operation of the passing loops and junction, until this was superseded in the early 20th century by a more modern L&NWR style signal box. The N&BJR line runs off towards Helmdon on the left, whilst the original route of the Buckinghamshire Railway continues to the right towards Verney Junction and eventually Bletchley. *Author's collection*

be surpassed for another twenty-one years. However, the vast majority of these additional passengers travelled in Third Class, so the effect on revenue was not proportionate, providing only a modest annual increase of around £300. Goods traffic, in particular coal and general merchandise, continued to flourish, with a pronounced increase in receipts over the previous year but, rather significantly, mineral traffic, the initial *raison d'etre* of the line, saw little overall improvement.

However, the new extension to Cockley Brake did find a somewhat surprising use by the Towcester Highways Board, who placed tenders in the local press in early 1874 for their annual supply of Hartshill stone for road dressing purposes. The Board required delivery of just over 500 tons to traditional local canal wharves such as Stoke Bruerne and Blisworth but the opportunity was also taken to bring the stone to more convenient locations, with 200 tons consigned to Wappenham station, 180 tons to Blakesley and a further 50 tons to Helmdon. All of this combined to provide the N&BJR with a comparatively bumper year, with an operating surplus of £1,448, again a result that would not be bettered for over twenty years.

However, not everyone was happy with the current arrangements for goods traffic. The *Mercury* reported '*great indignation*' at Towcester over what were considered to be most unreasonable terms imposed on the local carrier, Mr Tunnard. Tradesmen who had long submitted to the '*extortionate*' charges made by the railway company, as well as putting up with unreasonable delays, agreed that in the event of the railway not coming up with more reasonable terms, they would employ Tunnard to carry their goods directly to Blisworth in the future, stating that '*There is no doubt there is great room for improvement to the railway accommodation at Towcester*'.

Nevertheless, the N&BJR was obviously keen to carry as much traffic as possible, as evidenced by a notice announcing the Annual Provincial General Meeting of the Grand Lodge of Freemasons of Northants and Hunts at Towcester on Wednesday May 27th 1874. Attendees were advised that trains would be available from Blisworth to Towcester at 12 noon and 12.30pm. After the conclusion of the banquet, a return service was to be operated

at 7.12pm but for any stragglers '*a carriage will be attached to a goods train leaving Towcester for Blisworth at 8.30pm*'.

The close of 1874 brought the announcement of an interesting proposal for what appears to have been an independent Northampton & Blisworth Railway, albeit with echoes of a N&BJR scheme of three years earlier. The line was to run from a junction with the Bedford & Northampton Railway, just to the west of their new station in Northampton, to join the N&BJR route a short distance out from their Blisworth station, thus bridging the L&NWR main line. Junctions were also to be provided with the L&NWR at Northampton and Gayton Wharf, and provision was to be made for comprehensive running powers over the existing or proposed L&NW, Bedford & Northampton, Midland, N&BJ, East & West Junction, Evesham, Redditch & Stratford Junction, and Evesham & Redditch railways. Once again, the proposal did not come to fruition but efforts were obviously still being made to provide the long awaited through connection between Northampton and the west.

November 1874 also brought the deposition of plans for another railway scheme connecting with the N&BJR, namely the Buckinghamshire & Northamptonshire Railways Union Railway. This was to link the Aylesbury & Buckingham Railway with the N&BJR at Bradden and the East & West Junction line at Green's Norton, and also involved a new line running parallel to the existing L&NWR Banbury Branch near Buckingham, where a second station would be opened.

This somewhat understandably did not meet with the approval of the L&NWR, who after hearing that a Bill had been applied for in February 1875, mounted a strong opposition, resulting in the withdrawal of the scheme during 1876. Nevertheless, as will later be seen, there would be several, very similar proposals to open up this part of north Buckinghamshire over the following fifteen years, all connecting with the N&BJR; howevern none of them would be successful.

The year of 1875 saw a slight decrease in revenues from both passenger and goods traffic but although overall traffic volumes were being maintained, other costs continued to restrict any working profits to a minimum.

The N&BJR line was joined by the E&WJR route to Stratford at Green's Norton Junction, with trains then using a single line to and from Towcester station. With the junction in the background, a Banbury line train heads east on its way towards Towcester. Consisting of an L&NWR 0-6-0, four L&NWR six-wheeled coaches and a van, the photograph dates from the period between 1875 and 1910, when the L&NWR provided all of the rolling stock for its smaller neighbour. *Courtesy R. Wharton*

The L&NWR Takes Over

Against this background it was perhaps understandable that the N&BJR Board seems finally to have concluded that the cost of operation and maintenance of their own ageing locomotives had become an unnecessary burden on the company. A decision was therefore made to negotiate with their close neighbours the L&NWR and an agreement was duly concluded for the supply of engines at the rate of one shilling per train mile, including the provision of a driver and fireman. The footplate staff supplied were initially to be considered as *pro tem* servants of the N&BJR, with the L&NWR being absolved of all liabilities but, in due course, the L&NWR did in fact take over the employment of the existing N&BJR crews.

Payment was made fortnightly to the L&NWR at Bletchley and the arrangement was approved by the L&NWR Locomotive Committee on the understanding that trains would be hauled by one locomotive. A subsequent L&NWR Committee minute recorded commencement from 1st March 1875, although formal approval was not given by the Railway Commissioners until 26th October 1876. The rate per mile was increased to 1s 2d in 1877 and it seems likely that this was to cover the provision of passenger rolling stock, as well as the locomotives. The N&BJR retained their passenger stock after the L&NWR began operating the line in 1875, and still had eight coaches and two brakes at the end of 1876; however these had disappeared by the close of the following year, and were probably replaced at that point by L&NWR stock.

This arrangement, together with the basic three train service to and from Banbury, with Thursdays only additions, was to endure for the next thirty-five years through to the amalgamation with the Stratford-upon-Avon & Midland Junction Railway. Many services were operated as mixed trains, conveniently combining both passenger and goods vehicles behind the same locomotive.

The photographer of this 1940s view was standing on the minor road bridge that crossed both the L&NWR main line and the N&BJR route just to the north of Blisworth station, behind the camera. The line to Towcester is off picture to the left and Gayton Loops signal box on the main line to Rugby is just visible in the distance beyond the Up goods train. Had any of the various schemes of the 1860s and 1870s been enacted, this scene would have been very different, with a long girder bridge spanning the four tracks of the L&NWR line, roughly half way along the length of the train, carrying a line connecting the N&BJR route with the Blisworth to Northampton branch line (see map overleaf). Ex-L&NWR 'B' Class 0-8-0 No. 1890 was reclassified as Class 'G1' by the LM&SR in 1924 and renumbered as No. 8901 in 1926. It was rebuilt to Class 'G2A' in early 1947 and withdrawn as BR No. 48901 in 1952. *Author's collection*

This E&WJR plan of 1874 is illustrative of several schemes that would have connected the N&BJR line with the branch to Northampton. The proposed new line would have extended from the existing N&BJR route as it began to curve down into Blisworth station and then crossed above all four tracks of the L&NWR main line on a girder bridge located halfway between Gayton Loops signal box and the minor road bridge to the north of the station. *NRO–DP*

a Mexican railway. This locomotive was somewhat larger and heavier than most of its British contemporaries and the N&BJR took issue with its use over certain sections of their track, in particular the platforms and sidings at Blisworth. The dispute was eventually referred to the Railway Commissioners, who undertook their usual thorough investigation of the complaint. However, after some consideration of the various circumstances, they adjudged that although the engine was somewhat larger than usual, most of the route on which it was used was only single line and as the Fairlie had already been in use for several months without undue incident, they supported its use by the E&WJR, stating that *'everyone would just have to be careful'* at the few locations where there might be potential problems.

The year of 1876 also brought more local difficulty for the N&BJR through another dispute with the E&WJR. The latter's Act of 1864 provided for running powers over the N&BJR from Green's Norton Junction and into Towcester and Blisworth stations. As was usual, the E&WJR were required to bear a proportion of the operating, maintenance and staffing costs at these locations. In the event, the two companies were unable to agree on the allocation of these costs and, in July 1873, the Board of Trade had appointed Robert Stanley Mansel as arbitrator. An acceptable solution was found and an agreement signed on 25th July 1873, covering an initial period of two years and thereafter until terminated on six months notice by either company.

The E&WJR, with their own financial problems to contend with, still delayed payment and eventually the N&BJR found it necessary to issue a writ against their neighbours in early 1876. The detail of their claim does give an interesting insight into running costs on the N&BJR at that time, with the amounts outstanding from the E&WJR for the two years being as follows:

- Costs in respect of the construction of
  Green's Norton Junction..£ 89 10s 6d
- Two years running expenses of
  Green's Norton Junction.......................................£340 0s 0d
- Two years running expenses of
  Blisworth and Towcester stations.........................£583 11s 5d
- Two years rent of Blisworth station......................£200 0s 0d

These costs were apparently offset to some extent by an initial payment of £300 claimed to have been made in early 1873 by Messrs Crampton & Sons, the E&WJR contractors, towards the cost of construction of the junction at Green's Norton.

The E&WJR, already in receivership for the past year, unsurprisingly disputed the overall sum owed but all became to some extent rather academic at the end of July 1877, when they ceased to use the N&BJR facilities, having been forced to withdraw their Blisworth to Stratford passenger services.

However, one immediate result of this new arrangement with the L&NWR was a major auction held at Towcester on 23rd August 1875, which included all five of the N&BJR locomotives, four carriages, and an assortment of engineering items *'connected with the engine shed'*. Most of the lots seem to have been successfully disposed of, with the exception of *'one valuable locomotive tank engine, six wheels, trailing and driving coupled'*, which was the subject of a further auction announcement two years later in November 1877; its fate is not recorded.

Alterations were also made to the departure and arrival times of N&BJR trains from the beginning of December 1875, in conjunction with modifications to the L&NWR timetable of connecting services to and from Northampton. In most cases adjustments of just a few minutes were made, but some slight acceleration does seem to have occurred on the N&BJR portion of the journey between Blisworth and Banbury, possibly owing to the provision of more capable L&NWR motive power.

At the close of 1875, the N&BJR were again involved in an unsuccessful scheme to connect their line with Northampton but, on this occasion, the new railway was promoted as an independent, the Duston Minerals & Northampton & Gayton Railway, with a Charles Bartholemew as engineer. The now familiar route left the N&BJR line in Gayton, crossed the L&NWR main line and continued on to Northampton, to a junction at the Bedford & Northampton Railway terminus.

Trouble With the Neighbours

As indicated earlier, the opening of the final section of the East & West Junction Railway route brought additional trains to the Towcester to Blisworth section of the N&BJR during 1873. The E&WJR suffered their own financial turmoils during their early years and, as with their neighbour the N&BJR, this resulted in them having to return their initial fleet of Beyer, Peacock locomotives to the makers and resort to hired motive power. E&WJR locomotive matters will be more fully dealt with later but one interesting side effect was a dispute with the N&BJR over the subsequent use of one of their hired engines over the line to Blisworth.

It has been well recorded elsewhere that the E&WJR obtained the use, for a short period around 1875, of an articulated Fairlie 0-6-6-0 engine, which had originally been intended for

Contraction

On 5th July 1876, the N&BJR secretary, J. Wilson Theobald, wrote to the Board of Trade from his office at Union Court, Broad Street, London, enclosing a copy of the Act of 1865 which had authorised extensions to the N&BJR system. The reason for his communication was to apply for a warrant to formally abandon the whole of the railways listed therein, the time allowed for completion having expired and no progress having been made with construction, with *'the company having no funds for the purpose, and no present means of obtaining them'*.

The warrant for abandonment was issued by the Board of Trade on 10th February 1877, after an investigation into N&BJR circumstances by General Hutchinson. This revealed that of the sum of £500,000 authorised by the 1865 Act, only £74,770 had actually been subscribed and of this, £34,770 had been credited to William Shrimpton, the bankrupted contractor of the first section of line from Blisworth to Towcester. General Hutchinson confirmed that no part of the capital raised had yet been expended on actual construction of any of the lines so authorised and that the portion of the line near to Chipping Norton was in fact being constructed by the Banbury & Cheltenham Railway Company, albeit on a slightly different route.

A subsequent declaration signed before a Commissioner of Oaths by George Porter, station master at Towcester, and Edmund Stanton, the N&BJR Traffic Superintendent, gives an intriguing insight into the public communication of the formal abandonment process that had then to be followed.

The two company servants were required to affix, on three successive Sundays, a printed copy of the Board of Trade notice on the *'outer doors of the churches'* in all of the parishes affected by the proposed railways. Finally, J. Wilson Theobald was himself required to confirm to the Board of Trade that suitable notices had also been published in local and national newspapers, the list including the *London Gazette, Northampton Herald, Gloucestershire Chronicle, Oxford Times, Warwickshire Advertiser* and the *Worcestershire Advertiser*.

The late 1870s were lean years for the N&BJR, with successive Directors' Reports indicating a fall in receipts due to a *'general great depression in trade'* and the failure of one of the major ironstone traders using the N&BJR caused a particular problem during 1877. Although traffic from that source was partially resumed later in the year, a bad debt of £200 had resulted, which was a considerable sum to a company the size of the N&BJR.

The rival Easton Neston Mineral, Towcester, Roade & Olney Junction Railway Bill was also passing through Parliament and was a cause of some concern to the N&BJR Board, who saw the new line as a threat to their own traffic. Nevertheless, the N&BJR were still concerned that their line should be kept in good condition and commissioned an independent report on the state of the permanent way. This revealed that some rails and a great many sleepers required replacement, particularly on the Blisworth to Towcester section, and the company therefore allocated a sum of £400 to carry out the necessary work.

The N&BJR were also obviously still experiencing some difficulties in disposing of the remnants of their previously owned rolling stock. Despite the fact that the arrangement with the L&NWR had been in place for over four years, there was still sufficient remaining for a further auction to be held at Blisworth

and Towcester stations on 4th October 1879. Messrs W.J. Peirce offered for sale four railway carriages, three pairs of carriage wheels and axles, a locomotive brake screw, engine and tender lamps, and wagon brasses. In addition, 2,500 sleepers, gates and various fencing components were also available, together with a large quantity of firewood and two ricks of hay; presumably the railway company were taking the opportunity to raise as much money as possible on the occasion.

Now that the L&NWR was providing the rolling stock, at last a reliable passenger service was being offered to the travelling public. By the end of the decade, three trains each day served the full length of the line, with a further two running just from Blisworth to Towcester and back.

The Green's Norton Accident

The opening of the route through to Banbury had initially brought an increase in revenue from passenger traffic but unfortunately this was not to last. With only a slow improvement in goods traffic, the finances of the N&BJR were still being stretched. However, although the company could never be considered as profitable in overall terms, at least the N&BJR management had been able to cover their annual operating costs since the particularly low point in 1872, when a deficit of just over £1,200 was recorded. The margin for error was never very great, to the extent that, in 1881, a further unexpected additional expenditure of £900 must have been most unwelcome, leaving the company to report an annual operating surplus of just £107. This occurred when the company was forced to pay personal injury compensation as a result of a derailment at Green's Norton Junction, which appears to be the only serious accident that occurred on the N&BJR, and certainly the only one that attracted the attention of the Railway Inspectorate, who published the findings of their investigation on 12th November 1880.

The accident report is interesting as it does give a glimpse of N&BJR working practices during a rather obscure period after the L&NWR had taken over responsibility for the provision of rolling stock and also whilst the neighbouring E&WJR had been forced to suspend their own passenger services. The train derailed was the 4.45pm down Blisworth to Banbury service on 30th October 1880, consisting of L&NWR McConnell 0-6-0 tender engine No. 747, nine loaded goods wagons and a set of four close-coupled L&NWR passenger coaches. With no passenger services operating at the time on the Stratford line, Green's Norton Junction signal box was regularly closed after the passage of the last E&WJR goods train of the day, at around 4.30pm. The junction points were then padlocked to allow N&BJR trains a through passage towards Banbury using just the Down line.

The passenger coaches at the rear of the N&BJR train became derailed at about 20mph after passing over the facing points leading to the E&WJR line, leaving the track to the right hand side. The locomotive and goods wagons had, however, travelled through without mishap. The train then ran on for a further 213 yards before being stopped. Damage was caused to the track over this distance, whilst of the passenger vehicles the composite coach was the most affected, being *'upset'* and losing one of its doors, through which a First Class passenger, one Aubrey Cartwright of Wardington, either jumped or fell onto the track, and was seriously injured.

The engine crew, consisting of driver John Labrum and fireman Frederick Cousins, both servants of the L&NWR, had joined the train at Towcester and were running under clear signals through the junction when, upon feeling a violent jerk, they immediately shut off steam and seeing that part of their train was off the rails, brought it to a careful halt. On walking back, Labrum found the train to still be coupled together but the composite coach was on its side and had fallen onto the parapet of the bridge over the bridle road from Green's Norton to Handley. After assisting some of the passengers, he then walked back to inspect the track and found the injured gentleman some distance to the rear of the train. The passenger was able to walk with assistance to Handley Cottages but there became unconscious and was attended by a local doctor, who diagnosed severe concussion. Mr Cartwright was reportedly in 'gravest danger' for a few days afterwards but was able to return to his home at Wardington near Banbury; the local press subsequently reported that he was 'going on fairly well' and making a good recovery. Other passengers received relatively minor injuries which were dealt with by N&BJR staff in the nearby Green's Norton signal box. A 'travelling crane' was summoned from Blisworth, and the line was cleared and opened for operations by 4.15pm on the Sunday afternoon.

Guard Stephen Gun, travelling in the rear carriage of the train, gave a similar account and stated that normally the train would stop at the junction to change the token staff but on this occasion, with the signal cabin closed, they were in possession of the staffs for both sections though to Cockley Brake.

John Salmon, a platelayer who was travelling home to Wappenham by the train, and George Kingstone, a foreman ganger, both stated that they had inspected the track as usual earlier in the day and had not found anything amiss. However, when Kingstone examined the track after the derailment, he found that both point stretcher rods were displaced, each with one of their nuts unscrewed. The right hand switch blade was padlocked tight to the rail but the other was about one inch open. Alfred Hebbs, the regular signalman at Green's Norton, also confirmed that he had noticed nothing wrong when padlocking the points, prior to closing the signal box after the passage of the last E&WJR goods train at 4.30pm, less than one hour before the accident.

Major Marindin visited the scene and concluded that the derailment was due to track stretcher rods working loose during the passage of the train, owing to their securing nuts being shaken off, thus allowing the tongue of the points to move out of position. The passage of the locomotive and goods wagons was then sufficient to allow the point blades to move and so derail the coaches. However, he could not account for the nuts being loosened, which was also contradictory to the statements made the various employees but he did note that the threads at the end of the stretcher rods were worn, and the nuts bore damage consistent with them being hammered rather than adjusted with the correct tool. He also commented that the goods wagons were not derailed and were undamaged, suggesting that they had run through the junction successfully but had nevertheless probably caused the stretcher rods to become displaced.

The Major considered that although it might be more convenient for shunting purposes for goods vehicles to be at the front of a mixed train, they should in future always be placed at the rear. The driver of the train also came in for criticism, in that the Major considered that he should perhaps have stopped his train more quickly, which may have saved the composite coach from being dragged along on its side after derailment.

The final recommendation was that 'the company should lose no time in making a thorough examination of the stretcher rods at all the switches on their line, and in providing some more reliable mode of securing them than the existing one, which may almost be said to be obsolete'. The N&BJR Board, although acknowledging that the company had no legal obligation, elected to negotiate a settlement with the injured parties, in an attempt to avoid any potential costs of litigation. A sum of £700 was put aside to cover this but in the event it appears that an additional £200 was eventually paid out.

Further Developments

The early years of the 1880s saw some welcome additional traffic for the N&BJR, provided by ironstone workings approximately one mile from Blisworth, known as Wheldon's Siding. The siding appears to have been open since at least 1878, when references appeared in a report by the Railway Commissioners, who arbitrated in a dispute over rates charged for ironstone and coal traffic. A Board of Trade inspection was made in March 1881 when the layout was altered and the siding was then relocated to a point closer to Blisworth in 1888.

An inspection was also made of new signalling arrangements that had been provided at Blisworth. Following recommendations received from the Board of Trade, a new frame had been installed in the signal cabin at the north end of the station, and new signals provided to govern the arrival and departure of trains. In addition, the permanent way between the signal cabin and the station had been 'more or less relaid' and was now 'in good order', reflecting earlier concerns over the condition of the rails and their fastenings. A lack of interlocking between two crossover roads and their signals had not yet been attended to but the N&BJR 'hoped to interlock the crossing roads near the platform before too long'.

Various official meetings of the N&BJR over the next few years provide interesting glimpses of the current state of the company, the first being the 43rd ordinary meeting of the directors, held on 28th February 1885.

W.A.Michael, the Deputy Chairman, presided and the Secretary W.J.Crick reported that the total receipts from all traffic for the half year to 31st December 1884 had been £3,955.10s.3d,

NORTHAMPTON, TOWCESTER, AND BANBURY.																	
Leave	a. m.	a. m.	a.m.	p. m.	p. m.	p. m.	p. m.	p. m.	Leave	a. m.	a.m.	p. m.	p. m.	p. m.	p. m.	p.m.	p. m.
NORTHAMPTON ...	8 40	11 20	1 15	4 15	...	7 18			BANBURY	...	10 30	...	...	4*15	...	6*25	
Blisworth............	9 20	12 30	1 50	4 45	...	8 0			Farthinghoe	...	10 37	...	...	4 22	...	6*32	
									Helmdon	...	10 51	...	...	4 38	...	6*45	
Towcester	9 36	12 55	2 5	5 5	...	8 15			Wappenham	...	11 0	...	...	4 48	...	6*56	
Wappenham	9 45	1 7	...	5 15	...	...			Towcester	8 30	11 10	3 10	5 10	...	...	7 15	
Helmdon	9 58	1 19	...	5 30	...	...											
Farthinghoe	10 10	1 40	...	5 45	...	...			BLISWORTH	9 25	11 50	3 50	5 45	...	...	8 0	
BANBURY ...	Arrive...	10 20	1 55	...	6 0	...	...		NORTHAMPTON arr.	9 35	12 0	4 0	5 55	...	...	8 10	
Cheap Market Trains run on Thursdays and Saturdays to and from Northampton and Banbury																	

*Thursdays only.
†Thursdays excepted.

By 1880, N&BJR line services from Blisworth to Banbury had dwindled to just three trains in each direction, with some others only operating as far as Towcester and one only running on Thursdays for Banbury market passengers. Significantly, the services were now shown as fully integrated with trains to and from Northampton, with convenient connections at Blisworth, a sign of the increased co-operation with the L&NWR, who were now providing rolling stock on the N&BJR line. *Author's collection*

The N&BJR line to Towcester passed through prime ironstone country, particularly at the Blisworth end of the route. Most of the quarries were at one time or another served by the N&BJR, in some cases by simple siding connections but occasionally more exotic arrangements existed, such as this example near Gayton. Ore was carted from the nearby quarries to the top of the railway cutting and there dropped into a small narrow gauge tub for the short journey across to a chute, from where the contents were then fed into standard gauge wagons in the railway siding below. *Courtesy T. Marsh*

a fall of £303 on the comparable six month period in the previous year. Expenditure was slightly increased from £3,566 to £3,772 over the same periods, and the railway was stated to have suffered from a decrease in traffic levels in common with many other railways, due to a general depression in trade.

Comment was also made on the number of Bills passing through Parliament at the time that had a potential effect on the N&BJR. These were five in number, ranging from major proposals for the Northampton, Banbury & Metropolitan Junction (NB&MJR) and Worcester & Broom railways, to minor legislation for diversions to the Stratford, Towcester & Midland Junction line and funding consolidations for the East & West Junction Company; fortunately, none were found to be prejudicial to the N&BJR.

The proposal for the NB&MJR involved the construction of a line from East Claydon, on the Aylesbury & Buckingham Railway, to join the N&BJR at a point 130 yards west of Green's Norton Junction. Running powers were be provided from

that point and over the N&BJR to Blisworth, where a further new railway was to be constructed to link with the Northampton &

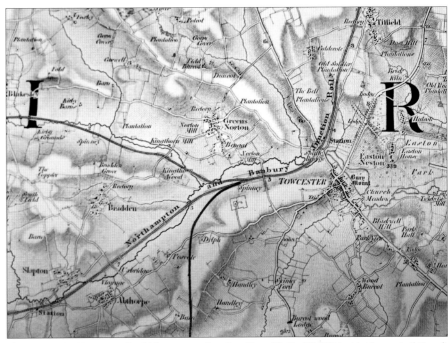

The 1884 NB&MJR proposal, which was to make a junction with the N&BJR just to the west of Green's Norton Junction, before heading off south-eastwards towards Claydon and Aylesbury. Had this line been built, Green's Norton Junction signal box would have become a much busier place. *NRO-DP*

Peterborough Branch of the L&NWR, close to the bridge over the Grand Junction Canal. The proposal also included a provision for the new company to repair, equip and improve the existing N&BJR route, and if required to lay down a second set of rails. However, by far the most interesting aspect of this scheme was a provision for the formation of a Joint Committee, consisting of the new company, plus the N&BJR; Evesham, Stratford & Redditch; East & West Junction; Stratford, Towcester & Midland Junction; Aylesbury & Buckingham; and Oxford, Aylesbury & Metropolitan Junction railway companies.

Strong opposition was mounted by the L&NWR and this, together with a congested Parliamentary schedule, meant that little progress was made and the scheme was eventually dropped during 1886. However, this potential amalgamation of the four local railways had rather unknowingly provided a fascinating glimpse of what the future actually held for those companies.

The meeting also heard that, although the N&BJR funds were not considered sufficient to allow for the payment of any dividend, hopes were expressed that the forthcoming resumption of passenger traffic on the neighbouring E&WJR would result in an increase in revenue. The E&WJR had to some extent moved on from their troubled period and were actually able to reintroduce their passenger services from the middle of 1885. This resulted in an immediate improvement in the number of passengers carried by the N&BJR, increasing from 62,000 in 1884 to 90,000 in 1886.

The 47th meeting of shareholders of the N&BJR then took place at their Tokenhouse Yard offices in London on 26th February 1887, where the deputy chairman, W.A. Michael, recorded the recent death of the Marquis of Ailesbury, who for many years had been chairman of the company. It was also reported that, owing to a 'slight accident' at Blisworth, it had been necessary to make further alterations to signalling and the N&BJR Board had been urged by the L&NWR, who operated the line, to install the block telegraph system over the route from Blisworth to Green's Norton; the directors indicated their intention to carry out this work as soon as was possible.

Another project for a new line affecting the N&BJR had also emerged, with plans deposited for the Towcester & Buckingham Railway on 28th November 1888. This line also commenced at East Claydon from a junction with the Aylesbury & Buckingham Railway and was to proceed

through Radclive, Stowe, Syresham and Silverstone to terminate at Towcester. Connections were to be made to the N&BJR and the authorised line of the Stratford, Towcester & Midland Junction Railway (ST&MJR) near Towcester and the Banbury Branch of the L&NWR at Radclive. Although the proposal passed through both Houses of Parliament in the 1889 session and an Act was obtained, sufficient investment was not forthcoming and once again the project was allowed to lapse.

The year also saw a report in the *Northampton Mercury* that the N&BJR had introduced a new train between Blisworth and Banbury, in which 'the third class compartments were just as cosy as the 2nd whilst the first class are of superior style'; presumably these new carriages were supplied by the L&NWR as part of their agreement to provide rolling stock.

The report of the 52nd general meeting of the N&BJR, held at their London offices at Palmerston Buildings in Broad Street in early September 1889, further indicated the current state of the company. The directors reported that, on the whole, traffic was satisfactory, with a 10% increase in expenditure being attributable to the maintenance of the permanent way, and necessary repairs to stations and bridges. In addition, legal expenses had arisen in connection with various other railway Bills which had some effect on the N&BJR. A slight drop in goods revenue was due to a reduction in the carriage of materials for the construction of the ST&MJR extension from Towcester to Ravenstone Wood Junction, whilst the junction with this new line at Towcester had recently been completed.

Formal opposition to the Bill for the E&WJR's Towcester & Buckingham line had been withdrawn following the inclusion of suitable protective clauses and the N&BJR board anticipated increased traffic on their own line to Banbury when the Buckingham and Ravenstone routes were opened. In addition, it was hoped that similar traffic would accrue from the Metropolitan Railway's latest proposal for a line from Canons Ashby, on the E&WJR, to Evenley on the L&NWR Banbury Branch, which was to include a junction with the N&BJR at Helmdon.

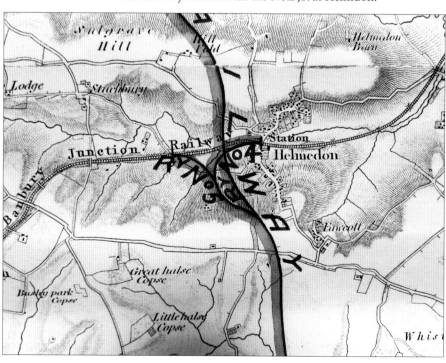

There were many proposals for new railways involving the N&BJR, including this scheme of 1889 for a northwards extension of the Metropolitan Railway. The new line would have crossed the N&BJR at Helmdon (spelt as 'Helmedon' on the map), with spurs providing through running to and from the Towcester to Banbury line in both directions. The rural nature of the village would have been somewhat disturbed had this line and its complex series of junctions been constructed. The coming of the Manchester, Sheffield & Lincolnshire Railway's (later renamed the Great Central Railway) London Extension line just a few years later would have completed the transformation, with the towering Helmdon Viaduct carrying the GCR line across the valley located just a short distance away to the west. *NRO-DP*

A late 19th century development at Towcester came with the construction of the Stratford-upon-Avon, Towcester & Midland Junction Railway route which joined the Midland Railway's Bedford to Northampton Branch at Ravenstone Wood Junction. After some reassessment of the original plans, this line formed a junction with the N&BJR just north of Towcester station, seen here on the right, with the original line to Blisworth on the left. The minor road to Tiffield crossed the line to Ravenstone Wood but not the Blisworth route and also served the station goods yard, off to the right. *Author's collection*

New Connections and Services

The year of 1891 did, however, at last bring a new connection to the N&BJR, with the provision of a junction just north of Towcester station with the E&WJR-promoted route of the Stratford, Towcester & Midland Junction Railway – the previously titled Easton Neston Mineral, Towcester, Roade & Olney Junction Railway. The line connected Towcester with Ravenstone Wood Junction on the Northampton to Bedford branch of the Midland Railway and was opened to goods traffic on 13th April 1891; it was also used by a short lived passenger service for three months from 1st December 1892. The new arrival did have some effect on the track layout at Towcester, which was modified to accommodate the new junction north of the station, with additional siding capacity also being provided.

The final decade of the 19th century also saw the welcome use of the N&BJR route, as far as Green's Norton, by a new L&NWR through service of Saturday 'Shakespeare Specials' from Euston to Stratford-upon-Avon. J.F Burke, the traffic manager of the neighbouring E&WJR, was instrumental in arranging for the L&NWR to operate these services, the first one of which left Euston station at 8.40am on 6th June 1891, with a return arrival at 10.40pm. The trains were aimed particularly at the American 'Shakespeare' tourist market and enabled the 'Premier Line' to offer a shorter route from the metropolis than the rival GWR. Although attractive fares and organised excursions from Stratford made this route competitive, the problem of having to shunt trains through the connection at Blisworth compromised the service. In addition, the L&NWR stock used was vacuum braked, whilst the local companies still operated on the Westinghouse system. Initially, L&NWR locomotives worked

their trains through to Stratford but in later years a selection of E&WJR engines were vacuum fitted and took over the trains from Blisworth.

More Legislation

Meanwhile, new railway legislation was also to provide the N&BJR with further obstacles to overcome. An earlier Regulation of Railways Act of 1873 had required all railway companies to submit an annual return to the Board of Trade, indicating their progress towards the goal of introducing interlocking of points and signals, and block signalling on all of their lines. The problems of variable operating standards across the railway system had been of concern to the Board of Trade for some time and, in addition, braking systems were also considered to be generally unsatisfactory, with many trains still only being controlled by a hand brake in the guard's compartment, or on the engine.

Railway companies were generally slow to comply with these recommendations and, at the time, the Board of Trade still had no powers of compulsion. It took the tragic events at Penistone in 1884 and Armagh five years later to eventually force the Government to act in the interests of passenger safety.

A further Regulation of Railways Act was passed in 1889, requiring railway companies to adopt, within one year, the block system of signalling for all of their lines open to passenger traffic. Also required, within eighteen months, was the interlocking of all signals and points, and within the same period the fitting of continuous brakes on all trains conveying passengers.

These mandatory requirements posed particular problems to a small, financially insecure railway such as the N&BJR and

Traffic volumes on the N&BJR line were always light and the running of mixed trains was often preferred, with this view taken in the 1930s at Towcester providing a good example. The unidentified locomotive is hauling three passenger coaches, a GWR cattle wagon, and a selection of open and sheeted goods wagons, probably having arrived from the Banbury line. Board of Trade regulations required that the goods vehicles should be attached behind the passenger stock, although this was not always too convenient for the shunting of traffic en route. *Author's collection*

they promptly made appropriate representations to the Board of Trade. An official response quickly accepted that the N&BJR had already installed interlocking between Blisworth and Green's Norton Junction, and so allowed an extension of time until 1st April 1893 for completion elsewhere. The Board of Trade also agreed that the requirement for the fitting of continuous brakes could be deferred to the same date. In addition, where traffic was insufficient to allow the separation of passenger and goods vehicles, unbraked vehicles could be added to passenger trains if their speed was to be less than 25 miles per hour. A similar relaxation was also allowed where passenger vehicles of a different company were attached that were fitted with brakes of a different kind.

Further communication resulted in the Board of Trade's suggestion that the N&BJR might be allowed to run just '*two mixed trains per diem in each direction*'. The N&BJR responded to the effect that although they did wish to run mixed trains over the whole of their line and over the L&NWR to Banbury, they should not be required to state the precise number of trains per day. Yet more correspondence ensued, with the N&BJR finally submitting an annotated copy of their timetable to the BoT, showing the trains that they wished to operate as mixed. The timetable, dated from 1st October 1892, reveals that four Up and Down trains were operated daily, departing Blisworth at 9.10am, 11.5am, 4.30pm and 7.22pm, and from Banbury at 7.30am, 10.45am, 3.12pm and 6.05pm, with journey times varying

slightly but averaging at just a few minutes over one hour.

Of these, the N&BJR requested that the 9.10am 'Parliamentary' train be mixed through to Banbury, the 1.15pm mixed from Towcester to Banbury only and the 4.30pm mixed throughout the journey on Wednesday and Saturdays only. In the Up direction, the 7.30am departure from Banbury would be mixed throughout to Blisworth and the 3.12pm train would convey cattle from Banbury to Blisworth on Thursdays only but be mixed just from Towcester on other days.

The N&BJR also requested that, owing to their method of operation, they be allowed exemption from the requirement for block signalling between Green's Norton Junction, Helmdon and Cockley Brake Junction.

The Board of Trade appears to have given agreement on these points and, on 28th December 1893, the N&BJR affirmed that the block system was in use on their line, with the exception of Green's Norton Junction to Cockley Brake Junction, which was being operated by '*one engine in steam*' at all times. All points and signals were also in the process of being interlocked but the Company again requested an exemption in respect of their sidings '*behind stations*', on the basis that all trains stopped at all of the stations anyway and that speeds were therefore low.

Confirmation was also given that all passenger trains were in fact fitted with continuous brakes, the reason for this being that all rolling stock had, for the past twenty years or so, been provided by the L&NWR who were fully compliant in that matter.

NORTHAMPTON AND BANBURY JUNCTION RAILWAY.

TIME TABLE

FROM 1st JULY, 1892, AND UNTIL FURTHER NOTICE.

Wiseacre and Sons Limited, Printers, London Wall, London.

DOWN. — WEEK DAYS ONLY.

	morn.	morn.	after.	after.		
LONDON (Euston) ...dep.	7 15	11 0	2 45	5 0	..	..
Willesden Junction ... „	6 18	11 11	2 57	5 12	..	..
Bletchley .... „	8 20	12 28	3 57	6 25	..	..
Wolverton .... „	8 29	12 37	4 6	6 35	..	..
Roade .... „	8 44	12 53	..	6 50	..	..
Liverpool (Lime Street) dep.	2 35	9 45	12 0	2 0	..	..
Manchester (London Road) „	12 0	10 0	12 0	2 10	..	..
Crewe .... „	a3 38	10 48	1 5	3 30	..	..
Stafford .... „	6 15	11 25	1 43	3 35	..	..
Derby .... „		8 25	1 5	2 55	..	..
Burton .... „		8 45	1 22	3 15	..	..
Leicester .... „	6 35	8 20	12 30	2 20	..	..
Wolverhampton........ „	7 0	11 15	1 25	3 15	..	..
Birmingham (New Street) „	7 30	11 50	2 0	4 0	..	..
Coventry .... „	8 0	12 25	2 36	4 41	..	..
Rugby .... „	8 25	12 44	3 8	5 30	..	..
Welton .... „	8 40	10 4	1 29	5 45	..	..
Weedon .... „	8 52	12 50	1 39	5 56	..	..
Stamford ....dep.	7 42	8 45	1 50	..	..	..
Market Harboro' ...... „		10 35	3 25	4 49	..	..
Peterborough ....dep.	6 35	10 55	2 59	4 30 5c45	..	..
Thrapston .... „	7 28	11 43	2 59	4 59 6c 9	..	..
Wellingborough ...... „	7 56	12 8	3 50	4 59	..	..
NORTHAMPTON (Castle Station) dep.	8 30	12 45	4 5	6 55	..	..
BLISWORTH (N. & B.) dep.	9 10	1 12	4 30	7 22	..	..
TOWCESTER .... „	9 25	1 27	4 45	7 37	..	..
WAPPENHAM ...... „	9 38	1 40	4 58	7 50	..	..
HELMDON .... „	9 48	1 52	5 10	8 2	..	..
FARTHINGHOE ..... „	10 8	2 5	5 23	8 19	..	..
BANBURY ....arr.	10 18	2 15	5 33	8 27	..	..

Miles from Blisworth (DOWN lower section): 4½, 8½, 12, 16¾, 20¼

UP. — WEEK DAYS ONLY.

	morn.	morn.	after.	after.		
BANBURY ....dep.	7 30	10 45	3 12	6 5	..	..
FARTHINGHOE ..... „	7 37	10 52	3 19	6 12	..	..
HELMDON .... „	7 52	11 7	3 35	6 26	..	..
WAPPENHAM ...... „	8 4	11 19	3 47	6 38	..	..
TOWCESTER .... „	8 20	11 35	4 0	6 52	..	..
BLISWORTH (N. & B.) arr.	8 35	11 50	4 15	7 7	..	..
NORTHAMPTON (Castle Station) arr.	9 14	12 5	4 50	7 25	..	..
Wellingborough ... arr.	9 46	12 36	6 32	9 9	..	..
Thrapston .... „	10 7	12 58	6 56	9 30	..	..
Peterborough .... „	10 52	1 48	7 55	10 17	..	..
Market Harboro' ... arr.	9 58	1 46	6 28	9 15	..	..
Stamford .... „	12 27	3 8	..	10 10	..	..
Weedon ....arr.	8 55	1 13	4 35	7 22	..	..
Welton .... „	9 19	1 23	B	7 35	..	..
Rugby .... „	9 30	1 36	4 55	7 52	..	..
Coventry .... „	9 59	2 11	5 42	9 16	..	..
Birmingham (New Street) „	10 35	2 45	6 35	9 50	..	..
Wolverhampton...... „	11 0	3 5	7 30	10 15	..	..
Leicester .... „	11 27	3 44	6 15	9 42	..	..
Burton .... „	11 8	2 56	6 55	..	..	..
Derby .... „	11 33	3 15	7 15	..	..	..
Stafford .... „	11 3	4 0	6 40	9 34	..	..
Crewe .... „	12 12	3 50	7 41	10 13	..	..
Manchester (London Road) „	12 40	4 20	8 15	2 55	..	..
Liverpool (Lime Street) „	1 30	4 50	8 40	3 0	..	..
Roade ....arr.	9 14	1 59	5 49	..	8 16	..
Wolverton .... „	9 29	2 15	6 4	..	8 34	..
Bletchley .... „	9 5	1 33	6 14	..	8 46	..
Willesden Junction ... „	9 56	2 28	6a23	..	10 2	..
LONDON (Euston) ... „	10 10	2 40	6a35	..	10 15	..

(A) Passengers for London travel to Weedon, and join the train leaving there at 5.5 p.m.   (B) Stops at Welton to down Passengers on previous notice being given to the Guard at Blisworth or Weedon.   (C) Saturdays only.

(a) Other days passengers leave at 3.38.

TRAINS ON SUNDAYS.

The usual charge for Booking is made for Parcels conveyed by Passenger Trains.
Return Tickets issued for distances up to 12 miles available for two days.
An Omnibus meets the Trains at Towcester, and takes Passengers and Parcels to and from the Station and any part of the Town. Fare 6d. each Passenger. Passengers wishing to be called for are requested to send word to the Pomfret Arms, Agent, R. McAuslin.

MARKET TICKETS.—Market Tickets, at Cheap Fares, available on any day of the week only will be issued by the following Trains, viz. :—

TOWCESTER CATTLE MARKET.—On Alternate Tuesdays.—Train leaving Northampton (Castle Station) at 12.45 p.m., returning from Towcester and back, 1s. 0d. Fare to Towcester and back, 1s. 0d. Also by the Train leaving Banbury at 10.45 a.m., Farthinghoe at 10.52 a.m., and returning from Towcester at 4.48 p.m. Fare to Towcester and back, 1s. 0d.

BANBURY MARKET.—On Thursdays only.—Train leaving Blisworth at 9.10 a.m., calling at all Stations, and arriving at Banbury at 10.18 a.m. Returning from Banbury at 3.12 p.m.—Fares to Banbury and back: From Blisworth, 2s. 4d.; Wappenham, 1s. 0d., Helmdon, 1s. 3d.

NORTHAMPTON MARKET.—On Wednesdays and Saturdays.—Train leaving Banbury at 7.30 a.m., calling at all Stations, and arriving at Northampton (Castle Station) at 9.14 a.m., Returning from Northampton (Castle Station) at 4.5 p.m.—Fares to Northampton and back, From Banbury, 4s., Helmdon, 2s. Wappenham, 1s. 10d., Towcester, on Saturdays only, 1s. 2d.

For further information apply to Mr. Edmund Stanton, Traffic Manager, Blisworth Station, or at the Booking Offices.

(BY ORDER.)

London Offices: 3, Great Winchester Street, E.C.

This *Working Time Table* of 1892 is an extremely rare survival of operational documentation from the Northampton & Banbury Junction Railway. An annotated copy was used as part of a submission to the Board of Trade for permission to run mixed trains, with pencilled notes indicating the various services which the company wished to operate as such. *Author's collection*

Change At Green's Norton

In June 1893 application was made to the Board of Trade to modify the junction arrangements with the E&WJR at Green's Norton. As it was no longer the practice to cross trains at the junction, the lengthy passing loops were thought not to be necessary. Plans were therefore submitted to shorten the existing loop at the Towcester end and also just beyond the junction with the E&WJR, and to close the eastern of the two signal cabins.

Major Hutchinson inspected the new arrangements and his report of 8th February 1894 revealed that the revised layout was now controlled by a single signal box at the site of the junction, containing sixteen levers, of which two were spares. A few small amendments to the levers were required and approval was given on the express understanding that '*no passenger, or passenger and goods trains, be allowed to pass each other at the junction if this involves the backing of a passenger train*'.

It was clear, however, that the N&BJR was still failing to be totally compliant with earlier Board of Trade requirements and the directors reported on June 11th that the urgency of funding improvements to their permanent way had prevented the completion of the interlocking required. Their financial position was such that it had not been possible to pay any interest on 'A' Debenture stock for over four years and there was little prospect for several years to come; in the meantime, they were doing everything possible just to '*improve their road*'. Indeed, in a report of an ordinary half year meeting at the end of August 1894, the directors commented that they had been able to put aside only £841 for repairs and renewals required by the Board of Trade, after allowing for payment of outstanding interest.

The question of the interlocking requirements was considered again in September 1894 but still all available funds were being used to improve the poor state of the permanent way. The Board of Trade continued to press the N&BJR, however, and in May 1895 the directors confirmed that they had requested their consulting engineer, Mr Richards, to prepare a report on the current state of affairs. They reaffirmed that a falling off in receipts had delayed improvement work but were hopeful that they could look forward to better times with the impending carriage of construction traffic for the new London extension of the Manchester, Sheffield & Lincolnshire Railway, which would cross their line at Helmdon.

Richards duly reported on 29th May that he considered the required improvements would mean considerable expenditure for what was now a '*small and struggling company*'. The report revealed that, at Blisworth, the facing points at the north end were '*worked from a cabin and interlocked and rodded as per requirements*' but at the south end the two facing points were only hand operated. Although speeds were low, this was not in his opinion totally satisfactory and a better arrangement would be to provide a new signal cabin in the middle of the layout to control both areas.

Richards indicated that arrangements were largely satisfactory at both Towcester and Green's Norton, and also at Wheldon's Siding, near Blisworth, which was operated by Annett's key attached to the single line staff. At Wappenham, the small volume of goods traffic was worked from a '*wire-locked ground frame*' and a proposal was made to dispense with the signals there, and lock the two sets of points with the single line staff.

The situation at Helmdon was slightly more complicated; although there was little goods traffic, there was a temporary junction for the connection to the MS&LR construction site, again operated by Annett's key. The old passenger passing loop had for some time been disused for its original purpose and had latterly been used as another temporary siding. Richards suggested that, on completion of the construction works, the loop should be removed completely, with the remaining goods traffic being controlled by removing the signals and locking the points by Annett's key on the single line staff.

In contrast, Cockley Brake Junction was reported as being '*operated by the L&NWR and first class in all respects*'.

The 'Last Main Line'

The above mentioned construction of the London extension of the Manchester, Sheffield & Lincolnshire Railway, which would later become the Great Central Railway, provided a welcome boost to N&BJR finances in the final decade of the 19th century. In fact, in 1895, the total receipts from all types of traffic exceeded the £10,000 threshold for the first time since 1874. This influx of new revenue continued for the next four years, until construction work finally ceased and annual receipts then returned to their previous levels.

Helmdon was chosen by contractor Walter Scott as a centre for his construction activities. A large depot and navvy encampment quickly grew up in the valley just beyond the N&BJR station in that village, with many local agricultural workers leaving the land to work on the new railway at higher rates of pay.

Steeply graded temporary connections were made to the new route, which was about to cross high above both the valley and

Helmdon was chosen by contractor Walter Scott as one of his depots for the construction of the London extension of the Manchester, Sheffield & Lincolnshire Railway. The new line crossed the N&BJR Towcester to Cockley Brake line on a high viaduct just west of the station in the village and temporary connections were made for the movement of materials, bringing welcome additional traffic to the minor line. This view, from the late 1890s, shows the N&BJR single track running through the middle of the construction site, whilst the newly completed viaduct on the extreme left awaits its first trains. *Author's collection*

The temporary connections between the N&BJR and the MS&LR works at Helmdon attracted the attention of the Board of Trade, who pointed out that the existing '*one engine in steam*' working of the line was being contravened by contractor's locomotives running down to the sidings at Helmdon station. As a result, the N&BJR were required to provide a new signal cabin, together with appropriate signalling and interlocking, to comply with regulations and to divide the line from Green's Norton to Cockley Brake into two sections. *Author's collection*

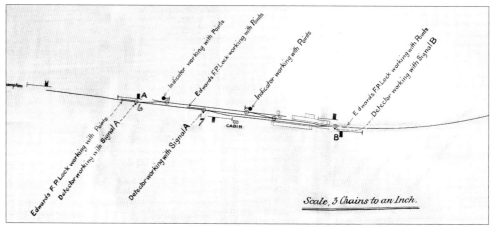

Scale, 3 Chains to an Inch.

This Manning Wardle 0-6-0ST, Works No. 583 of 1876 and named *Ciceter*, was one of the engines used by Walter Scott on the MS&LR contract at Helmdon. The engine, seen here beneath the shadow of the newly constructed viaduct, is one of the locomotives that would have been engaged in running over the temporary connection from the construction site to the N&BJR station sidings and in so doing incurring the wrath of the Board of Trade. Its name hailed from the engine's time working on the northern extension of the Midland & South Western Junction Railway, Ciceter being an old colloquial abbreviation of Cirencester in the late 1880s. Between 1902 and 1908, it was to be found working on the construction of the Cheltenham to Stratford railway. *Author's collection*

the N&BJR line, on a lofty blue brick viaduct. These allowed materials to be transported from the N&BJR and adjacent contractor's depot, to the level of the new works on each side of the valley. However, despite the temporary and rudimentary nature of the connections, proper procedures had still to be followed and the N&BJR initially fell foul of the Board of Trade in terms of the new arrangements at their station.

After confirmation from the N&BJR on 6th June 1895 that the link had been completed, the Board of Trade requested a plan, which was duly supplied one week later, showing full details of the station, signals, and two new junctions with the N&BJR line leading to the contractor's sidings.

However, Major Addison's subsequent report of 2nd July indicated that the N&BJR were violating a previous undertaking to operate their line with only one engine in steam at any time. It

appears that the movement of wagons between the works on the new line and the sidings at Helmdon station were being carried out by the contractor's engine, thus negating the use of one train staff for the whole line from Green's Norton to Cockley Brake.

Alterations were quickly carried out and an amended plan submitted to the Board of Trade, which showed the provision of full signalling and Edward's facing point locks, all controlled from a new signal cabin located on the Up side of the line to the east of the platform. Major Addison again inspected on 18th November and reported that, subject to a few minor conditions, he recommended approval of the new arrangements. It then remained for the N&BJR to request that their existing undertaking to operate the line between Green's Norton and Cockley Brake junctions by 'one engine in steam' be amended to take into account the new sections created on either side of Helmdon station.

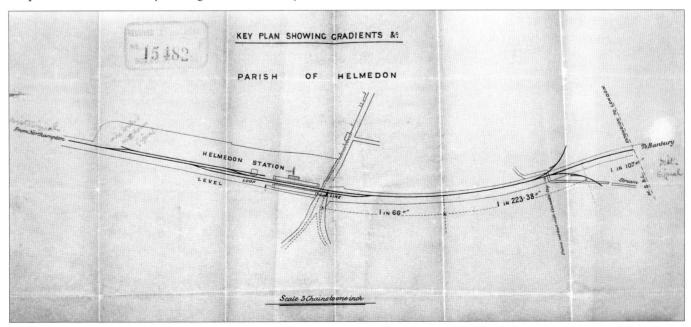

A plan of Helmdon from 1895, showing the temporary connections made to the trackbed of the new MS&LR main line at either end of the viaduct which would cross the N&BJR's route. The pencilled annotations indicate the new signalling requirements demanded by the Board of Trade. *Authors collection*

Public Disapproval

A letter to the editor of the *Northampton Mercury* of 11th October 1895 perhaps suggested that all was not well with the N&BJR and that the continual lack of funds had eventually left its mark on the everyday operation of the line. The writer complained:

'Sir – I shall be glad if you will call public attention to a public wrong. For many years I have travelled by this unpractical line two or three days every week, and the way in which business is carried out is most trying to one's temper and sometimes one's pocket. Having special business in London today I arrived at Towcester station at 8.10am and was booked to Blisworth by a train timed to leave Towcester at 8.15am and arrive at Blisworth at 8.30am. This train on the Company's bills is stated to run in connection with the London express leaving Blisworth 8.44am therefore allowing 14 minutes at Blisworth after arrival. Now this is the result: The train from Banbury arrived at Towcester 8.20am – that is, five minutes late. The engine was then detached from the train, and the shunting of cattle trucks and goods vans commenced, and was continued until 8.35am notwithstanding the anxious protestations of passengers who were naturally afraid they would miss the London train.

At 8.35am we left Towcester station and arrived at Blisworth 8.45 just in time to see the London train steam out of the station. I complained to the manager of this treatment and his reply was "If I had left the cattle behind I should have been wrong".

From first to last there was no accident, nor can there be any excuse whatever for the breach of contract and utter disregard for the passengers' interests. Why accept two contracts if one must be broken? Having paid my fare I have a right to expect to be carried to my destination but with reasonable certainty, barring accidents, but here was no accident, and I contend that such gross carelessness should be publicly protested against in the hope that some remedy may be found. I may add that this is not an exceptional instance, and possible litigation is the only resource left to the unfortunate traveller.

Yours obediently

Arthur Greville, Towcester, Oct. 9th 1895'

More Expenditure

The N&BJR Secretary, W. Leigh-Hunt, communicated with the Board of Trade on 5th March 1896, confirming that all of their outstanding requirements had now been complied with. However, within a few weeks, Major Addison, in assessing the progress made by the N&BJR, reported to his superiors that few steps had in fact been taken to attend to Richards' suggestions of almost a year earlier. He commented that almost five years had now elapsed since the first requirements were placed upon the N&BJR and in his opinion, it was now time to take stronger action.

Leigh-Hunt was asked for an explanation of the fact that his company had earlier reported compliance with all requirements. His reply to the Board of Trade, dated 14th April, revealed that *'there had been a misunderstanding due to erroneous information from our Traffic Manager'*, who had in fact reported that only the recommendations specific to Helmdon had been complied with; those put forward earlier by Richards had clearly not yet been acted upon.

As a result, Richards was again asked to provide an estimate of the costs involved in meeting the Board's requirements and,

on 5th June, he reported that the necessary new signalling and associated works would cost £486. He further estimated that the replacement of defective permanent way and repairs to bridges, which in his opinion were of greater importance than the Board of Trade's requirements, would cost an additional £2,864, allowing for the resale of any scrap metal and using company labour to carry out the work.

Faced with this daunting prospect, Leigh-Hunt responded to the Board of Trade that his directors estimated that they would be unable to complete the necessary relaying of the railway, together with the other mandatory improvements, for another eighteen months. He further commented that his directors had in fact been unable to pay even fractional interest on debenture stock over the past few years, such was the financial state of the company.

In the event, the above mentioned additional revenue from the MS&LR construction traffic did provide sufficient encouragement to allow the N&BJR Board to invite Messrs Stevens & Sons of Glasgow to submit their plans for improvements at Blisworth and Wappenham in June 1897. Blisworth was to receive a new signal cabin, with eleven levers, located in a central position as per Richards' suggestions, and both of the platforms were to be resignalled for the arrival and departure of trains. At Wappenham, the siding points were to be worked by a single lever each, unlocked by an Annett's key on the train staff. After completion of the work, Colonel Addison duly inspected the new arrangements and approved them subject to the provision of further stretcher bars at both locations; he also commented that although the requirements of the Regulation of Railways were now complied with, there were still some *'very bad rails'* on the sections inspected. However, throughout the latter years of the 1890s, the additional revenue from the construction traffic did also allow the N&BJR to address this problem by increasing their annual expenditure on permanent way, which reached a peak of almost £5,400 in 1897.

After 1901, with the renewals apparently completed, this expenditure returned to more normal levels. With traffic receipts being maintained, the company even experienced a few years of comparatively good operating surpluses, the high point being 1904, when a record figure of exactly £2,000 was achieved. However, their inability to make even modest annual payments to their shareholders over a number of years had resulted in huge arrears accumulating; this compounded interest meant that, by the last day of the 19th century, the N&BJR owed the considerable sum of £310,458 in interest across all classes of its debentures.

Another Proposal

Meanwhile, despite a quiet period of several years, before the 19th century drew to a close the promoters of new railways still had one more proposal for a scheme connecting with the N&BJR. Plans were deposited on 30th November 1899 for a Buckingham, Towcester & Metropolitan Junction Railway. This had distinct echoes of schemes of the 1880s, in seeking to connect East Claydon with both the L&NWR Banbury Branch and the N&BJR at Towcester, and a connection was again proposed to the now constructed Stratford, Towcester & Midland Junction line near Easton Neston. However, the recent opening of the MS&LR line had provided the area with sufficient new railway interest and the project attracted neither the required financial investment, nor the more important assent of the Select Committee at Westminster.

To end the 19th century on a somewhat lighter note, the secretary of the N&BJR, Leigh-Hunt, found it necessary to write to the Board of Trade, asking if they might be able to supply him with a copy of the N&BJR Official Byelaws, as the railway's own set had somehow been mislaid. It seems that the railway company wished to take proceedings against a group of men who had travelled without tickets from Helmdon to Cockley Brake Junction, where they then left the train presumably when it came to a mandatory stand before joining the L&NWR route to Banbury. Apparently, the N&BJR management needed to consult their own Byelaws in order to decide whether they should proceed against the men for travelling without having paid their fare, or for leaving the train at an unauthorised place.

The Final Years Of Independence

Although official records of the N&BJR are far and few between, fortunately the *Minute Book of Director's Meetings* for the years of 1907 to 1911 has survived. These meetings, held regularly at Baltic House, Leadenhall Street in London, do provide some interesting glimpses into the routine existence of a small and impecunious railway company during the early years of the 20th century and the lead up to the eventual amalgamation with the Stratford-upon-Avon & Midland Junction Railway.

J.W. Theobold had by now become chairman of the company, having served the N&BJR since 1863 as either secretary or general manager, and the other board members were Henry D. Kimber, R.H. Scott-Moncrieff and H.A. Vernet. The condition of their line was obviously still very much a concern for the directors, as in July 1907 they requested that Mr Burke, the engineer of the neighbouring East & West Junction Railway, should make an inspection on their behalf.

His report was reviewed by the Board on 29th August and this resulted in the purchase of rails and chairs for relaying approximately one mile of line between Blisworth and Towcester, and making repairs to various bridges and fences. Tenders were sought for the various materials required and rails were subsequently obtained from Guest, Keen & Nettlefold, sleepers from Burt, Boulton & Hayward and bridge timbers from Rowland Brothers.

Early in the following year, the Board met to consider the implications of a new Bill for the creation of the Stratford-upon-Avon & Midland Junction Railway, by the amalgamation of the East & West Junction, Stratford, Towcester & Midland Junction and the Evesham, Redditch & Stratford Junction companies. It was decided that the N&BJR should initially pursue a course of requiring the insertion of a clause in the Bill to safeguard their own interests but when this proved unacceptable to the promoters, the N&BJR Board decided to petition against the Bill. This resulted in further negotiations and, by late May 1908, agreement had been reached on a suitable clause and the N&BJR objection was withdrawn; the S&MJR Bill subsequently received the Royal Assent on 1st August.

That year also brought bad news when the wooden engine shed at Blisworth was destroyed by fire and the N&BJR had to fend off a resulting claim from the E&WJR for loss of their property in the blaze; fortunately, this had not been a locomotive. Tenders were subsequently sought for rebuilding the shed in a more substantial corrugated iron form and the work was finally awarded to R.B. Sparrow, who also operated an ironstone quarry at nearby Gayton, at a cost of £114 10s, plus a sum not to exceed £20 for '*certain extras*'.

The need for an impoverished company such as the N&BJR to closely control even the smallest items of expenditure was illustrated by the decision, in June 1908, to change the provision of vending machines from the incumbent supplier, the London & Provincial Automatic Machine Company, to the Nestle & Anglo Swiss Condensed Milk Company. The latter concern had negotiated to provide machines at Blisworth, Towcester, Wappenham and Helmdon stations at a rental of £10 per year per machine, thus undercutting the offer of the other supplier.

The later months of 1908 brought considerable discussion and correspondence on the subject of train services between

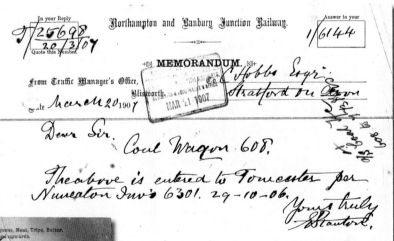

ABOVE: Examples of official N&BJR documentation are relatively scarce. This survival from 1907 covers the movement of a coal wagon from the Nuneaton area, which had arrived at Towcester over the neighbouring E&WJR route. *Author's collection*

LEFT: Despite the clear instructions given to the contrary at the top of this N&BJR waybill from 1893, the document was nevertheless utilised for the despatch of '*Birds tied*' from Blisworth to Kineton, via Green's Norton Junction and the East & West Junction line. *Author's collection*

Blisworth and Towcester. A letter had been received from the E&WJR, proposing alterations to their terms of use of the Green's Norton to Blisworth section of line, over which they had running powers. These proposals were rejected by the N&BJR Board and meetings were subsequently arranged between the chairmen of the two railways.

The E&WJR then seemingly backed down on what had initially been understood as having given one months notice of their intention to terminate an arrangement of 1891 between the two companies. It does, however, appear that they did make changes to their train timings, which then resulted in further discussion between the two companies, and also the L&NWR, over the resultant falling off in passenger numbers. It was then suggested that the E&WJR reverted to their previous timings and the L&NWR were requested to consider whether they could also alter the pattern of their services to Blisworth to help improve matters.

This was followed by a further suggestion from the E&WJR to reduce the overall number of trains over the Towcester to Blisworth section or, as an alternative, to terminate their own services from Stratford at Towcester. However, any further discussion was soon to become somewhat academic as, on 21st April 1909, the N&BJR Board held a special meeting to discuss a Memorandum of Terms that had been presented for the purchase of their company by the recently formed S&MJR. The N&BJR solicitors, Bircham & Co., were immediately instructed to contact their counterparts at the S&MJR, Bischoff & Co., to formulate a draft agreement. Clearly, the N&BJR were more than willing to fall gratefully into the arms of the prospective new owners.

The Formalities of Amalgamation

Although the N&BJR had hitherto doggedly maintained its independent existence against all the odds, incorporation into the newly formed S&MJR system was an entirely logical step. Their Blisworth to Towcester section actually formed an integral part, albeit by the use of running powers, of the S&MJR 'main line' to Stratford, whilst any thoughts of the N&BJR Cockley Brake Branch ever becoming part of a through route to the west had also long disappeared. The remaining months of 1909 therefore saw more meetings of the N&BJR directors, at which Bircham & Co. provided regular updates on the progress of negotiations for the sale of the company.

At the 92nd Ordinary General Meeting, J. Wilson Theobold reported that during the immediate half year, the company had made an excess of receipts over expenditure of just over £847.The Board considered that they had managed the line well, maintained it in a thoroughly good condition and, they believed, 'rendered the public some service'. He then confirmed a provisional agreement for the sale of the company to the S&MJR, remarking that it now seemed a perfectly natural thing that the two lines should come together as one undertaking. He did not, however, go so far as to suggest that the N&BJR were getting a very good deal but commented that it was 'the best arrangement that could be made at the time, and a fair one all round'.

September saw an exchange of draft agreements and after further negotiations, the N&BJR seal was formally attached to a finalised document. Harry Willmott of the S&MJR was also elected to the Board of the N&BJR, to fill a vacancy created by the death of Edwin Sloper.

On 29th November 1909, the N&BJR Board approved the submission of a petition to Parliament for leave to bring forward a Bill for the sale of their company. Various points of detail were considered over the following months and, with no objections having being raised against the proposal, Royal Assent was received on 29th April, with a completion of sale fixed for 1st July 1910. The sum agreed for the purchase of the N&BJR was £46,646. The financial affairs of the N&BJR were encapsulated in the opening pages of the Bill, which also confirmed the date for completion of all remaining formalities following the sale as 1st January 1911.

At this point in time the loan and share capital of the N&BJR stood at:

Irredeemable 5% 'A' debenture stock £115,930 3s 4d
Redeemable 5% 'B' debenture stock..............£170,057 13s 11d
5% first preference stock................................£145,000
5% second preference stock ....£ 74,770
Ordinary stock..£109,960

The Bill also necessarily extinguished all unexercised capital powers of the N&BJR that still remained from their Act of 1866, which authorised the raising of £550,000 for the construction of railways and works, none of which were ever completed.

A further provision of the Bill was for the new owners, the S&MJR, to widen the line at Towcester for a distance of seven furlongs and five chains between the Watling Street bridge and Green's Norton Junction, and to acquire certain specified parcels of land adjacent to their own railway at Old Stratford, Ettington and Kineton.

In addition, running powers over the old N&BJR lines were awarded to the Midland Railway but they were restricted from carrying any local traffic without obtaining further agreement; similar powers were also afforded to the Great Central Railway and the L&NWR. Provision was also made for all clerks, officers and servants of the N&BJR to be transferred to the new owners, with the exception of the secretary whose termination of office would be subject to no less than three months notice from the date of transfer. However, one immediate result of the impending changes was the resignation, and retirement, of Edward Stanton, who had been with the line since the very earliest days.

In the meantime certain other formalities now needed to be attended to. The agreement with the L&NWR for the provision of locomotives and rolling stock had been in place since 1875 but it having been arranged for S&MJR examples to take their place from 1st October, notice of termination was duly given to the L&NWR by letter of 11th May 1910. In addition, it was necessary for the N&BJR to terminate their membership of the Railway Clearing House and this was similarly dealt with on 2nd June.

The sale to the S&MJR was completed as planned on 1st July and the N&BJR Chairman then reported that he had been to William Deacon's Bank, where a deposit of £48,146 had been made to his company's account in respect of the purchase and other considerations. The formal winding up of the N&BJR was then put in hand, with W. Leigh-Hunt being required to swear an affidavit before the High Court of Justice Chancery Division on 20th June 1911. Arrangements were made for the distribution of moneys to shareholders, with the officers and directors of the N&BJR also being individually compensated by various sums totalling £1,000. However, the shareholders, although collectively holding a nominal value of £615,718 of N&BJR stock, only received a modest return for their troubles.

Bircham's had also arranged with the Board of Trade for the appointment of an independent accountant to oversee the issuance of the certificate required for the formal winding up of the N&BJR company. G.W. Knox, of Knox Cropper & Co. of Finsbury Circus, London, was approached and with the N&BJR being described as 'an impoverished concern', he eventually agreed to act for the sum of £10, which was duly provided by the board. Knox reported that there were only one hundred and sixty-five registered stockholders of the N&BJR and of these only one hundred and thirty-four could be traced; these were duly paid a total of £46,087 6s 5d and the balance of monies was paid to the Court, following which the Board of Trade issued the required certificate on 10th August.

Final handover of all corporate documents and the official seal of the N&BJR had been made on 25th July. A meeting of the N&BJR directors was then convened on 13th October 1910, to approve the very last half yearly accounts of their company. It was agreed at the same meeting that the office be removed to Leigh-Hunt's address at 62 London Wall, where he would be retained to act as required to complete the affairs of the company within a period not exceeding nine months from 30th September 1910.

The N&BJR was still not quite dead and a final meeting of a no doubt relieved Board of directors was held on 8th May 1911, where it was approved that the last remaining balance of £576 would be paid to the Paymaster General as provided for under the Act of Sale. The N&BJR therefore finally ceased to exist after a rather troubled life span of just forty-four years. It had managed to survive against all the odds and had at least retained the status of an independent railway company throughout this period of time. However, under the ownership of the S&MJR, much of its route was henceforth destined to become a rather insignificant branch line.

Some N&BJR Statistics

The N&BJR was never a prosperous railway and the revenues earned in the first few years now seem minimal by modern standards. In 1867, the first full year of operation, total receipts from all types of traffic amounted to £2,149, of which goods traffic contributed just over one half. The railway's locomotive (there was only one) ran 16,354 miles in that year and, quite understandably, it seems that all trains were operated as mixed passenger and goods. Passengers in all three classes totalled 34,562, with just one season ticket holder,

Early photographs of trains on the N&BJR route are practically unknown, so this view of E&WJR Beyer, Peacock 0-6-0 No.12, standing just inside the trainshed at Banbury L&NWR station, is one of the few that have so far been found. The precise date is unknown but must be after the amalgamation of the N&BJR into the S&MJR in 1910, when ex-E&WJR locomotives replaced the hired L&NWR stock on the trains from Blisworth and Towcester. *Author's collection*

yielding just £987 of revenue. Goods traffic amounted to some 11,600 tons, of which 7,300 tons were minerals, with 95% of that total being coal. The N&BJR's running costs for 1867 were £2,282, thus resulting in an overall operating loss of £133.

The line was extended from Towcester to Cockley Brake in 1872, and traffic volumes and receipts increased accordingly but with additional locomotives required and other costs increasing, an overall loss of £1,213 resulted. This would rather understandably prove to be the leanest year of the N&BJR's existence. However, the extended line soon bore fruit and total receipts rose above the £10,000 mark for the first time in 1874, to reach £10,022, with goods traffic contributing two thirds of that total. Nevertheless, the carriage of iron ore, the *raison d'etre* of the once-proposed extensions to South Wales, contributed only a small part of the receipts from mineral traffic. Passenger numbers, however, leapt to 115,144, a figure which would not be exceeded until 1895, and the total train mileage similarly increased to 65,225. The result was an operating surplus of £1,448.

In fact, from the low point of 1872 through to the amalgamation into the S&MJR in 1910, the N&BJR managed to keep its head just above water in terms of annual operating costs in each year, with the exception of just two. In 1895, a large increase in revenue from goods traffic, due to the construction of the MS&LR line through Helmdon, was rather unfortunately outweighed by increased operating costs. These resulted from the Board of Trade's requirement to upgrade the signalling arrangements there, to accommodate the connections to the contractor's sites. The year 1899 then saw a substantial reduction in goods traffic, possibly also due to the opening of the MS&LR, which may well have reduced local traffic on the N&BJR route. However, 1904 would probably be considered as the best performance by the N&BJR, with an operating surplus of exactly £2,000.

At the very end of the independent existence of the N&BJR, in 1909, the line carried just over 116,000 passengers and 142,000 tons of goods, although the total train mileage had reduced to just below 44,000, no doubt due to the running of heavier trains. Gross receipts from all types of traffic were £8,841, with passengers contributing one third of the total. This was another good year for the N&BJR, with an operating surplus of £1,510.

Although on the surface the N&BJR might appear to have operated efficiently, it was never able to make a return to its shareholders and was throughout hampered by underlying debts from its earliest years.

ABOVE: Sub-contractor Charles Noah Foster purchased a new Hunslet 0-6-0ST, Works No. 4, in late 1865 to work on his construction of the N&BJR line from Blisworth to Towcester and Cockley Brake. The locomotive, then named *Vulcan*, featured in the much reported legal proceedings of late 1866 when railway property, mistakenly including the engine, was seized in *lieu* of debts owed by the N&BJR. The locomotive pictured here was its immediate works predecessor, Hunslet No. 3, and thus probably nearly identical in appearance to *Vulcan*. *Author's collection*

BELOW: Contractor John Aird completed the construction of the N&BJR onwards from Towcester to Cockley Brake in 1872 and one of the locomotives known to have been used by him was an old L&NWR 0-6-0 hired from Isaac Watt Boulton. The engine, built as long ago as 1847, was named *Cotton* whilst in service with Boulton and was reportedly delivered to Blisworth in 1870. When construction of the line had been completed, it was then collected by Boulton himself and driven back home to Ashton-under-Lyne. *Author's collection*

Chapter 1.2
THE LOCOMOTIVES AND ROLLING STOCK OF
THE NORTHAMPTON & BANBURY JUNCTION RAILWAY

Of the four independent constituent companies that would later combine to form the S&MJR, only the Northampton & Banbury Junction and East & West Junction railways actually owned any locomotives or rolling stock. The early years of these individual companies were full of difficulties and always financially challenging; it was therefore inevitable that the provision of locomotives and rolling stock would reflect those circumstances. Initially, both companies placed orders with outside contractors for new locomotives to work their newly opened lines but, in an unfortunate parallel, both would later see them repossessed by the makers in *lieu* of payment.

Early records of both of railways are fragmented, and their locomotive and rolling stock history up to the end of the 19th century is therefore incomplete. In fact, if it were not for the annual statistical returns that were required by the Board of Trade, even less would be known. Any other early information that has survived has mostly been handed down over the years from usually anonymous original sources but, more recently, further details have been gleaned from new researches and this does at least help to provide a more complete record.

Comparatively little has been recorded about either the locomotives or the rolling stock of the N&BJR but fragments of available information can be pieced together to give something of a picture of the way that the trains were operated between the opening of the line in 1866 and the commencement of hiring from the L&NWR in 1875.

Contractor's Locomotives – *Vulcan*

Fortunately some details have survived of the locomotives used on the construction of both sections of the N&BJR line. Possibly the best known is the Hunslet 0-6-0 saddle tank Works No. 4 named *Vulcan*, which was supplied new to the sub-contractor C.N. Foster on 31st December 1865. Foster is known to have used this engine on the construction of the line from Blisworth to a point just beyond Towcester. It was to become the unintended focus of the earlier mentioned legal dispute, when the locomotive was incorrectly seized by the High Sheriff *in lieu* of a debt incurred by the N&BJR.

Vulcan went on to lead a varied life after the N&BJR, passing to another contractor, Leather Smith & Co. and being renamed *Portsmouth*, before then featuring with J. Firbank & Co. in September 1873; it was still with the latter company in 1901.

Contractor's Locomotives From Boulton's Sidings

Locomotives may also have been hired from Isaac Watt Boulton of Ashton-under-Lyne, who was a well-known dealer in secondhand and often heavily modified old engines; he is known to have had dealings with the N&BJR in its earliest days.

Alfred R. Bennett, in his book *The Chronicle's of Boulton's Sidings*, records the provision of an old Sharp, Roberts & Co. 2-2-2 tender locomotive, which was collected from Longsight as L&NWR No. 1125, on 28th February 1866 and driven to Blisworth by Boulton himself, with a stop on the way at Crewe to pay the required sum of £240. After a night at Blisworth, a start was made at 8.00am for Towcester, only to find the route blocked by wagons, no doubt engaged in the construction of the line which was still just over two months away from opening.

However, the issue is slightly clouded by the fact that Bennett states that the locomotive was on hire to the E&WJR; it is possible that this is an error or alternatively the engine may actually have been intended for use on the initial stages of construction of the E&WJR from Green's Norton.

Work was in hand on the second part of the N&BJR line from Bradden to Cockley Brake in the early part of 1870, under new contractors John Aird & Sons, although only one locomotive has been positively identified as being used by that company. This was another instance of a hiring from I.W. Boulton and was an old Longridge-built tender 0-6-0 from the 1840s, known to have been purchased from the L&NWR at Wolverton around 1870 and taken immediately to Blisworth. The engine, named *Cotton*, was then used on the construction of the line onwards from Bradden and after completion of the hire, Boulton, in his usual style, drove the locomotive home to Ashton-under-Lyne himself.

There is also the possibility of another Boulton locomotive being used; his No. 17, a small 3ft 0-4-0 saddle tank acquired in 1867, is known to have been supplied to John Aird in 1869, which could also just coincide with the recommencement of work on the N&BJR line.

N&BJR Owned Or Hired Locomotives:
The Neilson Engines That Never Were

In advance of the opening of their first section from Blisworth to Towcester in 1866, the N&BJR had placed an order for ten locomotives with Neilsons of Glasgow, consisting of five each of a standard design of 0-4-2 well tank and tender engine. The specification stated that the engines were to be painted in green, with brass numbering from 1 to 10. The purchase of ten locomotives for a line of only four miles might be considered an over provision but, at that point in time, the N&BJR was expecting to open as far as Banbury in the near future and had also successfully obtained powers to construct further extensions onwards towards South Wales.

Unfortunately, the financial crisis of 1866 crippled the newly opened line and it would be another six years before trains would even run as far as Banbury. The locomotive order was quickly cancelled and, in due course, Neilsons, with five engines already completed and standing in their yard, sought other buyers.

Intriguingly, an L&NWR Locomotive Committee minute of July 14th 1870 reveals that Neilsons had recently offered four locomotives to that railway; the opportunity was declined but the timing of the approach makes it interesting to consider whether these could have been the remainder of the engines originally intended for the N&BJR.

The Neilson 0-4-2 Well Tank Engines

The well tank locomotives were built to a specification provided by J.E. McConnell after he had left the L&NWR, explaining their similarity to that company's 'M' and 'N' classes, although having plain domes on the boiler and brass rims to the driving wheel splashers. They had driving wheels of 5ft 6in. diameter with a total wheelbase of exactly 17 feet, a boiler pressed to 130lbs per square inch supplying cylinders of 16in. x 20in.; the coal and water capacities were 25cwt and 450 gallons respectively.

There is some conflicting evidence about the original orders for these locomotives, with one source stating that all five were to be produced to Neilsons order No. E305 of

ABOVE LEFT: Prior to the opening of the first section of their line in 1866, the N&BJR had placed orders with Neilson & Co. of Glasgow for ten locomotives. Five were to have been built as 0-4-2 well tanks and this official photograph, taken by the manufacturer prior to delivery, shows the engine bearing a plate carrying No. 1. Two were completed but the order was then cancelled and the engines never reached Blisworth, eventually being sold by Neilsons to the Caledonian Railway. *Author's collection*

LEFT: The CR initially renumbered the two Neilson 0-4-2WTs as No's 540 and 541, and they received various modifications, including rudimentary cabs and stovepipe chimneys. No. 540 is pictured here at an early date, whilst still with its original chimney and painted style of numbering but with its new cab. *Author's collection*

BELOW: Both engines were moved on to the CR duplicate list in 1892 and given 'A' suffixes to their numbers. They were renumbered again in 1899, so this illustration of No. 541A (which became No. 1355) was thus taken between those two dates; withdrawal came in 1901. *Author's collection*

Another view of CR No. 541A, showing further modifications, such as the extended footstep and additional horizontal handrail on the bunker side, presumably provided for the use of shunters. *Author's collection*

1865 for the Athens & Piraeus Railway, with only the first, Works No. 1216, eventually being despatched to Greece. It is then suggested that construction of the remaining four was cancelled but subsequently resurrected under Neilsons order No. E318 for the N&BJR, with that order itself being cancelled when the company was unable to complete the purchase. However, two of the engines had actually been completed as Works No's 1217 and 1218, and these were then purchased in September 1870 by the Caledonian Railway against Neilsons order No. E366, after having been laid up in the works yard for some time and then fitted with rudimentary cabs before sale.

A photograph does exists of a cabless Neilson 0-4-2 tank locomotive in fully lined livery, bearing a cast number plate 'No. 1' but no other company identification and this has variously been reported as being a works view of either Athens & Piraeus Railway, N&BJR or even Solway Junction Railway (SJR) No. 1. The latter of these suggestions arises from the engines purchased by the Caledonian Railway having worked on the Solway line for a short period but it can be discounted as it is known that the SJR never owned any locomotives of their own and that their line was always operated by the Caledonian. The official photograph was therefore probably taken in anticipation of despatch to the N&BJR.

Having arrived with the Caledonian, the two well tanks were numbered as 540 and 541, later being transferred to the duplicate list as No's 540A and 541A in 1892. A further renumbering took place in 1899, to No's 1354 and 1355. They were eventually withdrawn from service in 1900 and 1901 respectively, after having worked at various locations including Rutherglen, the Dundee & Arbroath line, Millisle, Perth, Larbert and Methven.

The Neilson 0-4-2 Tender Engines

The tender engine design was similar to that of the well tanks, with the addition of a 4-wheeled tender of 8ft 10in. wheelbase, carrying $2\frac{1}{2}$ tons of coal and 1,700 gallons of water. The cylinders, motion, wheels and boiler were interchangeable between the two designs. An official works style photograph also exists of a tender locomotive of this batch but although the livery style appears to be the same as the well tank, there is no number plate fitted.

The two tender locomotives constructed before the N&BJR order was cancelled, Neilson Works No's 1219 and 1220, also joined the Caledonian Railway at the same time as their well tank counterparts, although apparently having been fitted with rather better cabs. They became No's 452 and 453, and were later successively renumbered as 322 and 323 in 1877, and 322A and 323A ten years later. A further change of identity followed in 1899, when the two became No's 1279 and 1280 respectively. The former was then withdrawn during the same year but the second locomotive survived to become No. 1323 in 1900, lasting in service until 1906.

These engines were initially – and rather ironically – employed on iron ore traffic on the Solway Junction line, the very purpose for which they had been intended on the N&BJR. However, they were moved away when that traffic declined and spent their years at Carstairs, Lanark, Muirkirk, Lockerbie and Brechin.

The other five locomotives from Neilsons were to have been tender versions of the well tanks but, once again, two were constructed before the order was cancelled; both again went to the CR. This is another official photograph but in this instance no numbering had been affixed. *Author's collection*

CR No. 1323, the final guise of Neilson Works No. 1220, at Carstairs in August 1902. The engine had previously been numbered 453, 323, 323A and 1280. These locomotives would have made a fine sight working between Blisworth, Towcester and beyond, although their haulage capacity on the anticipated heavy trains of iron ore, over what was a difficult route, must perhaps be questioned. *Author's collection*

Early Days on the N&BJR

The newly opened N&BJR was immediately faced with a locomotive shortage and it is not at all clear how services between Blisworth and Towcester were inaugurated. Fortunately, the statutory annual returns required by the Board of Trade do at least throw a little light on the situation. These confirm that the N&BJR owned just one locomotive, three passenger carriages, one other passenger vehicle and twenty wagons at the end of 1866. However, despite the statistical evidence provided by the returns, the identity of the sole N&BJR locomotive in these first few years is difficult to ascertain.

The one fact that can be stated with certainty is that this first locomotive must have been a tank engine. When Captain Rich of the Board of Trade inspected and approved the line prior to its opening, one of his stipulations was that the Blisworth to Towcester passenger trains must be operated by tank engines. At the time there was no means of turning engines at Towcester, so presumably the Captain was unhappy at the prospect of tender first operation over the newly constructed line.

One possibility is the use of Foster's engine *Vulcan* on N&BJR services during the first few months. It was quite usual for a contractor's engine to be used to operate a newly opened line and the fact that it was mistakenly impounded in October 1866 might add credibility to that suggestion. Regular use on their trains would quite possibly have conveyed the appearance of it actually being owned by the N&BJR.

A contemporary newspaper report also lends further weight to that theory, with the *Northampton Mercury* of 24th November 1866, stating that:

'*We are sorry to say that this railway, which for the short time that it has been opened has been found to be a very great*

accommodation to Towcester, has come to grief. Under an execution from the Sheriff the locomotive is in the spunging house and the traffic has been suddenly and entirely checked.'

There is one other unattributed record of an early engine used by the N&BJR and this is described as a '*decrepit antique*' known as '*The Owl*'. Although there is no other description available, one possibility is that this may have been an ex-Liverpool & Manchester Railway 0-4-2 of the same name, which is known to have been replaced in late 1853 and then sold in 1855 by the L&NWR. Up to six such locomotives were reputedly purchased

A Liverpool & Manchester Railway Sharp, Roberts 'Bird' type 0-4-2 engine of 1842. One of the class was named *Owl* and may have been the locomotive that worked on the N&BJR in its early days. Several of this type were acquired from the L&NWR by Isaac Watt Boulton during the 1850s and his dealings with the N&BJR are well known. *Author's collection*

by Isaac Watt Boulton and with his known connections with the N&BJR, it is just possible that one could have been hired or sold to the line.

Although it has also been identified as a possible candidate, it is unlikely that the earlier mentioned old Sharp, Roberts engine supplied by Boulton for construction work was used to operate services on the N&BJR. After delivery to Blisworth, the locomotive was found to have a cracked cylinder and was soon returned but it is possible that it came back to the N&BJR or Boulton may have provided another locomotive in its place.

An L&NWR Connection?

It is clear that the N&BJR could not have operated their services without some outside help at times, and it has been stated that the L&NWR provided locomotives and stock from 1st October 1866, although so far nothing has emerged from L&NWR minutes to confirm this. It is, however, quite possible, as was anticipated in the earlier mentioned newspaper report, that the L&NWR did assist on a temporary basis to keep services running on the line, possibly after the seizure and subsequent sale of *Vulcan*.

Although this is a quite logical suggestion and the L&NWR would indeed occasionally provide locomotives on loan in later years, it is still quite clear from annual returns that the N&BJR did in fact have their own locomotive between 1866 and 1868.

A further reference to the N&BJR operating their own trains is provided by the fact that a local engineering company, Harrison & Clayton of Northampton, is known to have maintained '*the locomotive operating between Blisworth and Towcester*' during these early years. Another local newspaper report also confirmed that the railway still only had a single engine in use during 1868, as it was reported to have failed at Blisworth, leaving passengers for Towcester stranded as no other engine was owned by the company.

The N&BJR did not provide a statistical return detailing the ownership of locomotives and rolling stock in 1868 but, in the following two years, they did report that these had in fact been hired, although the source is not known.

Other Early Locomotives

A few other references have been found to locomotives used on the N&BJR during the early years but these are also without substantial detail. A local newspaper announcement of 17th November 1866 listed an extensive range of what might be described as '*contractor's hardware*', which was to be auctioned by W.J. Peirce of Northampton '*in various parishes on the N&BJR line between Blisworth and Helmdon*'; the auction included a '*locomotive steam engine*'.

Unfortunately, no other information was provided but this was probably a contractor's locomotive that had been used on the construction of the Blisworth to Towcester line; however, it could just possibly have been an early unrecorded N&BJR-owned locomotive. The engine was not listed in a subsequent auction in December of that year, which merely appears to have been a clearance of the remaining impedimenta from the first sale.

It also seems that the L&NWR came to the assistance of the N&BJR on several occasions. It is recorded in their Locomotive Committee minutes of 13th August 1869, and again on 13th

January 1871, that an engine had been lent to their smaller neighbour '*for a few days*'. The cost was £4 4s per day, with the N&BJR providing their own fireman, which suggests that the hire also included an L&NWR driver; payment was to be made daily to the station master at Bletchley.

The same terms of hire were applicable in July 1872, when the L&NWR again provided assistance for five days. However, by this time the N&BJR were already assembling a locomotive fleet of their own, with one of their engines then being reported as under repair at Wolverton.

A More Identifiable Locomotive

A further auction announcement appeared in the *Northampton Mercury* of 22nd October 1870. The objective of this sale, to be held at Towcester station, was to dispose of a '*six wheeled, four coupled tank locomotive engine, now in the use of the said company, and distinguishable by the name 'W.A. Michael, owner, London'.*' The locomotive was to be sold '*with, and subject to, an agreement dated 14th September 1869, between Vincent James Barton, Merchant, of the one part, and the Midland Counties and South Wales (now the Northampton and Banbury Junction) Railway Company of the other part.*' It is rather difficult to understand just why this locomotive should have been made available for sale so soon after its apparent purchase, unless it had been found totally unsuitable for use on the N&BJR.

Walter Amos Michael was listed as a director of the N&BJR from 1870 until 1891 and was also secretary of the International Finance Society of Threadneedle Street, London. The Society had been involved with the financing of the N&BJR since the earliest days, when they advanced a loan to the contractor William Shrimpton, and they also featured in the restructuring of the company after 1869.

It would therefore seem likely that the IFS had arranged the provision of this and, quite possibly, subsequent locomotives for the N&BJR, using Barton as an intermediary. The fact that Michael's name appeared on the locomotive probably suggests that the IFS retained the ownership and that it was leased or hired to the N&BJR.

V.J. Barton, was an '*iron merchant and contractor for railway plant*', operating from 23 & 28 St. Martin's Lane, Cannon Street, London. He had earlier appeared as a partner of James Davis of Ulverston in 1858, then operating as iron and steel manufacturers, engineers, millwrights and founders, and later went into partnership with John George Barton, as iron brokers of 75 Old Street, London. However, there are no obvious traces of Barton dealing in locomotives in any of the usual trade journals of the period, whilst only a few references to his activities have been found in other sources. In 1868, he reneged on an arrangement to supply a locomotive and two carriages to the Thetford & Watton Railway, and eleven years later was known to have purchased two surplus broad gauge engines from the Cornwall Minerals Railway. It must be assumed, therefore, that he was not a regular dealer in locomotives, despite his obvious involvement in railway contracting.

Nevertheless, this is the first detailed evidence of any N&BJR locomotive and as will be seen, it was apparently not sold at the above mentioned auction. Furthermore, the N&BJR were instead about to embark on an enlargement of their locomotive fleet.

The Later Locomotives

The half yearly report by the N&BJR at the close of 1871 indicated that the railway then owned four locomotives, all of which were tank engines, one of them presumably being the subject of the above mentioned auction. One year later, this total had increased to five, with the newcomer being identifiable as a tender locomotive. However, by the end of 1873, whilst the total number of locomotives remained at five, the composition had changed with two now being tender engines, indicating that one tank engine had by then been disposed of. Fortunately, firm records have survived of the purchase of three of these five engines, which were obtained from the neighbouring L&NWR.

The first of these to arrive was an 1855 Tayleur 0-6-0 tender locomotive from the Vulcan Foundry, with 17in. x 24in. cylinders. This had once been No. 21 *Ajax* of the South Staffordshire Railway and had subsequently seen service with the L&NWR as their No's 306, 906 and 1227, before being sold to the N&BJR for £700. The sale was recorded by the L&NWR Locomotive Committee on 14th June 1872, although it is likely that delivery to the N&BJR would have been some months earlier.

Next was the second tender locomotive, a Hawthorn long boiler type 0-6-0 of 1849, with 18in. x 24in. cylinders, originally

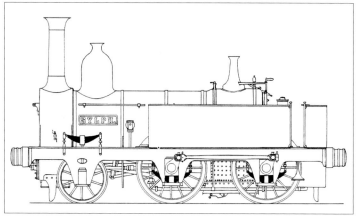

In 1873, a third purchase from the L&NWR was former SSR Sharp Bros 2-4-0T *Sylph*, built in 1851 and one of the first side tank locomotives in the country. This was allocated No. 3 in the N&BJR fleet. *Courtesy H. Jack*

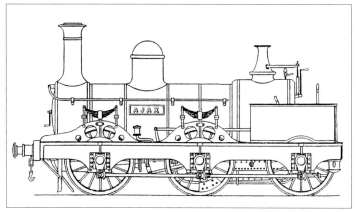

ABOVE: N&BJR operations were extended to Banbury in 1872, necessitating more robust motive power. One of the secondhand locomotives known to have been used on the line during that period was a tender 0-6-0 built at the Vulcan Foundry by Tayleur & Co. for the South Staffordshire Railway (SSR) in 1855. This passed into the stock of the L&NWR before being sold to the N&BJR in 1872, becoming No. 4 on that railway. *Courtesy H. Jack*

BELOW: Also bought from the L&NWR was a Hawthorn-built 0-6-0 tender engine of 1849, obtained by the N&BJR in early 1873, which became their No. 5. *Courtesy H. Jack*

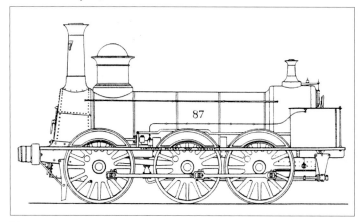

L&NWR No. 239, which had become No. 1849 by the time of its purchase by the N&BJR for £1,000 in February 1873.

Finally, as confirmed in L&NWR minutes of April 1873, the N&BJR purchased another South Staffordshire locomotive, their old No. 14 *Sylph*. This was a Sharp Brothers 2-4-0 tank engine of 1851, with 16in. x 22in. cylinders, and was one of the earliest of the side tank type to appear in this country.

This therefore leaves two of the five locomotives owned at the end of 1873 to be identified. These were two tank engines, one quite probably the same '*six wheeled, four coupled tank locomotive engine*' that was unsold at the 1870 auction.

Other minutes of L&NWR Locomotive Committee meetings during 1872 are also relevant to the N&BJR. On 10th May 1872, it was recorded that the L&NWR then had a locomotive under repair for the N&BJR at Wolverton. Two months later, minutes of 12th July revealed that a further two locomotives were being attended to on behalf of the same company. An interesting and rather cryptic comment is attached to the latter minute, stating that an L&NWR representative had '*told the secretary of that company* [the N&BJR] *that he cannot undertake any more repairs for them*' but the reason for this statement is not known. Possibly, the L&NWR knew that they would not in future have the necessary facilities at Wolverton, with the locomotive works and engine shed due to close down, or it may have been due to other problems between the two companies. It could also be interpreted as an indication that the relevant N&BJR engines were beyond further repair, which might explain the purchase in 1873 of the other engines from the L&NWR. The same minutes also show that the L&NWR had recently loaned two locomotives to the N&BJR for four days, presumably whilst the two at Wolverton were being attended to, significantly at a time when the N&BJR had just started to operate through to Banbury.

The chronology of these events possibly suggests that the single locomotive under repair in May could well have been the Tayleur 0-6-0, which is recorded as purchased by the N&BJR in June and was probably being fettled up before delivery. The two locomotives stated as being under repair in July may then have been the Hawthorn 0-6-0 and the 2-4-0 tank engine *Sylph*.

The Auctions

Further evidence that the 6-wheeled tank engine may not have been sold in the 1870 auction is then provided by the announcement of a forthcoming sale on 18th March 1873, at Wappenham station. Under the heading '*Northampton & Banbury Junction Railway*', this listed a selection of surplus materials and also included not one but two '*six wheeled, four coupled, locomotive tank engines, with copper fireboxes, and brass tubes*'. The materials were presumably the residue from construction of the line through to Cockley Brake but the '*six wheeled, four coupled tank locomotive*' from the 1870 auction had apparently been joined by another of the same general description.

The need to dispose of these two locomotives may well be explained by the fact that the N&BJR were by then operating trains through to Banbury, where the use of the L&NWR turntable was available and they would therefore no longer have been constrained by the earlier requirement to use tank engines.

These engines also represented two of the total of five that the N&BJR had reported as being owned at the end of 1873, with two of the remainder being the 0-6-0 tender engines and the other the 2-4-0 tank engine *Sylph*, that had only recently been purchased from the L&NWR. The annual Board of Trade statistics indicate that this situation was unchanged through 1874 and into 1875, and a further auction at Towcester on 23rd August 1875 confirmed the number of engines as still being five but, more importantly, provided more information on their details.

Various effects were listed as having been '*lately in use for working the Northampton & Banbury Junction Railway, but in consequence of other arrangements having been made, they are no longer required for that purpose*'. This refers to the decision made by the N&BJR during that year to request that the London & North Western Railway provide locomotives and rolling stock for the line.

Various items listed in the auction were of an engineering nature, and included an iron water tank, lathes, blacksmith's equipment, engine lamps and tools, all stated as having been connected with the engine shed. However, by far the most significant items were five locomotive engines and four carriages, fortunately on this occasion being described in much more detail:

'*A Locomotive Tank ENGINE, No. 1, six wheels, four coupled 15-in. cylinder,*

A Locomotive Tank ENGINE, No. 2, six wheels, four coupled 15½-in. cylinder,

A Locomotive Tank ENGINE, No. 3, six wheels, four coupled 16-in. cylinder,

A Locomotive ENGINE, No. 4, six wheels, all coupled, 17-in. cylinder, also Tender to same,

A Locomotive ENGINE, No. 5, six wheels, all coupled, 18-in. cylinder, also Tender to same

The above Engines, Nos. 1, 4, and 5 have lately undergone thorough repairs.

Four passenger CARRIAGES'

From the above descriptions, it is immediately possible, by reference to the wheel arrangements and cylinder sizes, to identify the three engines purchased from the L&NWR in 1872 and 1873. Thus No. 3 is the SSR 2-4-0 tank engine *Sylph*, No. 4 is the Tayleur 0-6-0 from the same source and No. 5 is the L&NWR Hawthorn 0-6-0. The other two engines, both described as '*six wheeled four coupled tank engines*', one having 15in and the other with 15½in cylinders, are clearly the two other locomotives that were unsuccessfully auctioned in 1873; in all probability one of them had also been the subject of the earlier sale in 1870.

One of these locomotives was disposed of, either at the auction or shortly afterwards, as at the end of 1875 the N&BJR stock had been reduced to one tender engine and three tank locomotives. Fortunately, it is known that the disposal was of the L&NWR Hawthorn 0-6-0, No. 5 on the N&BJR, which is recorded as having been sold to the Severn & Wye Railway, where it was later named *Ranger*. In addition, Harry Parr, in his 1963 history of the Severn & Wye, also comments that an N&BJR account of 1875 shows '*the balance of hire and purchase of engine No. 5 including repair £956 18s 11d, less realised by sale of same £800*', which confirms the sale of the Hawthorn. This also confirms that the numbers used to identify the five locomotives in the 1875 auction were in fact their running numbers on the N&BJR and not just a convenient means of listing them for the sale.

Whilst all of this was happening, the N&BJR had made an arrangement with their near neighbours the L&NWR to provide engines to operate their trains, which commenced on 1st March. However, despite this, the N&BJR was still in possession of the four unsold engines at the end of 1876, although this was reduced by the sale or other disposal of the remaining tender engine, the Tayleur 0-6-0, during 1877. At the end of that year the three remaining locomotives, all tank engines, were still reported as N&BJR stock, although one had been the subject of yet another auction on 14th December 1877. This announcement provided still more detail:

'*A Valuable Locomotive Tank ENGINE built by Sharp, Stewart, and Co., and re-built by the London and North-Western Railway Company in 1872. Six wheels, trailing and driving coupled, 5ft. 4in. diameter; leading ditto 3ft. 8in. diameter; copper fire-box and brass tubes; capacity of tank (side), about 1,000 gallons; 15-inch cylinders (outside), 22-inch stroke.*

The engine may be seen any day previous to the sale, on application to Mr. Porter, Traffic Superintendent, N. and B.J. Railway, Blisworth Station. Particulars may also be obtained of Mr. Vincent J. Barton, St. Clement's-Lane, London.'

Whatever the outcome of this particular auction, the remaining locomotive stock of the N&BJR was finally disposed of, by one means or another, during 1878, with the usual Board of Trade statistics indicating that no engines remained at the end of that year. The ultimate disposal of these remaining locomotives is not known but the fact that the Hawthorn of 1849, which was probably the oldest engine, did find another owner might suggest that the others could also have had a further life elsewhere, with at least one of the 2-4-0 tanks having received a thorough repair in 1872.

The N&BJR half yearly reports state that, in 1877, £1,572 was recouped from the sale of rolling stock. This could have related to the sale of either locomotives or other stock but the sum is perhaps rather high to have been merely scrap value. In the following year, a further £100 was received from the same source.

Research continues and it is to be hoped that somewhere a previously unidentified locomotive will appear, probably in non main line service, which may be revealed to have been one of the old N&BJR engines.

Possible Identities

The reference to Vincent J. Barton in the 1877 auction suggests that the fully described tank engine could be the same one that was purchased in 1869, appeared again in 1870 and was also engine No. 1 in the 1875 auction. The wheel arrangement, the Sharp, Stewart lineage and the mention of the L&NWR initially suggests that it might be the old SSR *Sylph* but that engine had somewhat smaller 5ft driving wheels and also 16in. cylinders, so can be discounted.

A detailed examination of the of the works lists of Sharp, Roberts and Sharp, Stewart does not reveal any obvious candidates for this locomotive. Also, L&NWR locomotive records do not align with the stated rebuilding in 1872 of any suitable Sharp product. The L&NWR did rebuild many of their own tender engines into 2-4-0 tanks but these were originally Crewe products and also do not fit the required dimensions.

The possibility has also to be considered of a major rebuild having completely altered the configuration and dimensions of an original engine, but this is probably rather unlikely considering the financial state of the N&BJR, and it was perhaps more likely that the L&NWR had merely overhauled, rather than completely rebuilt, this locomotive. However, if less emphasis is placed on the accuracy of the auctioneer's description of this tank locomotive, then another theory is possible.

According to their minutes of October 1868, the North London Railway (NLR) had just sold their locomotive No. 27 to a V.J. Barton. This was a former Northumberland Coal Company 2-4-0 tender engine, which had been released by its former owners on termination of their arrangement to work their own trains between their Thames wharves and the nearby NLR coal depots. Furthermore, the locomotive, seemingly an old Stephenson product, had been rebuilt as a 2-4-0 saddle tank prior to its sale and the reference to Barton makes it possible that this could be one of the two unidentified '*six wheeled, four coupled tank locomotives*' of the N&BJR.

This suspicion is further strengthened by the fact that the NLR minutes of 27th September 1869 then recorded a further sale to V.J. Barton, this time NLR No. 10, which was by then a 2-4-0 side tank engine, having been rebuilt thus at Bow Works from its original well tank configuration. The dimensions of this NLR class are stated as 5ft

Top: The N&BJR locomotive stock included two 2-4-0 tank locomotives of rather shadowy origins. A converted Stephenson 2-4-0 tender engine, formerly owned by the Northumberland Coal Company, was sold by the North London Railway in October 1868 to Vincent J. Barton, known to have had significant connections with the N&BJR. Although no photographic record has been found of that engine, it is quite possible that one of the two N&BJR tank locomotives was similar in appearance to the converted Stephenson 2-4-0 seen here in use at Pinnox Colliery, near Burslem. *Author's collection*

Above: Another view of a Stephenson 2-4-0 converted to a saddle tank is provided by *Cavendish*, a former L&NWR locomotive purchased by I.W. Boulton around 1870 and rebuilt before being hired out to the Cowbridge Railway. *Author's collection*

Right: The second mystery N&BJR 2-4-0 tank locomotive is fortunately somewhat easier to identify. Barton was involved in the supply to the line of an NLR 2-4-0 well tank, which had earlier been converted to side tank

configuration. The details and dimensions closely corresponds to an engine in the list of assets auctioned by the N&BJR in 1875. This photograph of an early model of the NLR class provides a useful illustration of the engine prior to its conversion to a side-tank. *Author's collection*

THE LOCOMOTIVES AND ROLLING STOCK OF THE NORTHAMPTON & BANBURY JUNCTION RAILWAY

3in. driving wheels, with 15in. x 22in. outside cylinders, being an almost exact match for the more fully described of the two N&BJR 2-4-0 tanks.

The one problem with this theory is that NLR No. 10 is recorded as being built in 1854 by Stothert & Slaughter and not Sharp, Stewart, although significantly the latter did construct further locomotives to exactly the same design for the NLR in 1855. However, the sales by the NLR to Barton and the corresponding dates of Barton's supply arrangement with W.A. Michael, strongly suggests that these were the two locomotives owned by the N&BJR.

One further helpful coincidence is that Barton also purchased four carriages from the NLR in September 1869 and these could also be the same four that were listed for auction by the N&BJR in 1875.

The actual appearance of these two engines is a little more difficult to define. Fortunately, however, it seems that NLR No. 10 was not the only locomotive of its class to be converted to a side tank and then sold. In 1869, the Whitehaven, Cleator & Egremont Railway took delivery of a similarly converted member of the same class, via the workshops of Fletcher, Jennings & Company at nearby Lowca. This locomotive then survived long enough to be taken into the ownership of the Furness Railway as their No. 12 *Marron* and it was duly photographed, albeit with the addition of a typical FR cab and other fittings, on its last legs at Moor Row shed, thus giving a possible glimpse of how N&BJR No. 1 might just have appeared.

The appearance of the other N&BJR tank locomotive is more difficult but there does exist a line drawing of the donor 2-4-0 tender locomotive, NLR No. 27, before its conversion to a saddle tank. There are also photographs of similar conversions of Stephenson 2-4-0 engines, including one that later operated at a colliery near Burslem, and this is probably as close as it will prove possible to get to the actual appearance of N&BJR No. 2.

The L&NWR Takes Over

As previously indicated, during the early part of 1875 the N&BJR Board decided that the provision and maintenance of their own fleet of locomotives and rolling stock was an unsustainable expense. It may be significant that the N&BJR had recently had to hire a locomotive from the L&NWR for sixteen days during October 1874 and again 'for a few days' in early 1875, which probably points to their own engines having become increasingly unreliable. A decision was therefore taken to request that the neighbouring L&NWR provide locomotives and stock for the line on a mileage hire basis.

A subsequent L&NWR minute confirmed the provision of locomotives from 1st March 1875, although the arrangement was not recorded by the Railway Commissioners until 26th October 1876. Thereafter, the N&BJR had all the appearance of a branch line of the L&NWR and even appeared as such in some published timetables, though the railway did retain its independent identity until merger with the S&MJR in 1910.

Very little is known of the locomotive types used by the L&NWR on the line, although one glimpse is given by an accident report of 1880, which confirms that a McConnell 0-6-0 tender engine was in use on passenger trains. A photograph is also known of a Webb tender 0-6-0 on an N&BJR line passenger train of a later era but otherwise it must be assumed that a typical variety of lightweight secondary L&NWR motive power would have been employed on the route.

After the purchase of the N&BJR by the S&MJR in 1910, the arrangement with the L&NWR was terminated and standard Beyer, Peacock 2-4-0 tanks and 0-6-0 tender engines of the new owners were then used on the old N&BJR line.

The Carriage and Wagon Stock of the N&BJR

If the history of the N&BJR locomotive stock is considered to be a little wanting in detail, then knowledge of the other rolling stock is even more nebulous. It is known that the N&BJR began operations in 1866 with three passenger carriages and one other passenger train vehicle, probably a full brake, and that twenty goods wagons were also used. It is also clear that these were all products of the Lancaster Wagon Company, the carriages actually being the first constructed by that concern. It seems likely that they were either hired or possibly obtained by hire-purchase, as when the N&BJR fell into financial difficulties in mid-1866, the Sherriff's officers were unable to seize the wagons in lieu of debts, as they could be proved to be the property of the Lancaster Company. It is recorded that seventeen wagons were quickly repatriated to Lancashire, so it is possible that the other three may have been owned by the N&BJR.

Two similar NLR 2-4-0 well tank engines were converted to side tanks before sale at around the same time, one of which subsequently became the Whitehaven Cleator & Egremont Railway's *Marron*. This survived long enough to be incorporated into the stock of the Furness Railway and was photographed at Moor Row in 1897. In all probability, it bore a close resemblance to the N&BJR example. *Author's collection*

Records are lacking for the years 1868 to 1870 but, by the end of 1871, rolling stock numbers stood at five Composite and one Third Class carriage, one passenger brake and one goods brake van, although no wagons are recorded at this date. One of the additional carriages is accounted for in an L&NWR minute of 10th March 1871, which confirms the sale of 'supplementary composite carriage No. 1430' to the 'Blisworth & Towcester Railway for £85'.

The N&BJR also purchased a further four vehicles from the L&NWR later in that year, with minutes of 12th September 1871 indicating the sale of two Composites, one Third Class and one brake van to the 'Towcester Railway Co.' for the sum of £385. One year later, the rolling stock had been increased to nine Composites, one Third and two passenger brakes, with just one goods brake. Doubtless the new arrivals were necessitated by the opening of the line through to Cockley Brake and Banbury. These totals were maintained for several years, until two Composite carriages were disposed of during 1876, possibly as a result of the auction held during 1875.

This still left eight carriages, two passenger brakes and one goods brake in N&BJR running stock at the close of 1876. It must be assumed that these were hauled by L&NWR locomotives after the agreement of March 1875 and continued to be used until that company also provided all rolling stock for the trains. Strangely however, despite the fact that these were no longer reported as part of the running stock at the end of 1876, four carriages still featured in one final auction sale of October 1879.

Little specific information is available on the carriages and wagons used on the N&BJR during the period when the L&NWR provided all stock and it must therefore be assumed that standard L&NWR vehicles were in use. However, the report of the Green's Norton accident of 30th October 1880 does provide some detailed information of the carriages then in use on the line. The train consisted of a set of four close-coupled L&NWR passenger coaches, comprising Third Class Break No. 3511, built in 1860, Composite No. 2276 of 1862, Third Class No. 339 from 1861 and another Third Class Break, No. 3510, also built in 1861,

A Northampton & Banbury Junction Railway 2d parcel stamp of circa 1900. *Author's collection*

all of which had been overhauled at Wolverton Works in July of that year.

The *Northampton Mercury* also reported on 19th May 1888 that the N&BJR had a new four coach set running on the line between Blisworth and Banbury, and that 'the 3rd class compartments are quite as cosy as the 2nd whilst the first class are of a superior style'. These must again have been provided by the L&NWR but were probably not new stock, having been relegated down to the N&BJR line after service elsewhere.

Liveries of the Northampton & Banbury Junction Railway

Very little is known about the liveries carried by the locomotives or rolling stock of the N&BJR. The Neilson engines ordered for the opening of the line in 1866 were to have been delivered in a lined green livery, with brass number plates, but no other details are available. The official works photographs of the two types do show a pale coloured base livery, although this could be the usual 'works grey'. The locomotives appear to be fully lined out in black with lighter outer bands, whilst the domes, safety valves, chimney top, and splasher rims are all burnished.

The random purchase and short life span of the few locomotives that were owned by the N&BJR in the late 1860s and early 1870s make it very unlikely that any form of corporate livery, or ownership, would have been applied. However, it is likely that the engines purchased from the L&NWR during that period would have arrived in that company's then standard 'light Brunswick green' livery, with the more recognisable black not having being adopted until around 1873.

It is also difficult to speculate on the livery of the small numbers of carriages used by the line. These are also likely to have continued to carry the livery of their previous owners, in particular the L&NWR and the North London Railway.

Regrettably, no photographic evidence appears to have survived of any N&BJR rolling stock to provide any visual evidence of livery or style. After 1875, L&NWR stock was used on the line, and so black locomotives, eventually hauling the typical 'plum and spilt milk' coaches, must be assumed to have been the norm.

ANALYSIS OF N&BJR LOCOMOTIVES AND ROLLING STOCK 1866 – 1878													
From yearly returns to the Board of Trade													
Totals as at 31st Dec:	1866	1867	1868	1869	1870	1871	1872	1873	1874	1875	1876	1877	1878
Engines / Tenders	1 / 0	1 / 0	1 / 0	hire	hire	4 / 0	5 / 1	5 / 2	5 / 2	4 / 1	4 / 1	3 / 0	0 / 0
Carriages	3	3	0	hire	hire	6	10	10	10	8	8	0	0
Other pass. vehicles	1	1	0	hire	hire	1	2	2	2	2	1	0	0
Wagons all types	20	20	0	hire	hire	0	0	0	0	0	0	0	0
Other rolling stock	0	0	0	hire	hire	1	1	1	1	1	1	0	0

Chapter 1.3
THE EAST & WEST JUNCTION RAILWAY

'The only result of obtaining a Receiver would be that it was found that there was nothing to receive.'

The story of the East & West Junction Railway has many parallels with its close neighbour – and eventual stablemate – the Northampton & Banbury Junction Railway. The early years of the E&WJR were similarly fraught with numerous financial problems, resulting inevitably in receivership and, during a particularly difficult period, even an eight year suspension of passenger traffic.

Despite these continual difficulties, the E&WJR nevertheless still managed to sponsor extensions at either end of its main route, thus providing at least the basis for the through traffic that was essential for its survival. These two nominally independent additions were operated as part of the E&WJR line and once internal squabbles had been resolved, all three companies eventually became united under the banner of a Joint Committee, providing a somewhat hesitant first step towards what a few years later would become the Stratford-upon-Avon & Midland Junction Railway Company.

The two sibling companies played an integral part in the development of the E&WJR after 1879 and it has therefore been considered prudent to present the following account on a mainly chronological basis, rather than make any attempt to untangle their individual existences from that of their parent company.

Early Schemes

Just a short distance away from the Northampton & Banbury Junction route, the East & West Junction Railway also experienced a remarkably similar and troubled evolution. Whereas early plans for a Northampton & Banbury Railway may, at least initially, have been intended merely to improve local transport links, the E&WJR was unashamedly promoted from the very beginning as a speculative venture to move Northamptonshire ironstone to those same South Wales furnaces that the N&BJR then targeted with their own plans.

Although their starting points in the east may have been similar, the route of the E&WJR was to follow a very different path. Whereas the N&BJR favoured an approach through Banbury and the Cotswolds, the E&WJR sought to reach South Wales by first heading more directly west to Stratford-upon-Avon.

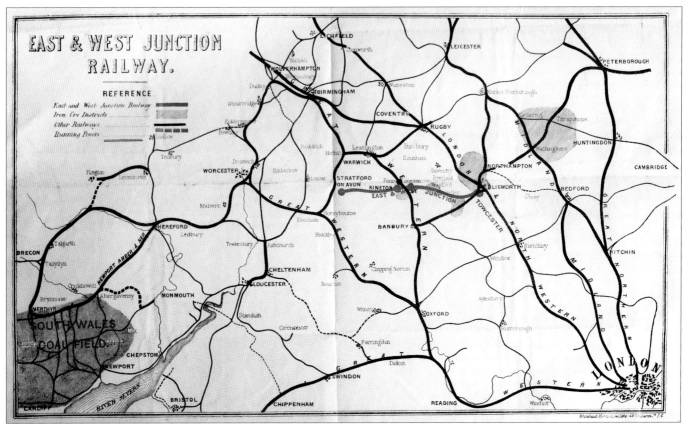

This early E&WJR prospectus map graphically illustrates the ambition of the promoters to connect the iron ore fields of Northamptonshire more directly with the South Wales coalfield and ironworks. The reduction in mileage offered by the new line, compared with the existing roundabout route by way of Rugby, Birmingham and Hereford, is clearly evident. However, any early optimism would soon be tempered by the opposition of both the London & North Western and Great Western railways, who were determined to protect their own interests and traffic volumes. In the event, only comparatively small volumes of iron ore would ever pass along the E&WJR route. *Authors collection*

Victorian splendour at Stratford-upon-Avon – a typical East & West Junction Railway train of the period stands in the Down platform after arrival from Blisworth in 1897. The casual observer would do well to determine the identity of the railway company, with no indication on the locomotive, one of the two Beyer, Peacock 2-4-0 tanks, to indicate E&WJR ownership. However, it would appear that the lower panels of the first 4-wheeled coach bear the circular belted insignia that was in vogue at one time. *Author's collection*

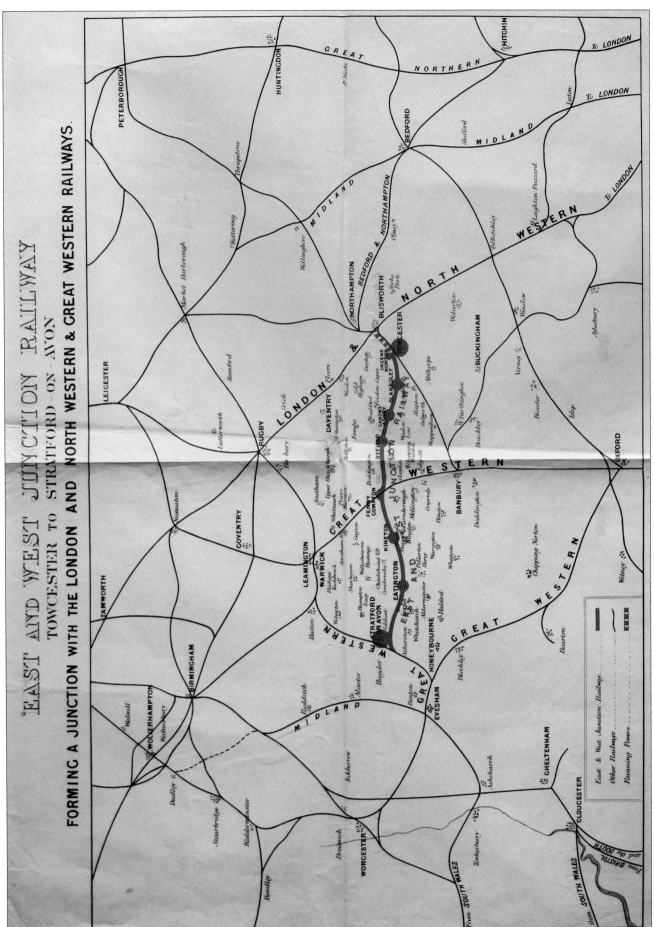

This early prospectus map for the East & West Junction Railway probably dates from 1873. Note that the station later to be known as Morton Pinkney is shown as 'Canon's Ashby'. Interestingly, there appears to be a station indicated at Green's Norton, probably corresponding with the proposal for a 'pick up platform' at nearby Kingthorn Wood.

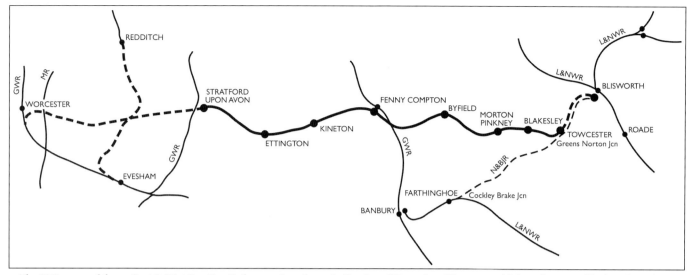

The 1862 proposal for an East & West Junction Railway envisaged a main line from Blisworth to Worcester, with branches to Redditch and Evesham. However, under the revised scheme of 1863, the line commenced at Green's Norton near Towcester and terminated at Stratford-upon-Avon, with the Northampton & Banbury Junction Railway actually constructing the section between Blisworth, Towcester and Green's Norton.

The pages of the *London Gazette* of 28th November 1862 first reveal the intention to apply to Parliament for an East & West Junction (Blisworth to Worcester with branches) Railway, with powers provided for the London & North Western, Great Western, West Midland and Midland railway companies to construct, subscribe and enter into working arrangements.

The scheme, which comprised of eight separate lines of railway, featured a main line extending from Blisworth to Stratford-upon-Avon, with junctions being made with the Great Western Railway *en route* at Fenny Compton and also at Stratford. A further line was to extend on from Stratford to Bidford, where three lines would continue northwards to Redditch, westwards to Worcester and southwards to Evesham. Extensions were also proposed from Canons Ashby to the Buckinghamshire Railway and Banbury, and also from Blisworth to Northampton. Plans for these railways were deposited on the following day but, in the event, the scheme failed to pass Parliamentary Standing Orders and no Act was obtained.

However, exactly one year later, on 30th November 1863, new plans were deposited for an East & West Junction Railway; these were very similar to the previous proposal but omitted the extension from Blisworth to Northampton, which was now part of a Northampton & Banbury Junction scheme. Although the new proposal did still extend west of Stratford to just beyond Bidford, the lines to Worcester, Redditch and Evesham were deleted. The application was successful, resulting in the passing of Acts *27 & 28 Vic.Cap.lxxvi* on 23rd June 1864.

The authorised length of the railway was 33¼ miles, with a share capital of £300,000 and powers to borrow another £100,000. James B. Burke was named as the engineer for this scheme, which was of rather simpler composition than the earlier proposal. The route would consist of just two railways, the first running from the proposed N&BJR near Towcester to a junction with the Honeybourne Branch of the GWR near to their Stratford-upon-Avon station. The second line extended westwards from that point, to a junction with the authorised route of the Evesham & Redditch Railway in the parish of Salford Priors.

In addition, running powers were awarded over the N&BJR

to Towcester and Blisworth, and also onwards to Northampton if and when that company constructed their proposed bridge over the L&NWR main line:

'*Railway No.1: A railway commencing by a junction or junctions with the authorised line of the Northampton and Banbury Junction Railway in the parish of Towcester, in the County of Northampton, in a field, No. 46, in the said parish, on the deposited plans of that railway and terminating by a junction with the Great Western Railway (Stratford and Honeybourne branch) in the parish of Old Stratford, in the county of Warwick, at a point about 35 chains south of the Stratford-on-Avon passenger station of that railway, and which said intended railway No. 1 will be made and maintained from, in, through, and into the several townships, parishes, extra-parochial and other places following, or some of them (that is to say) Towcester, Wood Burcote, Green's Norton, Bradden, Woodend, Blakesley, Plumpton, Adstone, Moreton Pinckney, Canon's Ashby, Eydon, Woodford-cum-Membris, Hinton, West Farndon, Byfield, Aston-le-Walls, Appletree, Boddington, Upper Boddington and Lower Boddington in the County of Northampton, Claydon, and Cropredy in the county of Oxford, Wormleighton, Farnborough, Fenny Compton, Burton Dassett, North End, Gaydon, Chadshunt, Kineton or Kington, Little Kineton, Butlers Marston, Combrook, Wellesbourne Hastings, Walton, Pillerton Hercy, Upper Eatington, Atherstone-on-Stour, Loxley, Lower Eatington, and Old Stratford in the County of Warwick, Alderminster, in the County of Worcester, and Preston-on-Stour and Clifford Chambers in the county of Gloucester.*

Railway No. 2: A railway commencing by a junction with the before-mentioned intended railway No, 1, in the said parish of Old Stratford, in the county of Warwick, in a field belonging to Charles Lucy, in the occupation of Joseph Southam, and about six chains eastward of Church Farm House, and terminating by a junction with the authorised line of the Evesham and Redditch Railway, in the parish of Salford Priors, in the said county of Warwick, in a field, No. 170, in the said parish, on the deposited plans of that railway, and which said intended railway No. 2 will be made and maintained from, in, through, and into the several parishes, townships, extra-parochial, and other places following or some of them (that is to say): Old Stratford Luddington, Binton, Temple Grafton, Bidford, and Salford Priors, in the said county of Warwick.'

The first prospectus for the E&WJR was unusually optimistic, anticipating gross revenue of just over £154,500 per annum. This was estimated to be sufficient to provide a net return to the railway company of some £87,600, which would in turn fund a healthy dividend to shareholders of nearly 20%.

However, behind these grand plans were flawed assumptions that the new East & West Junction Railway would ultimately capture all of the traffic in iron ore between Northamptonshire and South Wales, could also rely on significant tonnages of Welsh coal in the return direction and would have the cooperation of the Great Western Railway beyond Stratford.

The 'Pell Years'

The *Northampton Herald* of 12th March 1864, reporting on the progress of the E&WJR Bill through Parliament, included evidence presented by one George Pell, a local landowner, turned ironmaster and colliery proprietor. In 1857, Pell had erected ironworks at Heyford near Northampton and, in the following year, began working iron ore pits at nearby Gayton Wood and on land at Blisworth leased from Lady Palmerston, the wife of the then Prime Minister. Soon his quarries accounted for almost half of the iron ore production of Northamptonshire. He also owned brickworks and limeworks at Duston, on the outskirts of Northampton, and was renting the White Rose Colliery at Newport, Monmouthshire, from Lord Tredegar, which was producing 1,100 tons of coal per week by the early 1860s, much of which was used in Northamptonshire.

Pell already despatched ore from Northamptonshire to both the Staffordshire and South Wales ironworks, and his customers included the Chillington Works at Wolverhampton, Boulton & Watt's Soho Ironworks and Messrs Davis of Tipton. However, Pell was experiencing increasing difficulties in establishing a regular traffic to the South Wales area. On 23rd March 1858, he despatched a sample shipment of twenty wagon loads to the Dowlais Iron Company but, two years later, he was still trying to cajole them into becoming a regular customer. In fact, the South Wales ironmasters considered some of the Northamptonshire ore to be of comparatively low quality and also quite expensive, with transport costs representing approximately 70% of the price. Sales were therefore rather sluggish and unpredictable, except during 'boom' periods when demand was higher. The usual routing for Northamptonshire ore was by the L&NWR and GWR, via Rugby, Birmingham, Dudley, Stourbridge, Worcester, Ledbury, Abergavenny and Pontypool, a roundabout journey of some 150 miles.

Pell's rival in Northamptonshire was G.E. Bevan & Company, iron and tinplate merchants of Bristol, who enjoyed a rather better relationship with South Wales, regularly supplying 500 tons per week to Dowlais. In the autumn of 1860, Bevan had concluded a deal with the Dowlais Company and arranged for a daily train between Camden Town and Quaker's Yard. However, by 1863, Bevan was in communication with his customers with the observation that he was beginning to find the L&NWR rates for iron ore to be too high. He was therefore unable to compete with the lower rates offered for coastal deliveries and was considering giving up his supply to South Wales.

Pell and Bevan both subsequently tried to get the railway companies to reduce their rates, Pell applying without success for a shorter route via Rugby, Warwick, Stratford and Worcester. However, the opening of the Worcester & Hereford Railway in 1861 did partly assist by reducing the cost of Northamptonshire ore by 6d per ton.

This evidently helped to convince George Pell as to the desirability of a more direct line of communication with South Wales and he therefore began to lend his weight to the promotion of the E&WJR, opining that the proposed railway would probably save him 1s 3d per ton in transport costs. In fact, his involvement in the promotion of the line then became so significant that the E&WJR was to become known locally as 'Pell's Railway'. On becoming solicitor to the proposed line he stated:

'… *by these railways not only will through communication be established between the East of England, whence the lines centre, with the L&NWR at Blisworth and Worcester, at which city, railways are in operation to the west of England, South Wales, Herefordshire, and Shropshire and what is an especial feature of the plan the best and most direct communication will be obtained between the important manufacturing and agricultural towns and districts of Redditch, Studley, Alcester and Stratford-upon-Avon with the metropolis.'*

Although Pell was prepared to promote the new line he did not intend to finance it himself. As a result, he introduced Thomas Russell Crampton, the noted and somewhat eccentric engineer and contractor, to the E&WJR. Whilst the E&WJR Bill was under consideration in the House of Lords during May 1864, Crampton agreed to subscribe £175,000 of the total share capital of £300,000 for the construction of the line and purchased his stock at a discount of 30% on the nominal value. It was in fact Crampton's brokers, and not the E&WJR, who issued the first prospectus for the new line.

Five other initial subscribers were listed in the preamble to the Bill. Of these, Matthew Robert Bigge and Alfred Bate Richards had no particular connections with the area served by the new railway. The other three, however, had more significant local profiles: Sir Charles Mordaunt was the MP for South Warwickshire, Matthew Malcolm was the agent for Warwickshire landowner Sir Willoughby de Broke and William Addison was a surgeon residing at Kineton.

It also appears that neither Crampton nor Pell had any intention of operating the new line themselves. In due course, on 4th July 1864, together with James Staats Forbes, general manager of the London, Chatham & Dover Railway with which Crampton was closely connected, they met with the boards of both the L&NWR and GWR in an attempt to persuade them to run the line jointly. In the event, the GWR would not accommodate all of the L&NWR requirements and the proposal was dropped. The following year, the E&WJR themselves made similar overtures to the Midland Railway but they were also unproductive.

In addition to the anticipated volumes of iron ore and coal, a large volume of general traffic was also predicted and there was considerable interest shown by the inland port of Gloucester, which had just initiated a new traffic in cattle from Southern Ireland. Many of the beasts were taken on to pastures in Northamptonshire for fattening before being sold and although rail transport was easily available as far as Banbury, many stockholders then preferred to drive them on foot to Northampton, rather than use the lengthy route by rail via Birmingham. The proposed E&WJR route was seen as a great benefit, with the beasts then being able to arrive in Northampton more quickly and in much better condition.

In conjunction with other railway companies in the west, the E&WJR could also offer the shortest 'narrow gauge' route from London to South Wales, with the GWR still operating on Brunel's 7ft way. In addition, the L&NWR had at that time only a circuitous route to that area via Stafford and Shrewsbury, and they were therefore initially keen to support the E&WJR proposals. However, large volumes of iron ore traffic would soon develop from rail connected quarries around Northamptonshire and once the L&NWR realised that this traffic could potentially be lost to their own line, they became rather less amenable to the E&WJR.

The importance of the proposed new line was also recognised during the passage of the Bill through the House of Lords, where Lord Stradbroke lent his support by stating that he believed that the line would be one of the most advantageous, from a public point of view, that had recently been presented for approval. The GWR had also looked favourably on the early development of the E&WJR, seeing the line as a possible feeder to their own system but as soon as any intention for an independent line westwards from Stratford became apparent, they quickly became hostile.

The GWR thereafter opposed every application to Parliament made by the E&WJR and although overall they were largely unsuccessful in these actions, they did admit, under later cross examination by the Railway Commissioners, of 'trying to kill the E&WJR'. Their opposition increased as the possibility of the L&NWR obtaining access to Worcester became apparent and then was further magnified by the prospect of any potential cooperation between the E&WJR and the Midland Railway.

However, the GWR, with their amalgamation with the West Midland Railway having effectively provided them with a secure route to South Wales, were later able to come to terms with the L&NWR, who in return were then rewarded with a shortened route to that region by a connection with the GWR in the Birmingham area.

Further Extensions

Regardless of these various negotiations and machinations, Pell and Crampton had also arranged for the deposition of further plans on 30th November 1864, for an extension of their line towards the east: 'The same parties who have so successfully carried through the content for the East & West Junction Railway are taking steps to extend it from Blisworth through Northampton and Olney to Bedford.'

The new line was to form a triangular junction with the N&BJR route near Gayton, cross the L&NWR main line just north of Blisworth station and proceed towards Northampton, where it would also link with the L&NWR branches to Market Harborough on the southern side of the town and to Peterborough, a short distance further east in the parish of Great Houghton. The railway would then proceed in a south easterly direction to Olney and Turvey, eventually joining the Midland Railway near their Bedford station, thus covering much of the ground of the later Bedford & Northampton Railway.

Northampton Town Council met early in 1865 to discuss the relative merits of the three projected railway schemes that were currently planning to enter their town. These comprised the above mentioned E&WJR extension, the Bedford, Northampton & Leamington Railway and the Bedford, Northampton & Weedon Railway. The meeting adopted the E&WJR extension in preference to the other two and urged the three prospective railways to collaborate in the building of one line. As if in agreement, the House of Commons Standing Order Committee later threw out the Leamington scheme. The Bedford, Northampton & Weedon line was slightly more successful during the Parliamentary stages but eventually only the Bedford to Northampton section of the route was proved by the Committee.

However, February saw the *Northampton Mercury* report that the E&WJR proposal had been passed by the Examiner on Standing Orders and, with the company having made the necessary deposit to Parliament, no problems were envisaged in presenting the Bill. Ultimately, however, the Bill proved unsuccessful, whereas the Bedford & Northampton Railway proposal did receive Royal Assent on 5th July. Nevertheless, the E&WJR did gain the concession of running powers to Northampton over the existing L&NWR branch from Blisworth, in return for withdrawing their own plans for a separate line to the county town. The unfulfilled E&WJR scheme did, nevertheless, to some extent prophesy events of a quarter of a century later, when the company would eventually be successful in establishing a connection towards Bedford, although by a very different route.

The 30th March 1865 brought yet another proposal for a new railway linked to the authorised route of the East & West Junction line. James B. Burke, who was also an employee of George Pell at his ironstone works, was again the nominated engineer, on this occasion for a Chipping Norton, Banbury & East & West Junction Railway. The line was to begin at a junction with the authorised route of the E&WJR proper near Canons Ashby, and flirt with the borders of Oxfordshire and Northamptonshire on its way through Moreton Pinkney, Culworth, Thorpe Mandeville, Wardington, Chacombe, Neithrop and Warkworth, reaching the outskirts of Banbury at Grimsbury, where a junction with the GWR was to be made. A second line of railway would then proceed from this junction towards Adderbury and Bloxham, continuing by Hook Norton and Great Rollright to another junction with the GWR at their Chipping Norton station. Once again the project did not come to fruition, with no Act being obtained.

The almost ritual deposition of new plans by the E&WJR was continued on 30th November 1865, when a scheme for an extension to Hitchin was proposed, with George Pell again playing a significant role. Five sections of railways were planned, beginning with a line from their own, as yet, unconstructed route near Towcester to Wolverton, where a link would be made to the L&NWR main line. The new route would then continue from Wolverton, through Newport Pagnell to Steppingly, where the third railway would form an end on junction to continue to Hitchin and the Great Northern Railway. At Steppingly, there would also be a junction with the new Midland Railway extension from Bedford to London. This proposal was routinely objected to by the N&BJR, and also by the Newport Pagnell and Midland railway companies, as well as the usual clutch of individuals.

Another proposal of the same year was for a London, Worcester & South Wales Railway, which would extend from the E&WJR route at Stratford and Bidford to reach Claines, where a junction would be made with the GWR Worcester to Hereford line. The route was subsequently modified in 1866 but the proposal was then given up later in that year.

Thereafter, George Pell, with his health failing, ceased to take an active interest in E&WJR affairs and his business activities gradually dwindled away. His works at Heyford had already been temporarily closed between 1859 and 1863, and in 1865 he sold out his quarry and colliery interests to a new Heyford Iron Company. Pell, however, remained as a director of this new company, along with three directors of the E&WJR, Clarence Holcombe Judd, Samuel Isaac and William Forbes, until a petition by the Brecon & Merthyr Railway resulted in the dissolution of the Heyford Iron Company in December 1866.

A False Start

As mentioned earlier, George Pell had rented ironstone rich land in the Blisworth area from, amongst others the Prime Minister's wife Lady Palmerston. It was therefore fitting that the good lady was duly invited to initiate proceedings on the E&WJR by ceremoniously cutting the first sod on land at Cotswell Farm near Green's Norton, on Wednesday 3rd August 1864.

Illustrious guests travelled up from London by train, arriving at Blisworth station at 1.30pm, from where they were conveyed by road to Towcester. Triumphal decorative arches had been erected in the village of Blisworth and at several points in Towcester, where a banner proclaimed 'Success to the Railway'. The ceremony was performed using a specially prepared silver spade and mahogany wheelbarrow in the nominated field a mile or so west of the town. This was followed by the usual lavish luncheon and the customary speeches from the assembled dignitaries and officials. These included Sir Cusack Roney (the Chairman of the E&WJR) T.R. Crampton, Earl Pomfret, Lord Lyveden and, of course, the Prime Minister himself. Unfortunately, following these rather lavish inaugural celebrations, very slow progress was actually made on the line, with finance becoming very difficult to obtain.

The *Stratford-upon-Avon Herald* did report that the contractor, Thomas Crampton, had started local construction in that area during September 1864, with his engineer Mr Hughes taking up residence in Stratford. The *Leamington Spa Chronicle* of 27th May 1865 also commented on the disrepair of the old mill bridge over the Avon at Stratford, recommending that it be moved to the other side of the E&WJR bridge, which was '*now in the course of construction*', the foundation stone having been laid on 28th September 1864 by Charles Lucy.

A contemporary illustration of Lady Palmerston cutting the first turf of the East & West Junction Railway at Cotswell Farm, near Towcester on 3rd August 1864. Unfortunately, following these festivities, very little work was actually done over the next five or six years, apart from some initial construction activity at either end of the line, which included the building of the viaduct over the River Avon at Stratford. *Author's collection*

There is also evidence of work progressing at Fenny Compton, from a report in the *Oxford Chronicle* of 8th April 1865 of a fatal accident to a navvy in a cutting. At Goldicote, another workman was also killed in similar circumstances in October of that year. Work had also commenced further east, as in November 1865 it was noted that a skeleton had been unearthed during construction work on the line near Woodford-cum-Membris.

However, alongside this early progress the Directors of the E&WJR were still intent on pressing on with their plans for expansion. In November 1865, the company gave notice of an application to Parliament for an extension from a junction with their line to the west of Fenny Compton, through to the parish of Bishops Itchington, where they would join the authorised line of the Southam, Coventry & Great Western Junction Railway. The SC&GWJR scheme had been proposed to provide a shorter route to London for West Midlands coal traffic and once again the redoubtable George Pell was involved as solicitor for the E&WJR extension.

In the same month, solicitors Wright Dale & Co. of Royal Exchange Buildings, London, issued a prospectus for the raising of £300,000 additional capital for the E&WJR, by the issue of 15,000 shares of £20 nominal value. It was stated that '*arrangements had been made with Mr Crampton*' for him to complete the double line of the E&WJR within the limits of the additional capital and that he had agreed to pay interest at 6% per annum until a single line of railway had been provided; this was expected to be within eighteen months. The prospectus speculated that there was a potential annual demand of two million tons of iron ore from South Wales and that although Northamptonshire presently supplied only 200,000 tons, this figure could be dramatically increased by the provision of the proposed shorter line of the E&WJR. It was estimated that the double line could be built for £24,000 per mile but would provide a return of £90 per mile per week when fully opened, leaving an estimated £57,000 after expenses for distribution to shareholders; this represented a dividend of 13% per annum.

This optimism required a strengthening of the E&WJR Board, with William Staats Forbes and G.E. Surtees being nominated to

join the existing Stevenson Forbes, Samuel Isaac, Finlay Knight, Mathew Malcolm, Sir C. Mordaunt and Sir Cusack Roney at the next General Meeting.

The E&WJR Finance Bill was read for a third time and passed by Parliament on 7th June 1866, receiving the Royal Assent on 28th of that month. However, whilst all of that was taking place, wider events were already having a major effect on the plans of the E&WJR.

In May 1866, in the aftermath of the Overend, Gurney bank collapse, Crampton and his associates Peto & Betts were 'stopped' with liabilities of £4 million and construction of the E&WJR came to a halt.

In addition, the Imperial Mercantile Credit Association, who together with Crampton were deeply involved in the promotion of the London, Chatham & Dover Railway, also found themselves bankrupt with debts of over £4.5 million. As a result of this hiatus a new company, the Imperial Credit Corporation, was formed by IMCA shareholders and creditors, and their initial assets included a nominal £100,000 worth of E&WJR stock.

It appears that no work had in fact been carried out on the E&WJR after August 1866; a contemporary report stated that by the time work was suspended, 'the ground had only been broken in three places between Towcester and Fenny Compton' and that 'not a single yard of track had yet been laid'. This did not preclude the railway company from the attentions of the local Highways Boards, as on numerous occasions in 1865 and 1866 they were called to account for damage done to roads in parishes such as Appletree, Burton Dassett, Chadshunt, Gaydon and Northend.

Despite the fact that construction of their line was at a standstill, other issues continued to occupy the E&WJR management during 1866. In July, a court case ensued following a dispute with George Pell over the supply of bricks for construction work, whilst in Stratford, there was early speculation as to whether the E&WJR would join with the Stratford-upon-Avon Railway and the Great Western in the establishment of a joint station in the town. This question was destined to resurface some seven years later, when the E&WJR line was finally ready for opening.

It then seems that Thomas Brassey, the largest railway contractor in the country, briefly showed an interest in taking on the completion of the line. His company had survived the financial crash of 1866, although losing large sums of money, and his passing interest in the E&WJR may well have been due to the fact that he was then engaged as contractor for the nearby Evesham & Redditch Railway.

The *Gloucester Journal* of 11th July 1868 was the next to give an impression of imminent progress, when it intimated that '*a contractor has undertaken the works and it is expected that the distance from Stratford to Blisworth will shortly be completed*.' The identity of this contractor was not revealed but, within a year, Mr Justice Miller would preside over a hearing in which the E&WJR defended an action brought against them by a '*contractor for the line*' named Burke.

Problems continued and, in late 1868, the old E&WJR Board was ejected and replaced by representatives of the then major stockholders, under the leadership of Alexander Young, a public accountant from London, who had also acted as liquidator of the aforementioned Imperial Mercantile Credit Association.

The new board rightly considered that the only possible way to realise their assets was to enable completion of the line. Thus, with the E&WJR unable to pay their outstanding debts, a Scheme of Arrangement with the creditors and shareholders was proposed. This was subsequently heard before Vice Chancellor Sir William Milbourne James on 7th May 1869, where it was stated that the sum owed by the E&WJR to outside creditors was £46,377, with a further £35,000 in respect of land purchases that had not yet been completed.

It was confirmed that no work had been carried out on the line since August 1866, whilst only about 20 miles of the 33 mile route had been in any way started and that although powers had been obtained for the subscription of a further £300,000, none had so far been raised. The E&WJR were, therefore, totally unable to meet their liabilities and the directors proposed that they should be allowed to make an arrangement to complete the line and pay the creditors. Despite objections by some parties, the scheme was approved by Her Majesty's High Court of Chancery on 13th July 1869.

The restructuring authorised the company to enter into a contract for the completion of their railway within a period of two years, for a sum not exceeding £230,000, and also the raising of further capital by the issue of various categories of debenture stock totalling £600,000, in lieu of the original share capital and borrowing powers of 1866.

Once the E&WJR had been resuscitated, repeated attempts were made to issue unsold stock to help finance the completion of the line and numerous prospectuses were issued over the following few years. The first offered £318,000 of Perpetual 5% interest debentures, followed by another tranche of £210,000 of the same stock at a 10% discount, both issues being moderately successful. These were followed by a further two offers totalling £92,500 at lesser discounts. In addition, another application to Parliament was now required to allow a further two year extension of time for the completion of the line.

There was also much local unrest at the state of the works on the line. The *Leamington Spa Courier*, within its '*Town Topics*' column of 2nd July 1870, deplored what they saw as the proposed abandonment of the E&WJR, citing '*engineers who had vanished like so many fairies*' and '*vast mounds of earth left in an unfinished state, deep cuttings to be completed, and roads which had been diverted left to keep themselves in repair … a long line of country which had been enclosed within posts and rails has been left unkempt and uncared for, the earthworks have been overrun with weeds, several wooden bridges are gradually getting unsafe. Most certainly some notice should be taken as any objections to the line being abandoned must be made to the Board of Trade within a few weeks.*'

However, the very same journal was to report just a few weeks later that work on a cutting at Fenny Compton, which had been started some five or six years earlier, was about to be recommenced by the contractor T.R. Crampton.

A Fresh Start

Thomas Crampton, having been discharged from bankruptcy and now under the new guise of Crampton & Co., had accepted a new contract on 15th August 1870, to finish the E&WJR line for the sum of £157,000. Stephen Charles Best, late of the London, Chatham & Dover Railway, was appointed as chief engineer for the works. As a result of the delays, new Bills had also been necessary to allow for the revival of powers awarded under the previous Acts. These initially granted an extension of time for completion of the line to 23rd June 1871 and then during that year, a further extension of three years was obtained to 29th June 1874.

Advertisements soon appeared for the recruitment of up to 150 navvies for the Kineton to Fenny Compton section of the line and the local press were quick to relay news of progress. *Aris' Birmingham Gazette* cheerfully reported on 4th March 1871 that '… *many of our readers will be glad to learn that it is intended to open this railway as far as Kineton on 1st May, and that the portion of the line between Kineton and Stratford will in the course of the month, have its workings, which have stopped for some years, recommenced.*'

Another local organ, the *Leamington Spa Courier*, also rather more reservedly announced one week later:

'*It is somewhat consoling to hear a rumour which we trust is well founded that the works of the E&WJR are about to be resumed at the end of the line – it has long been a pitiable sight, and has been saddening to witness the rank weeds and grass growing over the partially made cutting near Cross o' the Hill. The large five arched brick bridge which spans the Avon is in an insecure condition, abruptly terminating in a small embankment. The Shipston road has been diverted, and has long been in a deplorable state, in the summer reminding one of Australia, by the immense quantity of dust raised by the mud, blinding travellers, and in the winter, the dust is converted to mud in the depth of some inches. There are many other features which could be pointed out, but as the works are to be resumed, we will content ourselves by pointing out some of the most objectionable, and we hope that in a few months all of these will have been removed. The line itself, as a commercial undertaking, is of value, it passes through a fine track of country and gives ready access for its produce to the various markets and will thereby benefit a large and industrious population.*'

Cross o' the Hill is a point just east of Stratford, close to the village of Clifford Chambers, where the new line encountered both the Banbury road and the Stratford & Moreton Tramway.

The *Courier* was slightly more positive in its issue of 6th May, expressing local relief that the '*terribly dilapidated and dangerous bridges*' were about to be put in order and that the deep cutting at Goldicote and the tumbledown bridge on '*the Shipston tramway*' were also in course of repair. It was also wryly suggested that improvements could be made to the E&WJR bridge over the River Avon at Stratford, which was '*one of the most unsightly bridges ever erected, blocking a fine view of Avon and weir brakes*' and hoping that the engineers '*might be good enough to consult an architect*'.

There was, however, a setback on 17th May, when a wooden engine shed located close to Kineton was destroyed by fire, causing considerable damage to the contractor's locomotive inside. The *Courier* also reported on another unfortunate accident at Kineton, involving one Henry Barber, a young man '*engaged on driving tip*', who tripped whilst running beside his horse and fell beneath a wagon. The badly injured youth was conveyed to the nearest surgeon at Stratford-upon-Avon by the rather unfortunately named William Death, a sub-contractor.

Death was also to feature in the local press for other reasons, when he was summoned for '*having exercised his usual calling and labour on 23rd April, that being the Lord's Day*'. An explanation was offered but the work was not considered to be either urgent or necessary and the bench deprecated his employment of a gang of men on the Sabbath; he was fined five shillings plus costs of eleven shillings.

Completion of the line was being considerably hampered by frequent and extensive earth slips in the cutting at Kineton but, nevertheless, local intelligence still considered that opening could take place, as had been anticipated, on 1st May. However, despite the progress that was now being made, the E&WJR directors decided to withdraw a proposal to extend their line westwards from Stratford to make a triangular junction with the Evesham & Redditch Railway in Salford parish.

A Partial Opening

The anticipated date of opening had clearly been somewhat optimistic and it was not until 26th May that Colonel Hutchinson was able to carry out his first statutory Board of Trade inspection of the new line. His report revealed that the 6 miles and 51 chains line was single throughout, with passing loops at either end; land had, however, been purchased and provision made for a double line at some future date. The new railway met the GWR main line from Birmingham to Banbury at Fenny Compton but only a simple siding connection was provided between the two routes, with no facility for through running. The permanent way consisted of 24ft lengths of flat bottomed rail weighing 69lbs per yard, fished at the joints and fixed by fang bolts and spikes to sleepers of creosoted Baltic timber, with the ballast being of '*burnt clay*'. The steepest gradient on the line was 1 in 100 and the sharpest curvature one of 40 chains, with all bridges and earthworks noted as having been substantially constructed.

However, the Colonel was not entirely happy with certain aspects of the new facilities, in particular the absence of a urinal and appropriate shed at Fenny Compton, along with the lack of a station nameboard and clock at the same location. The interlocking of points and signals at both stations also came in for criticism, together with missing fencing at certain points. In addition the ballast was reported as being '*insufficient in quantity and in certain places far too coarse*'.

The E&WJR provided a certificate stating that the line would be operated by train staff and by just one engine in steam at any time, and had also earlier provided details of the rolling stock to be used on passenger services. Colonel Hutchinson was, however, unhappy that no drawing had been included of a proposed Third Class carriage and required that this be supplied immediately. Overall, he was not satisfied that the line could be '*opened to passenger traffic without danger to the public using the same*', so declined to give his official sanction for the commencement of services.

A further inspection was therefore required and the Colonel duly carried this out a few days later, with his report being dated 3rd June. All of the requirements specified in the original report had been carried out, with the exception of the urinal and shed at Fenny Compton. In this connection, the E&WJR stated that, as they had a tentative agreement with the GWR for the erection of a new joint station, they expected that their passengers would be allowed

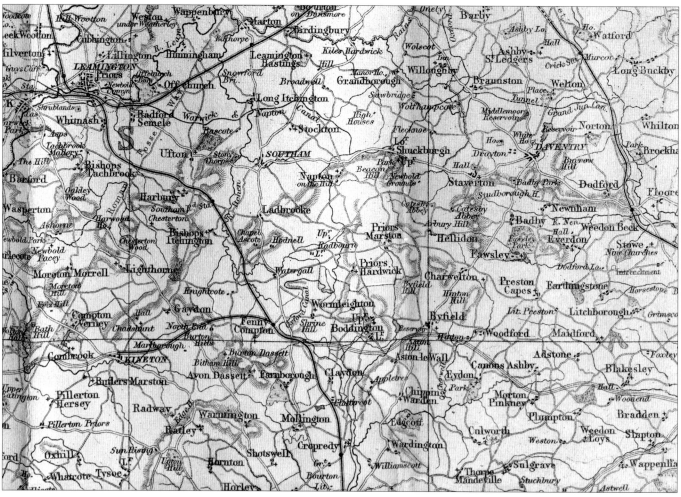

A section of an early map which shows the first section of the E&WJR from Fenny Compton to Kineton, opened on 5th June 1871. It would be another two years before the line was extended to Green's Norton and Stratford-upon-Avon to form a through route. *Author's collection*

the use of the existing GWR facilities in the interim. However, in the event of the E&WJR being disappointed in this expectation, their engineer did provide an undertaking to the Board of Trade to provide the necessary facilities on their own platform.

The opening of the line to passenger traffic was duly approved, and the *Leamington Spa Courier* of Saturday 10th June announced that the first trains had run on the previous Monday 5th June.

Colonel Hutchinson's two reports provided few other details of the facilities available at the two new E&WJR stations, but fortunately the local press were rather more forthcoming in this respect. *Aris' Gazette* duly recorded the opening, commenting that the main purpose of the new line was to convey Northamptonshire ironstone to South Wales, with over 300,000 tons having been sent during the previous year on the L&NWR and by way of Hereford. It was known that some difficulties had already been experienced with '*landslips in the cutting at Kineton*' but it was '*fully contemplated that the line will be completed throughout in the next 15 months*'. The report indicated that '*Kineton will be a large depot for corn and agricultural produce ... with a large goods shed, engine house and a handsome stone station with commodious waiting rooms nicely equipped with other conveniences and close to the town*' and that '*a joint station is about to be commenced at Fenny Compton for the exchange of traffic with the Great Western ... between Towcester and Fenny Compton there will be three stations at Blakesley, Canons Ashby,*

and *Byfield, and between Kineton and Stratford at Eatington*'. Passengers were to be provided with '*seven trains daily between Kineton and Fenny Compton, timed to catch the up and down trains of the GWR. Market tickets are to be issued at reduced rates on Thursdays and Saturdays for those attending Banbury and Warwick*'.

The *Leamington Spa Advertiser* also recorded events:

'*At length the old King's town of Warwickshire is joined by iron railway bands to the rest of the world. The Fenny Compton and Kineton section of the East and West Junction railway was opened for traffic on Monday, and in those places that event created not a little stir, and crowds assembled at both stations to witness the arrival and departure of the trains. The line was only passed by Colonel Hutchinson on Friday, and notwithstanding the short notice of opening the traffic on Monday was considerable, all the trains carrying a good many passengers, besides coal &c ... the rolling stock for the section just opened is complete, and comprises first, second, and third class carriages, wagons &c. and was built by the Midland Company, Birmingham ... Monthly livestock sales are to be held at Kineton, and the company are providing ample accommodation for taking away cattle from the station ...*'.

The *Banbury Guardian* added that '*... the Burton Hills have large deposits of ironstone and Lord Willoughby de Broke has made arrangements for working the mines and has entered into an agreement for the laying down of a tramway to the line.*'.

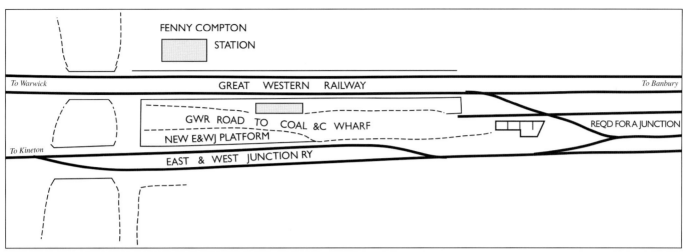

FENNY COMPTON

STATION

To Warwick　　　　　　　GREAT　　WESTERN　　RAILWAY　　　　　　*To Banbury*

GWR ROAD　TO　COAL &C WHARF

NEW E&WJ PLATFORM

To Kineton

EAST　&　WEST　JUNCTION RY

REQD FOR A JUNCTION

This drawing, based on a plan dated 8th September 1864, depicts the original simple arrangements at Fenny Compton on the opening of the first stretch of the E&WJR to Kineton in 1871. The short single '*new E&W Jc platform*' encroached into the existing GWR station approach road to their coal and goods wharf, whilst a rudimentary headshunt provided the only connection between the two railways. The GWR platforms were at this time opposite each other; the Down platform would later move to the far side of the road underbridge to allow for expansion of the GWR facilities.

This panoramic view of the two stations at Fenny Compton from the east shows the starting point of the first section of the E&WJR, opened in 1871 to Kineton. The GWR main line from Banbury to Leamington passes on the right, with the E&WJR running parallel through its own station on the left. The E&WJR facilities initially only comprised of the Up (right-hand) platform, which was restricted in width by the adjacent GWR goods yard and as such drew the attention of the Board of Trade inspector. However, despite his recommendations, nothing was ever done to rectify the problem until the platform was removed completely in the remodelling of the junction between the two lines in 1960. The GWR station had staggered platforms, that on the Down line being just out of sight behind the signal box, which itself was provided in 1931 as a joint venture between the LM&SR and GWR replacing two individual signal cabins operated by those companies. The original position of the E&WJR box is marked by the gap in the Down platform face, which once housed the signal and point wiring and rodding. *R.C. Riley*

A 1933 view of the E&WJR station from the eastern end of the platforms, showing the level crossing which also continued across the adjacent GWR main line. The girders of the adjacent road underbridge are also visible: it is not known whether the road traffic facilities were duplicated in this way owing to the propensity of the road to flood at this point, or whether restricted headroom under the bridge was also a factor. However, it seems that the original approach road to the GWR yard prior to the arrival of the E&WJR was from the south and this may have necessitated the provision of a level crossing over the latter line. *Author's collection*

Travelling on the New Railway

The Warwickshire press soon published letters from two of their readers relating their experiences on the E&WJR immediately after its opening, which provide a fascinating glimpse of how the line was operated in its earliest days. The first account was by a Mr Sidney Smith and appeared in the *Leamington Spa Courier* of 17th June 1871.

'Mr.Editor –

I have been a ride in the cars and a walk through the country and I am a wiser and sadder man. The last week my eyes have been assailed everywhere by red bills: "East & West Junction Railway Company. Opening of Fenny Compton and Kineton section. Timetable".

I also read accounts of this in the papers. At a cursory view it appears that the car takes an hour to run the distance (seven miles I am told).

The printed figures are also erased in places, and alterations made in writing. Altogether it is the greatest riddle I have seen for some time … so I started by the Great Western to Fenny Compton, where I found the East & West Railway Company represented by a platform, not long enough for a full sized train and a single track of rails. A small timetable, note-paper size, was pasted on a post, which was the only indication of business about the place. No name of station in letters a foot long, no byelaws setting forth pains and penalties, no list of tolls, no announcements that gratuities, smoking &c &c are defendu: none of those innumerable notices signed and countersigned which are scattered over all other depots in England; no station buildings, no agents, no clerks, no porters – simply the bare platform and the track, a peaceful calm reigning supreme.

I found I had some time to wait for a train, so went back to the Great Western depot and had a talk with the courteous agent there, who has embellished his platform with some fine flower beds and an arbour. He told me that he had that morning received orders to cut off the connection with the East & West by moving the metals on which trucks had previously passed from one line to the other, which would stop the traffic in coal &c.

A train at last came in sight. I returned to the platform and saw three passengers discharge themselves. The rolling stock of the company seems to consist of three cars and a brake van; their engine is a borrowed one, and does not consume its own smoke. I got into a second class car and inspected it – paint was the principal feature, the panels thin and weak, and in a collision would smash up sharp; however they don't sacrifice safety to speed. The first class is pretty fair, but not any stronger. The conductor, who also acts as a station master, booking clerk, and porter, came up and enquired "Ticket Sir?" I gave him half a crown … he was five minutes getting change.

At last we were off – 15 miles an hour, on the flat, full steam. A terrific run of 25 minutes brought us to Kineton, where there is a pretty little station, built in a hole. I guess there's some mud this weather. I found I had been the only passenger and felt proud accordingly.

There was a station master here to represent the company besides the conductor. He was not to be seen when I searched for him; no doubt the heavy traffic was too much and he had fled the spot to relieve his weary brain.

For a time the conductor told me they were not going on with the track beyond Kineton, the Directors doubtless intending to retire on their laurels and their dividends after opening the present section.

After liquoring in the village I returned and found the train on the go again, four passengers – immense excitement! Anxiety of engineer as to whether he had enough steam for the trip.'

The E&WJR appears to have exercised their right of reply in a rather sardonic letter published on 1st July and signed '*Blue Lias Cutting Kineton, E&W Junction 29th June*', inviting Mr Smith to revisit the line and make himself known to the management.

The second contemporary account appeared under the heading '*A novel railway journey*' in the *Warwickshire Advertiser* of 5th August 1871:

'*The E&WJR has opened their line from Fenny Compton to Kineton, a distance of 6½ miles. When the passenger for the latter place alights from the Great Western at their station at Fenny Compton he has only to cross the down line and pass through a*

£318,500 Perpetual 5 per Cent. First Debenture Stock,

BEING THE

EAST & WEST JUNCTION RAILWAY.

First Mortgage Charge upon the whole undertaking

The Directors of THE EAST AND WEST JUNCTION RAILWAY are prepared to receive Subscriptions for £318,500, part of the unissued balance of the £400,000 **First Debenture Stock** authorised by Scheme in pursuance of the " Railway Companies Act 1867."

This Stock, which at the price of issue pays £6 per cent., is the **First Perpetual Mortgage Charge** on a Railway 33¼ miles in length, the whole of which the Contractors are under penalties to complete and deliver to the Company (fit to be opened for public traffic) in the course of next year, nearly seven miles being already in working operation, and the works on the remainder in an advanced state.

The price of Issue is £83. 6s. 8d. per £100 Stock, payable as follows :—

£10	per Cent. on	Application.
10	,, ,,	Allotment.
25	,, ,,	September 30th, 1871.
20	,, ,,	December 31st, 1871.
18 : 6 : 8	,, ,,	March 31st, 1872.
£83 : 6 : 8		

Interest will accrue on the deposit and payment on allotment from the date of allotment, and on each subsequent instalment from the date of payment thereof, at the rate of 6 per cent. per annum, or subscribers can pay up the whole amount on allotment, in which case full Interest, at the rate of 6 per cent. per annum, will run from that date on the money paid, or 5 per cent. on each £100 Stock.

Applicants notifying their intention to pay up in full will be entitled to preference in the allotment.

The Interest will be payable half-yearly, on the 1st January and 1st July, at the Banking-house of Messrs. SMITH, PAYNE & SMITHS, 1, Lombard Street, E.C.

As a guarantee for due payment of Interest during construction of the Line, and for one year after completion (thus affording the Company ample time to develope its traffic), a sum equal to three years' Interest on the First Debenture Stock issued, will be invested in Consols or other Government Securities, in the names of

JAMES ATKINSON LONGRIDGE, ESQ., (the Chairman of the Company), and
ERIC CARRINGTON SMITH, ESQ., (Messrs. Smith, Payne & Smiths),

who have consented to act as Trustees, and who will apply the same, or such portion thereof as may be necessary, in payment of Interest as it falls due.

Certificates in respect of the amounts paid will from time to time be issued, and upon the payment up of all instalments they will be exchanged for Certificates, at the rate of £100 for every £83. 6s. 8d. paid.

The Acts of Parliament, Scheme, and Declaration of Trust, may be seen at the Offices of the Solicitors to the Company, Messrs. ASHURST, MORRIS & CO., 6, Old Jewry, E.C.

Applications in the annexed Form will be received by Messrs. J. and A. SCRIMGEOUR, 18, Old Broad Street, E.C., London, Brokers to the Company, or they can be forwarded to Messrs. SMITH, PAYNE & SMITHS, 1, Lombard Street, E.C. ; to the LONDON AND COUNTY BANK, Lombard Street, and Branches; or to the Secretary of the Company, CHARLES

East and West Junction Railway Company.

AUTHORISED CAPITAL.

		£
First Debenture Stock, having precedence of all other Debenture or other Stocks or Shares		
now offered		£318,500
Issued		19,000
Reserved		62,500
	Total	£400,000
Ordinary Shares Issued		400,000
Second Debenture Stock Issued		300,000
Third ditto		100,000
	Total	£800,000

DIRECTORS.

JAMES ATKINSON LONGRIDGE, Esq., 8, Poet's Corner, Westminster, *Chairman*.
MAJOR DICKSON, M.P., Waldershare Park, Kent.
CHARLES LÖWINGER, Esq., 1, Cadogan Place, S.W.
WILLIAM OWEN, Esq. (*Chairman of the Midland Waggon Company*), Clifton House, Rotherham.
HENRY TOOGOOD, Esq., 16, Parliament Street, Westminster, S.W.

ENGINEER.

JAMES B. BURKE, Esq., C.E., 11, Little Queen Street, Westminster, S.W.

BANKERS.

Messrs. SMITH, PAYNE & SMITHS, 1, Lombard Street, E.C.; and
THE LONDON AND COUNTY BANK, 21, Lombard Street, E.C.

SOLICITORS.

Messrs. ASHURST, MORRIS & CO., 6, Old Jewry, E.C.

BROKERS.

Messrs. J. & A. SCRIMGEOUR, 18, Old Broad Street, E.C.

SECRETARY.

CHARLES BANKS, Esq.

OFFICES—3, WESTMINSTER CHAMBERS, VICTORIA STREET, S.W.

The **East and West Junction Railway** is a line 33¼ miles in length, from **Towcester to Stratford-on-Avon, materially shortening the route via Blisworth, from London and the Northampton Iron Ore District, to the South Wales Coalfields.**

A section of the line between Kineton and the Fenny-Compton Station of the Great Western Railway has just been opened. The works on the remainder of the line are in an advanced state, and the Funds provided by the present issue will be amply sufficient for their completion.

The Midland Waggon Company of Birmingham have contracted to supply Rolling Stock for the working of the Line.

RESOURCES OF THE RAILWAY FOR TRAFFIC.

The East and West Junction Railway, by means of its running powers, joins the London and North-Western Railway at Blisworth. The Line passes through a rich agricultural and mineral district, via Towcester, Blakesley, Woodford, Byfield, Fenny-Compton, Kineton, to Stratford-on-Avon, and forms Junctions with the Great Western Railway System at Fenny-Compton, as well as at Stratford-on-Avon. Agreements exist with the Great Western Railway Company for facilitating the transfer of traffic to and from the South Wales and Monmonthshire Districts, and for affording service and accommodation for local traffic.

The Direct Route which this Line will open to the important port of Gloucester, from the Northampton and Bedfordshire Districts, will create a considerable traffic on the Line.

In the year 1869 a total of 540,259 tons of Northamptonshire Iron Ore was raised ; of this quantity the greater portion was carried to the South Wales District, where the demand for this Ore constantly increases.

By the route afforded by the East and West Junction Railway, the distance for through passengers, goods, and mineral traffic, from the South Wales Coalfields, Hereford, Worcester, and Gloucester, viâ Birmingham and Dudley, to the Northampton Iron Ore District, will be shortened by 25 miles, and this reduction in distance will undoubtedly secure a large through mineral traffic over this Line, both in Iron Ore to Wales, and in Coal from Wales to the above District and London.

Independently of the through mineral traffic, there are large iron-stone deposits along the course of the Line itself, and since the opening of the Fenny-Compton and Kineton section of the Line, arrangements have been made for the working of one of these mines, and the working of others only awaits the construction of the remainder of the Railway.

A careful estimate has been made of the minimum amount of traffic of this Line when completely open, with the following results :—

	£	s.	d.
Local Traffic, Passenger and Goods @ £23 per mile per week			
Minerals @ £14 ,, ,,	39,767	0	0
	24,206	0	0
	£63,973	0	0
Deduct 50 per cent. for Working Expenses	31,986	10	0
	£31,986	10	0
Interest on £397,500 First Debenture Stock, including present issue, @ 5 per cent.	16,875	0	0
Surplus Income	£15,111	10	0

As will be seen by the above, the estimated local traffic alone (independent of any through minerals) will be more than sufficient, after deducting working expenses, to provide for the annual Interest upon the first Debenture Stock now offered for subscription.

The Act of Parliament relating to the investment by Trustees in Railway Debenture Stocks, which the

---

An interesting early E&WJR prospectus of mid-1871 called for subscriptions for the remaining £318,500 balance of 5% First Debenture Stock. The pencilled comments appear to indicate the intention of a Mr Smith to apply for ten shares at a total cost of £833 6s 8d. The E&WJR were forever appealing to their shareholders for further injections of capital, initially to complete their route and afterwards to stave off receivership. *Author's collection*

wicket gate to gain the E&WJR train which is probably waiting with its little engine named "Kineton". Here is the train truly but where is the booking office? After vainly scanning every place where a booking office could be placed the said passenger makes sure of his journey by taking his seat and soon after doing which he is informed that the place for tickets is at the other end of the train. Pleasant Oliver Goldsmith in his "Deserted village" tells of a piece of furniture which "contrived a double debt to pay, a bed by night a chest of drawers by day" and something after the same fashion is the booking office in the guard's van.

Here by peering through a little orifice with a ledge to it the guard was to be dimly discerned fingering money and tickets. Having secured the necessary pasteboard, as you cannot yet book through to Kineton, you return to the composite carriage and await the starting.

Presently the aforesaid little engine moves off and you glide slowly through a rich agricultural district. You are aroused by the whistle from the engine which thereupon draws up quietly at a level crossing in the middle of fields. But on the other side is a small party of villagers who have come across the fields from Northend and scramble up to open doors very much in the same way as mounting the roof of one of the old red stage coaches. Meanwhile our friend the guard who bears E&WJR on his cap is down on the vacant cutting which will be hereafter occupied by a double line of rails, assisting the ladies to scale the carriage side. On goes the little engine again and your curiosity aroused you keep a look out ahead and perceive a countryman with uplifted arm signalling the train which obediently whistles and stops this time taking up a solitary lady. The train again proceeds passing under brand new railway arches, by embankments just out of navvy's hands, and helpless trollies lacking wheels apparently high and dry, to use a nautical phrase.

Kineton and its natty little station is at length reached and as you pass out of the station the appearances indicate that the line to Stratford is in a forward state. "When the way is opened from Stratford to Blisworth, Sir" says the guard "we will save twenty miles". "But the GWR will cooperate with you in price?" "Ah but Sir they cannot do it in the time, we shall beat them on that you know!"

From this same intelligent individual it was ascertained that

the novel conditions of travelling mentioned above were only temporary and that when the whole line is completed about this time next year passengers would not be able to command the steam horse by shouting or signalling at five bar gates in the open champaign. When that period arrives and the E&WJR has successfully overcome its difficulties we hope it may prove, by opening up a new district, a source of profit and remuneration to those who have waited long to see a return for the capital invested.'

Although facilities appear to have been reasonable at Kineton, the new company does seem to have initially provided far fewer creature comforts at Fenny Compton. However, this was undoubtedly due to the fact that it was originally intended to construct a joint station at the latter place, which would have served both GWR and the E&WJR lines. A plan of 1873 shows a central island platform for Up E&WJR and Down GWR trains, and a lengthy footbridge spanning the four tracks and platforms. In addition, a through running connection from the GWR is indicated from the Banbury direction, an unwitting portent of something that would not actually be achieved until 1960. In the event, a much simpler arrangement seems to have been in place for the opening, with just a basic platform being provided on the E&WJR line, adjacent to the existing GWR facilities.

The above accounts also indicate that just a single siding connection was provided between the two routes but the comment that the GWR agent had received instructions to sever this reflects the tensions that were already emerging between the two neighbours.

Mention was also made of the rolling stock for the new services. The E&WJR return to the Board of Trade at the end of 1871 confirmed the one Manning, Wardle locomotive purchased or borrowed from Crampton, two carriages, one other passenger type vehicle and just six wagons. A very early photograph of a train at Kineton station shows the contractor's 'borrowed' Manning, Wardle locomotive, with a crudely extended chimney, hauling what appears to be just three coaches, the first being a higher roofed vehicle and therefore probably a brake. However, this first vehicle could possibly be two separate carriages, thus corresponding with the above contemporary report, which speaks of 'three cars and a brake van'.

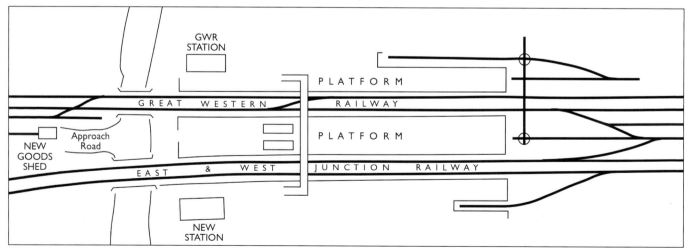

With the E&WJR approaching completion as a through route from Blisworth to Stratford, tentative arrangements were made for a joint station with the GWR at Fenny Compton. This 1873 plan illustrates how a wide central island platform would have been shared by the two companies, with a long footbridge connecting all four platforms. The GWR goods sidings and wharves, displaced by the new island platform, would have been moved beyond the road bridge. A through running connection from the GWR is shown a little further east on the original plan but this would not become a reality until 1960.

A few photographs have fortunately survived to illustrate the earliest days of the E&WJR; it is thought that this view of Kineton station pre-dates the opening of the first section of line in June 1871. An interesting mix of bystanders are present, ranging from the group of construction workers huddled together on the left, to the officials in the centre, gathered around what appears to be a surveyor's theodolite. The surroundings look very new and unfinished although at least the station nameboard is in place but work was obviously still under way in the background. *John Alsop collection*

A timetable in the *Leamington Spa Advertiser* of 10th June confirmed the planned seven trains in each direction. On weekdays, services departed from Kineton at 7.05am, 8.30am, 9.45am, 12.40pm, 2.05pm, 4.45pm and 7.05pm. In the opposite direction, departures from Fenny Compton were timed for 7.45am, 9.00am, 10.21am, 11.08am, 2.46pm and 5.33pm, with the last train of the day at 8.18pm. There were even three trains on Sunday, at 9.50am, 11.15am and 5.55pm from Kineton, returning from Fenny Compton at 10.28am, 11.55am and 7.17pm. However. the services on the Sabbath were not to last and had been withdrawn by September.

Two Up and three Down weekday trains conveyed all three classes of passenger but the remainder only catered for First and Second Class; on Sunday all were welcomed. The journey time in both directions was around twenty-five minutes, with the exception of the 2.46pm Down service which was scheduled to take only nineteen minutes to reach Kineton, whereas the first Up service of the day, the 7.05 from Kineton was for some reason allowed thirty-five minutes.

Excursionists were also being catered for, as evidenced by a notice in the *Leamington Spa Courier* of Saturday 5th August 1871, which reported on the Kineton Floral & Horticultural Show, held on the previous Wednesday. Apparently, '*for the convenience of late stayers a special train was engaged to run on the East & West Junction Railway, which left Kineton station at nine o'clock pm for Northend and Fenny Compton*'.

The station at North End is not listed in contemporary E&WJR timetables but the above reference would seem to confirm that passenger facilities were available there from the very earliest days of the line, although unusually no mention was made in the Board of Trade inspector's report prior to opening.

The above mentioned newspaper reports also refer to the ownership of wagons but as no working timetables of the period appear to have survived, there is no record of goods traffic. However, it is quite likely that, with only one locomotive available, mixed trains were run to also convey goods traffic, in particular coal, from the GWR at Fenny Compton.

This first part of the E&WJR was constructed by Thomas Crampton and one of his small Manning, Wardle 0-6-0 saddle tanks was appropriated to haul the inaugural passenger train; others of the type were still at work on the construction of the remaining sections of the line. However, with now only a few months remaining of the time originally allowed for completion of the line, another Act of Parliament was required to provide an extension of a further three years.

Thus the first chapter in the history of the E&WJR came to a close. At this point in time, the board of directors consisted of the chairman, James Atkinson Longridge of Poets Corner, Westminster, Major Dickson MP of Waldershore Park in Kent, Charles Lowinger of Cadogan Place, London SW, William Owen of Clifton House, Rotherham, and Henry Toogood of Parliament Square, Westminster. James B. Burke acted as engineer for the

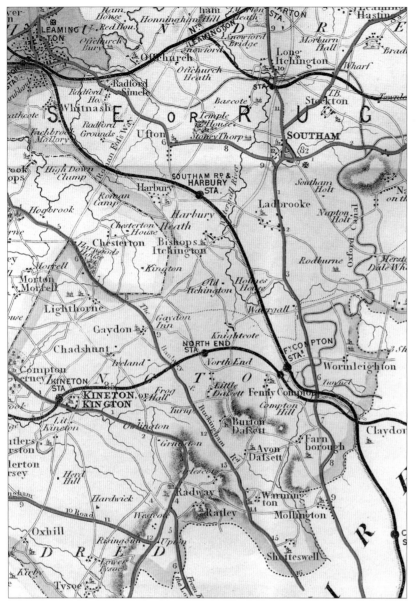

line and the secretary, operating from the company offices at 3 Westminster Chambers, Victoria Street, London, was Charles Banks.

Henry Toogood, acting as deputy chairman of a half-yearly general meeting on 3rd November 1871, reported that a Bill for an extension of time to complete the line had been passed despite 'great and strenuous opposition by the GWR'. He also stated that a further section of line to Eatington (sic) in continuation of that already opened would be ready in March next year but that the permanent junction with the GWR at Fenny Compton was not yet opened. Contractors Eyres, Crampton & Son had now received two new engines at Fenny Compton, one working 'the hill at Compton, and the other at Adston'. The company had, since the recommencement of construction, obtained possession of a considerable quantity of land for new works. They had also entered into a contract with the Midland Wagon Company for engines and rolling stock, on a principle of yearly payments extending over ten years, after which the stock would be owned by the E&WJR. Toogood also reported that 'Byfield people were anxious to see the line completed so that they get coal at 9d instead of the 15d last winter'.

At the close of 1871, an assessment of the potential of the line when fully opened gave an estimate of annual revenue for passenger and general goods traffic of £39,767 per annum, plus a further £24,206 in respect of the heavy mineral traffic that was expected to be carried. After a deduction of 50% for running expenses, the railway was expected to produce net revenue of almost £32,000, more than enough to pay a 5% dividend. Unfortunately, this was again to prove more than a little optimistic.

ABOVE: It has been difficult to find any documentary evidence of the existence of North End station, other than the entries in Bradshaw's timetables of the 1870s and occasional mentions in newspaper advertisements. This early map of Warwickshire does at least record its location midway between Kineton and Fenny Compton but there is no indication of Warwick Road station. *Author's collection*

RIGHT: Prospective passengers arriving at Kineton station from the road would have had this view of the main building, with the twin pavilions contrasting with the sloped gable ends on the platform side. The quite elaborate stone scrolls on the gable ends look as though they should perhaps have contained the letters 'E&WJR' and the date of opening in 1871 but they were forever to remain blank. *Author's collection*

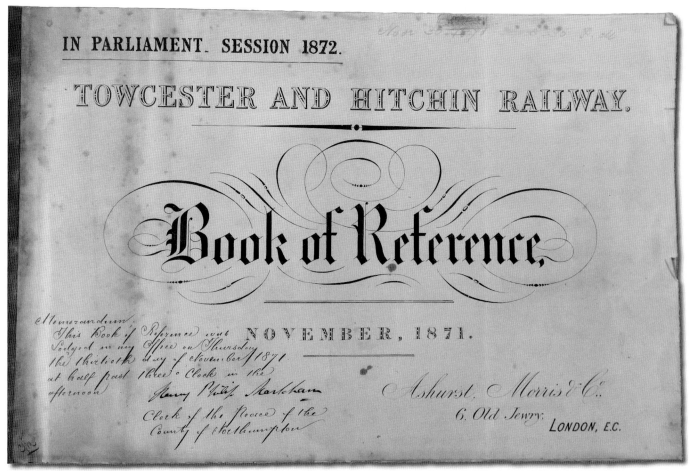

IN PARLIAMENT. SESSION 1872.

TOWCESTER AND HITCHIN RAILWAY.

Book of Reference,

NOVEMBER, 1871.

Ashurst, Morris & Co.
6, Old Jewry,
LONDON, E.C.

Further Plans

Meanwhile, James B. Burke and his brother Joseph F. Burke had been nominated as engineers for another proposal involving the E&WJR, for which plans were deposited in November 1871. The Towcester & Hitchin Railway was a resurrection of plans of 1865 and followed an identical path to the earlier scheme, although this later proposal consisted of just three separate railways instead of the original five portions of line.

The board of the E&WJR then met at a Special General Meeting on 2nd February 1872, to consider a proposal to construct a new line from Blisworth to Northampton. This was to leave the route of the Northampton & Banbury Junction Railway, over which the E&WJR held running powers, at Gayton and then cross above the L&NWR main line, after which an independent route would be followed to Northampton. However, instead of then continuing to Bedford, as in the scheme of 1864, a junction was to be made with the newly opened Bedford & Northampton Railway near to their St. John's Street station, after crossing the main thoroughfare of Bridge Street, some way north of the L&NWR station, on a single span iron bridge.

Also included in the plans deposited for this proposal was provision for a separate new line from the E&WJR at Byfield, past Charwelton, to terminate in a sparsely populated area near Hellidon a few miles further north. The purpose of this seemingly rather unlikely line was to tap large reserves of iron

The proposed 1865 extension to Hitchin would have left the E&WJR main line just west of Green's Norton Junction, crossed the Northampton & Banbury Junction line and then proceeded to the south of the town of Towcester, some distance away from the N&BJR station. It is interesting to speculate how station facilities at Towcester would have evolved had the extension line actually been built. *NRO-DP*

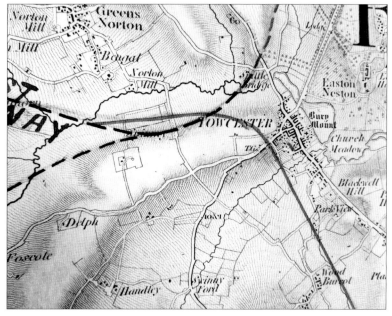

ore which were known to be available in the area and it seems possible from the details of the proposal that a narrow gauge route may have been under consideration. The vote was carried despite objections from some quarters but just over one year later the proposal would be withdrawn.

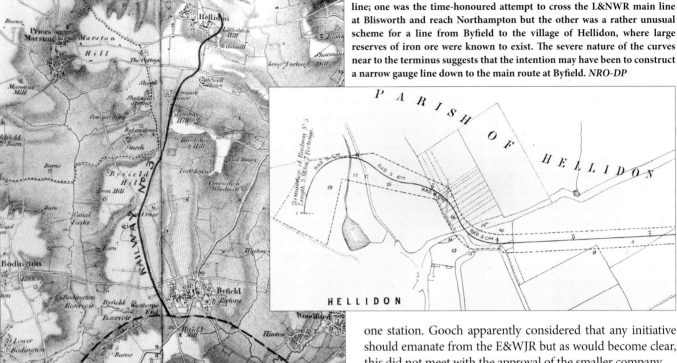

In 1872 the E&WJR proposed two extensions to their as yet uncompleted line; one was the time-honoured attempt to cross the L&NWR main line at Blisworth and reach Northampton but the other was a rather unusual scheme for a line from Byfield to the village of Hellidon, where large reserves of iron ore were known to exist. The severe nature of the curves near to the terminus suggests that the intention may have been to construct a narrow gauge line down to the main route at Byfield. *NRO-DP*

Trouble With the Neighbours

Construction continued on the unopened stretches of the E&WJR, as evidenced by Crampton's advertisement in the *Northampton Mercury* for '*rough carpenters for timber work and repairing earth wagons – apply on the works at Towcester. Blakesley, Byfield and Fenny Compton*'. In addition, the contractor had already ordered a further pair of suitable locomotives to assist in the construction work. Two small saddle tank engines were sourced from Neilson & Company, one arriving at Fenny Compton in September 1871 soon after the opening of the first section of line. The second, for the eastern part of the line at Towcester, was eventually supplied during 1872.

However, the apparent progress was not without incident. A report by the local constabulary at Stratford, on the problems of dealing with the navvy population in that area, revealed that '*the parties employed on the works band themselves together and by their acts prevent any process being executed against any of their gang by any one officer; in fact they are utterly lawless and worse by far than any class of like labourers who have been previously employed on works of like nature in our neighbourhood*'.

At the close of 1872, work was still in hand at various locations along the route and navvies were being sought in Byfield, Kineton and Stratford at wages of '*3/6d to 3/9d a day, according to merit – healthy localities and living cheap*'.

With the full opening of the through route from Green's Norton fast approaching, initial arrangements were tentatively made for the use of the Great Western station at Stratford, pending completion of the E&WJR facilities in the Old Town area. Stratford Town Council had met to consider the situation and, at the request of several gentlemen, the Mayor had spoken with Sir Daniel Gooch of the Great Western Railway, asking him to sanction the use of their station by the E&WJR, so the town could have just

one station. Gooch apparently considered that any initiative should emanate from the E&WJR but as would become clear, this did not meet with the approval of the smaller company.

The E&WJR had already purchased just over four acres of land in Stratford for their own station and yards from Charles Lucy, a local flour miller and former Mayor of the town, at a cost of £516 per acre. This represented a very good return for Lucy, as he had only purchased the land himself some ten years before at £170 per acre.

Early relations with the GWR in Stratford were to prove a little strained and contention over the wording of the agreement for use of the existing station, then jointly owned by the GWR and the Stratford-upon-Avon Railway, caused no little discussion and many exchanges of correspondence. An initial exchange of letters took place between Hobbs, the secretary of the E&WJR, and his counterpart at the GWR. The former had received a communication from Robert Gibbs, the Mayor of Stratford, on 23rd April 1872, indicating that the townspeople felt that: '*for the public accommodation and convenience it is most desirable that the E&WJR should have the joint use of the Stratford station of the GWR*' and that he had '*an interview with Sir Daniel Gooch on this subject, who expressed his willingness to enter into negotiations in this matter …*'.

The E&WJR board had initially concurred with this approach and, pending an arrangement being made, had decided to withhold any further work on the construction of their own station. The GWR wrote on 3rd May requesting details of the E&WJR requirements and terms for the use of their facilities but a prompt response from Hobbs pointed out that the initial proposal had in fact emanated from the Mayor and that '*the E&WJR had no wishes beyond consulting the inhabitant's wishes and conveniences*'. He stressed that the E&WJR Board only desired that a meeting should be held to discuss whether a mutually advantageous arrangement could be decided upon.

An agreement seemed close by mid July, with the respective solicitors having drawn up a form of words. This was on the point of being approved by the E&WJR Board, apart from '*… the alterations indicated in pencil having to be made*'.

However, those alterations were to prove to be the stumbling block to any agreement between the two companies. Hobbs insisted that the words '*the E&W company desire the use of Stratford station*' should be struck out and that it be made clear that the request for the use of the GWR station had been made solely by the Mayor and inhabitants of Stratford. If this stipulation was not met, the E&WJR would then consider negotiations to be at an end. The E&WJR concern was apparently that the insertion of their company name in any agreement would confer upon the GWR '*power to take an advantage which the circumstances do not warrant*' and that the correct way to proceed would only be on the basis of a mutual agreement.

A stalemate then ensued so, on 11th September 1872, Hobbs again wrote to the GWR, stating that unless agreement could be made within a week, the E&WJR would consider the matter closed and would continue with work at their own station. At this point, the Stratford-upon-Avon Railway company, who until now had been silent, attempted to mediate in the dispute, with a proposed form of words which they suggested might alleviate the E&WJR objections. A further attempt was made to reach agreement in January 1873 and this was still being discussed in May.

A matter of days before the first trains were due to run over the E&WJR line to Stratford, an inquest into the drowning of a young child in a well described the station as being '*now in course of completion*'. In the event, the unfinished E&WJR station was used and a Mr Golbourne provided an omnibus service to carry passengers to and from the GWR station.

This little local difficulty with the Great Western over station accommodation was, however, to be just a mere portent of more significant future problems between the two companies, involving through rates for ironstone traffic to South Wales, which would culminate in arbitration by the Railway Commissioners.

A Through Route

In due course, with construction on the two sections having been successfully completed, the E&WJR was able to make an application to the Board of Trade for sanction to open their through route from Green's Norton Junction to Stratford-upon-Avon. On this occasion, Colonel Yolland was delegated to perform the necessary inspection and his nine page handwritten report contains full details of his trip along the whole length of the E&WJR line on 26th and 27th June 1873.

The Colonel first commented that the

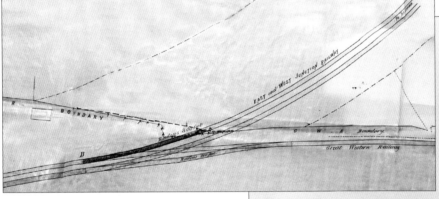

ABOVE: A plan of 1873 of the junction arrangement at Stratford between the E&WJR and the GWR's line to Honeybourne, which also incorporated the doubling of the existing GWR line through to their Stratford station. The initial intention was for E&WJR passenger trains to run through into the GWR station but disagreements between the two companies prevented this from taking place and the inaugural services from Blisworth used the part-completed E&WJR station in the Old Town area of Stratford instead. In the event, the connection between the two companies was only inspected by the Board of Trade for the carrying of goods traffic. *Author's collection*

RIGHT: The E&WJR's junction of 1873 with the Great Western's Honeybourne line was controlled by a typical GWR signal cabin of the period. This was originally known as 'Stratford-Upon-Avon E&W Jcn.' but after 1909 was changed to 'Stratford-Upon-Avon SM Jcn.'. By the 1950s date of this view, this change was still clearly evident from the patch on the nameboard. *Author's collection*

LEFT: The deep cleft of Goldicote Cutting, situated between Ettington and Stratford, caused a good deal of problems during the initial construction of the E&WJR line. Even in later years, it had to be carefully watched to ensure that falls of loose chalk did not endanger the railway. The line was often closed for periods at weekends so that workmen could dislodge suspect boulders from the cutting side, allowing them to then be collected from the track below. This was the only section of the E&WJR route that had been constructed as single track; elsewhere all cuttings, embankments and other infrastructure was wide enough to accommodate a second line of rails. *M. Mitchell*

BELOW: This poor quality but rare early view of the E&WJR station at Stratford from the eastern end of the Avon Viaduct illustrates the commencement of the original single line section to Clifford Sidings and the signalling allowing Up trains to depart eastwards from either of the two platforms. In 1942, the line was doubled from the station, across the viaduct and onwards to a revised layout at Clifford Sidings. *Author's collection*

section between the E&WJR station at Stratford and the junction with the GWR had been withdrawn from the application, as construction had not yet been completed. It was also an indication that negotiations over the use of the GWR station had failed.

The report went on to state that the new line was single throughout, with the exception of loops and passing places at all of the stations apart from Ettington, where there was a siding only. Once again land had been purchased and bridges constructed for the future provision of a double line of track, although in some cases the underline bridges had not yet been provided with the necessary girders for the second track. In addition, Goldicote Cutting had only been excavated for a single line of railway.

In common with the first short section to be opened, the trackwork consisted of 24ft lengths of rail weighing 69lbs per yard, secured with fang bolts and spikes. However, the ballast used on the new sections of line was either gravel or a gravel and stone mixture, instead of the burnt clay that had been used on the Kineton to Fenny Compton section.

Much of the line had been constructed through an area of blue clay bedrock, with some settlement having already taken place on embankments and the Colonel noted that this aspect might require careful attention in the future. Underline bridges were tested with a 'rolling load' and the deflection was found to be satisfactory, with the exception of a 15ft culvert at a point 29 chains from Green's Norton, which required immediate strengthening by the addition of the second set of girders intended for the future double track. No public level crossings were located on the line at the time of inspection but one authorised at 5 miles 68 chains from Green's Norton was then in course of construction.

Stations were noted at Blakesley, Morton Pinkney, Byfield, Ettington and Stratford, in addition to those already opened in 1871; the intention of opening a joint station with the GWR at Fenny Compton was again recorded. Significantly, however, again no mention was made in the Colonel's report of the existence of stations at either Warwick Road or North End,

although the latter had been indicated as a stopping place in the earlier mentioned excursion announcement.

The inspection revealed 'a good many small items' that still required attention. However, it was agreed with the E&WJR engineer, Mr Burke, that the line could be opened, subject to these being attended to by the time that the anticipated inspection was made of the connection to the Great Western at Stratford. These 'small items' included the fact that the E&WJR station building at Stratford 'was not yet all put up', the second platform was still under construction, and nameboards and station clocks were still to be provided. At Fenny Compton, station buildings and fences were in course of erection on the newly constructed Down platform, whilst in many other locations fencing was still to be completed.

Almost inevitably, attention was still required to the interlocking of points and signals at most locations, although the Colonel did not consider that any of these affected the safety of the travelling public. However, one interesting comment involved the interlocking of signals relating to a siding at Stratford, between the Up and Down lines, which may at last explain why

The exterior of the E&WJR station at Stratford-upon-Avon. The design was essentially an enlarged version of the 'standard' E&WJR station buildings which were to be found at all of the locations from Blakesley to Ettington, with the exception of Kineton. The rails set in the stone setts in the foreground served Lucy's Mill, on the nearby bank of the River Avon, and also in later years a large grain silo. On the right of the picture stands the original E&WJR signal box, replaced in 1919 by a new cabin just a few yards further west. However, the old box was not removed and continued to be used for a variety of alternative purposes for many more years. *Author's collection*

in subsequent years there was an unusually large gap between the two platform at this station.

At Fenny Compton, the Up platform was noted as having now been constructed for a length of 100 yards, although at one point the incursion of the fencing of the Great Western station approach road caused a considerable narrowing of the width available for passengers. It was recommended that the GWR should allow this problem to be resolved, otherwise the platform would have to be shortened again.

The E&WJR proposed to operate the full length of their line on the same train staff and ticket system that was in use on the original short length between Kineton and Fenny Compton but the Colonel recommended that the adoption of the absolute block system would provide for safer working of the line. The E&WJR, however, required more time to make this change, and it was therefore agreed that train staff and ticket could continue to be used for a period of six months from the date of opening.

A final recommendation was that the speed of all trains should be restricted to 25 miles per hour until the trackbed had compacted and, to assist this, gravel should be added to the areas ballasted only by stone to assist the consolidation.

The two remaining sections of the E&WJR single line, from Green's Norton to Fenny Compton and Kineton to Stratford, a total of 26$\frac{1}{2}$

miles, were therefore approved for opening to passenger traffic from 1st July 1873, with the Board of Trade inspector, Colonel Yolland, being moved to comment on the completeness of the works and permanent way.

The first train was a special service for the directors, which '*ran gently from Blisworth to Stratford and on return halted at Kineton for luncheon*' and the contractors, Crampton & Sons, hosted

A circa 1910 view of Blakesley station, looking west from the Up platform, with staff and locals in attendance. The station sign is the original, probably enamelled type and is mounted high on the station building. The early design of the Down starting signal is also of interest. The strange gabled structure and the Sykes banner signal are all part of the infrastructure of the Blakesley Hall Miniature Railway, which ran from its own small platform to the nearby stately home of the Bartholemew family. *Author's collection*

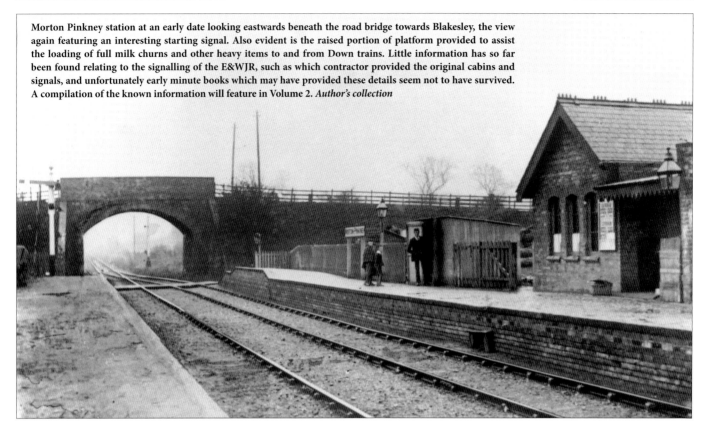

Morton Pinkney station at an early date looking eastwards beneath the road bridge towards Blakesley, the view again featuring an interesting starting signal. Also evident is the raised portion of platform provided to assist the loading of full milk churns and other heavy items to and from Down trains. Little information has so far been found relating to the signalling of the E&WJR, such as which contractor provided the original cabins and signals, and unfortunately early minute books which may have provided these details seem not to have survived. A compilation of the known information will feature in Volume 2. *Author's collection*

their own usual celebratory luncheon. The local *Stratford Herald* newspaper reported on the commencement of public services, noting that the E&WJR station was a '*small but substantially erected brick building standing on land formerly known as Church Farm*'. Other stations were decorated with flags and triumphal arches, the locomotives also being suitably embellished.

The *Herald* commented: '*We do not wonder that Tuesday was a gala day at Kineton. We hear of gay flags floating from the church tower, the bells ringing merry peals, and of triumphal arches being erected between the town and the railway. It must have astonished the founders of the old castle of King John, if they had been privileged to hear the roar of the steam monster in that quiet valley, and have seen the decking of evergreens to welcome the first train from Stratford at twenty two minutes past nine on the morning of the 1st of July. It was the day of free trips, and later on the contractors gave a dinner at the Red Lion Hotel Kineton to the principal inhabitants*'.

The report also reflected back to the opening of the original short stretch of line to Fenny Compton two years previously, and how: '*… this railway has been very accommodating … trains have stopped for passengers when passengers appeared, and as each train carried its own booking office, the result was one of simplicity of arrangement which would be much missed if this genial simplicity should give place to the ordinary routines of railway arrangement, now that the line is opened throughout its length …*'. Mention was also made of the introduction of '*pick up platforms*' at stated intervals, which would '*give the line an air of novelty, and a charm to picnic parties, which it will be in vain to expect from any of the older and more busy Companies*'.

This rather unusual method of operation might provide an answer to the apparent mystery of the two early

stations on the route at Warwick Road and North End, which may just have been of a temporary nature, in keeping with the above mentioned '*pick up platforms*', although it is not clear as to why these were not noted during either of the two statutory inspections of the line.

The *Banbury Guardian* added its own report on the new railway, again mentioning the '*novelty in railway travel of pick-up platforms at various points on the line, which will doubtless be found of great convenience to farmers and others on market days … these have been erected at convenient places and the promoters, having had the experience of the same thing at other parts of the line are sanguine of the success of the scheme when more extensively applied*'.

However, no evidence of plans to extend this scheme beyond the known examples at Warwick Road and North End has so far been found, with the exception of one proposal, noted by the *Bucks Advertiser* on 23rd August 1873, for '*a platform to stop trains by signal at Kingthorn Wood for the benefit of the Green's Norton district*'.

The *Banbury Guardian* also spoke of plans to lay down sidings for a large new brewery at Blakesley, arrangements for working ironstone from quarries at Culworth, the commodious goods shed, and cattle, timber and coal wharves provided at Byfield, a planned hotel at Fenny Compton and the impending erection of a new iron furnace at Towcester, all of which would benefit the new line.

The completed E&WJR line from Green's Norton to Stratford had finally cost almost £1 million to construct, against an initial estimate of £400,000.

Sec., C. Banks.										EAST and WEST JUNCTION.							[a Stop by signal]		
Fares.			**Down.**	1&2	1&2	1&2	1,2,3	1,2,3	1&2	1&2		**Up.**	1&2	1&2	1&2	1,2,3	1&2	1&2	1&2
1 cl.	2 cl.	3 cl.	Fenny Compton..dep	7 35	9	1021	1 1	4 46	5 38	8 13	Kineton ....dep	7	8 30	9 45	1230	2 10	5 07	
s.d.	s.d.	s.d.	Warwick Road........	a	a	a	a	a	a	a	North End	a	a	a	a	a	a	a
...	...	...	North End	a	a	a	a	a	a	a	Warwick Road........	a	a	a	a	a	a	a
1 6	0 10	0 6½	Kineton ....arr	8 0	9 30	1045	1 40	3 10	6 3	8 35	Fenny Compton 23, 20	7 23	8 55	10 8	1	5 2	35	5 25	7 5

Once again the station staff and a couple of locals are featured on this photograph of Byfield station, probably taken circa 1908 during late E&WJR days. They had all clearly been instructed to stand very still by the photographer, with the result that they have all adopted slightly odd rigid stances and stare resolutely off in to the distance. As in the case of Morton Pinkney, a raised area was provided on the platform for the loading of full milk churn but in this case it was on the Up side; this variation is probably due to the fact that the milk would be destined for London via the Great Central route. The original signalling is still present, whilst the small signal box had not yet been extended at both ends to provide space for additional instrumentation. The tall pumping house and water tank is prominent at the far end of the platform and this also supplied a water crane on the Down side behind the camera. *John Alsop collection*

A more comprehensive view of the facilities provided at Byfield, looking from the road overbridge at the eastern end of the station around 1910. Coal was clearly one of the staple commodities handled in the goods yard, with the Midland Railway wagon on the left probably having arrived from the East Midlands coalfield. Cattle traffic is also in evidence, with the whitewashed dock situated just beyond the goods shed. The main passenger access to the station was from the approach road leading to the rear of the building on the Up platform, whilst the goods yard entrance was off picture to the left. Passengers wishing to travel to Stratford had to cross the line by the timbered barrow crossing in the foreground – no E&WJR station was ever provided with a footbridge. The line curves away in the distance, passing beneath further village lanes before leaving Northamptonshire, to touch Oxfordshire and then pass into Warwickshire for the remainder of its route. *Author's collection*

Early Days on the Through Line

Initial reports suggested that the E&WJR were to run just three trains each way per day during July, '*so that everything may be got into working order*', and thereafter seven trains would be operated. However, a timetable for August 1873 shows four through trains in each direction on weekdays, but no trains on Sundays. Departures from Blisworth were at 9.10am, 11.00am, 4.50pm and 7.55pm, with eastbound services from Stratford at 6.25am, 8.55am, 2.20pm and 6.00pm; the journey time averaged around one hour and forty minutes.

The stop at Towcester was restricted to picking up passengers on westbound trains or setting down in the opposite direction, thus leaving local traffic to the Northampton & Banbury Junction Railway. There was also an additional local 'Market' service to Stratford on Fridays only, leaving Fenny Compton at 2.00pm.

In anticipation of the complete opening, the E&WJR had considerably increased their rolling stock. Seven locomotives were reported at the end of 1873, these being the Manning, Wardle 0-6-0 saddle tank owned by Crampton that operated the inaugural services in 1871, together with six new engines from Beyer, Peacock, comprising three 2-4-0 passenger tank engines and three 0-6-0 goods tender locomotives. Twenty carriages, eleven other passenger type vehicles and no less than ninety-three wagons completed the rolling stock. However, as will be seen, many of these vehicles would soon be repossessed, with the six new locomotives also being returned to their supplier.

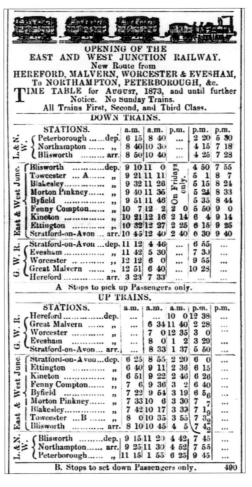

OPENING OF THE EAST AND WEST JUNCTION RAILWAY.

New Route from HEREFORD, MALVERN, WORCESTER & EVESHAM, To NORTHAMPTON, PETERBOROUGH, &c.

TIME TABLE for AUGUST, 1873, and until further Notice. No Sunday Trains.

All Trains First, Second, and Third Class.

DOWN TRAINS.

STATIONS.	a.m.	a.m.	p.m.	p.m.	p.m.
Peterborough ...... dep.	6 15	8 40		2 20	5 30
Northampton ...... „	8 40	10 30		4 15	7 18
Blisworth .... arr.	8 50	10 40		4 25	7 23
Blisworth ....dep.	9 10	11 0		4 50	7 55
Towcester ... A ... „	9 21	11 11		5 1	8 7
Blakesley .... „	9 32	11 26		5 15	8 24
Morton Pinkney... „	9 40	11 35		5 24	8 33
Byfield .... „	9 51	11 48		5 35	8 44
Fenny Compton... „	10 7	12 2	2 0	5 50	9 0
Kineton .... „	10 21	12 16	2 14	6 4	9 14
Ettington .... „	10 32	12 27	2 25	6 15	9 25
Stratford-on-Avon. arr.	10 45	12 40	2 40	6 30	9 40
Stratford-on-Avon...dep.	11 12	4 46		6 55	
Evesham .... „	11 40	5 30		7 30	
Worcester .... „	12 12	6 0		9 55	
Great Malvern ...... „	12 51	6 40		10 28	
Hereford .... arr.	3 23	7 33			

A Stops to pick up Passengers only.

UP TRAINS.

STATIONS.	a.m.	a.m.	a.m.	p.m.	p.m.
Hereford .... dep.			10 0	12 38	
Great Malvern ...... „		6 34	11 40	2 28	
Worcester .... „		7 0	12 35	3 0	
Evesham .... „		8 0	1 2	3 29	
Stratford-on-Avon. arr.		8 33	1 37	5 50	
Stratford-on-Avon...dep.	6 25	8 55	2 20	6 0	
Ettington .... „	6 40	9 11	2 36	6 15	
Kineton .... „	6 51	9 22	2 46	6 26	
Fenny Compton... „	7 6	9 36	3 2	6 40	
Byfield .... „	7 22	9 54	3 19	6 56	
Morton Pinkney... „	7 33	10 6	3 30	7 7	
Blakesley............ „	7 42	10 17	3 33	7 19	
Towcester ... B ... „	8 0	10 35	3 55	7 32	
Blisworth .... arr.	8 10	10 45	4 5	7 45	
Blisworth ....dep.	9 15	11 20	4 42	7 45	
Northampton...... arr.	9 25	11 30	4 52	7 55	
Peterborough...... „	11 15	1 55	6 25	9 45	

B. Stops to set down Passengers only. 490

An early boost to the newly opened line was provided by the L&NWR's realisation of the potential of tourist traffic from London to Shakespeare's birthplace. A handbill of August 1873 offered through fares and connections from London Euston and other L&NWR stations, by changing onto E&WJR trains at Blisworth. The journey from the metropolis could be achieved in a little over three and a half hours, and a Second Class return ticket could be obtained for 22s 3d or £1 11s 3d in First Class.

Every opportunity was taken to maximise the traffic potential, with fares and connections being shown from many other L&NWR served stations in the provinces, such as Stamford, Peterborough and Cambridge, as well as those closer to London, including Dunstable and St. Albans. Horses and carriages could also be accommodated, presumably for those wishing to stay longer in Stratford.

Somewhat closer to home, domestic services were soon disrupted by a derailment at Kineton on 2nd August 1873. The 6.00pm passenger train from Stratford had been delayed for some time at Ettington, waiting for two Down trains to pass but was finally allowed to proceed on its way almost half an hour late. On approaching Kineton, reportedly at high speed, the train left the track one hundred yards before the station but fortunately remained upright on the ballast.

A few weeks later, on 27th August, another derailment occurred at Kineton, which prompted a visit by Lt Colonel Hutchinson RE as inspecting officer for the Board of Trade. The

ABOVE: The E&WJR opened as a through route on 1st July 1873. The first timetable offered four trains in each direction between Blisworth and Stratford on each weekday, with an additional Friday afternoon only service from Fenny Compton to Stratford. A footnote indicated that E&WJR trains could not pick up or set down passengers to and from Blisworth on the N&BJR section of the route. There was also no mention of the stations at Warwick Road and North End. *Author's collection*

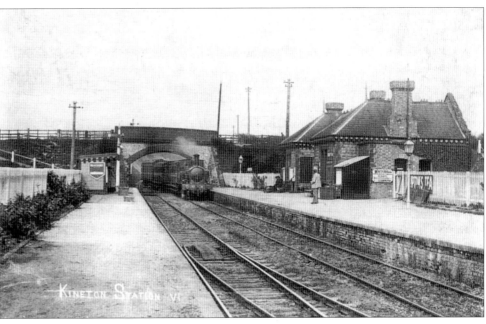

RIGHT: A train of mixed passenger stock, which appears to include a GCR through coach, arriving at Kineton station from the east during E&WJR days, circa 1908. The locomotive is one of the railway's two Beyer, Peacock 2-4-0 tank engines, either No. 5 or No. 6. *Author's collection*

Colonel's official report of 13th September revealed that the same 6.00pm Up passenger train from Stratford, consisting of a tank engine and five vehicles, left the rails when entering the passing loop line at the station. The driver saw that the points were half open but was unable to stop his train in time, and the engine and front brake vehicle were derailed, fortunately without any injury to passengers. Remarkably, the points and signalling had been tested that very morning by another officer of the Board of Trade who was making a routine inspection at Kineton. However, Colonel Hutchinson's investigation revealed that the points had failed to return to their correct position after an earlier Down train had passed through them. Theoretically, it should not have been possible for the signals to then have been lowered for the Up train, as the points and signals concerned were interlocked by means of bolts moved by wires. However, it was considered that a combination of new wires and the hot weather had conspired to make it possible for the porter to lower the signals without the problem being noticed. The Colonel commented that *this is a great cause of uncertainty in all signal arrangements, and the general introduction of some means of guarding against it is much to be desired*; he added that the Midland Railway had now adopted a system which seemed to be working well.

Another Connection to the Great Western

On 4th August 1873, the line was once more visited by Colonel Yolland of the Board of Trade, who took the opportunity to again travel the full length of the route from Green's Norton, whilst also attending to the main business of the inspection of the short connection from the E&WJR to the Great Western Railway at Stratford. The original plan had been for a simple junction at this location between the double line of rails of the E&WJR and the single track of the GWR line from Honeybourne, which had been completed in 1859. A station had originally been provided on the latter at Sanctus Lane but, in 1863, this was relocated to Alcester Road, which also then accommodated the Great Western operated Stratford-upon-Avon Railway branch from Hatton, after that line had itself moved from a temporary terminus slightly further to the north. However, an amended plan dated June 1873 shows the initial arrangement as having been changed to provide a second GWR line towards their own station, with the junction with the E&WJR being suitably amended.

The Great Western company had undertaken to construct the junction, associated sidings and signal work but the cost of £1,451 5s was borne by the E&WJR. The latter had, however, only applied for the opening of this connection for goods and mineral traffic, thus finally confirming that, following the earlier disputes, their passenger services would not be using the GWR station. The Colonel sanctioned the opening, subject to the moving of a GWR Up stop signal at the junction to the opposite side of the line, to provide better sighting from the signal box, and the interlocking of certain points and signals.

In travelling over the remainder of the E&WJR line, the Colonel noted the compliance with most of his earlier recommendations, although some attention was still needed to signals and points at both Ettington and Moreton Pinkney. However, a greater change was required to the track layout at Blakesley, where to obviate the need for a set of facing points on the running line, the goods

siding was required to cross the Down line and instead make a connection into the Up line. Once again a recommendation was also made as to the need to moderate the speed of trains, as in various places the trackbed was seen to have settled; the necessity of regular inspections being made to check for further subsidence was stressed.

During the month of October 1873, additional trains were added to the timetable to give better connections for passengers travelling to Birmingham, Oxford, Leamington and Banbury. A new service left Stratford at 8.30am, calling at Fenny Compton at 9.20am in time for the departure of the first Down GWR service, whilst later in the day another new train left the same station at 4.26pm, after the arrival of the GWR train from Oxford.

As if to conclude this stage of the E&WJR's development, on Monday 23rd February 1874, an auction was conducted by Fuller, Horsey, Son & Co. at Crampton's depot at Stratford, to sell the remaining equipment from the construction of the E&WJR. This continued on successive days at the other construction sites at Kineton, Fenny Compton and Byfield.

Items included a Manning, Wardle six-coupled saddle tank engine and three four-coupled locomotives by Neilson and Hawthorn & Co. Also listed were 400 end tipping earth wagons, 200 tons of bridge rails of varying weights, twenty crossings and 32 tons of permanent way fastenings. The remainder of the inventory featured the usual array of contractor's equipment, such as carts, harnesses, pumps, cranes, barrows, wheels and axles, sleepers, and a large selection of workshop tools and sundries. Buildings were also for sale and these ranged from modest huts, through to stables and *wooden locomotive sheds*.

A month later, on 18th April, the Manning, Wardle engine was again advertised for sale and this time was named as *Kineton*, the locomotive which had been used on the first train on the E&WJR but was now presumably surplus to requirements.

The Iron Ore Disputes

Despite the encouraging news of the full opening, problems were never very far away for the E&WJR, which was now being operated at a considerable loss. Perhaps understandably, the two years prior to full completion had revealed operating losses of £1,054 and £574 respectively but 1873 then produced a deficit of almost £9,500 or, expressed more succinctly, working expenses were over three times the total receipts for that year. There were, however, yet further difficulties on the horizon.

The E&WJR understandably now wished to offer lower rates for the carriage of iron ore over their new shorter route to South Wales, in addition to their other major market, the Staffordshire ironworks. The existing arrangement was for ore from the Blisworth and Towcester districts to be carried on the L&NWR directly to Staffordshire, or handed over to the GWR at Smethwick for onward carriage to South Wales, at previously agreed through rates. These rates had been in force for some years but faced with the E&WJR's proposal for lower rates, the L&NWR and GWR would only agree to a continuation of the rates currently in force.

The Great Western objected to the introduction of lower rates, as this would force them to compete by reducing their own prices, and so challenged the application made by the E&WJR. They, in turn and under the terms of the Railway Regulation

Act, attempted to compel the GWR to adopt the new route and rates. As the anticipated volume of iron ore traffic was of such fundamental importance to the E&WJR's survival, they felt it imperative to challenge their rival's stance.

The significance of these matters was encapsulated in one statistic that had been quoted during the Parliamentary enquiries into the proposed new loop line of the L&NWR through Northampton, to which the E&WJR had objected. It had been stated therein that, in the future, up to one million tons of iron ore per year would be despatched from the area surrounding Northampton. In fact, this level of output had already been achieved as early as 1872, having almost doubled since 1869 when 540,000 tons were produced. The E&WJR had always calculated that, due to their more favourable route, the majority of this traffic would pass over all of their line to South Wales, instead of the more circuitous route of the L&NWR and GWR alliance. They had estimated that if this level of traffic was achieved, after the deduction of operating expenses at their usual rate, they would have the benefit of a net return of some £43,000 each year – a handsome sum for a small railway.

The E&WJR were also aggrieved that they had earlier agreed to drop a proposal in their original Bill for an extension of their line to the Midland Railway route to Evesham. This was in return for the GWR agreeing to not oppose the overall E&WJR scheme and also to provide onward transport for iron ore traffic to South Wales at reasonable rates. However, the E&WJR had subsequently again indicated their intention to reapply for powers to extend their line westwards, thus alienating the GWR. The result was a long and complex process of arbitration through the Court of the Railway Commissioners, which would not fully conclude until May 1875.

The Railway Commissioners heard depositions from both sides and evidence was presented by no less than Mr Grierson, the general manager of the GWR. The commissioners summarised the situation as follows:

'The material question for us is whether the through rates proposed by the East and West Junction give the Great Western a lower mileage rate than they can reasonably be required to accept. They receive for mileage out of the existing through rates charged on iron ore sent from Blisworth or from Lloyd's Siding near Towcester via Smethwick, a sum which is at the rate of a half penny a ton per mile. That is the yield per mile and the proportion they receive of their agreed through rates with the North Western Company, and the through rates proposed by the East and West Junction, though their gross amount is about 10¹/₂d less than these. North Western through rates would give the Great Western the same rate of a half penny per mile from Stratford: and as the Great Western carry for near equal distances in both cases, the same rate per mile that is remunerative to them in one case must be so in the other, provided the quantities carried do not greatly differ. The North Western rates for iron ore carried from the district of Northamptonshire into South Staffordshire range between .48 and .56 of one penny per ton per mile, with distances by no means as great as those run over the Great Western lines to South Wales. Where a line is opened by which distance and cost are lessened, it seems a reasonable consequence that the rates charged to the public, who are in a position to avail themselves of the shorter route, should be also in some measure reduced. No doubt, as we have said, the quantity carried is an element in the cost of carriage, and equally with distance affects the rate at which the work can profitably be done.

While therefore we grant the rates proposed by the East and West Junction Company, we are of opinion that they should only take effect when there is a traffic of 500 tons per week: and supposing the rates received and the quantity forwarded at the end of a year to fall short of that amount, we think that the East and West Junction should pay to the Great Western Company the difference between their receipts at the new rates and what they would have received at the existing rates, or at the rates of any less amount which may be charged on the other route.'

However, that was not to be the end of the matter and a further dispute followed. The two companies could now have no disagreement over the rates for carriage of the ore but as the cost of carriage was also apportioned according to the mileage travelled on each system, the GWR were understandably keen to receive the traffic from the E&WJR at the more easterly of the two junctions between the two companies at Fenny Compton, rather than that at Stratford.

The inevitable result was a further arbitration by the Railway Commissioners in 1874. The Commissioners pronounced that they would not allow the Stratford route to the exclusion of Fenny Compton, although they did consider that the route from the latter was the more natural one; the E&WJR in turn proposed a compromise of using a combination of both routes. However, the Commissioners did allow a mileage proportion to the E&WJR by both routes and also decreed that, in the case of the route that gave least mileage to the E&WJR, they would reallocate a certain number of miles out of the GWR route to them. Judgment was postponed for a period of ten days to allow the two companies to negotiate.

The Commissioner's eventual recommendation was, however, 'that both routes should be made available for through rates and that the through rates should be so apportioned as to put the two routes on a par as far as the two companies were concerned, leaving the public and the owners of the minerals free to consign their traffic by whichever route they preferred'.

Unfortunately, all of this had coincided with the start of a major depression in the iron trade, with the result that overall demand was significantly reduced; this was not good news for the E&WJR.

Receivership

The E&WJR received another unwelcome setback on Saturday 21st March 1874, when the station building at Fenny Compton was destroyed by fire. The stationmaster left for home in the nearby village just after 9.30pm but around 2.00am on the Sunday morning a GWR policeman discovered the interior of the building to be on fire. He ran to the village to raise the alarm but, by the time that he returned with help, the roof had collapsed and only the walls remained standing. Fortunately, all was insured with the Pheonix Fire Assurance Company but parcels stored in the office and railway paperwork were all destroyed.

Efforts were still being made to attract additional traffic to the line and to take advantage of the connections afforded to other parts of the country by adjacent railway companies. A

typical example was an excursion announced by the E&WJR for Whit Monday 25th May 1874. Cheap fares were offered from Northampton, Blisworth, Towcester and all E&WJR stations, to Stratford-upon-Avon and onwards to Evesham, Worcester and Malvern. The special train left Blisworth at 7.40am, whilst departure times for the return journey were from Malvern Link at 6.30pm, Worcester Shrub Hill 7.00pm, Evesham 7.30pm and Stratford at 8.15pm.

The financial situation of the E&WJR still being difficult, the year of 1874 brought another proposal for an Act to 'keep open the railway, to work it to better advantage, and to pay their debts and liabilities'. Although the Act was passed and the issue of new debentures up to £100,000 was authorised, unfortunately the money could not be raised. Nevertheless, a timetable of 9th

January 1875 still revealed a seemingly healthy service of five Down trains each weekday from Blisworth to Stratford, with an additional service in the Up direction; no trains were run on Sundays.

However, as will be seen, this situation was not to last and with the straitened financial circumstances continuing, a suit by a First Mortgage Debenture holder resulted in the appointment by the Court of Chancery of Major Alexander George Dickson MP as receiver on 29th January 1875. Henry Merrick, a relative of the E&WJR solicitor, was installed as general manager. Charles Banks, who had been with the company since 1864, continued in his role as secretary and was supported by Joseph Francis Burke, who had replaced his own brother James as traffic manager after his death in the previous year. Burke aptly summarised one of the

ABOVE: Pictured just after leaving Stratford-upon-Avon around 1893, E&WJR Beyer, Peacock 0-6-0 No. 4 heads east with a short train of elderly 4-wheeled stock bound for Blisworth. The journey would take an hour and a quarter with seven intermediate stops. *Author's collection*

LEFT: E&WJR Beyer, Peacock 2-4-0 No. 5 awaits departure from Stratford with an Up service. The tank engine carries no corporate identification, with just a painted number on the bunker side. The livery appears to be black with broad reportedly green lining on the tank and bunker side, and with much polished brightwork also on display. *Author's collection*

major problems encountered by the now floundering E&WJR company, when he stated that since opening 'the line had not carried an ounce of through traffic'.

Vice chancellor Malins, in conducting the court proceedings, observed that 'the only result of obtaining a receiver would be that it was found that there was nothing to receive' and that he 'could not help thinking that if these gentlemen who had lost their money would endeavour to assist in improving the works, the concern might still be made to yield a profit'.

Further problems soon ensued. On 6th February 1875, the E&WJR's Beyer, Peacock locomotives and other rolling stock was seized by the Sheriff's officer at the behest of the 'Birmingham Waggon Company', who had provided the finance for their purchase. This led to an immediate suspension of services and

an attempt was made by the E&WJR to mitigate any adverse publicity. They issued a statement via telegram to various agencies, stating that the sudden lack of trains was due to the company returning rolling stock that was previously on hire and thus needing to obtain replacements, rather than being due to any seizure of their assets or financial crisis.

The *Birmingham Daily Post* then carried a report on Saturday 13th February to the effect that services were to resume on the following Monday, with the necessary rolling stock having been secured, one report suggesting that the L&NWR may be about to step into the breach. However, another two weeks were to elapse before a further *communiqué* was issued, stating that services had been resumed on Monday 1st March, with two trains in each direction. Whether this was with their own locomotives and rolling stock is not clear but five days later, the *Northampton Mercury* advised that 'arrangement has been made for the L&NWR to supply sufficient engines for the line by which greater regularity in arrival and departure will be endured'. It is also recorded that the E&WJR did approach the Northampton & Banbury Junction company for the temporary loan of a locomotive but they were unable to assist; at the

ABOVE: Looking eastwards from the end of the Up platform at Fenny Compton station, showing the crossover road leading to the E&WJR goods yard on the Down side. The GWR cattle dock and coal staithes are visible to the left of the picture, behind the E&WJR Up platform, and beyond is the Banbury to Leamington main line. The point just visible beyond the Up Starter signal was for the exchange siding connection between the two railways, hidden behind the fences. It was only sufficient to allow the handling of a few wagons at a time, greatly restricting the exchange of traffic, although in truth this was never extensive anyway. Smoke drifts across the E&WJR line heading away to Banbury, from fires set by the local permanent way gang burning off some of the vegetation on the side of the bank. *Author's collection*

RIGHT: A view eastwards from the Southam to Banbury main road bridge, illustrating how the E&WJR line from Byfield ran parallel to the GWR's Banbury to Leamington main line on its eastern approach to Fenny Compton. The single line of the E&WJR had just crossed over the GWR line and the adjacent Oxford Canal in the far distance, then turned westwards to gradually descend down to the station. *Author's collection*

A 1930s view eastwards from between the rails through a neatly kept Kineton station, with Crampton's siding just visible beyond the road bridge, after which the line ascends a noticeable gradient towards Fenny Compton. Here both platforms feature a raised section to ease the loading of heavier items. One of the familiar diamond shaped weight restriction signs juts up alongside the right-hand bridge parapet. *Author's collection*

Beyer, Peacock 2-4-0T No. 5 or 6 taking water whilst awaiting departure from Stratford with an unusually lengthy Up working to Blisworth circa 1900. The train comprises the majority of the company's smart 6-wheeled coaching stock, flanked by a brake vehicle at each end. The locomotive is in original condition, with 'E&W' ownership plates on the tank sides and an indecipherable number on the bunker together with the builder's works plate. *Author's collection*

E&WJR No. 5 pictured just west of Stratford-on-Avon station in 1902. The locomotive bears the corporate identity and running number on cast plates on the tank and bunker sides respectively, and the number is also carried on the bufferbeam in raised and polished numerals. A re-railing jack is usefully positioned on the front footplate to deal with the seemingly inevitable *contretemps* on the lightly laid track of the period. *Author's collection*

time, the N&BJR were in fact about to begin hiring engines from the L&NWR themselves.

Presumably this was a temporary situation, as over the next few months the E&WJR is known to have obtained the use of a varied assortment of motive power, including two elderly French engines and a distinctive Fairlie's patent 0-6-6-0.

A column in the *Ipswich Journal* of 23rd November 1875 rather aptly summarises everyday events on the E&WJR at this time. Under the heading '*Rambles to famous places XI – Stratford-upon-Avon*', the report states that '*on leaving Kineton station we jog slowly, stopping continually for our engine is much in need of repairs, though that seems to trouble our companions little, as they tell us that is only their everyday experience*'.

Inevitably, the everyday E&WJR travelling public were not exactly enamoured of the unreliability of the services and one '*Inconvenienced of Kineton*' was moved to write to the editor of the *Leamington Spa Courier* on 3rd April 1875:

'*Sir, Few persons have cultivated the useful accomplishment of 'how not to do it' more effectively than the Chief Manager of the East & West Junction Railway.*

In what we thought were its palmiest days, when four trains ran in either way every day, they were so admirably timed that about one was of much use to local passengers who might be going to

Leamington or west of Didcot … the first train up from Stratford is timed to be at Fenny Compton about half an hour after the GWR has left it for Leamington. An ordinary manager would have arranged for their train to have left Stratford half an hour earlier, and waited to take passengers forward to Blisworth.

The second train is a goods leaving at 11.30, and the third leaves at 5.30 bringing the Kineton letter bag, three minutes before the outgoing mail leaves. We cannot get to Leamington via Stratford till 2.30, and the wretched want of punctuality has shaken the confidence of everyone, that few would care to risk it.'

An E&WJR timetable, showing only departure times and published in the same newspaper on 17th April, reflects the correspondent's comments. The first train from Stratford was at 9.15am, with the second at 11.30am. In view of the reference in the above letter to this being a '*goods*' it seems possible that this service may in fact have been a mixed train. The third and final train of the day left Stratford at 5.30pm.

Curiously, however, this and other timetables of the period depict the services as being operated in two sections, from Stratford to Fenny Compton and then onwards from Fenny Compton to Blisworth, with the same arrangement applying to services in the opposite direction. As an example, trains from Blisworth to Fenny Compton departed at 11.30am, 5.00pm and 8.00pm, with onward services for Stratford then leaving Fenny Compton at 12.40pm, 7.25pm and 9.10pm. It is possible that this was so arranged to offer the best connection options to and from GWR main line services at Fenny Compton; E&WJR trains did in fact operate as through services between Blisworth and Stratford, albeit with a layover at Fenny Compton.

On the financial front, the problems continued to mount, typified by the E&WJR being summoned before Banbury magistrates on 26th March for failing to pay a 'poor rate' at Claydon; a letter was read from the company secretary stating that they were unable to pay owing to their being in Chancery, with a receiver having been appointed to handle their affairs.

More Proposals – and a Way Forward?

Vice-chancellor Malin's earlier comments in fact set the pattern for the next few years, with the continually troubled E&WJR repeatedly trying to cajole their shareholders into providing more funds and to forego their dividends or interest payments. A communication of August 1875, sent to influential shareholders, reiterated that the current financial problems had arisen from the combined hostile behaviour of the GWR and L&NWR companies, the former in violation of an earlier agreement, and also the unprecedented stagnation of the iron trade, all of which 'could not fairly have been anticipated'. The continued opposition of the larger companies was thought to be inevitable and insurmountable, and the future prospects of the E&WJR therefore rested on their ability to enable the construction and operation of extensions to their own line in order to generate further through traffic. These objectives, it was thought, would be best met by a connection in the west with the Midland Railway branch from Redditch to Evesham, which would provide a friendly route towards Gloucester, Bristol and South Wales. In the east, another connection to the Midland Railway, on their Northampton to Bedford Branch, would similarly give access to potential traffic from the London area, and a combination of the two extensions would also enable the Midland to route their own Bristol traffic away from their

East & West Junction Railway Company.

HALF-YEARLY GENERAL MEETING OF SHAREHOLDERS.

3, WESTMINSTER CHAMBERS,

VICTORIA STREET, WESTMINSTER, S.W.,

ADJOURNED TO 15th NOVEMBER, 1876.

REPORT OF THE DIRECTORS.

The Accounts for the past Half-year, which ended on the 30th June last, audited and certified, are appended hereto. The gross receipts and earnings for the 6 months on Revenue Account amounted to £4,620, as against £3,181 in the corresponding period of the preceding year, and as against £4,490 for the half-year, which ended 31st December, 1875. The payments and expenditure attributed to Revenue Account amounted to £6,178 (or £1,558 more than earnings) as against £5,206 for the corresponding period of the preceding year, and £6,238 for the half-year which ended on the 31st December, 1875. It will thus be seen that there has been an increase of £130 only in the earnings over the last half-year.

The earnings have been taken by the Receiver appointed on behalf of the 1st Debenture Stockholders by the Court of Chancery, and the working expenses paid, as far as possible, by him.

Since the date of the last Report no improvement has taken place in the state of the Iron Trade; on the contrary, things have been getting worse, and to such an extent, that it is considered by many doubtful whether the South Wales Iron Trade will ever recover, consequently the Iron Ore traffic on this line, which it was expected by this time would have increased to a large extent, has not done so, £2,384 only having been earned during the past 6 months as against £2,103 for the half-year ended 31st December, 1875, and £1,274 for the half-year ended 30th June, 1875.

Having regard to these and other difficulties attendant on the working of the line, (particularly the practical impossibility owing to the large Companies, of obtaining the general through traffic which ought properly to pass over this line), which render it a matter of great difficulty to keep it going, the importance of extensions of this Company's system, so as to bring them into direct communication with other outlets and sources of traffic, dwelt upon in previous reports, cannot be over-rated.

The Directors of the Evesham, Redditch and Stratford-upon-Avon Junction Railway (which is to be worked by this Company as a part of their system) in their Report recently published, state that the whole of the then unissued Share Capital of that Company had been taken up, and that their Company had entered into arrangements for securing the completion of the railway and works (with a single line of permanent way as originally contemplated) fit for opening to the satisfaction of the Board of Trade by the 1st August, 1878, and within the time limited by that Company's Special Act.

The mid 1870s were troubled times for the EWJR. The extracts, above and above right, from a report by the directors in late 1876, after the company had fallen into receivership, bemoaned the difficulties caused by the attitudes of the 'larger companies' and the continuing problems with the iron trade but looked forward to the opening of the Evesham, Redditch & Stratford Junction Railway's route to Broom Junction. However, within a year, passenger traffic would be suspended on the E&WJR line and a new low point reached. *Author's collection*

circuitous route via Wigston and Birmingham. The way forward therefore seemed clear.

In addition to these proposals, the end of the previous year had also brought forth an echo of earlier N&BJR schemes, with a

REPORT OF THE DIRECTORS.

The Accounts for the past Half-year, which ended on the 30th June last, audited and certified, are appended hereto. The gross receipts and earnings for the 6 months on Revenue Account amounted to £4,620, as against £3,181 in the corresponding period of the preceding year, and as against £4,490 for the half-year, which ended 31st December, 1875. The payments and expenditure attributed to Revenue Account amounted to £6,178 (or £1,558 more than earnings) as against £5,206 for the corresponding period of the preceding year, and £6,238 for the half-year which ended on the 31st December, 1875. It will thus be seen that there has been an increase of £130 only in the earnings over the last half-year.

The earnings have been taken by the Receiver appointed on behalf of the 1st Debenture Stockholders by the Court of Chancery, and the working expenses paid, as far as possible, by him.

Since the date of the last Report no improvement has taken place in the state of the Iron Trade; on the contrary, things have been getting worse, and to such an extent, that it is considered by many doubtful whether the South Wales Iron Trade will ever recover, consequently the Iron Ore traffic on this line, which it was expected by this time would have increased to a large extent, has not done so, £2,384 only having been earned during the past 6 months as against £2,103 for the half-year ended 31st December, 1875, and £1,274 for the half-year ended 30th June, 1875.

Having regard to these and other difficulties attendant on the working of the line, (particularly the practical impossibility owing to the large Companies, of obtaining the general through traffic which ought properly to pass over this line), which render it a matter of great difficulty to keep it going, the importance of extensions of this Company's system, so as to bring them into direct communication with other outlets and sources of traffic, dwelt upon in previous reports, cannot be over-rated.

The Directors of the Evesham, Redditch and Stratford-upon-Avon Junction Railway (which is to be worked by this Company as a part of its system) in their Report recently published, state that the whole of the then unissued Share Capital of that Company had been taken up, and that their Company had entered into arrangements for securing the completion of the railway and works (with a *single line of* permanent way as originally contemplated) fit for opening to the satisfaction of the Board of Trade by the 1st August, 1878, and within the time limited by that Company's Special Act.

The Directors of this Company look forward with some degree of expectation to the opening of the above line, which, although having such an important bearing on the future of this undertaking and on the individual interests of the proprietors, has not been supported by them as might have been expected, it appearing that but for the extraneous support which the new line obtained on its own merits there would have been no chance of carrying it through—the support actually rendered by the general body of proprietors of this undertaking being insignificant.

plan by the E&WJR to construct a new branch from the N&BJR line near Blisworth station, across the L&NWR main line to a junction with that company's branch to Northampton. A special general meeting of the E&WJR Board was held in February 1875, with Thomas Hillas Crampton in the chair, for the purpose of approving a submission to Parliament for this scheme. The board approved the proposal, noting that the extension to Northampton would almost double the potential volume of ironstone traffic carried by the E&WJR. Support was also forthcoming from the Northampton Chamber of Commerce, where local Member of Parliament Pickering Phipps championed the cause.

The *Northampton Mercury* also reported in June 1875 that the new proposal was '*now before the House, and in three weeks will be before the Committee*'. This new link, of '*only three furlongs and a few chains*' was to cost '*only £20,000*' and apparently the only objectors to the proposal were the L&NWR, who feared for their own mineral traffic, the GWR who '*always opposed the E&WJR, and always would*' and the N&BJR, who were described as being '*tools of the L&NWR*'.

The month of June did see the Bill before the House Select Committee and amongst those giving evidence was John Hickman, who claimed to be one of the first to send iron ore from Northamptonshire, back in 1852. He stated that he had generally found the trade to be unsuccessful due to the length of time taken to reach the ironworks, which sometimes extended to as much as nineteen days from despatch from his quarries. He had given up that traffic in 1857 but opined that he would be glad to resume it if a more direct route from the Northampton area could be provided and so was greatly in favour of the new E&WJR proposal. Similarly, Edward Siemen, a farmer of Fenny Compton, regularly sent cattle by rail to Northampton market. He was also unhappy with the delays in transit, particularly due to the connection required at Blisworth and often preferred to walk his beasts to market by road, rather than despatch them by rail. The case for the new stretch of line seemed sound but the Select Committee found that the preamble had not been proved and the Bill was lost.

In the meantime, the passenger timetable had been given a few modifications, with an extra through train in each direction being introduced in the middle of the day. In addition, there was a rather unusual extra working leaving Stratford at 8.30am and travelling only as far as Fenny Compton; this train then appears to have waited there, being overtaken at 9.38am by the next through service from Stratford but then continued its journey on to Blisworth at 10.25am. There was, however, no corresponding return service, apart from a train at 3.19pm from Byfield to Stratford.

The E&WJR was then badly affected by serious flooding across the Midlands during the weekend of 9th and 10th October 1875. The last train from Blisworth at 7.00pm on the Saturday evening, had to cautiously pick its way through up to eighteen inches of water in places and, on the following morning, it was found that over three quarters of a mile of track had been washed away between Green's Norton and Blakesley, where the line ran close to the River Tove. Ballast was scattered up to fifty yards across the adjoining fields, leaving track suspended and disrupting services for several days.

As if this was not enough for the beleaguered E&WJR, they were shortly to be embroiled in a spat with their neighbours the N&BJR, over the use of their recently acquired 'Fairlie' locomotive which, it was claimed, fouled the platform edges at Blisworth and Towcester. The E&WJR were forced to again take their case to the Court of the Railway Commissioners early in 1876, and were no doubt relieved when judgment was made in their favour and they were allowed to continue using the locomotive over the

N&BJR, with just certain restrictions in the sidings at Blisworth.

The passenger timetable had also of necessity been revised and a local advertisement of 11th November 1876 revealed a paltry daily service of just two trains in each direction. Departures from Stratford were at 8.35am and 4.45pm, and from Blisworth at 11.30am and 7.00pm.

As usual, further problems were never very far away and more severe weather during the first few days of 1877 caused the line to again be swept away near Towcester, with serious flooding also affecting Fenny Compton, all resulting in a temporary suspension of services. This, however, would shortly become permanent for entirely different reasons.

ABOVE: The original locomotive shed at Stratford-upon-Avon was a decidedly cramped and ramshackle affair, as can be seen from this early view featuring three of the Beyer, Peacock 0-6-0s. Note the ash-ballasted track which, together with the rather primitive coaling arrangements on the right and the rather strange gabled end to the wooden running shed, all contributed to an air of pleasant antiquity. *Author's collection*

LEFT: The interior of the shed was just as fascinating as the exterior and it is apparent that quite significant engineering tasks were undertaken here, despite the somewhat primitive appearance of the equipment and a lack of working space. A small and impecunious railway company such as the E&WJR needed to carry out as much maintenance as possible 'in house' and usually only major jobs were sent out to contractors. *Author's collection*

Passengers No More

Passenger services somehow struggled on into 1877, with a timetable of 21st January still giving times from Blisworth to Fenny Compton and then separately onwards to Stratford. A passenger train was derailed at Kineton on 3rd February and the usual routine enquiry by the Board of Trade was then soon followed by another visit, reported by the *Leamington Spa Courier* of Saturday 26th May 1877. Officials had carried out a full inspection of the E&WJR route from Green's Norton to Stratford, concluded that the line was '*unsafe for rapid travelling*' and had imposed a maximum speed of 15mph. The *Courier* drily added that the Board's intervention was '*a work of supererogation, for we verily believe that that speed had never been exceeded, if ever it had been attained*'.

A timetable of 7th July published in the local press revealed changes to the departure of passenger trains to accommodate the longer journey times. The 11.45am from Blisworth was unchanged but the afternoon train was retimed from 5.40pm to 6.05pm; in the opposite direction, the old 8.35am and 3.30pm departures from Stratford became 7.55am and 2.53pm. In all cases, the overall journey time was extended from 1 hour 50 minutes to around 2 hours and 40 minutes.

Undoubtedly, the permanent way was in a poor state of repair and the situation cannot have been assisted by the recent severe flooding on certain parts of the line. Patronage was reported as being very low, with many trains carrying less than half a dozen passengers and even their confidence in the line had rapidly dwindled after certain occasions when they had even been '*called upon to assist the propulsion of the train to get it to journeys end*'.

Somewhat inevitably, as the end of July approached, the directors announced that '*on and after Monday last 23rd inst. all passenger traffic is suspended*', with the result that a large number of employees were '*thrown out of work*'. Although the fact that passenger receipts had, for some time, been insufficient to cover the running expenses has often been cited as the cause of the suspension, it nevertheless appears that the poor condition of the track was the main reason. Goods traffic was stated to be '*tolerably respectable in the amount*' and being unaffected by the Board of Trade ruling, was continued. An increase in mineral traffic had to some extent obscured a fall in passenger receipts since 1874 but, overall, the finances of the E&WJR were still stretched, with operating costs still averaging one and a half times the annual revenue.

A report from the directors accompanied by a statement of accounts following the half yearly general meeting of shareholders on 15th November 1876, confirmed this situation and makes interesting reading. The directors again stated that no improvement had taken place in the iron trade generally and it was considered doubtful whether the South Wales iron ore traffic would ever recover. In fact, it was now becoming apparent that an increasing amount of the ore used in South Wales was being imported from Spain. This was due to the wider adoption of the Bessemer process of steel manufacturing, for which Northamptonshire ore was far less suitable. Even the passage of the Spanish Civil War did not greatly affect the downward trend in demand but the railway company still clung to the hope that the local ores, which had once promised so much, would eventually again prove useful in South Wales.

The directors further reported difficulty in obtaining other through traffic, owing to the attitude of the '*larger companies*' and that the importance of extensions to the E&WJR system could not be overrated.

Following the suspension of passenger services, a further circular was sent out by a then reconstructed board, again explaining the current position of the company. This once again reiterated the difficulties being experienced with the opposition of the GWR and L&NWR but added that the directors still foresaw a situation where, with the aid of extensions, the line could prosper. This was particularly supported by a recent '*friendly agreement*' reached with the Midland Railway, who would use the route for their through traffic.

The directors were not, however, of the opinion that they could continue to operate without further financial assistance but that a relatively small sum was all that would be needed to ensure immediate stability. They therefore resolved to make a last appeal which, if unsuccessful, would result in the line being closed and probably abandoned. Shareholders were asked to complete a form which would indicate their agreement and to return it by 29th December 1877. It appears that the appeal fell mainly on deaf ears and was largely unsuccessful but the company was at least favoured with sufficient contributions to enable a less expansive alternative scheme, which, with some difficulty, would keep the line open for a further period of time.

Another consequence of the dire situation on the line was a notice of the sale of '*superfluous lands of the East & West Junction Railway*' by George Clark & Son of Tower Street, London

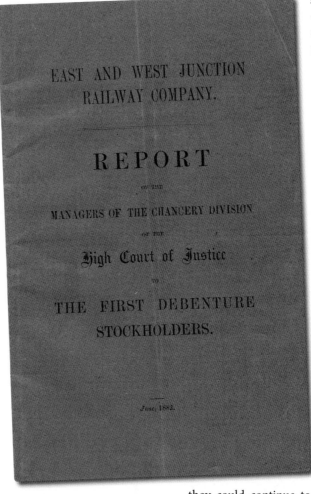

EAST AND WEST JUNCTION RAILWAY COMPANY.

REPORT

OF THE

MANAGERS OF THE CHANCERY DIVISION

OF THE

High Court of Justice

TO

THE FIRST DEBENTURE STOCKHOLDERS.

June, 1882.

The E&WJR stumbled into the early 1880s managed by a committee installed by the official receiver and a report to the shareholders of the company was issued in June 1882. This called on the recipients to give up the interest and arrears on their holdings for the next five years, to enable the E&WJR to merely continue operations. Such appeals were a constant feature over the next few years and were generally unsuccessful, although enough funds were raised to just keep the railway going. *Author's collection*

31

CIRCULAR LETTER

(ACCOMPANYING THE FOREGOING REPORT).

EMBODYING THE PROPOSED SCHEME,

AND

ASSENT THERETO FOR SIGNATURE BY FIRST DEBENTURE STOCKHOLDERS.

EAST AND WEST JUNCTION RAILWAY,

Office of the Managers and Receiver of the Chancery Division of the High Court of Justice,

PALACE CHAMBERS, BRIDGE STREET,

WESTMINSTER, S.W.,

June, 1882.

DEAR SIR,

I forward to you as a holder of First Debenture Stock, by book post, a pamphlet containing the Report which has been prepared by my colleagues and myself, as the Managers administering the affairs of the Company, appointed by the Court.

When a Company carrying on a commercial enterprise, under the Limited Liability Acts, becomes unable to discharge its obligations, the natural and general result is for it to be wound up, and its debts liquidated by the eventual distribution of such a Dividend amongst the Creditors as the realisation of the property and assets of the Company will allow, but, as shown in the Report, such a course is not applicable in the case of a Railway Company, and the complications in the present case are such that, as matters stand, the First Debenture Stockholders must personally agree to some method for improving the value of their

holdings, and preventing them from continuing, as at present, unsaleable and practically worthless.

After careful consideration of the case in all its bearings and matured deliberation, we have arrived at the conclusion that—as the only feasible means of dealing with the exigencies of the case—First Debenture Stockholders should agree to give up to the Managers the Interest on their Holdings (including arrears) down to the 1st January, 1887; such interest to be dealt with by the Managers in such way as they consider most desirable for or towards the discharge of the Company's liabilities, and the obligations entailed by the working of the line, the development of the undertaking, and such further purposes as they may consider beneficial for the furtherance of the First Debenture Stockholders' interests generally, and in consideration of First Debenture Stockholders to an amount which we consider sufficient assenting to this, we are willing, during our period of office, to undertake the administration of the fund entrusted to us.

If this proposition be given effect to, we believe the maximum benefit may be secured for the First Debenture Stockholders. On the other hand, should it not be adopted, or should not some more effectual measure involving greater assistance be substituted for it, then having regard to the conflicting interests of the various parties interested, and the other special difficulties of the case dealt with in our report, we consider that it will be impracticable to continue the working of the line in the interests of the First Debenture Stockholders.

It rests with the First Debenture Stockholders themselves by assenting, or not assenting, to decide the result. We can only urge you in your own interest to support the proposition, and to return us the enclosed post-card, signed by you, by an early post.

I am, dear Sir,

Yours faithfully,

A. G. DICKSON,

Manager and Receiver.

EC1. The auction, held at Towcester on 25th September 1877, consisted of twelve lots of '*freehold meadow land all having frontages onto the railway at Old Stratford, Upper Eatington, Butlers Marston, Farnborough, Aston-le-Walls, Moreton Pinkney, Blakesley, Braddon, and Green's Norton*.'

From this point onwards, the evolution of the E&WJR entered a very complicated and fragmented period. Despite their precarious existence, the company somehow managed to involve themselves in the promotion of the vitally necessary extensions at either end of their own main route. Initial proposals for these two extensions had, in fact, first emerged many years before the lines were finally constructed. The western extension to Broom had first been promoted in 1873, when the E&WJR had only just opened as a through route. Similarly, the line eastwards from Towcester to Ravenstone Wood was first conceived in late 1878 but construction would not commence for another decade.

The opening of these two additions to the E&WJR empire would then allow the formation of a Joint Committee to operate the resulting three lines as one. Even then, however, progress towards this seemingly logical goal was to be slow and fraught with difficulties.

An Extension to the West – the Evesham, Redditch & Stratford-upon-Avon Junction Line

The Evesham, Redditch & Stratford-upon-Avon Junction Railway (ER&SJR) line, effectively a western continuation of the existing E&WJR route, had first been proposed as far back as 1873, by '*the proprietors and other persons interested in the E&WJR*', partly as a replacement for an abandoned scheme for a London, Worcester & South Wales Railway. The prospectus for the new company spoke of the new line being '*physically an extension of the E&WJR and in conjunction with that line giving direct through routes for traffic between the Eastern district, the Midland Counties, West of England, and South Wales …*'. The line was to be '*worked by the E&WJR as part of their system, and with rebates granted by that company and also by the Evesham & Redditch company guaranteeing dividends*'. The new line also offered an advantage of 47 miles over the GWR route between Stratford and Bristol, and a significant reduction in mileage

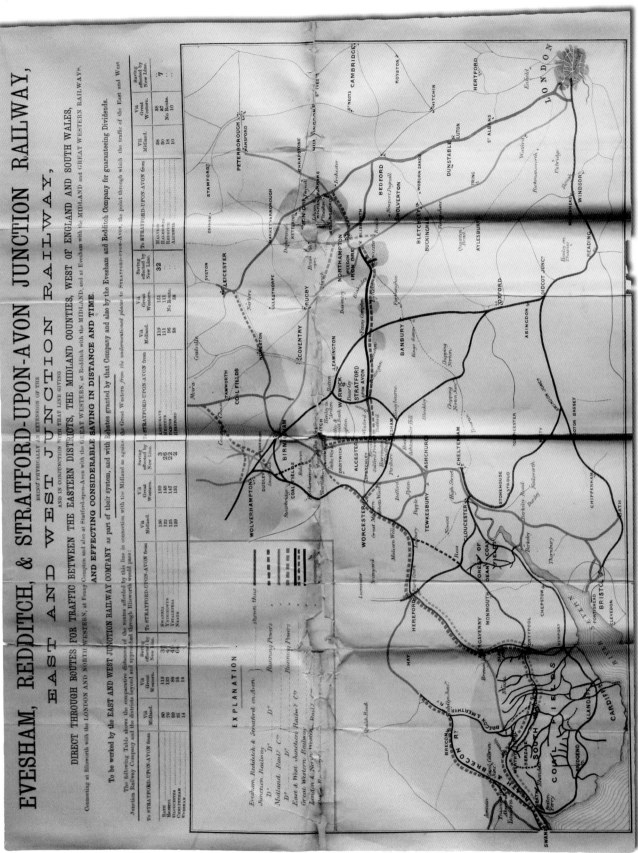

This prospectus map for the Evesham, Redditch & Stratford-upon-Avon Junction Railway is a fragile and rare survival, with any documentation from that company proving extremely difficult to find. The map shows the new line as an extension of the existing E&WJR route, together with running powers to Redditch and Evesham. The accompanying text confirms that the line was to be worked by the East & West Junction Railway, with 'rebates granted by that company and the Evesham & Redditch for guaranteeing dividends'.

This panorama from the western end of the Up platform at Stratford shows the Evesham, Redditch & Stratford Junction Railway's line to Broom Junction climbing to cross the GWR in the left background of the picture, between the signal post and the water column. The connection to the GWR line at E&W Junction runs off to the right behind the signal box, whilst the access lines to the engine shed can be seen just behind the Down platform end. The rather basic locomotive coaling stage was located adjacent to the Broom line. *Author's collection*

The ER&SJR line continued from the western end of the original E&WJR route at Stratford-on-Avon and immediately climbed to bridge the GWR's Stratford to Honeybourne line, a few chains south of the physical meeting point of the two railways at E&W Junction. This 1950s view is looking west up to and over the bridge, towards Broom Junction. *Author's collection*

to South Wales. Ystalyfera Ironworks was stated as being just 125 miles away by the new line and the Midland Railway, whereas the existing GWR route was 22 miles longer.

One of the main promoters was Samuel Lloyd, who leased iron bearing land at Easton Neston from Sir Thomas Hesketh and had also purchased 49 acres of similar land at Byfield in March 1873. Also involved were John Nuthall Brown, a Birmingham merchant and manager of the Cannock Chase Coal Company and a director of the Cannock & Wolverhampton Railway Company, William Dundas Gardner, a London barrister, and William Morris, a solicitor whose clients included the E&WJR. Other interested parties included Messrs Penton, Reid, Richard Rowson, Herbert Barnard, Kenneth Bouverie, H. Emmanuel and G.H. Herbert.

A line of 7³/₄ miles was proposed from Stratford westwards to the Evesham & Redditch Railway in the parish of Salford Priors. The latter route had been opened from Evesham to Alcester in June 1866 and then extended through to Redditch two years later. Connections at Barnt Green, to the north, and Ashchurch, in the south, then provided a loop line duplicating the Midland main line from Birmingham to Bristol. The MR worked the Evesham & Redditch line from opening and would ultimately officially absorb the smaller company in 1882. The promoters of the ER&SJR apparently held the prospect that their own company would also eventually be absorbed by the MR for '*a first class price*' but it seems that this was just a ruse to attract interest and investment, and was without foundation, although it did serve to somewhat sour relations with the Midland.

The ER&SJR Act was duly authorised on 5th August 1873, with powers to issue a share capital of £90,000 and raise borrowings of a further £30,000. An arrangement was also made for the completed line to be operated by the E&WJR for a period of ten years. This agreement allowed for that company to retain a proportion of the receipts from the new extension to assist them in keeping their own line open. Running powers were also granted to the ER&SJR over the route operated by the Midland Railway between Evesham and Redditch.

The share capital was quickly taken up but it was not until 1876 that it would prove possible, with the assistance of various classes of E&WJR shareholders, to make some initial arrangements for the actual construction of the line. The company then applied to the Board of Trade for a Certificate of Deviation of 2 miles 7 furlongs and 8 chains from the original route, between Binton and Old Stratford, so taking the line further to the north. Also included in the application was the deletion of a south facing curve at Broom, which would have formed a triangular junction.

This was a rather surprising omission as, even allowing for the fact that ironstone traffic to South Wales had not reached anticipated levels, the major traffic flow was still expected to be westwards towards Evesham and Bristol, and not northwards to Redditch and beyond.

The land required for the construction of the line was purchased from the owner, the Marquis of Hertford, for a total of £7,844 1s 3d, with options of further areas of land being taken if required, at an additional payment of £225 per acre. The transaction was completed by the Marquis' land agent and the Hon. Robert Henley Eden of Minchinhampton, a director of the ER&SJR.

On 6th April 1877, the *Worcester Herald* reported that Messrs Berkeley & Little [*sic*] of London had commenced construction of the new line on the previous Friday; in fact the name of the main contractor was Liddell & Barkley of Westminster. The actual work was carried out by two sub-contractors – one part of the line was constructed by James Cooper of Summer Hill, Bidford, and the other portion by '*Mr. James of Stratford*' who '*will complete the earthworks beyond Luddington*'. The construction of the bridges was carried out by Messrs Wincote Bros. of Leamington. Liddell employed Douglas Austhwaite Stanley as engineer for the line, whilst William Hayden Gates, who had entered the service of the East & West Junction Railway only a few months earlier, was placed in charge of the drawing office.

After some consideration, it was thought advisable that the ER&SJR should exchange goods and passenger traffic at the actual junction with the Evesham line rather than exercise their running powers to the adjacent stations of Wixford or Salford Priors. Any capital outlay so involved would be much less than the cost of using the Evesham line and better suited the proposed method of operating the passenger services.

The ER&SJR accordingly entered into a contract with the Gloucester Wagon Company in April 1878 for the provision of two signal cabins and associated signalling equipment, and it was also agreed that the necessary turntable and sidings at Broom would be provided by the ER&SJR but located on Midland land. The ER&SJR also purchased a small area of land at the

ABOVE: When it first opened, the only intermediate station on the ER&SJR route to Broom Junction was at Binton, seen here from the east during the early 1950s, although little of substance would have changed since the line was opened. The compact station building and commodious goods shed, located immediately alongside the Stratford road, were both built of local stone and a small goods yard completed the facilities. At one time a small signal cabin stood on the platform, but this was taken out of use in the 1930s. *Author's collection*

LEFT: The roadside elevation of Binton station reveals the solid stone built construction, quite unlike anything on the 'parent' E&WJR system and perhaps more reminiscent of small branch line stations in the Cotswolds. The approach road, which also served the goods yard, ran parallel to the main Stratford to Evesham road, with the village approximately half mile away to the north. *Author's collection*

Redditch end of the site for further sidings. However, the goods wharves and approach road were constructed by the Midland Railway at their own cost; agreements were made as to the use and maintenance of the various goods sidings. The single island platform station at the junction was also constructed by the MR on behalf of the ER&SJR, once again on Midland land.

Construction of the line was straightforward and good progress made. The ER&SJR's solicitors, Merrick & Co., were soon able to indicate to the Board of Trade that the directors considered that their line was almost ready for opening and, on 1st July 1878, gave the required one month's notice to allow the BoT to arrange an inspection. In fact, it was not until 23rd September that Major Hutchinson was appointed to inspect the line, following a second formal notice of opening from the

new company. It appears from correspondence that the Major had already discussed matters during a recent visit to the nearby E&WJR line and, as a result, the inspection was then deferred until 4th October at the request of the ER&SJR.

The subsequent report stated that that the new railway was of 7 miles and 44 chains length, with a steepest gradient of 1 in 60 and that, as usual, sufficient land had been purchased and bridges constructed to allow for the doubling of the line at some future date. Nine overbridges spanned the line and there were also nineteen underline bridges, the largest of which had a 35ft span. In addition, there were eleven large culverts, two of which were reported as needing 'careful watching'. There were no tunnels or crossings of public roads and signalling was carried out from two cabins at Broom Junction, one at Stratford and a

RIGHT & BELOW: A further, albeit rather small, station was added on the ER&SJR route in 1881 at Bidford, adjacent to the existing Wixford Road bridge. In fact the station used the spare second arch of the bridge to house the booking office and other facilities, although these were, to say the least, decidedly spartan. Initially just a single bench was provided for waiting passengers on the basic timber-faced platform, where empty fruit baskets can be seen awaiting return to the nearby growers, right. The boarded up arch must have been rather uncomfortable for both staff and the few waiting passengers but things did get slightly better in later years, with the opening being partly bricked up and additional accommodation provided on the platform by a selection of huts and disused carriage bodies. *Author's collection*

signal frame at Binton station, with engine turntables provided at both ends of the new line at Broom and Stratford.

The new line began from an end-on connection with the existing E&WJR route at Stratford and continued in a westerly direction, immediately rising to cross above the GWR line to Honeybourne. A '*neat looking stone structure containing all of the requisite conveniences*' was provided for passengers at '*Binton Bridges*'. After passing through the line's only major engineering feature at Summerhill Cutting, trains crossed the River Arrow and then used a 5 chain length of Midland Railway metals from the junction to access a simple island platform provided for interchange with Evesham line services.

Major Hutchinson also commented specifically on the layout of the loop at Broom station, where he considered that the reverse curves were not suitable for fast running. However, this seemed unlikley to be a problem, as there was no necessity to

run through trains around the loop. He suggested that, pending any alterations to the layout, ER&SJR trains should terminate in the loop platform and Midland services would use the through line. Modifications were also required to the signalling at Broom and gauge ties were needed on some points, with attention being necessary to the blocks of wood between the girders of the River Arrow bridge.

At Binton, a locking rod needed to be painted white and the signal apparatus covered over, with more gauge ties also being required. The inevitable gauge ties were also found wanting at Stratford, together with attention to the interlocking of several signals, whilst the removal of branches was required from an inconveniently placed tree, to ensure clear sighting of the signals.

The report also commented that '*no arrangements have yet been concluded for the working of the traffic*'; due to the incompleteness of the works and the lack of rolling stock, the line was not yet considered fit for opening to passengers. However the Major did enclose with his report an undertaking from the ER&SJR to work the line using a train staff combined with the absolute block telegraph system.

The Board of Trade therefore issued a statutory order for the postponement of opening for one month. Further delays ensued, resulting in postponement notices being issued in November and December. On 4th December, the ER&SJR reported that, owing to '*differences with their contractor*', certain requirements had still not been met. However, on 20th December the Company were at last able to report that they had complied with all requirements, although they still awaited confirmation from the Midland Railway that certain works at Broom had been completed. The situation dragged on as a result, with further postponements issued in January, February and March, until finally the MR stated that they would shortly be carrying out the required repositioning of signal No. 17. This was completed on 29th March and the line was at last ready for use.

The local press carried an announcement by the E&WJR that the extension to their route would open to goods and passenger traffic on Whit Monday 2nd June. This therefore produced the rather incongruous situation of the E&WJR operating passenger trains on a subsidiary route, whilst its own services were still suspended due to the state of their track. The opening was also

BROOM STATION.

BROOM JCT S.

ABOVE: ER&SJR services ran over a few chains of Midland metals to reach what was originally an exchange platform at Broom but later became a public station named Broom Junction. This view from the adjacent road bridge shows a train bound for Evesham and Ashchurch waiting in the through road of the island platform, behind MR '1798' Class 0-6-0 No. 3460, whilst the E&WJR connecting service for Stratford can just be seen standing in the loop platform alongside. No. 3460 was renumbered from No. 361 in 1907, whilst the interesting cyclecar just glimpsed in the right background would probably date the picture as around 1912. *Neil Parkhouse collection*

LEFT: Broom South Junction signal box was located at the point where the ER&SJR line joined the MR's Redditch to Evesham route. The first cabin was replaced in 1892 by this later design, which itself was then superseded in 1931, together with a box to the north of the station, by a single LM&SR designed signal box in the same position. This was then re-designated Broom North after the opening of the southern connection to the Evesham line in 1942. *The Lens of Sutton Association*

recorded by the *Leamington Spa Courier*:

'*The new line between Stratford and Broom was opened on Monday, having been commenced about two years ago, the contractors being Messrs. Liddell and Barkley of Westminster, who sublet the work in two portions. There is a new and commodious station at Binton Bridges to accommodate Welford and the adjacent villages. The railway will be worked in connection with the train services of the Midland Railway. The opening was unaccompanied by any demonstrations, there being however a large number of spectators at the Stratford station to witness the departure of the first train. Mr. J.F. Burke of Stratford is the Company's engineer and Mr. D. Stanley the contractor's agent.*'

The trains, operated by the E&WJR, ran into the new exchange platform at Broom. This was initially just an unadvertised facility for interchange with Midland Railway trains but, from 1st November 1880, as Broom Junction, it became a public station in its own right. The regular service, calling en route at Binton, consisted of five trains per day in each direction. This was enhanced on the opening day by a special excursion from Birmingham New Street to Stratford.

In order to inaugurate the new service to Broom, additions were required to the sparse selection of E&WJR rolling stock. Somehow, the impecunious company managed to obtain a brand new Beyer, Peacock 0-6-0 saddle tank locomotive and additional

A delightful circa 1908 track level view of Broom Junction station, showing the massive Midland style platform running-in boards, which were erected in pairs and angled slightly to aid sighting from the train. They almost dwarfed the station building here, not to mention the grounded coach body, which looks to be an MR Passenger Brake Van of mid 1870s vintage, which was presumably placed here for use as a parcels office and goods store. No goods shed was ever provided at Broom. The sidings on the right were shared between the Midland and the ER&SJR and used for the interchange of local traffic, although most of the goods services on the Stratford line were through trains that reversed at Broom and continued on to Evesham, Gloucester and the Bristol area. A number of generally well-dressed passengers can be seen waiting on the island platform, possibly for services on both the ER&SJR line, on the far side, and the MR route, on this side. Broom Junction North signal box can just be seen beyond the far end of the platform and note the enamelled advertising signs attached to the fence facing the station, as well as to the buildings themselves. *John Alsop collection*

A general view from the bridge just to the south of Broom Junction station, which carried a minor road between Broom village and the hamlet of Dunnington, with the single line of the ER&SJR veering away towards Bidford, Binton and Stratford on the left, and the Midland route heading south towards Evesham on the right. The turntable provided for ER&SJR line locomotives was particularly necessary for the Beyer, Peacock 2-4-0 tank engines, which were barred from running bunker first on this section of line. The table remained in use until the 1930s, after which engines ran tender first in one direction on the Stratford route. The South Curve, which would have made a direct connection allowing ER&SJR trains to run south but that was deleted from the projected line in 1876, would have run from left to right across the field in the background, just in front of the trees in the distance. It would eventually be built in 1942 during the Second World War, to facilitate the running of iron ore trains to South Wales. On the left, Broom Junction signal box is the cabin opened by the LM&SR on 6th May 1934, probably not long before this picture was taken and which replaced the South and North boxes. It was renamed again in 1942, as Broom North, with the opening of the South Curve. The bridge from which this picture was taken has been flattened since closure of the line, whilst the dual carriageway of the re-routed A46 now runs just to the west of the railway, through the field on the right. *Author's collection*

coaches, although it is recorded that the inaugural train was headed by one of the old French locomotives.

An additional but very basic single platform station was later added at Bidford in 1881, with booking facilities provided within the bricked-up second arch of the adjacent road overbridge, which was not required for a line of track. A short distance to the east of the road bridge a connection was also provided into the siding of the Canada Brickworks Company. This had been approved by the Board of Trade on 8th November 1879, the inspecting officer's report indicating that there were no signals at the siding and that the points were worked by a single lever, on a frame unlocked by the single line train staff. A plan accompanying the report shows a simple layout consisting of a single gated siding and headshunt on the Down side of the line, adjacent to the brickworks.

Although the ER&SJR were awarded running powers over the Midland Railway line from Broom to Evesham and Redditch, there is no record of these ever being exercised. However, an intriguing announcement in the *Leamington Spa Courier* of 17th April 1880 did nevertheless state that, in connection with a performance at the Stratford Memorial Theatre on 23rd of that month, the E&WJR would run a special train to Redditch.

The purchase of the Beyer, Peacock saddle tank was followed in 1880 by the arrival of another locomotive from the same company, with 0-6-0 goods engine No. 2 being obtained to augment the rapidly failing French locomotives. However, the new line to Broom was soon to attract unwelcome publicity on two occasions later in the same year.

In November, a local youth from Luddington was detained for throwing stones at a train as it passed under the bridge at that point on the line. Driver Thomas Robson of the E&WJR duly gave evidence on behalf of the railway company at the Local Assizes in February 1881, with the result that the culprit was sentenced to fifteen months imprisonment.

The second occasion, on 18th December 1880, the line made the national headlines, when it was claimed that the notorious 'Solihull Murderer' had been apprehended at Binton station. This proved to be incorrect but the rumour was probably due to the fact that a Birmingham haberdasher, John Hooman, had been detained at the station for obstructing John Darby, a porter. Despite Hooman being something of a lesser catch, the Bench still considered the crime serious enough to warrant a fine of £3 12s 6d.

Then to the East – the Easton Neston Mineral & Towcester, Roade & Olney Junction Railway

The *Buckinghamshire Herald* of 16th November 1878 carried a notice of a proposal to apply to Parliament for powers to construct the Towcester, Roade & Olney Junction Railway. This would connect Towcester with the existing Bedford & Northampton Railway line at Ravenstone Wood, near Olney, and en route serve the brick and ironstone industries that had developed on the Easton Neston Estate. The Bedford & Northampton Railway had been operated from opening in 1872 by the MR and this new line would thus be the final link in an east-west connection between two Midland routes.

The nominal promoter of the new company, with offices at 22 Spring Gardens, Trafalgar Square, London, was William Merrick, already solicitor to the E&WJR, acting together with 'other interested persons'. These comprised local landowner Sir Thomas George Fermor Hesketh, Baronet, who had undertaken to provide one third of the costs of promotion, Frederick Gretton, a partner in the brewing firm of Bass, Ratcliff & Gretton & Co., who would provide another third, and Samuel Lloyd, an ironmaster, who together with sundry other gentlemen from the Birmingham district, were to contribute the final third. William Merrick was not an active partner, although his firm was to act professionally for the new company.

Sir Thomas Hesketh owned a considerable portion of iron ore bearing land, through which the new railway was intended to pass. Samuel Lloyd and his associates had already developed the ore, and Frederick Gretton had also acquired a large interest in the area and had already undertaken works which included a light mineral railway at Easton Neston, some of which was intended to form a part of the new through route. The Easton Estate Mining Company premises consisted of a surface area of approximately twenty five acres, with an estimated mineral bearing resource of over 1,600 acres, and included deposits of ironstone, limestone and other minerals. A substantial ironworks with two rotary furnaces stood nearby, as did productive brickworks which utilised raw material from the local clay beds. The whole of the area was already intersected with some two miles of internal railways and sidings, and was connected to the outside world at Lloyd's Sidings, on the Northampton & Banbury Junction line just to the north of Towcester.

Lord Hesketh was stated to be willing to take payment in shares in return for land required for the railway, whilst the line would be supported by all of the other affected landowners. The Duke of Grafton had withdrawn his initial objections and support was also forthcoming from the Reverend Sir Henry Gunning, with the line running through some five miles of his estate at Horton, which included valuable timber and limestone resources. It was also agreed with him that a convenient station would be provided, adjacent to the nearby Northampton to Newport Pagnell road.

The connection with Bass & Company was also considered to be a great benefit, as they were a major customer of the Midland Railway, who could be influenced to support the scheme, and pass their traffic over the new line and thence the E&WJR.

With their Broom line nearing completion, an extension to the east was now a rather pressing requirement for the E&WJR. As a result, the E&WJR Board proposed to their shareholders that they should thereafter give up certain proportions of their income and shareholdings to help facilitate the development of this new railway.

Plans were deposited on 30th November 1878 for an application to Parliament in the 1879 session to sanction the 10½ mile line. The preamble for the Bill was passed in early May 1879, read for the third time on 15th May, and Acts *42 & 43 Vic.Cap.ccxxiii* were duly obtained on 15th August. Initially, the new company was to be titled the Towcester, Roade & Olney Junction Railway but as an afterthought, the prefix of Easton Neston Mineral was added, as it was considered that mention of the already existing light railway might encourage some local interest in the line and lessen any potential opposition.

The Acts authorised no less than eight separate lines of

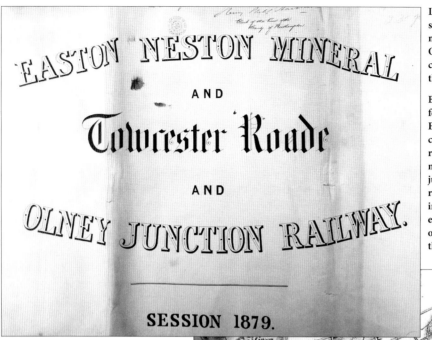

LEFT: The title page of the deposited plans for the 1879 session of Parliament, prepared for the extravagantly named Easton Neston Mineral & Towcester, Roade & Olney Junction Railway. The use of the name of the mineral company was a late addition to encourage local interest in the scheme. *NRO-DP*

BELOW: The original plans for the ENM&TR&OJR featured a new line at Towcester, linking the existing E&WJR line near Green's Norton Junction directly to a complex junction arrangement with both the N&BJR route to Blisworth and the existing Easton Neston Estates mineral railway. The N&BJR line would have been bridged just to the north of Towcester station, with the mineral railway upgraded to main line standards and incorporated into the new line onwards to Ravenstone Wood. In the event, most of these plans were abandoned, leaving just one new line to be constructed eastwards from a point on the N&BJR just to the north of Towcester station. *NRO-DP*

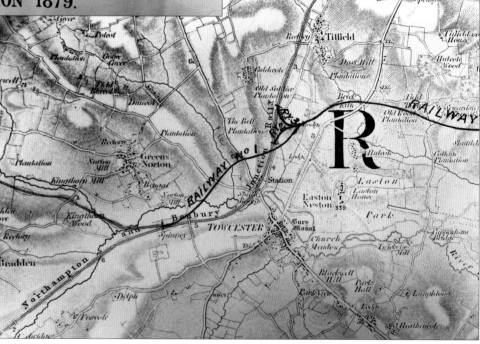

railway, running from Towcester to the Bedford & Northampton Railway at a point three miles west of Olney, with various other connections as follows:

Railway No. 1 – A line of 1mile, 6 furlongs and 9 chains, from a junction with the E&WJR and terminating at or near the private railway of the Easton Estate & Mining Company.

This section would have left the E&WJR route 95 yards west of the Home signal at Green's Norton Junction, before crossing the valley of the River Tove on an embankment. The route then bridged the N&BJR just north of Towcester station and terminated at a junction with the existing private mineral railway of the Easton Neston Estate at a point 865 yards from that line's junction with the N&BJR at Lloyd's Siding.

The line was never constructed and was replaced by a more straightforward connection with the N&BJR just to the north of Towcester station, authorised by an amendment of 1884.

Railway No. 2 – A line of 2 furlongs and 6.5 chains, from a junction with the N&BJR and terminating in a junction with the private railway of the Easton Estate & Mining Company.

This line was purely for the accommodation of the N&BJR should they require to use it and involved a steep climb, so would only have been suitable for mineral traffic. The route was a south to east curve extending from a junction with the N&BJR 600 yards north-east of the platform at Towcester station, to a junction with the private Easton Neston mineral line 550 yards from their junction with the N&BJR at Lloyd's Siding.

Railway No. 3 – A line of 3 furlongs and 8.5 chains from a junction with the N&BJR and terminating at a junction with Railway No. 1

A railway already existed on this site as a mineral line from Lloyd's Siding to the Easton Neston Estate, although the gradients were steep and thus unsuitable for through traffic in its present state. The route was to be upgraded to form a triangular junction with the N&BJR together with line No. 2.

These two sections were never constructed and were effectively replaced by the 1884 line from just north of Towcester station.

Railway No. 4 – A line 3 miles, 5 furlongs and 3.3 chains in length, commencing from a junction with railways No's 1 & 3, and terminating 180 yards eastwards from the point at which the stream that forms the boundary between the parishes of Stoke Bruerne and Roade is carried by a culvert beneath the public road from Stony Stratford through Roade to Northampton.

This line onwards towards Stoke Bruerne incorporated a short stretch of the existing Easton Neston mineral line, east of the proposed triangular junction with the N&BJR, which would also be suitably upgraded for main line use.

Railway No. 5 – A continuation of 6 miles, 1 furlong and 8.4 chains from a junction with railway No. 4 to a termination with the Bedford & Northampton Railway Company.

This section continued from Stoke Bruerne to join the Bedford & Northampton Railway, at a point 11 yards from a distance post on that line indicating $12^{1}/_{2}$ miles from its point of commencement. The resulting junction was initially referred to in various communications as Horton Junction but later became known as Ravenstone Wood Junction.

A passenger station, goods exchange sidings and other facilities at the junction were provided for in the Act but were never constructed, with running powers over the Midland Railway to Olney being substituted instead.

Railway No. 6 – A curve of 3 furlongs and 2.10 chains from a junction with Railway No. 4 to a junction with the L&NWR Company at Roade station.

Initially this line was to just run down to join the outer Down siding of the L&NWR at a point approximately 10 chains short of the Down platform of their station. At the time of the proposal the precise future layout of the L&NWR at Roade had not been determined, with the main

line due to be widened on the eastern side and the station rebuilt accordingly.

A station and exchange facilities at the ENM&TR&OJR end of the curve were proposed but never constructed; in the event, a later agreement was made with the L&NWR to extend the curve into their station to a new bay platform on the Up side. This was constructed but never used by the intended passenger service.

Railway No. 7 – A line of 2 furlongs and 0.9 chains length from a junction with Railway No. 5 to a junction with the Bedford & Northampton Railway.

This would have formed a triangular junction at Ravenstone Wood, running north-west from the new route at a point 470 yards before the junction with the Bedford & Northampton Railway, to join that line 520 yards further on towards Northampton. This was never constructed, having been abandoned by an Act of 1889.

ABOVE & LEFT: The original proposal was for the ENM&TR&OJR line to terminate at Ravenstone Wood, in a triangular junction with the Midland Railway's Bedford to Northampton line, with sufficient land also being purchased there for a station and sidings. However, once again the plans were revised and running powers to Olney station were substituted for the facilities at the junction. Railway No. 7, the northern arm of the junction, was also considered unnecessary and was thus subsequently deleted from the scheme. *NRO-DP*

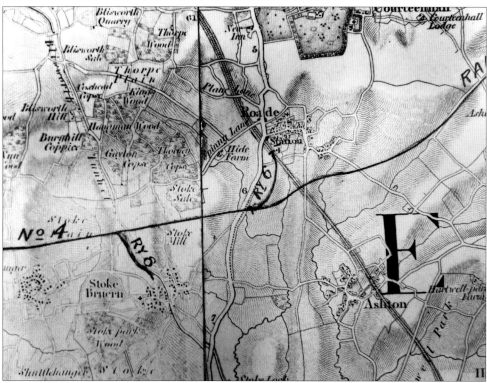

Railway No. 7. This is a fork joining the Midland in a westerly direction in addition to the main line which joins it to the Eastward.

Midland Railway   Station

No. 7

There is no probability of any traffic westwards and it could be exchanged at Station A   if there should be any it could

LEFT: This extract from a Stratford, Towcester & Midland Junction Railway document of 1889 states the reason for the abandonment of the proposed Northampton-facing spur (Railway No. 7) at Ravenstone Wood Junction. It also indicates that provision for a station had been made at the site of the junction. *Author's collection*

BELOW: A few miles further east, the ENM&TR&OJR would have thrown off a short branch down to the Grand Junction Canal at Stoke Bruerne Wharf (Railway No. 8) but this proposal was also later abandoned. However, the curve down to the L&NWR goods sidings at Roade was built, although on a slightly revised alignment and with a further extension into the L&NWR station, where a bay platform had been constructed for a proposed passenger service between Towcester and Roade. *NRO-DP*

Railway No. 8 – A branch of 3 furlongs and 5.10 chains from a junction with Railway No. 4 to terminate near the Grand Junction Canal to the south-eastwards of the southern end of Blisworth Tunnel.

This steep and sharply curved short line would have left the main route at a point 280 yards north of Stoke Plain farmhouse and then plunged southwards down a 1 in 40 gradient to a wharf on the bank of the Grand Junction Canal, 375 yards from the southern portal of its tunnel at Stoke Bruerne.

This line was also never constructed, being abandoned by the Act of 1889, by which time it was considered superfluous, with terms also being difficult to agree with the canal company.

Running powers were provided over the Bedford & Northampton line to both of these county towns, over the N&BJR from the junction of Railway No. 3 to the E&WJR and over the E&WJR itself.

The Bill had come before Parliament during the first few days of May and was passed by the Select Committee despite initial opposition from both the neighbouring N&BJR and L&NWR. The L&NWR were persuaded to withdraw their objection and the opposition of the N&BJR was disposed of by the abandonment of one of the proposed lines, Railway No. 1. This spur had been of considerable importance to the N&BJR but they eventually relented after the new company had threatened a severance of any future friendly relations.

The authorised share capital was set at £230,000, with loans of £70,300, and the engineers for the construction of the line were J.H. Shipway and Lionel Henry Shirley. Considerable support was forthcoming from Northampton, where the Town Council memorialised the House of Commons to pass a resolution in favour of the new line. However, just one member of the council was against the proposal – Mr Markham, a director of the

Bedford & Northampton Railway, felt that the new line would actually take traffic away from the town and preferred that his company's route be extended to Blisworth instead. The MR were already operating the Bedford & Northampton Railway and were paying the princely sum of £15,000 per annum for the privilege but early receipts from the traffic carried had fallen well short of this figure, such that any additional revenue would have been welcomed. However, it appears that the Midland already had an agreement with the L&NWR to not extend beyond the town of Northampton.

The directors and First Debenture stockholders of the E&WJR also supported the new scheme and many agreed to give up rights to interest payments to assist the project but once again nothing was immediately achieved.

At this point in time, the first board of directors of the newly formed company consisted of the chairman, Sir Thomas George Fermor Hesketh, and Alfred Barrett, Samuel Lloyd, Frederick Gretton, John Princep and Edwin Wellington Simkin; the company secretary was Herbert James Edden.

Back on the E&WJR

Despite the fact that only limited goods services were being operated, a further Beyer, Peacock 0-6-0 tender engine, similar in specification to No. 2, was purchased in 1881 and was logically allocated No. 3 in the E&WJR fleet. However, the difficulties of keeping open the line continued to increase, with hostile action being taken by some creditors, as a result of which further measures were taken by the Receiver, resulting in Alexander George Dickson, George Hall, Thomas Hillas Crampton, Meredith Meredith Brown and Thomas Coombs being appointed as joint managers of the undertaking; Crampton was actually the eldest son of the engineer Thomas Russell Crampton, who had built the E&WJR line and he was destined to remain with the company until 1908.

A further lengthy report and appeal was issued by the Receiver and managers during 1882, from which it also emerged that there were instances of landowners still being unpaid following the construction of the line a decade earlier. Although the company had appeared to be in possession of a continuous line of railway, in certain cases conveyance of title had still not taken place and continuity was theoretically vulnerable to the sale of isolated stretches of trackbed – a remarkably similar situation to that which had plagued the neighbouring Northampton & Banbury Junction Railway.

The appeal for funds concluded by urging E&WJR First Debenture stockholders to give up to the managers the interest on their holdings, including arrears, for the next five years, to aid the further development of the line; yet another convenient form was duly attached for their assent to this course of action.

On 10th August 1882, a further Act was promoted to reduce the authorised share capital of the proposed new eastern extension line to £200,000 and the loans and debentures to £60,000. This also renamed the Easton Neston Mineral & Towcester, Roade & Olney Junction Railway to a more manageable Stratford-upon-Avon, Towcester & Midland Junction Railway. In addition, the head office was relocated to another London address, at 21 Great St. Helens Street, EC.

The ever watchful *Northampton Mercury* then reported in early December, that the E&WJR were believed to be preparing a Bill for the sale of their railway to the L&NWR and Midland companies, and that following completion of any agreement, construction would begin on the new line to Olney. In the event, this was more than just a local rumour, as within a few months Parliament had actually approved a Bill to vest the company into the Midland Railway but there does not appear to have been any further development of this proposal.

Away in the west, the agreement for the working of the now three years old Broom extension was also an issue, as although the E&WJR were entitled to retain just 50% of the receipts, they had in fact so far contributed nothing back to the ER&SJR, who as a result were by then experiencing difficulties with their own creditors. In addition, the agreement for the working of the line by the E&WJR, initially for a ten year period from 1873, had not been renewed. It was felt that there was a very real danger of the

A Midland Railway service to Evesham leaves Broom Junction station, headed by the unusual combination of an 0-4-4T and a goods 0-6-0 – rather an over-provision of motive power for the usual branch train, so perhaps this was a special of some sort. The ER&SJR line curves away towards Stratford above the locomotives, with milepost 67 indicating the distance from London Road Junction at Derby; thus even a minor branch of the Midland Railway was constantly reminded of the presence of 'headquarters', whilst 'Up' was always in the direction of Derby, rather than towards London on most other English main line railway companies. The Stratford service, consisting of a locomotive and single coach, is standing in the sidings just beyond the turntable and will reverse into the loop platform when the Evesham train has cleared the junction. *Author's collection*

The original Midland signal box at the north end of Broom Junction station was installed in 1879, opening on 2nd June concurrent with the Stratford line. It was replaced by this later style of cabin on 3rd September 1913 but was then rendered redundant in 1934 by the opening of the new LM&SR signal box just to the south of the station. This view, showing track renewal and maintenance underway, was taken in 1936. *Author's collection*

shareholders of the ER&SJR therefore becoming hostile to the E&WJR company and with their line already being shown on Midland Railway timetable maps as an extension of that system, there was concern of a possibility of a defection to MR ownership. In fact, despite authority being obtained to raise further money by an issue of debenture stock, the ER&SJR would soon rather inevitably fall into receivership.

Towards a Re-Opening?

The next significant development was an Act of 25th August 1883, nominally promoted by the earlier mentioned Stratford-upon-Avon, Towcester & Midland Junction Railway Company (thereafter referred to in correspondence and other documents as the 'Stratford Company') This provided for the creation of £120,000 of share capital and £40,000 of loans, for building the proposed eastern connection from Towcester to the Midland Railway, and to also repair and upgrade the East & West Junction Railway main line, which had by then slipped into an almost derelict state.

Once those aims had been achieved, the Act provided for the formation of a joint committee to collectively manage and operate the ST&MJR, E&WJR and ER&SJR. The shares carried a guaranteed 5% return per annum in perpetuity, secured against the total receipts of the E&WJR and shareholders were also to benefit from any future surplus income from the newly formed ST&MJR company. The directors of the ST&MJR were, by this time, Sir Thomas George Fermor Hesketh of Easton Neston, R.W. Abbott of Bass, Ratcliff & Gretton, Alfred Barratt, a Birmingham councillor, Henry Downing, a director of the Stratford-upon-Avon Railway, Thomas Coombs, of the Evesham, Redditch & Stratford Junction Railway and George Hall of the E&WJR.

The E&WJR was by now finding it increasingly difficult to maintain even their small remaining amount of local mineral and goods traffic, which amounted to only one train per day from Stratford to Towcester and back. The company had, of course, not received any revenue from passenger traffic since the suspension of services in 1877, and were now facing the distinct prospect of their line being closed and even abandoned completely. The track was reported to be in a derelict condition, with sleepers rotted and the spiked rails displaced and worn. There was poor drainage, subsidence and falls of embankments contributing to the general malaise, whilst missing fencing in many locations resulted in cattle regularly grazing on the little used and grassy tracks.

Faced with this deteriorating situation and unable to raise any funds themselves, the E&WJR had little choice but to encourage the ST&MJR to exercise the powers granted under their 1883 Act. Under this scheme, activated in October 1883, the E&WJR were also required to nominate four persons to act alongside another two from the ST&MJR in forming the joint committee. This committee would then appoint a standing arbitrator for the resolution of any future differences.

The ST&MJR lost no time in making arrangements for the commencement of the various works, issuing a prospectus for subscription to a new issue of shares. Watson, Smith & Watson were appointed as contractors for the repair of the E&WJR and the construction of the new line to the junction with the Midland Railway, at a cost of £160,000. Engineers took up residence in Towcester, and surveying and other preliminaries were reportedly due to commence 'very shortly'.

Watson, Smith & Watson were also soon advertising from an office at 15 College Street, Stratford-upon-Avon, for clerks, time keepers and platelayers for the upgrading of the E&WJR route, and shortly afterwards for platelayers from a contractor's site at Kineton. Charles Liddell was appointed as engineer for the project and was assisted by R.C. Turner as consultant engineer.However, by the end of the year, a further agreement was necessary to extend the time available for the completion of the work and also to allow that company additional time to settle various outstanding land purchase claims.

Unfortunately, various prospectuses issued by the ST&MJR had included claims that the Midland Railway had agreed to support the venture by guaranteeing to run their traffic over the line when completed. In fact, the Derby company refuted this statement and were even moved to place letters in the *The Times* newspaper to state their position. The result was that some shareholders of the ST&MJR opposed the raising of further capital, considering that without the support of the Midland, the line's future would be compromised.

Eventually, however, work commenced on the renovation of the E&WJR on 8th May 1884, with the thirty-three mile line divided up into four sections. The Green's Norton to Byfield length was managed by Beverley Griffin, Byfield to Fenny

Compton by John Gadsden, the next section as far as Ettington was overseen by C.S. Williams, and the final stretch to Stratford by W.W. Strover. Work initially consisted of reballasting the E&WJR trackbed and relaying the line with new sleepers and 80lb steel rails. Stations, bridges and fencing were then improved, and by the time that the E&WJR directors, together with their new company secretary Captain Hunt, made a preliminary tour in June 1884, renovation of eight and a half miles had already been completed, and a thousand men were at work on the project.

As usual, the work was not without human cost and the local press highlighted an unfortunate sequence of fatalities of labourers working on the line. On 28th August 1884, Job Kingston of Blakesley was run over by the ballast wagons that he was helping to unload, whilst on Friday 5th September, John Perryman, a ganger, slipped under the wheels whilst trying to board a moving train at the same location. In addition, another navvy was killed by a bar of iron falling upon him and a colleague was decapitated by a train after falling asleep on the track.

The directors made a further tour of inspection in September, when the work was approaching completion. A contractor's Manning, Wardle 0-4-0 saddle tank engine, bearing the name *Hesketh*, was brought up from Stratford to Blisworth with a carriage conveying a small party of Watson, Smith & Watson staff, meeting the directors and other invited guests who had arrived by the 11.25am train from Euston. The completed party consisted of Messrs D. Barratt, B. Dale, J. Watson, J.B. Smith, J.L. Watson, Sidney Smith, T. Coombes, W. Hawkes, Samuel Lloyd, G.A. Dean, G. Hall, H.W. Downing, G. Boyden, B. Griffin, J. Gadsden, C.S. Williams and W.W. Strover.

Additional open wagons fitted with seats were attached and the train made its way back to Stratford, with brief stops at Towcester and Green's Norton, before joining the E&WJR line proper to inspect the new works. At the latter junction, considerable improvements had been made to alleviate the continual problems caused by flooding, with a new larger culvert being provided to carry off water and the nearby river bridges being strengthened.

New '*single headed steel rails of a new design*' had been laid, together with chairs and crossings of a type recently introduced on the Kettering to Manton line of the Midland Railway. However, there were still some uncompleted sections, which provided the party with a graphic illustration of the significant upgrading that had already taken place. Drainage and embankments had been improved and fencing repaired, with many signal posts also being replaced by the Railway Signal Company

of Fazakerley, Liverpool. All stations had also been renovated, whilst at Fenny Compton, a major improvement had been made by replacing the old wooden viaduct over the Oxford Canal and GWR line with a new girder structure.

Stratford was reached at 3.00pm and a late lunch taken at the Shakespeare Hotel, the directors stating that they were well satisfied with the progress made. The special train then took just 1½ hours to return to Towcester, where it connected with the 6.52pm N&BJR train to Blisworth.

The half-yearly meeting of the directors of the ST&MJR, which took place at Great Winchester Street, London, on 21st October 1884, duly reported that the line was now ready for inspection by the Board of Trade. Reopening was expected by 1st November, in anticipation for which arrangements for new locomotives and rolling stock had been put in hand. It was reported that good progress was also being made with the new extension to Olney and that possession had already been obtained of a three miles length of the necessary trackbed, with negotiations for the remainder taking place.

As usual, the announcement of the reopening of the E&WJR was a little optimistic, with Board of Trade approval not being received until 18th December 1884. Major Hutchinson arrived at Towcester by the 9.24am service from Blisworth, and was joined by a large party of E&WJR officials and others on a special train that would traverse the new route. The E&WJR chairman, Major Dickson, was supported by one of his directors, Mr Hunt, and his traffic manager Joseph F. Burke. Messrs J.L. Watson and R.C. Turner represented the contractor, with three inspectors of works Beverely Griffin, W.W. Strover, and C.S. Williams. In addition, Mr Edwards, who had '*fixed the locking gear of the line*', and Charles E. Spagnoletti, telegraph superintendent of the GWR and a consulting telegraphic expert, also joined the party. The train apparently steamed out of Towcester station towards Stratford in a heavy storm of snow and rain, returning in the early afternoon after a successful inspection. In the event, although reopening was approved, passenger services between Stratford and Blisworth were not actually reintroduced until 22nd March 1885.

The delay after the successful inspection in December was probably due to the wait for the two new Beyer, Peacock 2-4-0

This early view of Beyer, Peacock 2-4-0T No. 6 unusually provides good detail of the rear of the locomotive, as it waits around the turntable at Stratford-upon-Avon in company with one of the earlier 0-6-0s provided by the same manufacturer. The E&WJR's arrangements for coaling, by hand using wicker baskets, is clearly visible on the left of the locomotive. *Author's collection*

tank locomotives, No's 5 and 6, to haul the trains. New carriages were being obtained as well, whilst goods rolling stock, which had been reduced to a mere dozen wagons by the end of 1884, was also enhanced for the reopening.

The reinstated passenger service consisted of a basic service of four trains daily in each direction, with the exception of Sundays when no services were operated. The last train from Blisworth ran at a slightly later time of 8.10pm on Saturday evenings, whilst on Monday mornings only, an additional service ran from Stratford at 7.05am; the average journey time was around 1 hour 25 minutes.

The company celebrated their reopening to passengers by issuing a quite lavish thirty page booklet entitled *VIEWS and DESCRIPTIONS of the places of interest on the EAST and WEST JUNCTION RAILWAY*. This contained details of the route between Blisworth and Broom, individually attached real photographs of the major tourist attractions and a current timetable, showing connections with the main line companies. However, as

A SHORT DESCRIPTIVE GUIDE

OF THE

EAST & WEST JUNCTION RAILWAY

BEING THE SHORTEST AND MOST DIRECT ROUTE FROM

LONDON TO STRATFORD-ON-AVON

via

LONDON & NORTH WESTERN RAILWAY

INCLUDING NOTICES OF

STRATFORD-ON-AVON

(The birthplace and grave of the Immortal Bard, WILLIAM SHAKESPEARE)

BROOM, BIDFORD,
AND THE VILLAGES ADJACENT, OF PEBWORTH, MARSTON,
HILLBOROUGH, GRAFTON, EXHALL AND WIXFORD
(Known as Shakespeare's Country)

SULGRAVE

(The ancestral home of the WASHINGTON family)

KINETON

(Where the Battle of Edgehill was fought)

TOWCESTER

(Where CHARLES DICKENS laid the Election scene of Mr. Pickwick, with Sam Weller,
and other members of the Pickwick Club)

AND OTHER PLACES OF HISTORICAL OR ANTIQUARIAN INTEREST
NEAR WHICH THE LINE PASSES

The Illustrations are from Photographs by Messrs. F. Frith & Co.

LONDON

MACFARLANE AND CO.

4 ADELAIDE STREET, CHARING CROSS, AND NEW YORK

1886

Entered at Stationers' Hall

LEFT & BELOW: The E&WJR promoted the reopening of their line to passenger traffic in 1885 by the introduction, one year later, of a comprehensive guide book. This also included timetables featuring connecting services over the L&NWR and Midland Railway to such far-flung destinations as Euston, Bristol, Cambridge and even Dublin. *Author's collection*

TIME TABLE

Showing Train Service to and from Stratford-on-Avon and other East and West Junction Stations, and the principal Stations on the London and North-Western and Midland Railways.

Subject to alterations, for particulars of which see Time Tables for current month.

UP

STATIONS.	A.M.	A.M.	P.M.	P.M.	P.M.
BRISTOL ... dep.		8 0		3 20	
Clifton Down ... ,,				2 50	
Bath ... ,,		7 35		3 0	
Gloucester ... ,,		9 5		4 36	
Cheltenham ... ,,		9 20		4 46	
Great Malvern ... ,,		8 25		3 23	
Tewkesbury ... ,,		8 58		4 50	
Ashchurch ... ,,		9 50		5 15	
Evesham ... ,,		10 30	B1 52	5 53	
Broom Junction ... arr.		10 46	2 8	6 10	
Derby ... dep.		6 40	11 40		3 45
Burton ... ,,		7 5	11 58		4 3
Birmingham (New Street) ... ,,	6 40	9 43	1 35		5 15
Redditch ... ,,	7 47	10 38	2 18		6 1
Alcester ... ,,	8 6	10 56	2 37		6 21
Wixford ... ,,	8 12	11 3	2 42		6 26
Broom Junction ... arr.	8 16	11 6	2 45		6 30
BROOM JUNCTION ... dep.	8 27	11 7	2 46	6 11	6 32
BIDFORD ... ,,	8 30	11 10	2 49	6 14	6 35
BINTON ... ,,	8 33	11 17	2 56	6 21	6 42
STRATFORD-ON-AVON ... arr.	8 45	11 24	3 6	6 29	6 50
,, ,, ... dep. (A.M. 7 5)	8 55	11 26	3 5	6 32	
ETTINGTON ,,	7 16	9 6	11 36	3 15	6 42
KINETON (for Edge Hill) ,,	7 25	9 15	11 45	3 24	6 51
FENNY COMPTON ... ,,	7 36	9 26	11 56	3 35	7 2
BYFIELD ... ,,	7 50	9 42	12 11	3 49	7 18
MORTON PINKNEY (for Sulgrave) ,,	7 58	9 51	12 19	3 57	7 26
BLAKESLEY ... ,,	8 6	9 59	12 26	4 4	7 33
TOWCESTER ... arr.	8 14	10 8	12 33	4 12	7 40
BLISWORTH JUNCTION ,,	8 29	10 23	12 48	4 27	7 55
Blisworth Junction ... dep.	8 44	10 36	1 10	4 35	8 0
Northampton ... arr.	8 55	10 46	1 20	4 45	8 10
Peterboro' ... ,,	10 50	12 40		7 55	10 10
Market Harboro' ... ,,	9 58	All 28	c3 50		8 55
Blisworth Junction ... dep.	a8 45	10 28	12 52	4 30	8 0
Rugby ... arr.	A9 34	11 2	1 30	5 2	A9 40
Nuneaton ... ,,	A9 59	11 37	2 50	7 20	All 12
Stafford ... ,,	10A53	12 31	3 45	7 4	A1 6
Crewe ... ,,	11 35	1 13	3 43	7 39	A1 30
Chester ... ,,		1 55	4 15	8 35	12 31
Manchester ... ,,		2 30	4 15	8 15	2 55
Liverpool ... ,,	12 40	2 40	4 40	8 30	3 0
Dublin ... ,,					D6 45
Blisworth Junction ... dep.	9 6	10 34	1 10	4 35	8 0
Bletchley ... arr.	9 38	11 15	A2 10	A5 52	8 36
Bedford ... ,,	10 54	11 56	5 0	7 0	9 55
Cambridge ... ,,		1 5	6 15		
Blisworth Junction ... dep.	8 58	10 47	1 4	4 35	8 0
Willesden ... arr.	10 18	11 55	2 17	7 3	9 57
Broad Street ... ,,	10 42	12 40	12	7 40	10 40
Kensington (Add. Road) ,,	10 43	12 12	2 33	7 20	10 32
Victoria ... ,,	10 49	12 49	3 14	7 49	10 49
EUSTON ... ,,	10 30	12 10	1	A7 15	10 10

(Railway groupings, top to bottom: MIDLAND RAILWAY · EAST & WEST JUNC. RY. · LONDON & NORTH WESTERN RAILWAY · LONDON)

MONDAYS ONLY. — C—On Saturdays arrives at 3.15 P.M. — B—On Tuesdays only. — E—North Wall. — D—Westland Row. — N.B.—For Conditions under which Tickets will be issued see the Company's large Time Tables. — A—Viâ Northampton. — NO SUNDAY TRAINS.

DOWN

STATIONS.	A.M.	A.M.	A.M.	P.M.	P.M.	P.M.	P.M.	P.M.
EUSTON ... dep.		7 15	A9 30	1 30	3 0	6 0	6 0	
Victoria ,,		8 54		12 54	2 24	5 24	5 24	
Kensington (Add. Road) ,,		9 25		1 18	2 42	5 42	5 42	
Broad Street ,,		9 6		12 55	2 25	5 30	5 30	
Willesden ,,	6 18	9 41		1 42	3 12	6 12	6 12	
Cambridge ,,		7 50		10 20	1 55	4 40	4 40	
Bedford ,,	7 30	8 51		11 19	2 58	5 41	5 41	
Bletchley ,,	8 25	10 14		2 43	4 8	7 20	7 20	
Blisworth Junction arr.	8 57	11 30		3 20	4 30	7 50	7 50	
Dublin ... dep.	P.M.	E7 0				D6 45	D6 45	
Liverpool ... ,,	A.M.	2 35		11 5	12 0	4 5	4 5	
Manchester ,,		7 45		11 15	12 0	4 15	4 15	
Chester ,,		2 35		11 30	12 0	4 0	4 0	
Crewe ,,		3 55		12 7	1 5	5 7	5 7	
Stafford ,,	4 33	8 25		11 33	1 45	5 25	5 25	
Nuneaton ,,	7 32	9 15		12 43	2 42	6 15	6 15	
Rugby ,,	8 20	10 20		2 5	A3 15	6 50	6 50	
Blisworth Junction arr.	8 56	10 47		2 45	4 25	7 35	7 35	
Market Harboro' ... dep.	8 5	10 46		12 30	2 46	6 55	6 55	
Peterboro' ,,	6 45	8 45		11 35	1 55	3 35	3 35	
Northampton ,,	8 50	11 20		3 5	4 15	7 35	7 35	
Blisworth Junction arr.	8 58	11 30		3 15	4 25	7 45	7 45	
BLISWORTH JUNCTION dep.		9 3	11 33	3 25	4 40	7 58	8 10	
TOWCESTER ,,		9 18	11 48	3 40	4 55	8 13	8 26	
BLAKESLEY ,,		9 26	11 56	3 50	5 4	8 22	8 35	
MORTON PINKNEY (for Sulgrave) ,,		9 33	12 2	3 58	5 11	8 29	8 42	
BYFIELD ,,		9 41	12 12	4 7	5 19	8 37	8 50	
FENNY COMPTON ,,		9 52	12 55	4 21	5 33	8 51	9 4	
KINETON (for Edge Hill) ,,		10 5	12 36	4 32	5 44	9 1	9 15	
ETTINGTON ,,		10 12	12 45	4 41	5 54	9 10	9 24	
STRATFORD-ON-AVON arr.		10 22	12 55	4 50	6 5	9 20	9 33	
,, ,, dep.	7 50	10 24	2 20	3 30	5 40			
BINTON ,,	7 57	10 31	2 29	3 45	5 47			
BIDFORD ,,	8 5	10 39	2 37	4 0	5 55			
BROOM JUNCTION arr.	8 10	10 42	2 40	4 5	5 58			
Broom Junction ... dep.	8 16	11 6	2 45		6 30			
Evesham ... arr.	8 33	11 23	3 3		6 46			
Ashchurch ,,	9 4	11 54	3 50		7 20			
Tewkesbury ,,	9 51	12 18	4 20		7 43			
Great Malvern ,,	10 25	1 55	5 50		8 15			
Cheltenham ,,	9 31	12 19	4 25		7 50			
Gloucester ,,	9 53	12 40	4 43		8 10			
Bath ,,	12 3	3 20	6 8					
Clifton Down ,,	11 48	2 20	6 30					
Bristol ,,	11 40	2 5	6 0		11 30			
Broom Junction ... dep.		10 45		4 24	6 10			
Wixford ... arr.		10 50		4 28	6 14			
Alcester ,,		10 57		4 33	6 20			
Redditch ,,		11 15		4 54	6 41			
Birmingham (New Street) ,,		12 13		6 0	7 45			
Burton ,,		2 16			9 26			
Derby ,,		2 40			9 55			
Dublin (via Broom & B'ham) ,,			A.M.	E8 45				

(Railway groupings, top to bottom: LONDON & NORTH-WESTERN RAILWAY · EAST & WEST JUNC. RY. · MIDLAND RAILWAY)

SATURDAYS ONLY. — EXCEPT SATURDAYS. — SATURDAYS ONLY.

usual not everyone was happy with the service. The Towcester column of the *Northampton Mercury* of 7th March 1885 carried a letter from '*Olim Juvenis*' who related how '*Once more the metals of the E&WJR are daily being run over and the brand new light brown carriages steaming into and out of the station have been the highlight of the week. But the company might let us get down to Stratford for less than 4s 6d and to Blisworth for something under a shilling*'.

A few weeks later a letter from '*Cheap fares*' headed '*Stratford-upon-Avon Steeplechases*' complained '*Sir – A bill announcing that cheap tickets will be issued from Towcester and other places on the E&WJR is in circulation. How the fares from Towcester can be called cheap is difficult to understand as on the bill 3 shillings is the charge, and on every Friday a market train runs from Towcester and the fare is 2s 6d. If 3 shillings is charged on the days of Towcester steeplechases many will not go. The fares are generally too high and I venture to say the line would earn more at lower rates with the same expenses*'.

However, despite the complaints, things were at last returning to something like normal, at least on the old main line of the E&WJR.

Another Setback

Watson, Smith & Watson, having completed the renovation of the E&WJR route, then turned in earnest to the construction of the new ST&MJR extension from Towcester to the east, where a start had been made and a '*few yards of the first cutting*' were already to be seen close to the Towcester to Northampton road. However, yet more difficulties were soon on the horizon.

The *Northampton Mercury* of 26th September 1885 carried a report of '*An important case under the law of distress*' with the Easton Neston Estate & Mining Company having been summoned by the Western Wagon & Property Company of Bristol. It was stated that Easton Neston had, in May 1885, seized from Watson, Smith & Watson a locomotive named *Gavin* in lieu of unpaid rent for a brick engine shed used by the contractor. However, the engine did carry a plate stating its ownership by the Western Wagon Company and the resulting legal case became the first ever to be heard under the Act of Railway Rolling Stock Protection 1872. Watson, Smith & Watson had hired the locomotive for the construction of the new line but had then fallen into arrears with their monthly payments for the engine shed. After some considerable legal discussion as to the actual status of the shed, the magistrates found for the Western Wagon Company and ordered the return of their locomotive.

This proved to be indicative of the poor financial state of Watson, Smith & Watson and, before long, an auction of '*highly important railway plant … under the execution of the Sheriff*' was held by W.J. Peirce & Thorpe at the contractor's work site in a field adjoining the Towcester to Northampton road. The extensive list of items included 550 double rails '*as laid*', sleepers, building bricks, coping stones, slates, iron girders, centres, trestles, scaffolds, switch and lever boxes, trolleys, fencing and many other materials associated with the construction of a new railway, plus a slated carpenter's shop, blacksmith's shop and an 8hp portable engine.

Watson, Smith & Watson formally forfeited their contract in

July 1885 and a meeting of creditors took place at the London Bankruptcy Court on Friday 4th September, with a receiving order being made against the company by James Cox, a timber merchant of Stratford-upon-Avon. The debts were stated to be largely owed to creditors in Cirencester, Gloucester, Burton on Trent, Leeds and Manchester, and a public examiner was appointed on 10th September. A further auction sale of furniture and surveying equipment was held on 21st October at a house in Park Street, Towcester, '*lately in the occupation of Messrs. Watson Smith & Watson*'; this had presumably been used as an office.

The legal proceedings were finally completed in November with the result of Watson, Smith & Watson being declared bankrupt with gross debts of £186,360.

The delays to the construction of the new line meant that another Act had been necessary to allow for an extension of time allowed for completion, which also included amendments to the planned route. The proposed connections with the N&BJR, which would have formed a triangular junction with that line some distance on the Blisworth side of Towcester station, were deleted and the direct connection from the E&WJR near Green's Norton was similarly withdrawn. All were replaced by a straightforward new two mile line from a junction with the N&BJR just north of Towcester station, to connect with the originally planned route near Easton Neston.

Meanwhile, on the E&WJR, the year of 1885 also saw two new but ultimately unfulfilled proposals involving the line. A fourteen mile extension of the E&WJR from Broom to Worcester, promoted by shareholders of the Railway & General Company, was ultimately authorised by Parliament, despite strong opposition from the GWR, into whose station at Worcester running powers were to be provided. A second scheme, associated with the Worcester & Broom proposal, presented the possibility of a connection towards London, with the Metropolitan Railway, having seen off the objections of the GWR and L&NWR, proposing to extend their own line beyond Buckingham to a link with the E&WJR at Morton Pinkney. However, both schemes eventually failed.

Further, any optimism engendered by the two proposals, along with the reopening of the E&WJR line to passengers, was immediately tempered by the fact that the Evesham, Redditch & Stratford Junction Railway finally fell into receivership on 2nd January 1886.

As if to draw a line beneath this rather unproductive period, the remnants of the Watson, Smith & Watson tenure were finally auctioned in Miller's Field, near Towcester, by Fuller, Horsey, Sons & Castell from 2nd June 1886 onwards. The lots included the usual selection of contractor's plant, track and chairs, as well as three tank locomotives. These have been identified as a Hunslet 0-4-0ST named *Bruce*, a Manning, Wardle 0-4-0ST *Hesketh* and the Black, Hawthorn 0-6-0ST *Gavin*. It seems likely that all three were later employed on the construction of the Towcester to Ravenstone section by the replacement contractor.

The year of 1886 also brought the arrival of Charles Hobbs, who was appointed as E&WJR accountant and would, within two years, also assume the role of secretary following the departure of Charles Banks. Hobbs was often described as a '*somewhat irritable man*' and '*a most awkward gentleman to deal with*' but he would serve the company well through some difficult years.

Incidents and Accidents

Whilst the construction of the long awaited extension to the east was again being delayed, life continued much as usual on the main section of the E&WJR. A welcome renewal of relations with the L&NWR brought better news in the form of the introduction of a new goods service over the line from Blisworth to Broom during 1887. However, traffic was never very plentiful and the service was destined to only last for one year.

The E&WJR did, however, enhance their own goods services, with an overnight train from Stratford to Blisworth, to expedite traffic from Bristol, Gloucester and other West Country depots to London. In addition, an improvement was made to the passenger timetable with the addition of a 6.12pm departure from Blisworth to Stratford, which gave a better connection with the important 4.30pm L&NWR service from Euston.

The year also saw an unfortunate sequence of accidents and incidents on the E&WJR line, beginning with a burst tube on the engine of a Stratford to Broom passenger train on 11th January 1887, which brought the train to a stand some distance from the latter junction. Once advised that no further progress would be made for some time, the passengers decided to take matters into their own hands and walked the one and a half miles along the track, in an attempt to catch their intended train to Alcester and beyond; unfortunately, the connection was missed.

Just over six months later, on 26th July, travellers were once again forced to descend to the trackbed when an E&WJR passenger train left the rails at Towcester station, in the process completely closing the line by the Watling Street bridge. Passengers were escorted on foot to reach hastily arranged trains on either side of the blockage, while a breakdown crane was summoned from the L&NWR depot at Northampton Bridge Street to replace the errant vehicles. The next incident was not long in arriving, as just a few days later, the obviously hard working locomotive of an E&WJR excursion train, bound for Birmingham, managed to set alight a whole field of barley situated three miles from

Stratford; fortunately, the field was isolated and no damage to other property ensued.

Finally, on 26th September, a more serious accident occurred at a point near Stratford known as Kennels. A special goods train travelling towards Broom left the rails and ran into the embankment, the engine tipping over and causing much damage to the track. A temporary loop was constructed to carry traffic whilst the recovery and repairs were put in hand. The subsequent investigation revealed that the derailment had been due to platelayers failing to replace bolts after working on the track.

The year also brought more bad news for the E&WJR, with the death of Alexander George Dickson, following which the remaining four joint managers and the Receiver continued to run the line.

After leaving Stratford-on-Avon station and crossing the Avon viaduct, the line became single track, with the route curving away to pass beneath the bridges carrying first, the old Stratford & Moreton Tramway, and then the Shipston road, prior to arriving at Clifford Chambers Siding. *Author's collection*

This historically interesting photograph provides a closer view of the E&WJR engine shed at Stratford and reveals how the building was originally accessed from the turntable. Manning, Wardle 0-6-0ST No. 1, which had hauled the inaugural train from Fenny Compton to Kineton in 1871, shares the premises with the much later built Beyer, Peacock 0-6-0 No. 15. The large jib prominent in the right foreground is from a crane that probably belonged to the permanent way department. The whole site was rather discreetly hidden from the view of passengers on the adjacent Down platform. *Author's collection*

Eastwards From Towcester

A further Act had been necessary during March 1887, to extend the time allowed for the completion of the Ravenstone Wood line and to approve further share capital and borrowing powers. At this date, the ST&MJR had expended approximately £160,000 on the refurbishment of the E&WJR line but only £18,000 on construction of their own line to the east and they were unable to raise any further funds. It was decided that the only way to raise capital for the construction of the ST&MJR was now to issue a new class of stock, ranking above all others in claim on the net revenue of E&WJR. The new arrangements authorised the raising of £200,000 by an issue of debenture stock, whilst at the same time cancelling all unfulfilled share and borrowing powers left from their previous Acts.

A new contractor was also required and, on 5th August 1887, Saul Isaac, of Bloomfield House in the City of London, was appointed to complete the line. The close of the year brought encouraging news, with a report in the *Northampton Mercury* of 3rd December stating that work was about to recommence on the new railway and that navvies were already on site awaiting instructions.

Isaac was a Justice of the Peace, and Member of Parliament for Nottingham from 1874 to 1880. He was associated, with his brother Samuel, in the formation of Isaac Campbell & Company, a firm of army contractors based in Jermyn Street, London. Samuel was also involved in railway contracting, being a prime mover in the promotion and construction of the Mersey Tunnel, and had also been an early board member of the East & West Junction Railway. Saul Isaac took on the ST&MJR contract as a speculative venture, with payment being made by way of debentures issued to him at a large discount of some £40,000. He would later sell on all of these to other private investors at a premium, using the services of the then well known intermediary George Edwin Taunton.

The engineers for the new line were named as Liddell & Richards. Isaac also announced that he had retained the services of Beverley Griffin, who had recently successfully supervised the relaying of the track on the E&WJR route whilst in the service of Messrs Watson, Smith & Watson; he had also worked on the Metropolitan Railway extension to Rickmansworth.

A large crowd assembled at one o'clock on 15th December 1887 in a field adjoining Towcester station, to witness the *'turning of the first sod'* by Sir Thomas Hesketh, with a prayer being offered by the Rev'd H. Delafons of Tiffield. This was followed by the usual largesse for three hundred invited guests at a *'recherché luncheon'* at the Towcester Conservative Club. Saul Isaac presided over the proceedings, and was ably supported by Sir Thomas Hesketh, Sir Rainald Knightley MP, Mr Pickering Phipps, Mr C.W. Bartholemew and other local notables.

The actual construction was sub-contracted to the experienced firm of Baldry & Yerburgh, with Griffin acting as their resident engineer and work was reported as having just commenced during January 1888. The new contractors were early users of steam navvies for the excavation of cuttings and several were purchased, together with locomotives, from Messrs Kirk & Parry after the completion of their Barking to Pitsea contract on the London, Tilbury & Southend Railway.

The local newspapers were, as usual, quick to report on

developments. The *Northampton Mercury* of 12th May 1888 advised that rapid progress was being made on the new line but also begged the question '*... but why don't they pay their navvies better? It is because of the numerous applications they have made for employment. I am pleased to say that they have set on many local labourers who have been out of work for some little time previous ... Towcester station is to be greatly improved, and no less than £6,000 is to be expended on the alteration of sidings etc'.*

In fact, the initial progress was soon to be interrupted by what the *Banbury Advertiser* would describe as '*little hitches*', amongst which was a dispute over the price of land payable by the railway company to Pickering Phipps, now the owner of the Horton Estate. In the meantime, however, yet another Act of Parliament had been necessary to provide an extension of the time for completion until 15th August 1890, which also authorised the abandonment of several more portions of the proposed route. These were the western side of the intended triangular junction at Ravenstone Wood, the short branch down to the Grand Junction Canal at Stoke Bruerne and the upgraded section of the original mineral line from the N&BJR to Easton Neston. In addition, the constitution of the joint committee was also amended to require four members from the E&WJR and three from the ST&MJR, making a new total of seven delegates, the ER&SJR being left out in the cold.

Meanwhile, an ordinary general meeting of the ST&MJR on 8th December 1888 was informed that approximately eight miles of earthworks for the new line from Towcester to the Midland Railway had been completed, leaving just $2^1/_2$ miles to be constructed, although no track had so far been laid. The Midland Railway had, however, been busy with arrangements at their own end of the line. On 13th December, Major Marindin visited Ravenstone Wood to inspect the newly installed connection with the still to be completed ST&MJR route. The Major found a Midland style signal box opposite the new junction, containing twenty levers, with six spares, controlling signals and points, all correctly interlocked. There were as usual a few requirements; 'runaway' points were needed on the Down line a train length outside of the Down Home signals and it was suggested that No. 8 signal should be a disc rather than a semaphore. Use of the connection was sanctioned but it was stipulated that, if the new line was to be opened for contractors or goods traffic before a full inspection for passenger use had taken place, then 'safety points' should be inserted on the branch.

Shortly afterwards, with the line almost ready but still awaiting Board of Trade inspection, Saul Isaac was sufficiently encouraged to arrange a tour of his new railway for '*a select company of gentlemen*'. The party journeyed from Euston to Towcester in a special train provided by the L&NWR, which was then drawn over the line by the contractor's engines. After the run to Olney and back, Isaac hosted the usual festivities at the Pomfret Arms, Towcester.

On 12th September 1889, the *Banbury Advertiser* was also able to report on a private tour of the progress of the works. This was arranged by Mr A.A .Davis and Mr J.H. Frogley, respectively the agent and engineer of Baldry & Yerbergh, and Mr H.O. Baldry, the inspector of works. Note was made of the improvement of facilities at Towcester, including the provision of a substantial footbridge and a new waiting room on the Down side, with the

The Easton Neston Mineral & Towcester, Roade & Olney Junction Railway, latterly known as the Stratford-upon-Avon, Towcester & Midland Junction Railway, met the Midland's Bedford to Northampton branch at Ravenstone Wood Junction, a solitary outpost, surrounded by woodland on the Buckinghamshire and Northamptonshire border. This view, looking westwards towards Northampton on Sunday 25th September 1960, captures the loneliness of the location and the alpine nature of the Midland line, as it dips sharply and then climbs again to reach Piddington station. The lodge of Cowper's Oak foot crossing stands in the angle between the ST&MJR line to Towcester and the Midland branch. It being a Sunday, the signals in both directions on the Midland line had been cleared and the signal box 'switched out' of circuit. *Author's collection*

platforms having been raised and their surface considerably improved. The station at Stoke Bruerne was reported as being ready for use, whilst Salcey Forest was 'in course of erection' and approached by 'an excellent road formed out of the old coach road used before traffic was diverted'. From that point onwards the line was only temporarily made but ground had been laid out at Ravenstone Wood for the provision of sidings.

Following the completion of construction, the usual inspection was carried out by Major Hutchinson of the Board of Trade on 31st December 1889, with the Midland Railway assisting by providing two locomotives and an officer's saloon, the locomotives being used to test the various bridges on the line. A contemporary newspaper report stated:

'A start was made from the Olney end at nine o'clock, and Towcester was reached about half past one o'clock. The inspector tested the bridges, especially the one near Roade, and the bridge over the Northampton & Banbury Railway just below the Towcester station, upon which he had placed a couple of the Midland Railway Company's largest engines. The bridge has recently been strengthened and stood the test satisfactorily. Major General Hutchinson was some considerable time examining the points &c at the junction with the Northampton & Banbury line above Towcester station, where the run is very sharp. Mr. Saul Isaac, who accompanied the Inspector, informed our representative that, in his opinion, the Inspector was satisfied with the way in which the line has been made. It is doubtful whether the new railway will be opened this month.'

The new line did not of course bridge the N&BJR line at any point, whilst the reference to the use of two large Midland Railway engines probably refers to the testing of the long girder bridge over the L&NWR main line at Roade. The location of a bridge 'just below the Towcester station' would seem to indicate either the one over Watling Street or the nearby crossing of the River Tove but these bridges are unlikely to have been inspected as that part of the line was N&BJR territory and therefore theoretically outside of the inspecting officer's remit.

The Major's report as usual listed the salient features of the line, including a steepest gradient of 1 in 76 and a sharpest curve of 12 chains at Ravenstone Wood Junction. Towcester station had recently been improved and provided with a footbridge, and the other stations were recorded at Salcey Forest and Stoke Bruerne. In addition, there were intermediate sidings at Easton Neston and a branch line down to the L&NWR at Roade, where the main line was crossed by a girder bridge of 73ft span.

Signalling of the new junction was controlled by a cabin at Towcester with sixteen levers, including two spares. Signal boxes were also located at both Salcey Forest and Stoke Bruerne stations, both containing ten levers and two spares. The siding points were operated by ground frames released by the train staff, and the Major also noted that the junction and signalling with the Midland Railway at Ravenstone had previously been approved for use. As was usual, there were a few stipulations made before opening could be sanctioned. These included attention to the conflicting positions of the signals for the Blisworth Branch

The ST&MJR line crossed the L&NWR West Coast main line at Roade on a substantial girder bridge, spanning the pairs of fast and slow lines, and also a long siding on the Down side. Roade station is in the distance beyond the sets of signals on the gantry which controlled the Down main line and Northampton loop respectively. Roade goods yard is off to the right of the picture, opposite the connection down from the ST&MJR, which was originally planned to run into the siding on the Down side, just beyond the L&NWR signal box; in the event, the spur was continued on into a newly constructed bay platform in Roade station. *Author's collection*

and the new line at Towcester, and inevitably the provision of gauge ties on many of the points. Additional but more basic requirements were the provision of buffer stops for the siding at Salcey Forest and attention to fencing at various points.

Overall the Major was satisfied but was still unable to sanction opening for passenger traffic owing to the *'want of rolling stock'* and the incompleteness of certain works. However, Baldry &

Yerbergh obviously considered their involvement to be at an end as, on 14th December, an auction of *'valuable horses'* was held at the Northampton Horse Repository, in consequence of the contract for the construction of the ST&MJR having been completed. Over the next few months, the opening of the line was repeatedly postponed until, with the satisfactory completion of the outstanding works, approval was finally forthcoming on 17th May 1890.

The ST&MJR's spur to the L&NWR main line at Roade was initially intended for goods only but was soon upgraded to carry passenger traffic, the intention being to provide a service from Towcester. The work required another Board of Trade inspection, carried out by Major Hutchinson on 16th August 1890, which was fortunately captured in a unique series of photographs. In this first view, the photographer had positioned himself a few yards down the curve to the L&NWR and is looking back at the new, to an extent unfinished works at the junction with the Towcester to Ravenstone Wood line. The pristine cabin, supplied by the Railway Signal Company, worked the two tall signals in the distance which controlled access towards Ravenstone Wood and the curve to Roade respectively; also prominent is the rodding and quadrants operating the points on the curve, which became double track a few yards further on. *Courtesy T. Marsh*

A short distance down the steeply graded 22 chain connecting line, it became double track. The ST&MJR main line runs across the top of the picture, with the signal box on the right. The cabin contained fifteen levers for the operation of the points and signals at the junction and along the curve, whilst the already extant L&NWR Roade Junction signal box controlled matters down at the main line end of the connection. *Courtesy T. Marsh*

This wider view of the connection at Roade was taken from the opposite side of the L&NWR main line, which the ST&MJR route crossed via the girder bridge seen on the previous page, which is here just out of picture on the left. The wagons in the foreground are located on a siding serving a limestone quarry and note too the single wagon in the centre of the view, standing next to a signal on the curve up to the ST&MJR. *Courtesy T. Marsh*

The lower end of the connecting curve at Roade, with contractor's workmen still very much in evidence. The line runs behind Roade Junction L&NWR signal box, where what appears to be a contractor's tank locomotive can be seen, standing in front of the village footbridge which spanned the tracks at the southern end of the station. The ST&MJR line continued under the extreme left hand arch into the new bay platform. The L&NWR main line, itself newly widened to accommodate the recently opened Northampton loop, is on the right, with wagons again standing in the limeworks siding on the far side. *Courtesy T. Marsh*

The photographer had then moved down to the aforementioned village footbridge, so this view is looking back towards Roade Junction L&NWR signal box and beyond to the 73ft span of the ST&MJR girder bridge spanning the main line. A locomotive, which appears to be an L&NWR tender type, has brought a short train down to the junction, which was almost certainly conveying an official inspection party. The work was all in vain, however, as the bay was never used by passenger trains. The connection up to the ST&MJR route saw intermittent use for the exchange of goods traffic but even that only lasted until 1917, when the track was removed and reused elsewhere. Incidentally, the locomotive cannot be one of the three ex-L&NWR Class 'DX' 0-6-0 goods engines that worked on the E&WJR, as these were not acquired until over a year later, in December 1891. The limeworks siding, complete with loading chute, is again prominent on the left of the picture. *Courtesy T. Marsh*

A closer view of activities, with much brickwork remaining to be done; everyone has paused, however, for the photographer. A small contractor's locomotive occupies the bay, where it was hoped that trains from Towcester would soon terminate. The engine appears to be a Manning, Wardle old Class 'I' 0-6-0ST and is possibly Works No. 92 of 1863, which is known to have been in use by Baldry & Yerbergh around this time. *Courtesy T. Marsh*

OPPOSITE PAGE TOP: Roade Junction L&NWR station from the village footbridge, showing the construction of the retaining walls for the new bay platform for ST&MJR trains still under way. An L&NWR local train is signalled on the Up line from Northampton, the signal indicating that it was to cross to the Up main line immediately after passing the photographer. *Courtesy T. Marsh*

Taken on 14th August 1938, nearly fifty years separates this view of Roade from that page left, with the bay platform having been filled a few years earlier, leaving an area of rough ground in between the Down main line platform and the retaining wall. Only a few Bletchley to Rugby local passenger services, using the 'old line' via Weedon, ever called at the main line platforms here, with most stopping services being routed by the Northampton loop line on the right of the picture. The houses on the right all appear in the earlier picture but those on the left are new. *Author's collection*

Saul Isaac then issued a prospectus in various newspapers for the raising of further capital, announcing the issue of £75,000 debenture stock, stated to rank in priority over all of the issued capital of '*a line of railway of 43½ miles running from Stratford to Ravenstone, which was now fully open and available for traffic*'. This brought an immediate response from the E&WJR, who pointed out that they in fact owned all but ten miles of the railway in question, had no involvement in the promotion of the new issue of stock and would accept no financial liability, being '*at direct issue upon various matters, which can only be settled in the highest courts of law*'.

There then followed a series of letters in *The Times* newspaper, with both parties stating their own positions with regard to the issue of the stock. Feelings were obviously running high, with terms such as '*malicious libel*' being bandied about and legal proceedings were threatened. Matters appeared to have calmed but Isaac continued to circulate further private prospectuses and eventually the E&WJR commenced proceedings on 19th June, to restrain him from further misrepresentation. Ultimately, Isaac's involvements with the ST&MJR would be a major factor in his collapse into bankruptcy, with gross debts of almost £32,000.

The ST&MJR had also by then independently negotiated running powers with the Midland Railway over the 3½ miles of their line to Olney. This had not been included under the provisions of the original Act, which instead allowed for the provision of the necessary facilities for the exchange of traffic

at Ravenstone Wood. The new agreement also provided for the use of the Midland Railway station and other facilities at Olney, with additional siding capacity and a small engine shed being provided by the ST&MJR for their new traffic.

However, the connection provided down to the L&NWR at Roade was initially intended to be used only for the exchange of goods traffic and so was not yet sanctioned for use by passengers. After negotiations with the L&NWR, it was subsequently agreed that the proposed link with their sidings should be extended by a few chains, to terminate in a new bay platform to be constructed at the rear of the existing Down main line platform of Roade station, thus providing the required facilities for passenger traffic. This also involved some upgrading and realignment of the existing curve down from the ST&MJR route and work had progressed sufficiently by 8th July 1890 for an application for another inspection to be made to the Board of Trade.

Correspondence from the ST&MJR revealed that more land had been acquired for the doubling of the curve at Roade and for additional sidings. Also, that the line was to be constructed using 80lb bull head rails, with the final extension into Roade station using heavier main line track of L&NWR pattern.

The application for the inspection details five sets of facing points on ST&MJR property, with a further pair on the L&NWR section. Interestingly, their positions were now indicated as distances from the junction with the N&BJR at Towcester,

An elevated view of Roade Junction, looking south towards Bletchley, showing the remains of the ST&MJR bay platform on the far, Down side. Note the platelayers hut positioned at the south end of the filled in bay. The curved arch of the village footbridge was only ever used by a few construction and inspection trains from the ST&MJR line. *Author's collection*

whereas when initially inspected in the previous year, the line of the new railway had been calibrated from the junction with the Midland Railway at Ravenstone Wood. It was the stated intention to work a passenger service to Roade from Towcester, a distance of under five miles, using tank engines, there being no turntable accommodation at either station.

The requested inspection finally took place on 16th August 1890, with Major Hutchinson again officiating, and his report provides interesting detail of the new works:

'This spur line is 21.85 chains long and connects the main line between Towcester and Olney with the L&NWR at Roade station … the new line is partly double and partly single and the sharpest curve has a radius of 10 chains and the steepest gradient an inclination of 1 in 80. The position of the spur has been considerably altered from that shown on the parliamentary plans and though no sharper curve has been introduced, the gradient of 1 in 80 for 13.6 chains has been substituted for the authorised one of 1 in 105 for 9 chains. As there are gradients on the main line of 1 in 76 and 1 in 82.5 no objection need be taken to this unauthorised gradient of 1 in 80 but it should not have been introduced without the consent of the Board of Trade being previously obtained.

The only works on the line are a brick culvert and a brick retaining wall at the back of the line along the Roade platform … the former has been substantially constructed and the same remark applying to the latter as far as completed.

There are no level crossings of any description and the signal arrangements are carried on in a new cabin at the junction with the main line and in the existing Roade station cabin. The former

contains 15 working levers and the latter 64 levers all in use.

I noticed the following requirements: Gauge ties are required to the facing points at Roade Junction and station … interlocking of the levers in Roade station cabin requires completion … Check rails are required around the curves of 10 chains radius … some rails require lifting and regulating … a clock is required at the junction cabin and the signalman's sight of the distant signal should be improved by the removal of some branches of trees. It is proposed that the traffic should in the first instance be worked by trains from Olney to Towcester, from Towcester to Roade, and from Roade to Towcester. To carry out this arrangement there is at present no rolling stock but the ST&MJR are prepared to supply this failing any agreement being come to on the subject of rolling stock between them and the EWJ Co.

The spur line is worked on the one engine system and an undertaking to this effect is to be supplied.

Subject to this undertaking and the prompt completion of the above mentioned requirements I can recommend the Board to sanction the Roade spur line being passed for public traffic upon the understanding that proper rolling stock for working is provided as soon as the necessary arrangements can be made.'

Official approval for opening of this section was duly provided on 17th September 1890 but it is not clear who was responsible for these final alterations to the line, with Baldry & Yerbergh apparently having completed their initial contract some months earlier. It is possible that the railway company used their own labour resources, or perhaps Baldry & Yerbergh were re-engaged to complete the work.

A closer view of the main line platforms at Roade, showing the massive construction of the retaining wall built for the ST&MJR bay platform, which was carved from the existing embankment. The curve up to the ST&MJR route left the station through the arch of the footbridge, to pass behind Roade Junction signal box and then climb up to the Towcester to Ravenstone line in the right background. *Author's collection*

Everyday E&WJR

Although official documentation relating to the E&WJR in the last decade of the 19th century is extremely scarce, fortunately a *Working Time Table* of July 1890 has survived, which provides a fascinating glimpse of operations on the line just before through traffic began to operate on the new extension to Ravenstone Wood.

The passenger services followed a predictable pattern, with Blisworth to Stratford trains departing at 8.55am, 11.35am, 2.50pm and 4.57pm, with the last train of the day at 7.07pm (not Saturdays) or 8.47pm (Saturdays only). Of these, only the 8.55am ran right through to Broom Junction. In the Up direction, however, three services ran through from Broom to Blisworth, leaving at 11.07am, 2.48pm and 6.14pm, whilst a further two, at 7.20am (on Mondays only) and 8.40am started the journey from Stratford. Curiously, the 7.20am Mondays only service is noted in the timetable as '*to run with the N&B train between Towcester and Blisworth*'. The N&BJR service in question was the 7.30am departure from Banbury, so this shared working is an unusual

incidence of cooperation between the two companies, for which there is no apparent explanation.

The passenger services on the E&WJR were completed by the short distance trains from Stratford to Broom and back. In the Down direction, these departed from Stratford at 7.45am, 2.15pm, a mixed passenger and goods service at 3.30pm and 5.40pm. In the Up direction, trains left Broom at 8.25am and 6.31pm. The latter service is indicated as using the carriages from the 3.30pm Down mixed train.

Whereas the profile of the passenger service is quite recognisable, the goods traffic is somewhat less so. In the Down direction, the first train of the day was a 1.00am through goods departure from Blisworth to Broom, which is noted as stopping at Towcester to pick up traffic for Stratford and beyond only. This was followed down the line by a 6.30am pick up goods service to Stratford, which paused at all stations for a short period for the exchange of traffic. Both of these services are shown as not running on Monday mornings but did operate on Sundays '*unless otherwise advised*'. A further, as required, through service from Blisworth to Stratford

EAST AND WEST JUNCTION RAILWAY.

WORKING TIME TABLE for JULY, 1890, and until Further Notice.

Private—Not for Publication.

(Stamp: EAST AND WEST — SINGLE POST LETTERS BY RAILWAY — 2 D. — FEE. — JUNCTION RAILWAY)

DOWN.

Distance from M. CH.	Station		Through Goods 1 (morn.)	Pass 2 (morn.)	Goods 3 (morn.)	Pass 4 (morn.)	Goods 5 (morn.) A	Pass 6 (morn.)	Pass 7 (aft.)	Goods and Pass 8 (aft.)	Pass 9 (aft.) Saturdays only	Pass 10 (aft.)	Goods 11 (aft.) A	Pass 12 (aft.) Not on Saturdays	Pass 13 (aft.) Saturdays only	Goods 14 (aft.)
	Blisworth	dep.	1 0		6 30	8 55		11 35	2 50		4 57		5 12	7 7	8 47	
...	Lloyd's Siding	arr./dep.														
4 20	Towcester	arr./dep.	1 15 / 1 20		6 42 / 6 46	9 10		11 50	3 5		5 12		5 27 / 5 30	7 24	9 01 / 9 02	
5 14	Junction	arr./dep.	1 23		6 49 / 6 54	9 12		11 52	3 7		5 14		5 33	7 29 / 7 30	9 15 / 9 16	
8 35	Blakesley	arr./dep.	1 31		6 57	9 19 / 9 20		11 58 / 11 59	3 13 / 3 14		5 21 / 5 22		5 43 / 5 53	7 35 / 7 36	9 18 / 9 26	
11 46	Morton Pinkney	arr./dep.	1 41		7 7 / 7 15	9 28 / 9 29		12 4 / 12 5	3 19 / 3 20		5 29 / 5 30		6 16	7 43 / 7 44	9 26 / 9 27	
15 58	Byfield	arr./dep.	1 51 / 1 57		7 28 / 7 36 / 7 48 / 8 30	9 37 / 9 38		12 11 / 12 12	3 26 / 3 27		5 38 / 5 39		6 25 / 6 35	7 57 / 7 58	9 39 / 9 50	
22 42	Fenny Compton	arr./dep.	2 18		8 50 / 9 26	9 50 / 9 51		12 26 / 12 27	3 39 / 3 40		5 51 / 5 52		6 55 / 7 10	8 7 / 8 8	9 49 / 9 50	
28 72	Kineton	arr./dep.	2 24		9 46 / 10 26	10 0 / 10 1		12 36 / 12 37	3 49 / 3 50		6 2 / 6 3		7 24 / 7 40	8 15 / 8 16	9 56 / 9 57	
32 72	Ettington	arr./dep.	2 34		10 40 / 10 55	10 7 / 10 8		12 45 / 12 46	3 58 / 3 59		6 11 / 6 12		7 53 / 8 27			
...	Clifford Siding	arr./dep.														
38 8	Stratford-on-Avon	arr./dep.	2 45 / 3 0	7 45	11 7 / 11 12	10 17 / 10 20	11 45	12 55 / 2 15	4 8	3 30 / 3 45	6 22	5 40	8 47	8 26	10 6	8 15
41 70	Binton	arr./dep.		7 56	11 15	10 30	11 56	2 26	4 0			5 51				
...	Bidford	dep.		8 6	11 7 / 11 12	10 38	12 6	2 36	4 0			6 1				
45 52	Broom	arr.	3 25	8 10	11 15	10 42	12 10	2 40	4 5			6 1			11 45

UP.

Distance from M. CH.	Station		Through Goods 15 (morn.) Stops at Bidford when required.	Goods 16 (morn.)	Pass 17 (morn.) Mondays only B	Pass 18 (morn.)	Pass 19 (morn.)	Pass 20 (morn.)	Goods 21 (aft.) A	Pass 22 (aft.)	Goods 23 (aft.)	Goods 24 (aft.) Not on Saturdays	Goods 25 (aft.) Saturdays only	Pass 26 (aft.)	Pass 27 (aft.)
	Broom	dep.	12 20	4 30						2 48	4 30			6 14	6 31
	Bidford	dep.								2 52	4 40			6 19	6 36
62	Binton	arr./dep.	12 42 / 12 54	4 55		8 40				3 9 / 3 10	5 0	6 10		6 27	6 46
7 44	Stratford-on-Avon	arr./dep.			7 20	8 40 / 8 50	8 40			3 9 / 3 10	5 10	6 10	6 50	6 37 / 6 40	6 56
...	Clifford Siding	arr./dep.													
12 60	Ettington	arr./dep.	1 14		7 28 / 7 29		8 49 / 8 50	11 37 / 11 38	1 15 / 1 25	3 19 / 3 20		6 30 / 6 58	7 10 / 7 20	6 48 / 6 49	
16 60	Kineton	arr./dep.	1 24		7 37 / 7 38		8 58 / 8 59	11 46 / 11 47	1 38 / 1 50	3 28 / 3 29		7 25 / 7 25	7 30 / 8 0	6 57 / 6 58	
23 10	Fenny Compton	arr./dep.	1 39		7 47 / 7 48		9 8 / 9 9	11 56 / 11 57	2 5 / 2 15	3 38 / 3 39		7 42 / 8 34	8 17 / 8 34	7 8 / 7 9	
29 74	Byfield	arr./dep.	1 55 / 1 56		8 3 / 8 3		9 21 / 9 22	12 11 / 12 12	2 35 / 2 50	3 51 / 3 52		8 27 / 8 46	9 0 / 9 30	7 23 / 7 24	
34 6	Morton Pinkney	arr./dep.	2 5		8 10 / 8 3		9 29 / 9 30	12 19 / 12 20	3 0 / 3 21	3 59		8 57 / 9 15	9 41 / 9 51	7 34 / 7 36	
37 17	Blakesley	arr./dep.	2 12		8 16 / 8 17		9 35 / 9 36	12 25 / 12 26	3 29	4 6 / 4 7		9 25 / 9 33	10 0 / 10 10	7 41 / 7 42	
40 38	Junction	arr./dep.	2 19		8 23		9 42	12 31	3 37	4 13		9 43	10 20	7 48	
41 32	Towcester	arr./dep.	2 22 / 2 25		8 25		9 44 / 9 45	12 33	3 40	4 15		9 46 / 9 51	10 23 / 10 30	7 50	
...	Lloyd's Siding	arr./dep.													
45 52	Blisworth	arr.	2 40		8 40		10 0	12 48	3 55	4 30		10 6 / 10 10	10 45	8 5	

NOTES.—

No. 1 stops at Towcester to attach Goods Traffic for Stratford and Stations beyond only.

A To run when required. Whenever No. 21 is to run through to Bisworth, Stratford must Telegraph all Stations, including Green's Norton Junction, not later than 11 a.m., for Staff purposes.

Strict punctuality must be observed in the working of Trains No. 1, 11, 15, and 21.

Nos. 1, 3, 15, and 16, will not run on Mondays. These Trains run on Sundays unless otherwise advised.

B Binton will be switched out each night after last stopping Train, and Trains after that will be signalled between Broom and Stratford.

B To run with the N. and B. Train between Towcester and Bisworth.

Engine Drivers must pass cautiously over facing points, both up and down.

Thick lines thus —— indicate where the Trains cross or pass each other.

In descending the inclines between Blisworth and Towcester, the rate of speed both for Passenger and Goods Trains must be so reduced that the Trains shall be completely under control; special caution being observed in running through Gayton Cutting, one mile from Blisworth Station.

A fixed Green or Caution Signal is placed at the summit of the incline between Blisworth and Towcester, to indicate where the Engine-driver and Guard are to regulate the speed of Trains.

In the event of Trains being *Late*, the Engine-driver is not to endeavour to make up lost time by running at an excessive speed.

☞ The following are the Train Staff Stations, and the Staff Regulations must be strictly observed:—Blisworth, Towcester, Green's Norton, Blakesley, Morton Pinkney, Byfield, Fenny Compton, Kineton, Ettington, Stratford-on-Avon, and Broom.

ABOVE: This *East & West Junction Railway Working Timetable* of July 1890 is a scarce survivor and provides a fascinating window into the operation of that line, just before the Stratford, Towcester & Midland Junction Railway extension to Ravenstone Wood Junction was opened to traffic. *Author's collection*

RIGHT: An East & West Junction Railway 2d letter or parcel stamp of circa 1900. The Post Office only held a monopoly over the sending of letters, not parcels. The use of such stamps to send parcels, newspapers or other items (newspaper and miscellaneous items stamps differed in design from parcel stamps) by rail dated back to the mid 19th century but were only officially sanctioned and issued under government control from 1891. There was also no regulation over their design; most were quite plain, such as this example, and few featured any railway aspect to their design apart from the company name. They form a collecting field in their own right and due to the lack of regulation when they were issued, they are far from as well documented and catalogued as ordinary stamps. *Author's collection*

The two Beyer, Peacock 2-4-0 tanks, No's 5 and 6, operated through E&WJR passenger services between Blisworth and Stratford for many years after their purchase in 1885. In this view, probably taken during the late 1890s, the locomotive bears no sign of ownership, just a painted number on the bunker side. In later years, the builder's plate would move to a position on the outside framing of the leading wheels and a cast number plate would take its place. The location is undoubtedly Blisworth, with the tall L&NWR main line signals in the right background, one with a circular 'slow line' ring on the arm, being unmistakeable. *Author's collection*

During the 1890s, one local pick up goods train a day served Clifford Siding, situated just east of Stratford-upon-Avon, adjacent to the overbridges of the Shipston road and the old Stratford & Moreton Tramway. This early view, looking eastwards from the road overbridge, shows the single siding controlled by a ground frame, with a horse-drawn cart loading goods from a wagon; most of the traffic was derived from the surrounding agricultural community. The line from Stratford was doubled to this point during the Second World War and the siding capacity considerably extended. *Author's collection*

ran at 5.12pm. Other, more local, non-passenger operations in the Down direction were an 11.45am from Stratford to Binton, Bidford and Broom, the aforementioned mixed service at 3.30pm and an engine and van movement from Stratford to Broom at 11.15pm, which picked up traffic at Binton when required.

This latter operation provided the locomotive for the first Up goods service of the day, which left Broom in the early hours at 12.20am and ran right through to Blisworth. Next was a 4.30am working from Broom to Stratford only, which picked up at Bidford when required, and there was then a gap until the 12.28pm, as required, pick up service to Blisworth. These first three Up goods services were all denoted as not running on Mondays but again would operate on Sundays unless otherwise advised. A footnote instructed that when the 12.28pm service was to run right through to Blisworth, staff at Stratford were to telegraph all points, including Green's Norton Junction, to advise them of the running of the train. A final pick up goods left Stratford for Blisworth at 6.10pm or 6.50pm on Saturdays. The Up goods services were completed by a 4.30pm local goods between Broom and Stratford only.

Another footnote in the *Working Time Table* indicated that '*a fixed green or caution signal is placed at the summit of the incline between Blisworth and Towcester to indicate where the engine driver and guard are to regulate the speed of trains*' and a warning was also given to crews to observe special caution when travelling through the cutting at Gayton. It was noted too that Binton's signals would be switched out each night after the last passenger service, with trains afterwards being signalled through from Stratford to Broom; no mention is made of any signalling at Bidford.

On the main line of the E&WJR, the same year also saw the welcome introduction of Saturday L&NWR excursions from Euston to 'Shakespeare Country'. The first such service ran on 26th July, leaving the capital at 8.45am and arriving at Blisworth at 10.10am, where the train was divided into two portions. The first ran onto the N&BJR line, proceeding via Towcester and the E&WJR route. After arrival at Stratford at 11.30am, tourists were

The western end of the Up platform at Stratford-upon-Avon circa 1906, featuring the original E&WJR signal box and a rather insubstantial canopy tacked on to the front of the station building, sheltering the waiting passengers; this would later be replaced by a more effective structure. The unusual design of water crane is also of interest, with a built-in brazier basket to prevent freezing but with a supplementary three-legged brazier at ground level. Note, too, the rather uncommon location of the loading gauge, over the Down passenger line and also that the signal box, as well as being festooned in enamelled advertising signs, boasts two nameboards, each carrying a slightly different version of the station's name! *Author's collection*

Another early 20th century view of Stratford engine shed, revealing an array of E&WJR Beyer, Peacock motive power, with two 2-4-0 tanks and an 0-6-0 tender engine on show. The original shed consisted of the two left-hand bays, with their rather unusual arched cutaways to clear the locomotive chimneys. The two bays on the right were a later addition of more suitable construction, with the higher section housing an engine hoist. Note the whitewashed walls and edging to the turntable pit and also the base of the yard lamp and telegraph pole, no doubt carried out to prevent shed staff and enginemen from the possibilty of accidents at night time. *John Alsop collection*

conducted around the usual attractions and then conveyed by road to Warwick, Kenilworth and Guys Cliffe.

Meanwhile, the second portion of the train had continued from Blisworth to Warwick Milverton station by way of Rugby and those passengers followed a reversed itinerary, arriving lastly at Stratford. From here they returned to Blisworth, where the train was reunited for the return to London, which was reached at 10.40pm. The E&WJR at this point in time used the Westinghouse brake on their rolling stock and locomotives, whereas the L&NWR was a vacuum braked line. Initially, therefore, L&NWR locomotives were used to work these new services through to Stratford.

A Joint Approach?

Meanwhile, in anticipation of the opening of their new route from Towcester to Ravenstone, the ST&MJR had, on 24th October 1889, made a formal request to the E&WJR to nominate their four members of a joint committee as provided for under the 1883 Act. This should have heralded a new era in the operation of the railways but, instead, the E&WJR members continually declined to meet with their counterparts, challenging various assertions made by the ST&MJR and alleging that there were still unfulfilled obligations on the part of that company.

The ST&MJR then served a further request on Christmas Eve of the same year, again with no result. With patience beginning to run out, a legal remedy was thought necessary and an application was made to the Queen's Bench for a Writ of Mandamus, requiring the E&WJR to comply. This was heard on 1st March 1890, before the Lord Chief Justice and Lord Justice Fry, with counsel for the

ST&MJR producing maps and plans, and claiming that there was an urgent need for the joint committee to be formed as soon as possible, with their line expected to be passed for full operation in the near future.

However, the E&WJR continued to maintain that their understanding, under the provisions of the original Act, was that the ST&MJR should have provided an exchange station and other facilities at Ravenstone Wood Junction, where land had been acquired for the purpose, instead of negotiating running powers over the Midland Railway to Olney. In addition, they claimed that those running powers were also, in fact, only available to the ST&MJR, thus theoretically restricting the East & West Junction, and the Evesham, Redditch & Stratford Junction railways in their running over the new line.

The E&WJR also claimed that additional train mileage of up to 12,000 miles per annum would be incurred, over a steeply graded and difficult to operate stretch of line, by running through to Olney instead of exchanging traffic at Ravenstone Wood.

It was further claimed that similar exchange facilities should have been provided on the new line at Roade and the E&WJR were unhappy that the full potential of this connection was not yet being fulfilled. They had anticipated that it would replace their hitherto rather unsatisfactory and costly arrangement with the N&BJR at Blisworth, where they annually exchanged in excess of 40,000 passengers and 30,000 tons of general merchandise with the L&NWR. The E&WJR was concerned that their own traffic potential would be lessened by these omissions and their expenses increased by the exchange of traffic at the 'foreign' stations, instead of on the ST&MJR line.

Ravenstone Wood Junction and the Midland signal cabin that controlled it, looking from the ST&MJR line eastwards towards Bedford. Early plans indicated a triangular junction, station and sidings at this location but running powers over the Midland to Olney were substituted instead. *M. Mitchell*

They also complained that the new line had not yet been completed as a double line of railway throughout and, furthermore, that they were in danger of being dispossessed of land that they did own through the actions of unpaid vendors.

The differences appeared insurmountable and, as a result, it was determined that there was little alternative but to present the case to the Court of the Railway Commissioners for judgement, which was heard on 13th August 1890. The E&WJR were given fifteen days to reply to the ST&MJR claim that they had withdrawn from their obligations of agreeing to form a joint committee and they duly responded in considerable detail in their answer to the Railway Commissioners. This lengthy document again asserted that the ST&MJR had failed in their own obligations and challenged various points submitted by them to the court. A further contention was that the ST&MJR had, subsequent to Board of Trade certification, allowed their new line to become unsafe for traffic through lack of proper maintenance. In support of this, the E&WJR directors had instructed their own engineer and traffic manager, Joseph Burke, to inspect and report on the condition of the ST&MJR line.

Burke's report speaks of the track being *'irregular in line and level, and the ballast being insufficiently broken and packed under the sleepers'*. In some places the embankments were said to have settled considerably, probably due to lack of maintenance since the Board of Trade inspection, and *'loose walls of pliable local limestone have been built up (in some places to a height of three or four feet) to hold the ballast, which is also of the same perishable description and is rapidly deteriorating, and the vibration of the trains will undoubtedly cause these loose walls to fall away and leave the permanent way insecurely supported'*.

Burke considered that before trains could be run at any speed, the railway would need lifting and repacking, and adjusting to correct line and level, with curves properly super-elevating. In particular, the Down line to the L&NWR at Roade still required the provision of a check-rail as indicated earlier by the Board of Trade and the whole of that part of the line was considered *'quite unsafe to run over'*. Some of the culverts were reportedly in a very bad condition and dire consequences were also forecast if one particularly suspect culvert, close to the L&NWR main line, were to collapse. Gates did not close properly owing to their posts drawing and where the line was crossed at Ravenstone Wood by a public roadway, only ordinary field gates had been provided and no gate keeper's lodge erected.

Burke rather pointedly stated that he would decline to comment on the absence of *'such obviously requisite matters such as stations, sidings, turntables, water supplies, and other accommodations at the junctions with the LNW and Midland railways'* or on the large expenditure required on rolling stock, with the E&WJR stock already having been found insufficient for even their own purposes. Some of the stock was only hired and most was not yet fitted with the continuous brake. Burke also considered it impractical to work the Roade Branch in connection with a through service of trains between Towcester and Ravenstone. He unsurprisingly concluded that *'after a close personal inspection at present it would be quite unsafe to run trains over it, and with the consequent danger to life and limb apart from pecuniary and other risks involved, as your Engineer and Traffic Manager, I should feel compelled to decline to take part in the working of any line in the condition in which the railway between Towcester Roade and Ravenstone is at present'*.

A postscript to the report also stated that there were several other serious objections stated in his director's earlier answer to the Railway Commissioners, with which he also entirely concurred. He was of course, rather understandably, only telling his own directors exactly what they wished to hear.

Burke's report was duly forwarded to the Board of Trade by the E&WJR solicitors Merrick & Son, on 30th October, with a request that '*it may receive your attention*'. Another letter from Merrick's then followed on 5th November, informing the Board of Trade that at the sitting of the Court of the Railway Commissioners on the previous Monday, the application of the ST&MJR against the E&WJR had been dismissed, although the former had indicated that it would make another application to the Court. Despite the fact that the Board of Trade had given their formal approval for the line to be opened as long ago as May, this ongoing dispute between the E&WJR and the ST&MJR had so far prevented the actual use of the route for regular traffic.

After more legal argument, a final resolution of the situation came on 29th January 1891, when Lord Chief Justice Wills decreed that there should be no further impediment raised against the formation of the joint committee. In giving judgment, with costs, in favour of the ST&MJR, he also criticised the conduct of both of the parties and the way in which the overall defence of the E&WJR had been presented. Faced with this decision, the E&WJR had finally to agree to nominate four of its managers to join the two ST&MJR representatives in forming the long awaited joint committee.

Speaking at the annual meeting of the ST&MJR on 2nd July 1891, the chairman, Dr Barratt, who had taken over that office from Sir Thomas George Fermor Hesketh, was then at last able to state that their new line had now been '*absolutely finished*' and had again been inspected and approved by the Board of Trade on the previous evening. The joint committee with the E&WJR had also been formed and began to function from 13th April 1891. An agreement had already been concluded with the Midland Railway for running their goods

After the formation of the joint committee, the E&WJR and ST&MJR names soon appeared together on documentation and also on this ubiquitous style of bridge weight restriction sign. When first built, these bridges were only required to support the weight of horse-drawn carts but the coming of steam driven road wagons and then motor vehicles required the imposition of even more severe weight restrictions. *Author's collection*

traffic from London to Bristol over the new line.

The new committee immediately styled itself as the East & West Junction & Stratford-upon-Avon, Towcester & Midland Junction Railway, with the poor Evesham, Redditch & Stratford Junction Railway again nominally being left out in the cold. This new heading soon appeared in full on various official documents and forms but, within a short space of time, the company had tired of their extravagant title and it often was abbreviated to the '*East & West Junction &c. Railway*'.

Passengers to Olney

At last a compromise had been reached and the joint committee could function, with the line then opening to through goods services from 2nd July 1891. However, some local traffic, probably coal, appears to have been operated since April, when the line had initially been approved for use by the Board of Trade. The Midland Railway also commenced using the route as planned for their through service from Bristol to London, with the resulting

The ST&MJR built two intermediate stations between Towcester and Olney, at Stoke Bruerne and Salcey Forest, for their short-lived passenger service. The two were identical in construction and appearance, and in some views are difficult to tell apart. This is Salcey Forest, looking east towards Ravenstone Wood Junction. Apart from the short platform, the only other facilities were a brick built hut alongside the single goods siding located behind the platform, whilst initially, a small signal cabin had also been provided, on a site just off picture to the right. *Author's collection*

ABOVE: Salcey Forest station from the east in 1939. This was a particularly isolated spot, reached only by a field footpath from the main Northampton to Newport Pagnell road, which bridged the line at Horton. Little changed here for many years but the platform edge had mostly gone, although the building itself, which only saw passengers for a few months in the 1890s, remained in railway use until demolition in the mid 1950s. *Author's collection*

ABOVE: Stoke Bruerne station was identical to its twin at Salcey Forest but at least was adjacent to a minor road, even if the eponymous canal village was still a mile or so downhill from the line. The building was eventually sold out of railway use and remains today as a private residence. *L. Hanson*

LEFT: The road approach to the station was only used by railway passengers from December 1892 until the end of March in the following year, when services between Towcester and Olney were withdrawn due to a lack of patronage. Thereafter, a permanent way worker lived in the premises, whilst the approach road was used intermittently by the few traders that used the goods siding located just beyond the far end of the station building. *Author's collection*

Stoke Bruerne from the adjacent minor road bridge, showing the small goods yard and sidings. Unlike Salcey Forest, the yard here continued in use until closure to common user traffic in 1952. A few coal wagons are visible, and there appears to be a motorised permanent way trolley parked on the running line, which continues towards Towcester beneath another overbridge in the distance. The track layout as originally provided had comprised a loop with two short sidings running off either end. The points at the western end of the loop were taken out at the end of September 1912, with the signal box being closed at the same time and replaced by a ground frame just glimpsed here to the right of the point on the running line. *Author's collection*

agreement entitling the joint committee to retain two-thirds of the receipts from this traffic.

However, problems soon arose after a heavy Midland goods train from London to Bristol was derailed on the E&WJR route between Kineton and Ettington early on the morning of 13th October 1891. The permanent way was considerably damaged and the line blocked for most of the day. The accident was, however, to have greater consequences, when engineers sent by the Midland Railway to inspect the scene reported that the track was in such a poor condition that they did not consider it safe to run their own heavy locomotives over it. The Midland Company therefore quickly reconsidered their existing agreement with the joint committee and stated that their locomotives would no

longer work the through traffic after December 1891.

The joint committee therefore had to act quickly to obtain additional and more suitable motive power to continue to operate these services and, accordingly, three ex-L&NWR Class 'DX' goods 0-6-0s were obtained. However, this development also caused a serious drop in revenue, with the new arrangements for carrying the Midland traffic being far less favourable. In addition, the joint committee locomotives often struggled with the heavier trains and on many occasions required banking assistance from a Midland engine to tackle the stiff climb from Olney to Ravenstone Wood. This, of course, introduced another unwanted expense and further reduced the already depleted profitability of the Midland traffic.

Three L&NWR 'DX' Class 0-6-0s were purchased by the E&WJR in 1891 to handle through goods traffic from Stratford to Olney, although only No. 7 was destined to have a long career on the line. This circa 1900 view at the west end of Stratford features either No. 8 or No. 9 at the head of a string of wagons on the spur from the Great Western. The line to Broom Junction heads off picture to the left. *Author's collection*

At least, with goods services having been successfully initiated, attention could now turn to the use of the line for passenger traffic, serving en route the two substantial stations that had been provided at the lonely locations of Stoke Bruerne and Salcey Forest. The joint committee, still short of suitable locomotives and rolling stock, therefore arranged to hire two trains consisting of a tank engine and three carriages, somewhat ironically from the Midland Railway, to inaugurate a passenger service from Olney to Towcester. The E&WJR company was, however, able to supply engine crews and the service began, with little ceremony, on 1st December 1892.

On the following day, the *Northampton Mercury* recorded the commencement:

'... the first train starting from Olney shortly before nine o'clock. This short line, it is only 12 miles in extent, has had several vicissitudes and has practically been complete for months. Goods trains passed over it twelve months ago, but it was not until today that the public (save we believe in one excursion train) have had the privilege of passing over the line ... four trains are arranged per day for this month at least. All trains stop at all stations, and most of them are timed to do the distance in 32 minutes. They are all in connection with the Midland or other lines and experience will probably show that the travelling public will largely avail themselves of the new line, a veritable short cut. For goods traffic it is bound to be of much use, for extra journeys of 35 miles for each goods train are not jokes even to a wealthy company like the Midland.'

The *Mercury* continued:

'... the Olney people did not take much notice of the start, none going down to the station to see the train off and only two booking by it. Owing to the breakdown nearer Bedford, the train was despatched to time 8.41 without waiting for the down train from Bedford. It started with four passengers, two with tickets to Towcester, one booked for Salcey Forest, and one to Stoke Bruerne. The train consisted of three renovated Midland carriages, drawn by a Midland tank engine. The journey was very easy and the time well kept. There was a minutes stop at Salcey Forest station, where no-one was booked. At Stoke Bruerne, eight took tickets for Towcester, a 3$^1/_2$d ride, but only seven entered the train, one man who had secured the first ticket No. 0000 keeping it as a relic. At Towcester the engine was put on the other end, and the return journey with eleven passengers, commenced at 9.26. Inspector Sawkins of the Midland Railway accompanied the train.'

The breakdown near Bedford was in fact a far more serious occurrence than the description might have suggested. Earlier that morning, an overnight Midland goods train from Gloucester to London was derailed close to Bedford and a mile of track damaged, resulting in services on the Northampton and Bedford line also being suspended.

However, the new passenger service was not the success that the *Mercury* had predicted with, perhaps unsurprisingly, few passengers using the trains after the inaugural journey. Receipts did not cover the Midland Railway accounts for the hire of the stock and the service was therefore summarily withdrawn, with the closure to passengers of the two stations en route.

The *Mercury* of Friday 31st March 1893 recorded the cessation of services, stating that '*passenger trains will cease to run along*

The short-lived passenger service from Towcester terminated at Olney, on the Midland Railway branch from Bedford to Northampton. Here the ST&MJR also provided a small shed to service and stable the branch engine and additional sidings for their goods traffic. The locomotive shed, topped by a distinctive water tower, can be seen on the left of this view of the station, opposite the goods shed and sidings. This 1950s view is looking south-east towards Bedford. Closed to passengers on 5th March 1962 and goods on 6th January 1964, nothing remains of the station today. *Author's collection*

This closer view of the ST&MJR's locomotive facilities at Olney reveals the simplicity of operations here. The turntable led directly into the brick-built single road shed, which also acted as a support for the water tank; an inspection pit was available between the rails, whilst a simple lean-to store and a couple of gas lamps completed the site. Although officially closed in 1928, which meant that engines were no longer out-stationed here, the shed and yard were still in regular use through to the mid 1950s. *Author's collection*

that line after tomorrow Thursday', the inference being that the report had been drafted earlier in the week after the receipt of advance information from the railway company. The end of services has, however, been reported, in usual railway parlance, as being with effect from the 1st April. The stated cessation '*after Thursday*' initially seems unusual but when it is realised that Friday 31st March was actually Good Friday and no trains would normally have been run on that day, it becomes clear that it was considered convenient to end operations instead on the Thursday; in fact, the *Mercury* had itself appeared a day early that week for the same reason.

As a direct result, the proposed passenger service to Roade L&NWR station, where a bay had been specially constructed in the Down main line platform, was never introduced. It would in any case have been difficult to integrate with the Towcester to Olney service, with trains having to retrace their steps up from the L&NWR to regain their own line and continue their journey.

Services on the E&WJR proper continued much as before, with a core of four trains each way per day between Blisworth and Stratford. An additional early train ran from Stratford at 7.05am on Mondays only, whilst on Saturdays only two extra services ran at 4.45pm and 8.45pm. Otherwise, the first trains in either direction left at 8.55am, with the corresponding last returning train departing at 6.37pm from Blisworth and three minutes later from the other end of the line at Stratford. This pattern of service continued, with just minor variations through the period of the mid 1890s.

Excursion traffic was also popular, a prime example being during July 1894, when the E&WJR organised a day trip to the Malverns. The train left Blisworth at 6.45am, with many passengers travelling from Daventry to join en route. An hour was spent at Tewkesbury during a drive around the area, with the return train leaving Malvern at 7.00pm, and all passengers were back at their starting points by 9.30pm. As an interesting operational aside, this excursion would have used the direct connection at Ashchurch Junction between the Evesham and Malvern branch lines, which crossed the Midland's ex-Birmingham & Gloucester Railway main line on the level.

Operational Matters

In October 1891, the E&WJR secretary, Charles Hobbs, acting on behalf of the joint committee, approached the Board of Trade for approval to introduce a new method of train control on their lines. Hobbs' letter stated that the committee wished to introduce the Webb & Thompson system of electric train staff for the absolute block working of single lines, in place of the existing ordinary train staff or 'one engine in steam' arrangements. The intention was to eventually introduce the new equipment on all lines but initially to just upgrade the section from Towcester to Ravenstone Wood.

The BoT offered no objection to the proposal but commented that it would be desirable to work the system '*with two wires*', as recent experience elsewhere had shown this to be preferable. In addition, the joint committee were requested to provide a sealed undertaking to comply with the necessary regulations. This, however, was to prove a problem as Hobbs had to report that, as the joint committee was not a corporate body, they had no official seal to affix. In the event, the BoT were prepared to accept a formal undertaking and this was duly provided, signed by Hobbs and Saul Isaac. The BoT then responded with their approval for the line to be worked by the Tyer's Train Tablet system; Hobbs was typically quick to correct the error.

However, before the new installation had been made, the joint committee reported to the BoT that they now considered that it would be more convenient to work only the section from Towcester to Salcey Forest by the new electric train staff system and to continue the use of the existing arrangements onwards to Ravenstone Wood Junction. It is not clear from the correspondence whether this was due to cost or operational requirements but the matter seems to have been concluded satisfactorily by October 1892, when a revised undertaking was submitted.

Subsequently, the joint committee did gradually extend the use of the new electric train staff over much of their system and, in May 1894, the Board of Trade was again approached to sanction its use between Ettington and Stratford-upon-Avon. The following year then saw a further extension between Byfield and Moreton Pinkney, whilst in April 1897, the section from Byfield to Ettington was included.

Through this period of the mid 1890s it had also somehow been found possible to further enhance the E&WJR locomotive fleet, with further goods 0-6-0s , No's 10 and 11, arriving from Beyer, Peacock in 1895 and 1896 respectively. In comparison with the situation of ten years earlier, the motive power department now had a far more modern and reliable appearance.

Internal Wrangling

Despite the joint committee having theoretically been in operation since early 1891, internecine wars still rumbled on, with various squabbles continuing to surface. Authority was given to appoint an arbitrator in an attempt to alleviate some of the disputes but, in the event, even this seemingly sensible solution failed to materialise. The ER&SJR were also to complain that they had no representation on the committee, as an original clause allowing for this had at some stage been withdrawn from the agreement as a result of objections from other quarters.

A second approach was then made to the Railway Commissioners by the promoters of the ER&SJR, these comprising Messrs Penton, Reid, Rowson, Barnard, Bouverie, Emmanuel and Herbert, who between them held £200,000 of debenture stock. Mr Justice Wills severely criticised the voluminous objections raised by the E&WJR, granting the ER&SJR application and awarding costs against the E&WJR, which were ultimately to remain unpaid.

The ST&MJR were the next to raise objections, on this occasion against the appointment of Merrick, the E&WJR company solicitor, to the post of general manager of the joint committee at an

ABOVE: A few miscellaneous documents have fortunately survived from the joint committee era, including this privilege ticket order issued in September 1907 to Mr H.J. Hill, a clerk at Stratford-upon-Avon, for a journey over the GWR line to Birmingham. *Author's collection*

ABOVE RIGHT: Luggage labels were also issued by the joint committee, such as this example produced for traffic between Ettington and Towcester. *Author's collection*

RIGHT: A large package, weighing 142lbs, was conveyed between Stratford and Kineton by the East & West Junction & Stratford-on-Avon, Towcester & Midland Junction Railway on 24th November 1893; the carriage fee was three shillings. *Author's collection*

annual salary of £200. The E&WJR representatives already on the committee were Messrs Brown, Crampton, Coombes and Hall, and together with Merrick, they were also the receivers and managers of their own line. It is not difficult to see why equitable solutions to the various problems were difficult to reach, with so many vested interests involved amongst the still nominally independent companies.

A measure of the difficulties between the companies can be seen in an exchange of correspondence between one Thomas Wilkins, by then a director and receiver of the ST&MJR company, and certain official bodies. On 4th September 1893, Wilkins wrote, obviously in some desperation, to the Registrar of Joint Stock Companies at Somerset House, apparently in response to an earlier demand for mandatory returns:

'*Dear Sir: Your favour 518R is before me. You are possibly aware that under this company's special act their railway had to be placed under a joint committee of two members of this company and four members of the East and West Company for the two railways to be worked and managed as one: saving only "separate establishment charges of the two companies".*

That joint committee has under the insistence of the four East and West members employed as its own officers the officers of the separate establishment of the East and West Company. It has also insisted on working the Evesham, Redditch and Stratford Junction Railway without any authority to do so and has made the fact of there being no agreement between that company and the two companies an excuse for retaining what the joint committee's executive asserts to be net revenue. Hence this company is without funds. The small portion of stock and the shares issued are in consequence of the uncommunicative working of the joint committee wholly unmarketable so that the company is practically kept penniless by the joint committee.

This company owes one and half years for services of the registered officer and secretary and office room. The registered officer therefore has practically ceased to act although he still retains control of the issue of certificates by keeping the seal key.

I am dubious what steps to take. I have been a Director and Receiver without remuneration for some years but have received nothing. Solicitors are unwilling to act when they can see no immediate fund for expenses and even arbitration cannot be sought without money. It seems to me there must be some special course available where Parliament practically takes the control of our property and its revenue out of our hands. There must be some way of getting justice done. As to stock and loan accounts there is no difference between now and last return. The difficulty is to get a registered officer to fill up and make returns when there is no money to pay him. Can you advise me what might be done?'

A reply was obviously quickly received as on 6th September Wilkins wrote again:

'*518R. Sir: I am obliged by yours of 5th and have written to the Assistant Secretary Railway Department Board of Trade to ask what is to be done to put this company in funds to enable it to perform the duty you mention.*

So long as we are prevented from using or receiving revenue from our line by an Act of Parliament I fail to see that we can be considered liable for not performing duties entailing an expense which we have not the funds to meet.

The company would be homeless but for my giving it a home and if this is to incur trouble with the authorities I shall take its name down and resign my connection with it.

I have been striving for 6 years to get common justice done to the people who have put their money with this company on the faith of the East and West Company's guarantee of 5% and am getting very sick of working for nothing and struggling against the shameful treatment we get under our act.

Except its line the company possesses nothing so I don't see how a penalty can be enforced.'

Eventually, in late March 1894, a Bill was put before a Parliamentary Select Committee to reconstitute the joint committee and give a greater influence to the ST&MJR, who had become unhappy with what they considered to be continual obstruction by the E&WJR and ER&SJR members. The creation of the joint committee had also changed the financial fortunes of the ST&MJR, although they considered themselves to be something of a senior partner.

At the first sitting, the chairman of the Parliamentary Committee pointedly commented that the members of the joint committee appeared to be continually fighting amongst themselves and that he could not remember another case being submitted to Parliament for the settlement of such an internal dispute. In the event, it was judged that the preamble to the Bill had not been proved, the application was thrown out and so matters continued much as before.

The Regulation of Railways Act 1889

Although recent attention had largely focussed on the upgrading of the E&WJR line and the machinations of the formation of the new joint committee, further problems were never far away. As usual, this meant unwelcome and unplanned expenditure.

The Regulation of Railways Act of 1889 empowered the Board of Trade to require all railway companies to make certain provisions, within a prescribed timescale, in connection with public safety. These covered the introduction of block signalling, the interlocking of points and signals, and the provision of continuous brakes on passenger trains, which now became a statutory requirement. The effects of this Act on the neighbouring Northampton & Banbury Junction Railway have been recorded earlier and the E&WJR understandably had similar difficulties in complying with these edicts from higher authority.

As a result, the E&WJR secretary, Charles Hobbs, initially communicated with the Board of Trade on 23rd December 1889, indicating that the company concurred with certain representations and objections already made on behalf of similarly impecunious lines by the Railway Companies Association earlier that month. He further stated that, in consequence of the already unprofitable nature of the E&WJR passenger traffic, his directors felt that they may in future be forced to run only mixed trains of goods and passenger vehicles. However, if the new requirements for continuous braking were to be adhered to, it might then leave them no alternative but to abandon the passenger traffic altogether.

As a result of these discussions the Board of Trade agreed to allow the E&WJR to convey non-continuously braked vehicles on passenger trains in cases where the traffic was urgent or of a perishable nature, subject to the company strictly limiting the number of those occasions. The rules were similarly relaxed for the running of mixed trains where it was necessary for the convenience of the public and the E&WJR were also allowed to continue using four of their existing passenger carriages, (No's 1 to 4) which were not fitted with continuous brakes, on the basis that they were old and of limited value and lifespan, and would not therefore bear the expense of fitting the brake.

Despite these concessions, however, Hobbs again conveyed representations to the Board of Trade in a lengthy letter of 21st November 1890. It was pointed out that the E&WJR interchanged traffic on a daily basis with the Midland, Great Western and London & North Western railways, all of whom had adopted the vacuum brake on their vehicles, whereas the E&WJR was still a Westinghouse braked line. It was held that the E&WJR would be disadvantaged in that they would still be unable to convey through traffic from those companies, and would therefore be forced to offload and reload vehicles with the attendant costs and delays. The other companies could convey each others traffic or induce the public to use only their lines rather than send via E&WJR routes, and this was considered unfair and prejudicial to the state of the E&WJR finances.

Hobbs further pointed out that the E&WJR passenger traffic was already so small that a tank engine, two carriages and a brake usually sufficed for each train. However, there were frequently occasions when family saloons, horse boxes, carriage trucks and hound vans from other companies with different brake arrangements were attached to E&WJR trains. If the proportion of unbraked or differently braked vehicles on trains was restricted, then a considerable curtailment of facilities to the public would follow, with further consequent loss to the E&WJR.

The company therefore requested that the BoT allow the number of vehicles not fitted with continuous brakes and carried at the rear of trains to be increased to three, with the addition of another brake vehicle in the rear. This relaxation, it was claimed, would also be of great convenience to local farmers, who often wished to send an odd vehicle of perishable or cattle traffic on the next possible train.

It was also claimed that another requirement, to position passenger carriages of mixed trains between the engine and the goods vehicles, would be potentially dangerous on the E&WJR, owing to the many changes of gradient on the line. The alternate uphill and downhill stretches would subject the passenger carriages to the whole weight of the goods vehicles and possibly cause snatching of the couplings on certain stretches of line; it was felt that some of the stock was not substantial enough to stand those stresses. Mixed trains were greatly appreciated by the public in the district and should the E&WJR be forced to curtail or discontinue them, it was again felt that this would cause another considerable inconvenience.

The directors also suggested that, with the company already in Chancery, they would have insufficient funds to allow the fitting of additional engines with the required brake appliances or to fit their stock with continuous brake pipes. Indeed, any further curtailment of the E&WJR revenue would seriously increase their financial difficulties, to a point where it would probably once again be necessary to consider withdrawal of passenger facilities completely. In further support of their representations, the E&WJR concluded that, judging from published returns,

they had already complied with the Board's requirements to an extent which compared favourably with many other similar small railway companies.

Unfortunately, this appeal fell mostly on deaf ears and the Board's reply of 28th November 1890 stipulated that they were unable to agree to any further modification of the schedule of requirements served on the E&WJR under the terms of the Act. However, they did allow the company some breathing space by amending the dates for the compliance until 28th November 1891 for the adoption of the Block System, and to 28th May 1892 for the interlocking of points and signals on all lines, and the introduction of the continuous brake.

A further concession indicated that the requirements for the interlocking of points and signals would not be applied where use of an Annett's Key, or Train Staff, had previously been approved by the Board of Trade. It was also clarified that the proportion of unbraked vehicles on trains should not exceed one in four vehicles on passenger trains running a distance less than ten miles without a stop, or one in six on trains exceeding ten miles without a stop.

The Board of Trade did agree that a limited number of mixed trains could be run where the goods wagons did not have continuous brakes, subject to the engine, tender and passenger vehicles having such brakes. However, they reiterated that in such cases, the goods wagons should be conveyed behind the passenger vehicles, with a brake van provided for every ten vehicles of the train. Further stipulations were that the total number of vehicles in a mixed train should not exceed twenty-five and that the maximum speed between stations should not exceed 25 mph. In addition, all trains were required to stop at all stations or at intervals not exceeding ten miles or, if the stations were more than ten miles apart, then at all stations. The Board also indicated that they would reserve the power to designate the number of mixed trains or the portions of lines on which they were to run.

The date for compliance with the regulations for the fitting of continuous brakes was fast approaching when Hobbs again wrote to the Board of Trade on 13th May 1892. He pointed out that the E&WJR had already complied with the requirements for block signalling and interlocking but that it had not yet been possible to fully comply with the braking requirements and requested an extension of a further year. He stated that 61% of E&WJR vehicles had so far been fitted with the continuous brake and that arrangements had also been made to equip another engine. However, the continuing poor financial situation of the company and the paucity of receipts had rendered them unable to do more than pay their working expenses.

In reply, the Board of Trade allowed the requested extension of time but also added that they were still unable to settle the numbers of mixed trains to be allowed until the requirements of the N&BJR were known, as a portion of the running line was common to both companies. The E&WJR were requested to send a list of the trains that they wished to be mixed but, somewhat surprisingly, their prompt reply of 12th August instead informed the Board that they no longer proposed to run any mixed trains.

Rather inevitably, further correspondence then ensued and, on 25th November, Hobbs stated that, owing to the fact that the E&WJR ran for almost the whole of its length through favourable hunting country, they were often called upon to convey a considerable number of horse boxes on their passenger trains. The E&WJR had normally been able to accommodate this traffic but were now faced with the difficulty that the stock of other companies was not fitted with the Westinghouse brake. The E&WJR were therefore unable to take the horse boxes forward, causing considerable inconvenience to their public and the Board were asked to agree to such traffic being taken on passenger trains without limiting their speed to 25mph.

Change at Morton Pinkney for London and Birmingham?

As mentioned previously, in March 1883, the Imperial Credit Corporation, a major shareholder in the E&WJR and its associated companies, had been wound up and its assets were transferred to the Railway & General Company in May of that year. The Railway & General was a finance house that specialised in railway speculation, cheaply buying up shares in run-down lines and attempting to sell them on at a profit to larger neighbouring concerns.

In 1885, two of the major shareholders of the R&G Company, Henry Pigeon and John Turton Woolley, had been involved in the promotion of an E&WJR Worcester & Broom Railway scheme, which would have formed an end-on junction with the existing line at Stratford. Three years later, a Worcester & Broom Railway (Extension) scheme was proposed, to link the E&WJR line near Morton Pinkney, with the Metropolitan Railway at Aylesbury, thus forming a potential through route for the Metropolitan from London to Stratford and Worcester.

However, the plans were interrupted when the principal shareholder of the R&G, Benjamin Piercy, died in 1888. The R&G then turned for support to Sir Edward Watkin, chairman of the Metropolitan and the Manchester, Sheffield & Lincolnshire railways. Watkin sensed an opportunity and, before too long, William Pollitt, the general manager of the MS&LR was installed as a director of the Railway & General Company, followed shortly afterwards by his fellow board member J.W. McClure. At this point in time, the Railway & General held £108,479 of E&WJR stock and a further interest of £42,895 in the ER&SJR.

The proposal for the extension from Morton Pinkney, together with a rival scheme by the E&WJR for their own Towcester & Buckingham line, was brought before the House of Lords on 30th May 1889. However, the presentation for the Worcester & Broom Extension Railway caused considerable unintended amusement, when the promoters produced their plan of the route in the form of a modified L&NWR timetable map. The committee decided to consider the two new proposals as conflicting Bills and eventually the Worcester (Extension) Railway Bill was rejected by Parliament on 27th June, whilst the rival Towcester & Buckingham scheme was approved.

A meeting of the Railway & General Company on 17th February 1892 then revealed how their board had in fact been making strenuous efforts

to gain control of the E&WJR and ER&SJR over the past few years. However, they had found it impossible to learn much of the internal affairs of these companies which, having been in the hands of receivers for many years, had published no accounts or held any meetings for shareholders. As a principal shareholder, the R&G were concerned to discover that the railways had made, without consultation, arrangements with the Midland to allow running over their lines. A more vigorous approach was felt to be required and it was decided that they should take the necessary steps 'to deal with the remaining Directors of the E&WJR'. In addition, two directors of the R&G were also appointed to the board of the ER&SJR, in an attempt to exercise more control over that portion of their assets.

This, however, was the last attempt by the Railway & General Company to influence the development of the railway network in the South Midlands. In 1893, they sold their holdings in the E&WJR and ER&SJR, a nominal asset value of £337,316 9s 8d, to the Manchester, Sheffield & Lincolnshire Railway for just £20,000. This expenditure had been approved by the MS&LR Board in May of that year, as a means of cheaply obtaining a majority shareholding in the E&WJR and its associated companies. The MS&LR outlay purchased 2,608 preference and 5,861 deferred £5 shares in the ER&SJR, and over £280,000 nominal worth of a variety of E&WJR stock; also included was an E&WJR certificate of indebtedness for £9,385 to Thomas Russell Crampton, dating back to 1881 and 1883, when Crampton had hired locomotives, rolling stock, and materials to the company.

The MS&LR then supported a new proposal of 1892 for a Birmingham, North Warwickshire & Stratford-upon-Avon Railway. This was to have branches from Wotton Wawen to the GWR's Alcester Branch and from Stratford to link with the E&WJR, and included a provision for the MS&LR to work over the new line. Once the MS&LR had forged southwards from

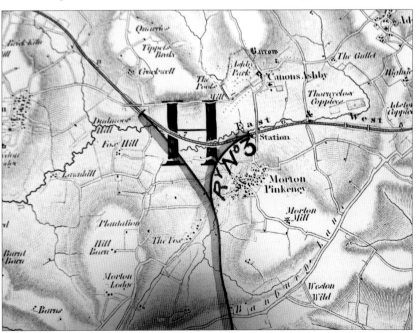

The 1889 extension of the Metropolitan Railway to join the E&WJR at Morton Pinkney would have certainly increased the traffic at that remote location, although it is perhaps doubtful whether the station itself would have seen much additional business, with most trains probably using the western side of the proposed triangular junction to reach Stratford and Birmingham, rather than Towcester and beyond. *NRO-DP*

the Nottingham area, this would have created the potential for a through route from Birmingham to London via Stratford and the E&WJR at Woodford. It would have furnished a competitive route from London to Birmingham of 116¹/₂ miles, shorter than the Great Western and only 3¹/₂ miles more than the L&NWR. The E&WJR and the ST&MJR both registered objections to the Bill, which was also opposed by the Midland and Great Western companies.

The MS&LR Board accordingly gave authority for moves to establish greater links with the E&WJR and ER&SJR, and a subsequent Act of 29th June 1893 provided powers for the MS&LR to subscribe to and run their trains over their smaller neighbours' lines. Provision was also made for the MS&LR to subscribe £50,000 to the ordinary stock of the E&WJR and ER&SJR, and £100,000 to the Worcester & Broom project in addition. The MS&LR would, if the subscription was realised, then appoint two of their own directors to the boards of the E&WJR and ER&SJR, and three to the board of the Worcester & Broom company.

Railway industry gossip of late 1894 then hinted that the MS&LR were even likely to seek powers in the next session of

Parliament to amalgamate the E&WJR, ST&MJR and ER&SJR lines, and then to take the combined group into their own fold. However, before long the MS&LR cooled off in their attempts to reach Birmingham themselves, with the prospect on the horizon of an agreement with the Great Western Railway to provide a new joint line into London. In addition, to avoid antagonising their new allies they also decided not to further exploit their holdings in the E&WJR and ER&SJR.

However, the eventual construction of the MS&LR extension to London, in the guise of the Great Central Railway, did provide the E&WJR with some welcome revenue for a while. In 1895, with construction proceeding apace, temporary single line gated connections were provided between the E&WJR and the new railway near Woodford-cum-Membris. For the next few years, a considerable amount of construction traffic traffic was carried over the E&WJR.

These two links were eventually upgraded to main line status and soon after the opening of their London Extension to passenger traffic, the newly formed Great Central Railway

ABOVE: The double track northern curve between the E&WJR and the Great Central Railway joined the main line just to the south of the station then known as Woodford & Hinton and was used until 1947 for passenger traffic, and thereafter just by freight until closure in 1964. This early view shows the newly completed trackwork, with the railway settlement around the station and the village of Woodford Halse still developing in the background. *Author's collection*

RIGHT: The new GCR main line was linked to the E&WJR at Woodford West Junction by means of two connections. The south curve was only used for traffic for a very short period of time after the opening of the GCR line in 1899 and was then disconnected at the main line end, thereafter being used as a long siding from Woodford West Junction. This view, taken on 1st March 1959, shows the GCR main line to the right and the bufferstops in the left distance denoting the end of the long siding on the curve. *M. Mitchell*

RIGHT: The Great Central main line burrowed beneath the E&WJR mid way between Morton Pinkney and Byfield stations. This view, taken in the late 1890s, illustrates how the existing E&WJR line had to be slewed to one side to allow for the construction of a girder bridge over the cutting of the new railway. The bridge was constructed to accommodate double track to align with the engineering of the E&WJR route, although a second line would never be laid. *Fielden's Magazine*

ABOVE: The two connections from the Great Central main line converged with the E&WJR at Woodford West Junction, where a GCR design signal box was erected to control the traffic. This view, taken in 1933 from a nearby bridle road footbridge, shows the northern link to Woodford & Hinton station on the left, the E&WJR line to Morton Pinkney continuing straight ahead and the disused southern spur holding just two wagons to the right. The massive blue brick span of the Eydon road bridge crosses the latter two routes in the background. Both of the connections were built as double track, although the E&WJR was just a single line at this point. *Author's collection*

RIGHT: A closer view of the southern curve between the E&WJR and the Great Central Railway at Woodford, with the latter line just out of sight beyond the bufferstops in the distance. The two sidings were used for the exchange of traffic between the two routes until the closure of the E&WJR line in 1964 but here, on 23rd May of that year, were now in use for the storage of wagons. *Author's collection*

LEFT: The northern connection between the E&WJR and GCR carried passenger traffic to and from Woodford & Hinton station. This included both domestic E&WJR trains and through carriages travelling between London and Stratford-upon-Avon. Here, the E&WJR's only true passenger locomotive, Beyer, Peacock 2-4-0 No. 13, has been attached to a through coach from the Great Central route and will shortly depart for Stratford-upon-Avon. *Author's collection*

BELOW: A view of Ettington station from the road bridge, probably in the late 1920s when old Midland Railway 0-6-0 goods locomotives had been introduced on the route to replace withdrawn E&WJR types. No. 3551, a '1798' Class built in August 1897, carried MR. No. 2265 until renumbering in 1907. Seen here awaiting departure with a Stratford train, the locomotive had just completed sixty years in service when withdrawn in October 1957. *Author's collection*

utilised the southern spur to the E&WJR. This occurred in August 1899, when the 5.20pm passenger service from Marylebone was operated directly through to Byfield, where an E&WJR train was provided onwards to Stratford. This arrangement was, however, to prove very short lived as, in September, the through service to Byfield was amended to work, on Saturdays only, via Woodford & Hinton station and the northern curve instead. In the following month, the connection was then made at Woodford station itself.

The south curve thereafter fell into decline, being taken out of use from 22nd October 1900 and was disconnected at the GCR end, with the remnant continuing as exchange sidings operated from Woodford West Junction.

As will be seen later, a renewal of interest from the Great Central would then see through coaches operating between Marylebone and Stratford via Woodford from 16th June 1902, around the same time as the L&NWR through coach from Euston, via Blisworth, ceased to operate. The Marylebone service would ultimately run for many years, with as many as four through coaches each day at times, until finally withdrawn in 1936.

More Schemes – and Some Local Sensations

In 1896, the joint committee made one last and ultimately unsuccessful attempt to associate themselves with another company, in order to extend their catchment area and so attract more through traffic to the line. Discussions apparently took place with the Midland & South Western Junction Railway, whose sphere of influence extended from Cheltenham, through Swindon and onwards to Southampton. An alliance would undoubtedly have attracted some additional traffic to the line but it appears that the M&SWJR were not sufficiently interested to pursue the proposal.

Tragedy then struck in three rather different ways during the latter part of 1897. On 14th August, the *Leamington Spa Courier* reported the death of Harry Freeman, a porter at Binton. A part of his work at the station was to lower the signal for approaching trains and having done so on this particular occasion, he had then tried to '*run across the metals to reach the opposite platform*' [*sic*] but had been caught by the locomotive and run over. There was, of course, only ever one platform at Binton.

Three months later the same newspaper reported on another similar incident, when Edward Jessett, of Bedlam Farm, Burton Dassett, was killed by the 3.00pm train from Stratford at Tomlin's Crossing on the Chadshunt road. These two unfortunate occurrences could probably be described as occupational hazards of the time but the '*Ettington Horror*' featured in the *Northampton Mercury* on Saturday 19th November was a far more sensational affair altogether.

Elizabeth Brandish, a nurse from Clent, was arrested for the

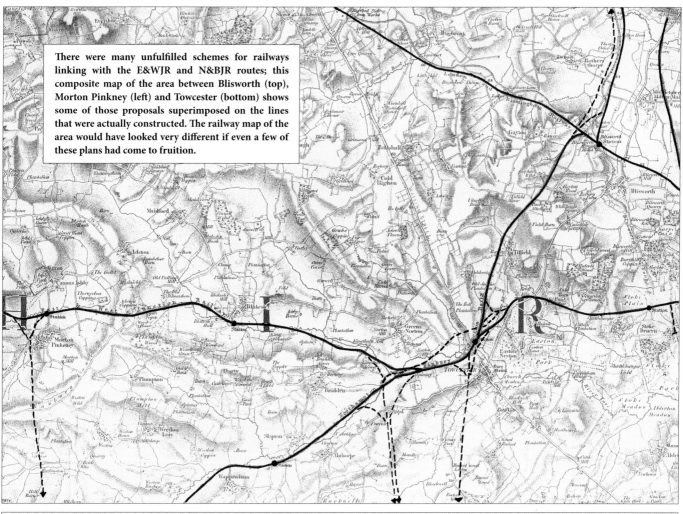

There were many unfulfilled schemes for railways linking with the E&WJR and N&BJR routes; this composite map of the area between Blisworth (top), Morton Pinkney (left) and Towcester (bottom) shows some of those proposals superimposed on the lines that were actually constructed. The railway map of the area would have looked very different if even a few of these plans had come to fruition.

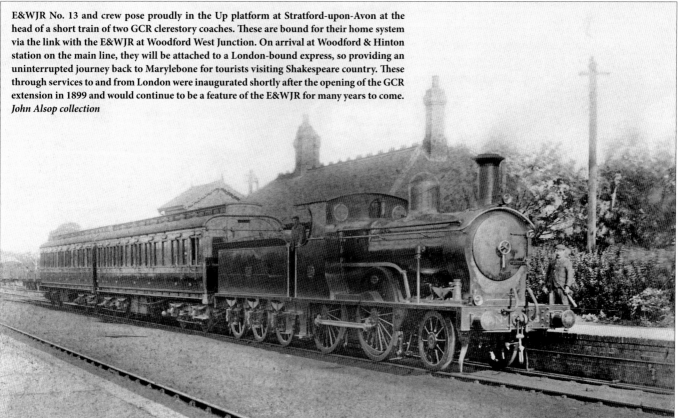

E&WJR No. 13 and crew pose proudly in the Up platform at Stratford-upon-Avon at the head of a short train of two GCR clerestory coaches. These are bound for their home system via the link with the E&WJR at Woodford West Junction. On arrival at Woodford & Hinton station on the main line, they will be attached to a London-bound express, so providing an uninterrupted journey back to Marylebone for tourists visiting Shakespeare country. These through services to and from London were inaugurated shortly after the opening of the GCR extension in 1899 and would continue to be a feature of the E&WJR for many years to come.
John Alsop collection

This delightful Edwardian coloured postcard promoting the charms and railway connections of Ettington contained a vignette of the station, with an arriving E&WJR train from Blisworth just visible being in the background. John Alsop collection

murder of her 2¹/₂ year old illegitimate child on an E&WJR train somewhere between Towcester and Ettington. The mother was noticed acting strangely at both Blisworth and Towcester stations and at the latter was seen boarding a Stratford train with her child, and also carrying a large tin trunk. When the train arrived at Ettington, the woman was seen without the child but now carrying a parcel wrapped in white material. At the station she refused assistance with her luggage, and was then seen to place the parcel in the trunk, before being collected and taken to Drybank Farm where her brother resided. After an investigation by the local police, during which evidence was given by E&WJR guard John Wakefield Days, the body of the child was found buried in quicklime at the farm.

On a more positive note, during August 1898, the E&WJR reinstated a connection at Burton Dassett with the disused iron ore workings. Quarries had been opened on the nearby Burton Hills in the early days of the line but had subsequently been abandoned. Messrs Attenborough & Timms, under the style of the Burton Hill Iron Company, were preparing to reopen the quarries and had requested a connection to their siding, which itself was served by a new aerial ropeway leading down from the hills above. Plans provided to the Board of Trade for approval show that a previous double line section of the E&WJR at this point had been removed, and that a new loop and headshunt was to be constructed on the Down trackbed to service the siding. Unfortunately, the new operation proved to be short lived and production ceased after around four years. The siding then became disused but would later be resurrected.

A further and again ultimately abortive scheme involving a connection with the E&WJR then appeared in November 1899, with the deposition of plans for a Buckingham, Towcester & Metropolitan Junction Railway. This comprised four separate sections of railway, linking the Metropolitan line at East Claydon with Towcester, where junctions would be made with both the ST&MJR and N&BJR routes. As was usual with these schemes, the L&NWR Banbury Branch was also joined, on this occasion near Radclive. Inevitably there were a number of objections to the proposal, on this occasion including from the E&WJR, ST&MJR, ER&SJR, Stratford-upon-Avon Railway and the Great Central Railway.

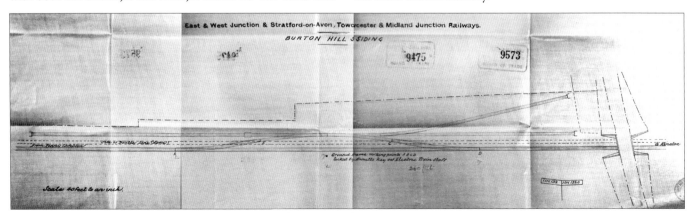

In 1898, the E&WJR reinstated sidings at Burton Dassett to handle iron ore traffic from the reopened quarries on the nearby Burton Hills. This plan shows the new sidings superimposed on the trackbed of a second line of rails, close to the point where the line is crossed by the main Warwick road. It was in this area that the short-lived Warwick Road station once stood, although its precise location is still unclear.

RIGHT: In 1899, yet another ambitious proposal for a new railway was put forward. The Buckingham, Towcester & Metropolitan Junction Railway was to link the Metropolitan line at East Claydon with the N&BJR and ST&MJR lines near Towcester. This map illustrates how the railway geography of Towcester would have been considerably changed, with another bridge over Watling Street within a few yards of the existing N&BJR structure and a duplicate line to the east of Towcester station to join the ST&MJR route. *NRO-DP*

BELOW: An E&WJR Beyer, Peacock 0-6-0 is seen apparently running round its two coach train, comprising a 6-wheeled coach and a bogie clerestory carriage, standing in the Down platform at Blakesley station in 1914. However, no services are known that started or terminated at Blakesley, although it is possible that it is a short distance working to Towcester or a special train. It is also possible that the locomotive has been detached to engage in shunting in the goods yard beyond the signal box and will shortly continue its journey. Hudson & Co's sack hire depot was to be found in the usual corrugated hut, situated behind the Up platform. *John Alsop collection*

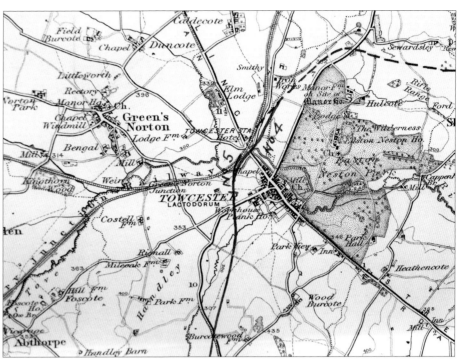

Train Working in the Early 20th Century

The E&WJR *Working Time Table* for July 1901 shows relatively few changes from that of a decade earlier, despite the fact that an influential new neighbour had recently appeared on the scene in the shape of the Great Central Railway, with a connection being available to the E&WJR line at Woodford West Junction.

The overall pattern of passenger services and timings in July 1901 was broadly similar to that of 1890, with some variations to specific departure times. Five down trains continued to run between Blisworth and Stratford with, as before, only the first train of the day continuing on to Broom. However, in the return direction, four of the five trains now ran over the full length of the line from Broom to Blisworth, with only the first train of the day starting from Stratford. There were now no Up trains from Broom terminating at Stratford, although there were two local Down services between those points.

Byfield Up platform, station building and signal box, with the station staff, including the signalman, posing for the photographer. The picture can be dated quite precisely, as the L&NWR noticeboard behind the signalman carries a poster with a date of 'April 24 1897' clearly readable on it. The staff took a pride in their station and Byfield was to be a regular recipient of 'Best kept station' awards. The platform barrow is loaded with several boxes of biscuits, whilst in the right background is Holy Cross church. *Neil Parkhouse collection*

The timetable footnotes then reveal that, in the Down direction, the 4.55pm departure from Blisworth (7.07pm on Saturdays) conveyed an L&NWR through coach from Euston to Stratford, which was returned as part of the next day's 11.10am train from Broom Junction.

However, the opening of the ST&MJR extension from Towcester to Ravenstone Wood Junction had brought new goods traffic to the E&WJR line. In the Down direction, trains left Olney for Broom at 2.20am and 3.45am, with a further service as far as Stratford only at 5.45am. None of these trains ran on Monday mornings, although on Sundays there was a 1.30am service from Roade to Towcester, which could start from Olney when Midland Railway traffic was available for collection. Separate goods services also ran between Blisworth and the west, comprising a 1.30am train (not on Monday but it did run on Sunday) to Broom and a 6.15am departure for Stratford, which ran 45 minutes earlier on Sundays. The pattern of E&WJR Down goods services was completed by 3.30am and 11.05pm (the latter as required) trains from Blisworth to Towcester, and 12.15am, 1.00pm, 3.25pm and 7.45pm local goods from Stratford to Broom.

The traffic pattern in the opposite direction did not quite mirror the Down services. Trains left Broom at 1.15am (not Mondays) and 9.45pm (not Saturdays) for Olney, together with a 10.00pm (Saturdays only) to Blisworth. Several additional trains ran between Broom and Stratford only at 4.55am (Sundays only), 5.30am with two engines (not Mondays), 8.40am (Mondays only), 2.50pm and 4.30pm. Up services starting from Stratford comprised a 5.50am to Blisworth (ten minutes later on Saturdays but only running as far as traffic necessitated), 7.10pm to Blisworth and 9.00pm for Olney (not on Saturdays). Finally, local Up services ran between Towcester and Blisworth only at 4.20am, 12.25am (when required), plus the outward journey at 12.15am, which would terminate at Roade Junction but could continue to Olney as and when cattle or Midland traffic was to be conveyed.

Several of the above through trains were indicated as calling, when traffic required, at Woodford West Junction and Burton Dassett Siding. On the Ravenstone line, one train in each direction would call at Stoke Bruerne and Towcester Brick Siding, with traffic also being exchanged at Roade Junction on certain services.

The Midland Junction Railways (Sales) Bill of 1901

Ownership of the remnant E&WJR, ST&MJR and ER&SR companies was now becoming increasingly difficult to establish. Somewhat inevitably, the ST&MJR had followed its two companions into receivership on 27th May 1898. It was also by then on its seventh company secretary since the inception of the post back in 1879, with most incumbents having only stayed the course for two or three years before giving up the struggle.

The financial state of the three concerns was fast becoming irrecoverable, with receipts hardly covering the normal running costs of the railways. The joint committee had for almost the whole of its existence been unable to allocate any funds towards essential repairs and renewals, or to service its many outstanding debts. Money owed to creditors amounted to upwards of £150,000 and the collective accumulated interest overdue to the shareholders of the three constituent companies was now close to one million pounds.

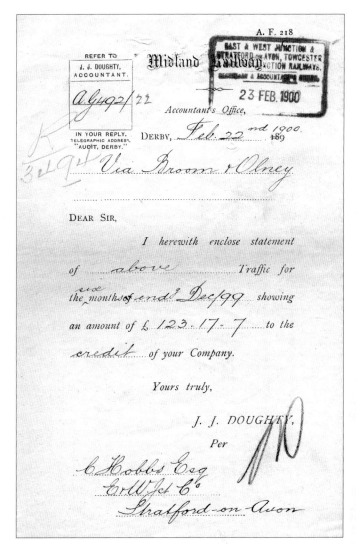

Through goods traffic to and from the Midland Railway was always of great importance to the joint committee. This interesting MR pro-forma of 1900 indicates that the sum of £123 17s 7d has been credited to the account of the joint committee in respect of Midland traffic carried via Broom and Olney, during the six month period to 31st December 1899. *Author's collection*

Drastic action was obviously necessary and although past attempts had been completely unsuccessful, it was once again decided to try to attract the interest of other larger railway companies. The Midland Counties Junction Railways (Sales) Bill was therefore promoted to empower the joint committee to sell the three railways to one or more of the Midland, Great Western, L&NW, Great Central or Metropolitan railway companies and the Act was duly obtained on 17th August 1901. This Bill was, in fact, not promoted by either the joint committee or any of the individual constituent railway companies but instead by third parties who held preponderating interests in those companies. It was effectively a means of clarifying the now somewhat complicated ownership titles of the joint committee and the individual companies, and to render the whole a more attractive and marketable commodity. The Great Western and Great Central railways did initially oppose the Bill but these objections were later withdrawn.

The first schedule attached to the Bill concisely summarised the financial position of the three components of the joint committee. The East & West Junction Railway had issued a total of £668,687 of debenture stock since 1869 and a share capital of

£300,000. The comparable statistics for the ER&SJR, referred to in the Bill as the 'Evesham Company' were £40,900 and £90,000 respectively, whilst for the ST&MJR or 'Midland Junction Company' they were £400,000 and £175,000. This represented a total of £1,474,937, plus a sum of £100,000 for holders of Lloyd's Bonds and other creditors, making the total value £1,574,937; an average per mile of railway of £30,287.

The main line companies were obviously maintaining a watching brief at this stage, as minutes of a Great Central board meeting do reveal that they had decided not to present any proposal to their shareholders; this was in line with all of the other major companies, who had taken a similar stance. Ultimately, however, no firm interest in purchasing the ramshackle group was shown by any of the railway companies nominated in the Bill.

On a more parochial level, a local scandal then emerged on the E&WJR during the latter part of 1901. A goods guard by the name of Harry Cooke was suspended after being found drunk on duty at Stratford; the theft of fifteen bottles of spirits, in transit from London to Cheltenham, was subsequently discovered. Cooke was tried and sentenced to three months hard labour for his misdemeanours but his accomplice, a telegraph linesman named Arthur Wellesley, immediately absconded and was not arrested until he returned to Stratford early in December; he was later sentenced to a month in gaol.

The E&WJR company were themselves involved in a court appearance in August 1902, when they were charged, along with a Somerset farmer, with moving sheep to Kineton contrary to animal movement restrictions then in force. The railway company were able to mount a strong defence, in that they had merely received a wagon from the GWR at Fenny Compton for onward transit and did not transship the sheep. The case against them was dismissed but the farmer was fined one shilling.

Railway Races to Stratford

The *Railway Magazine* in 1902 reported briefly on the status of the E&WJR line in an article on the railways of Warwickshire, which was understandably dominated by descriptions of the operations of the GWR, L&NWR and Midland Railway. However, mention was made of the fact that the E&WJR had been participating in a new service of through coaches from London to Stratford-upon-Avon since 16th June of that year. These were worked to and from Marylebone station by the Great Central Railway and the E&WJR were then responsible for the section between Woodford & Hinton and Stratford, calling only at Kineton en route.

Stratford-upon-Avon was one of the few major towns to which the GCR could claim the shortest route from London, with their distance of 93¼ miles via Aylesbury and Woodford beating the then GWR route through Oxford and Honeybourne by 17½ miles. The GCR was therefore able to claim the fastest time between Stratford and the capital, with a service of 2 hours and 20 minutes. Up to four such through coaches were offered from Marylebone, one of which was operated as a slip coach and detached just south of Woodford & Hinton station.

A scene full of interest at Stratford-upon-Avon during E&WJR days. Passenger 2-4-0 No. 13 waits in the Up platform with a similar, somewhat ill-matched combination to that seen at Blakesley a few pages earlier, of a 6-wheeled coach and a much more prestigious clerestory type. The latter is probably a through carriage from the Great Central Railway. A Down train stands in the opposite platform, beneath the oddly positioned loading gauge, whilst in the background, one of the E&WJR's secondhand L&NWR 'DX' Class 0-6-0s waits with a goods train. *Author's collection*

RIGHT: No. 13 features again in this early 20th century view of a Down train approaching Stratford-upon-Avon, shortly after passing under the Stratford & Moreton Tramway bridge near Clifford Chambers Siding. The first coach is possibly an L&NWR vehicle. *Author's collection*

BELOW: This general view of Kineton station from the north end of the road bridge in 1899 shows passengers awaiting both Up and Down services, and there appears to be plenty of activity around the goods shed and yard. Some of the wagons are undoubtedly for coal traffic but it is not entirely clear as to what is stacked on the bank beyond the sidings; it may be stacks of timber or possibly bales of hay, large quantities of which were gleaned from the embankments alongside the line and sold as fodder. Kineton served as the terminus of the first section of the E&WJR line from Fenny Compton for two years from 1871 to 1873. *Author's collection*

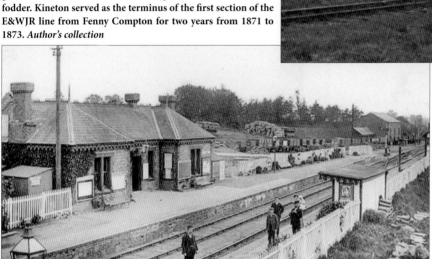

These new services were in addition to the existing daily through coaches to and from London Euston, by way of Blisworth and the L&NWR main line, which offered a three hour through service. In fact, by this means, E&WJR passengers could also avail themselves of a novel through service by the L&NWR route, with the 11.45am departure from Stratford connecting into a through coach for London Victoria at Blisworth, thus dispensing with a tedious crossing of London for travellers to the south of England.

However, the GWR, who had long considered Stratford to be their home territory, could only offer a best journey time of twelve minutes in excess of the L&NWR train and almost an hour more than the GCR upstarts. In addition, convenient connections were introduced at Woodford & Hinton into several other trains in both directions on the Great Central route and later a through coach from Stratford to York and Scarborough was also provided. The GWR response to this intrusion was to accelerate their own services to give a new time of 2 hours 35 minutes from Paddington. However, the Great Central, determined to keep their advantage, added a new through coach to and from Stratford in 1904, which reached the capital in 2 hours 10 minutes and was later accelerated by a further five minutes.

At this time, the E&WJR used the Westinghouse brake, having only a few locomotives fitted with the vacuum brake system, which was then in use by both the GCR and L&NWR. The through carriages to and from the Great Central Railway were therefore usually operated in isolation by E&WJR engines

to and from Woodford & Hinton, whereas the L&NWR stock, which was dual braked, could be worked to and from Blisworth as part of a normal E&WJR train.

More Rolling Stock

The usual financial problems were still hampering the joint committee during 1903, with solicitors reporting that they had finally succeeded in resolving questions arising out of the contract for new engines recently placed with Beyer, Peacock. However it seems that this then cleared the way for delivery of the new locomotives and, on 17th July 1903, the line's first true passenger engine, 2-4-0 No. 13, was delivered. It was soon followed by 0-6-0 goods engine No. 14 in early November.

Mr Burke was also authorised to obtain prices and specifications for further new locomotives and these were duly tendered for by both Beyer, Peacock and Robert Stephenson & Company. The Birmingham Railway Carriage & Wagon Company also offered to supply the required seventy-five 10-ton goods wagons at £65 10s each, whilst a tender of £101 was accepted from the Avonside Engine Company for the provision of '*power brakes*' for engines No's 2 and 3, to comply with '*prevention of accident rules*'. This completed the upgrading of brakes on all of the locomotives with the exception of No. 8, an elderly L&NWR 'DX' 0-6-0, whose wooden tender frame was not considered strong enough to bear the weight of the extra equipment.

Engine No. 15, another 0-6-0 goods type, duly arrived from Beyer, Peacock in early 1904, with the joint committee having paid a quarter of the purchase cost on delivery, the balance being paid at three monthly intervals over four years.

Company secretary Charles Hobbs also informed the E&WJR's insurers during 1903 that it was intended to install electric light at Stratford. When their surveyor visited in June, he reported that the signal box, main building, waiting room and refreshment room were electrically illuminated from batteries in the carriage accumulator shed. The engine shed was, however, still oil lit, although electricity was available in the adjacent workshop, which had its own generator.

The photographer had managed to gain the attention of everyone in this view of Kineton station, which was taken looking east towards Fenny Compton in 1905. The permanent way gang display a variety of headgear, with the 'bowler' in the foreground probably being the foreman. The signalman looks on from one of the front windows of his box, whilst the rest of the station staff have also emerged, along with a couple of locals, to ensure that they too feature in the picture. With wagons featuring on both running lines, it is likely that this was a Sunday with no trains scheduled to run. *Author's collection*

Away from locomotive matters, an issue from as far back as 1882 was then to resurface during 1905, when the joint committee's solicitor, Merrick, raised the question of old unsettled land claims against the E&WJR. These, he considered, required '*early consideration*', as they would have to be resolved to ensure the future working of the railway. He pursued the matter again at the committee meeting of 6th April, when a particularly urgent case involving a Mr Faircloth was reported. Two and a half years rent was owed by the joint committee, despite a reduction to £28 per annum, and the term of the agreement had now expired. However, this potential problem was given short shrift by the committee, who objected strongly to the acceptance of any liabilities carried by the constituent companies in respect of unpaid land.

Matters also came to a head in 1904 over the operation and financing of the two interfaces with the Midland Railway, at Broom Junction and Olney station. It appears that for some years there had been no proper agreements in place as to the apportionment of costs and responsibilities for maintenance at these two locations, where the E&WJR had originally provided many of the facilities when their two extension lines had opened. Hobbs therefore made contact with his opposite number at Derby, John Mathieson, in an attempt to rectify the situation and voluminous correspondence then ensued over a period of some months. E&WJR ownership of various facilities, such as the turntable and sidings at Broom, and engine shed and additional sidings at Olney, were re-established, and eventually agreements were reached as to the sharing of maintenance and staffing costs at both locations.

It was even proposed that staff at Broom would be provided with 'joint' Midland and E&WJR uniforms, although it is unclear as to whether this was ever enacted. However, what was agreed was that the Midland should pay what was apparently a standard rate of six pence per locomotive for use of the E&WJR turntables at both places. It does appear though that the overall financial situation of the E&WJR was now becoming more manageable and, subsequently, orders were soon placed with the Birmingham RC&W Co. for new horse boxes, timber and cattle wagons, and brake vans.

Engine No. 16, another standard Beyer, Peacock 0-6-0 product, was placed in traffic on 28th March 1906. Intriguingly, some consideration was apparently being given to the purchase of a further 2-4-0 passenger locomotive, similar to No. 13. A decision on this matter was, however, deferred and instead, prices were sought for two further goods locomotives of increased power. As a result, the two were ordered from Beyer, Peacock at a cost of £3,035 each, whilst two 15-ton 6-wheeled brake vans were also obtained from Harrison & Camm.

Whereas the indigenous rolling stock may have been sufficient for day to day services, it was quite another matter when such events as race meetings or the annual Stratford 'Mop Fair' increased passenger numbers. On these occasions, coaching stock was borrowed from far and wide, with Great Central, London & North Western and Midland railway sets added to the E&WJR stock to produce longer trains. These often greatly overlapped platforms and thus had to be drawn up twice for passengers.

In 1903, C.W. Bartholemew installed a complete miniature 15-inch gauge railway system in the grounds of his home at Blakesley Hall. One branch of the system terminated at Blakesley E&WJR station, where a small passenger platform was provided adjacent to the Down main line. Another branch served the station goods yard, where coal and other consumables were transshipped on to narrow gauge wagons for conveyance up to the hall. The miniature line saw considerable use by excursion parties, with special fares being offered by the E&WJR from local stations. This superbly crisp circa 1905 Locomotive Publishing Company photograph shows E&WJR No. 4 waiting at Blakesley (note the size of the lumps of coal in No. 4's tender) with a three coach train from Blisworth to Stratford, whilst a small group stands adjacent to some carriages in the miniature railway platform. The unusually shaped boxes in the siding next to the miniature platform are in fact a rake of side-tipping wagons, which were used on the line for the conveyance of coal. The shed hidden in the bushes on the right, with the rustic triangular façade jutting up above the roof, was the station building for the miniature railway. Blakesley Hall became a military hospital during the First World War and the miniature railway was used in the rehabilitation of the wounded. The line continued after Bartholemew's death in 1919, with his widow remaining at Blakesley Hall but saw little use after the mid 1930s. The last of the track was finally lifted in 1946 and the surviving wagons scrapped. The Hall became uninhabited from 1947 and fell in to dereliction; it was demolished in 1957 but permission has now been granted to rebuild it. *John Alsop collection*

This circa 1905 view, from High Street bridge at the west end of Blakesley station, provides a clearer view of the miniature railway platform and the waiting shelter, before it became surrounded by the shrubs and bushes seen in the picture on the previous page. The two routes ran side by side beneath the road, separated only by the iron fence, with the miniature line then swinging away into the hall grounds. The bridge still survives today but the station site is now occupied by a large private residence and there is little evidence of the existence of the minature railway. *John Alsop collection*

Another Plan

There was now a pressing need to take some form of action to bring to an end the continual wrangling between the constituent companies of the joint committee, and to secure a more stable financial and operational position. Charles Hobbs took the initiative on 31st August 1905, by issuing a letter to all First Debenture holders of his company. The communication began:

'As your name appears on the books of the company as one of the first debenture stock holders of which there are 795, I am directed by the Board to remind you that it is upwards of 30 years since any funds were raised by the issue of capital and that owing to the failure of the objects of the line the receipts from it have never sufficed to pay any interest.'

Hobbs continued: '... it is therefore with a certain amount of satisfaction that my Board directs me to inform you that for the first time in the history of the company there is a possibility, as a result of a prospective change in circumstances and revised measures, of some return being obtained by the proprietors, if the opportunity is taken advantage of promptly by them. If on the other hand should it be passed by, the position is such that all chances of getting anything in the future threaten to be indefinitely postponed if not extinguished.'

Appended were details of the nature of the proposition, which

The rather unwieldy title of the East & West Junction, Stratford, Towcester & Midland Junction Railway soon became abbreviated, as seen on this July 1907 *'Schedule of Wagons passing'* Broom and Olney, submitted to the Railway Clearing House. The route of the wagon in question is also of interest, being a Midland Railway vehicle that had been consigned from Bristol Avonside Wharf to London Blackfriars on the South Eastern & Chatham Railway. *Author's collection*

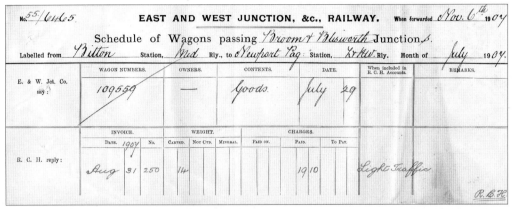

No. 22/6608

EAST AND WEST JUNCTION, &c., RAILWAY. When forwarded *Feby 13th 1908*

Schedule of Wagons passing *Broom & Olney* Junction.

Labelled from *Tewkesbury* Station, *Mid* Rly., to *Croydon* Station *LB&SC* Rly., Month of *October* 1907.

E. & W. Jct. Co. say:	WAGON NUMBERS.	OWNERS.	CONTENTS.	DATE.	When included in R. C. H. Accounts.	REMARKS.
	12945	*Mid*	*Goods.*	*Oct* *15*		*Tewkesbury to St Pancras* (mid) (mid)

R. C. H. reply:	INVOICE.		WEIGHT.			CHARGES.			
	DATE. *1907*	No.	CARTED.	Not Crd.	MINERAL.	PAID ON.	PAID.	TO PAY.	*Settled Privately*
	Octr 15	*541*		*30*			*2 4 6*		*R.C.H.*

LEFT: MR wagon No. 14945 made use of the E&WJR during October 1907, on a journey from home territory at Tewkesbury to Croydon, on the London, Brighton & South Coast Railway. The route taken was along the Midland line as far as Broom Junction and then, after traversing the full length of the E&WJR to Ravenstone Wood Junction, MR metals were regained through Olney and Bedford to reach London St. Pancras goods depot. From there the wagon would have been forwarded beneath London onto the Brighton line. *Author's collection*

RIGHT: The E&WJR's route was frequently used for Midland traffic from the Bristol area to London but, occasionally, other destinations are to be found. This wagon was consigned from Bitton, on the MR line between Bristol and Bath, to Newport Pagnell, the terminus of the short L&NWR branch from Wolverton. It is therefore quite possible that the vehicle may have been routed through the little utilised connection between the ST&MJR line and the L&NWR at Roade. *Author's collection*

No. 55/6465

EAST AND WEST JUNCTION, &c., RAILWAY. When forwarded *Nov 6th 1907*

Schedule of Wagons passing *Broom & Blisworth* Junction.

Labelled from *Bitton* Station, *Mid* Rly., to *Newport Pag* Station, *L&NW* Rly., Month of *July* 1907.

E. & W. Jct. Co. say:	WAGON NUMBERS.	OWNERS.	CONTENTS.	DATE.	When included in R. C. H. Accounts.	REMARKS.
	109559	—	*Goods.*	*July 29*		

R. C. H. reply:	INVOICE.		WEIGHT.			CHARGES.			
	DATE. *1907*	No.	CARTED.	Not Crd.	MINERAL.	PAID ON.	PAID.	TO PAY.	*Light Traffic*
	Aug 31	*250*	*14*				*19 10*		*R.C.H.*

stated that a new spirit of cooperation now existed between the E&WJR, the ER&SJR and the ST&MJR companies, who although nominally partners in the joint committee, had long been at loggerheads. All had their differences and it was stated that, in particular, the ST&MJR had been for some time engaged in hostile measures, including court actions and applications to Parliament, intended to '*wipe out the E&WJR*'.

However, a truce had now been established and there was a willingness to finally unravel the intricacies of the ownership of the three companies. Instead, the plan was to substitute an arrangement which would replace the multitude of individual holdings with a new issue of consolidated stock on a reduced capital basis. Hobbs concluded by offering the shareholders a somewhat rose tinted view of the future possibilities of receiving a return from their long held investments and requesting that they completed an attached postcard to indicate a willingness to participate, or alternatively to opt out by taking a reduced cash value for their holdings.

Obviously a sufficient number of positive responses were received, as Hobbs then issued a further circular on 1st November detailing a proposal

to establish a new Joint Stock Company, divided into 200,000 nominal £1 shares, which would be issued to assenting stockholders in proportion to their existing holdings. Acceptance was recommended, as it was considered that this was a last opportunity to put an end to conflicting interests and although a good deal still remained to be done, it represented the best deal available to the E&WJR proprietors; the usual postcard was provided indicate a preference.

This represented the first small step along the road towards the eventual formation of the Stratford-upon-Avon & Midland Junction Railway company. However, despite the through traffic potential now offered by the Midland Railway at either end of their system and the new opportunities provided by links to the Great Central, the joint committee still found themselves deeply in debt to various creditors.

Amalgamation at Last

Change was now very definitely on the agenda and at last there were positive signs that there might be a way forward from the seemingly irretrievable situation that had gradually overtaken the joint committee. New and forward looking

London and North Western Railway.

PASSENGER TRAIN RATES & FARES OFFICE,
(8079)

EUSTON STATION,

PLEASE REFER TO
F /17.2.08.
1 /397959.

LONDON, February 17th. 190 8.
N.W.

Your R.6635/08

DEAR SIR,

EAST & WEST JUNCTION STRATFORD-on-AVON, TOWCESTER & MIDLAND JUNCTION RAILWAYS. SECRETARY & ACCOUNTANT'S OFFICE FEB 19 1908

Kineton **Horse** with **Great Harwood**

I agree to your proposal so far as this Company is concerned, for this occasion only.

Yours truly,

HENRY PARTINGTON

per

C Hobbs Esq.,

Stratford on Avon.

Horse box traffic was also of great importance to the E&WJR, as in this case, where a horse was conveyed between Kineton and Great Harwood, near Blackburn in Lancashire, quite possibly on behalf of Sir Willoughby de Broke. Presumably the E&WJR had proposed a rate to which the L&NWR agreed, as per this document. *Author's collection*

An interesting scene at an immaculately kept Byfield station circa 1925 – the platform barrow on the left is lettered 'LMS', so it is post-Grouping – even though there is a total absence of fare paying passengers. The goods yard is shared by horse boxes, coal wagons, sheeted wagons and a van, whilst the ex-Midland Railway goods 0-6-0 on the Down line beyond the water tank is in the process of shunting the daily pick-up goods. Note the nearest private owner wagon, partly obscured by the station nameboard, belongs to local coal merchant A. Russell, whilst the one at the rear of the yard is lettered for Oxford-based coal merchants Stevens & Co. The pivoting operating arm of the massive brick water tank house is prominent in the foreground; Byfield was originally the only place between Blisworth and Stratford where water was available to locomotives, until similar facilities were later provided at Towcester. The picture, by Rugby-based photographer and postcard publisher Victor W. Long, was taken from Church Street bridge, at the east end of the station, looking towards Fenny Compton. The bridge has been demolished since the closure of the line and whilst the site has not been built on, nothing remains of the station apart from a section of the Down platform. *John Alsop collection*

RIGHT: Harry Willmott was the father figure of the E&WJR and, subsequently, the S&MJR, acting as chairman of both railways. Together with his son Russell and deputy chairman Sidney Herbert, he must be credited with the transformation of the fortunes of these railways from 1908. *The Locomotive Magazine*

LEFT: Inter-company documentation was not confined to goods traffic, as this memo of 1902, bearing the full title of the East & West Junction & Stratford-on-Avon, Towcester & Midland Junction Railway shows. It dealt with a query over a through fare between Kineton and Woolwich Arsenal station. Interestingly the journey was made via Woodford and the Great Central line. *Author's collection*

BELOW: Arthur Ernest Diggins was born in King's Lynn in 1872. After a year in charge of the Stores Accounts office in Manchester for the GCR, he was appointed as accountant of the newly formed Stratford-upon-Avon & Midland Junction Railway in December 1908, becoming secretary in July 1909. Diggins took early retirement in July 1923, shortly after the S&MJR's amalgamation into the LM&SR and he died in 1955, at the age of 84. *The Locomotive Magazine*

management was urgently required, and the E&WJR quickly obtained this with the appointment of Harry Willmott and Sidney Herbert to their board, the former also being nominated as an E&WJR representative on the joint committee.

Willmott had started his railway career with the Great Eastern in 1865 and rose to the position of goods manager of the London District, before leaving to become general manager of the Lancashire, Derbyshire & East Coast Railway in 1895. However, when the LD&ECR was taken over by the Great Central in 1907, he was moved to the position of agent for the Sheffield District, something which he seems to have considered as a demotion. As a result, within twelve months he resigned from his post with the GCR to take on the new challenge of resuscitating the E&WJR.

Sidney Herbert JP, the owner of a London stockbroking business, provided the perfect foil for Willmott's progressive management style by bringing much needed financial acumen to the company. He also brought considerable railway experience, being at one time or another a director of the Didcot, Newbury & Southampton, Mold & Denbigh and the Isle of Wight Central railways, and would later become chairman of the Association of Minor Railway Companies.

Another important appointment was that of Arthur E. Diggins

as accountant. Diggins hailed from King's Lynn and spent his early railway career with the Eastern & Midlands Railway, where he spent ten years before moving on to the Lancashire, Derbyshire & East Coast Railway as book-keeper and chief clerk. Once that company had been taken over by the Great Central, he transferred to Manchester but only spent one year with his new employers before rejoining Harry Willmott on the E&WJR.

Within a few months Harry Willmott had become chairman of the E&WJR, with Thomas Hillas Crampton indicating his intention to resign from that post on 15th July 1908. One of the new chairman's first involvements was in the formation of the Midland Counties Junction Railways Securities Company. This was designed to facilitate the long overdue official amalgamation of the three components of the joint committee into a single railway company, and the acquisition of their assets in exchange for cash and shares in the new body.

The resulting Stratford-upon-Avon & Midland Junction Railway Amalgamation Act of 1st August 1908 duly authorised the merging of the Stratford-upon-Avon, Towcester & Midland Junction, the Evesham, Redditch & Stratford Junction and the East & West Junction railways. The Act also awarded running powers to four of the large main line companies: the Midland, L&NW, Great

BELOW: Russell Wilmott was born in 1879 and began his railway career in his father Harry's office on the LD&ECR. After a short time he became articled to Messrs Fowler & Marshall, a firm of engineers, surveyors, architects and land agents in Sheffield, and at the expiration of his articles, he was appointed assistant in the engineers office of the LD&ECR, where he remained for two years. In 1903, he accepted a post in the surveyors office of the Great Northern Railway but a few months later transferred to the engineer's office of the Great Northern, Piccadilly & Brompton Railway, an underground line then in course of construction. After two years he took a position with Baker, Mott & Hay who were constructing the City & South London Railway, another underground line, from the Angel, Islington to Euston. In 1906, he was appointed assistant engineer with the LD&ECR and when they were taken over by the GCR in 1907, he became one of their district engineers. His next move was to rejoin his father and take charge of the traffic and engineer's departments of the S&MJR in 1909. He left the company to join the Isle of Wight Central Railway on 1st January 1912 but was paid a retainer by the S&MJR to continue as a consultant. He died in office with the IWCR at the early age of 40 on 25th June 1920. *The Locomotive Magazine*

Central and Great Western railways. The MR obtained running powers over the whole of the new S&MJR system, although they were not permitted to carry local traffic without written consent.

In the case of the L&NWR, running powers were available for coal and coke traffic only, between Stratford-upon-Avon and the junction with their own main line at Roade. However, a further clause allowed for full running powers for any type of traffic over those lines, should the Railway & Canal Commissioners decide that reasonable facilities had not been made available to them. The Great Central Railway were also granted comprehensive running powers over the S&MJR but the Great Western were to some extent repaid for their earlier hostilities, by only being allowed to run over the section between their two junctions with the S&MJR at Stratford and Fenny Compton.

The joint committee minutes of 5th August duly recorded the Amalgamation Act and also the willingness of Mr Burke to resign his post of engineer in two weeks time. This was accepted and an agreement made to pay him three months salary upon his departure. Clearly the new broom was intending to sweep very clean indeed, as the new chairman also indicated that he would 'arrange to serve upon, or accept, any suitable notice of resignation of his office on or from any officer or member of the staff'.

A replacement for Burke was also not long in arriving, as after making perhaps rather superfluous enquiries and conducting interviews, the committee then appointed the chairman's son, Russell Willmott, as traffic manager and engineer from 24th August, at a salary of £350 per annum. Russell Willmott had to some extent followed in his father's footsteps, by starting his railway career with the LD&ECR company, before moving on to the Great Northern and then acting as engineer for two London underground railway schemes. Afterwards, he returned to the LD&ECR for a time, before following his father to the E&WJR.

The *Leamington Spa Courier* aptly summarised all of these latest developments:

'The *Stratford-upon-Avon & Midland Junction Railway Company* – in this title we have the latest phase of the evolution of a district railway company. The system has passed through three phases as follow: The Evesham, Stratford & Redditch Junction; The East & West Junction; The Stratford Towcester & Midland Junction.

In accordance with the Act of Parliament the above companies will be amalgamated on 1st January into the Stratford-upon-Avon & Midland Junction Railway. The Traffic Manager and Engineer is Russell Willmott, the secretary C. Hobbs, Accountant A.E. Diggins, and the chief offices will be at Stratford.'

The new regime was placed firmly in the public eye when board approval was given on 29th September 1908 to put the company's new identity, in the form of the initials 'SMJ', on locomotives and rolling stock.

RIGHT: A sylvan setting a few yards to the east of Stratford E&WJR station circa 1912, with a goods train crossing the River Avon viaduct just behind Lucy's Mill Bridge, a public footbridge. The open wagon nearest the engine looks to be an MR vehicle but the following tow are both lettered 'E&W'. The young bystanders leaning over the railing appear to be more interested in how their friends are doing with their fishing than the passing train. A footbridge still exists here today, although it has been rebuilt from the form seen here. However, the railway bridge survives, duly strengthened for the carriage of vehicular traffic on Seven Meadows Road, which now runs along the old trackbed from the location of Clifford Sidings, through the station site and to a roundabout close to the point where the Broom line once crossed the GWR. *Author's collection*

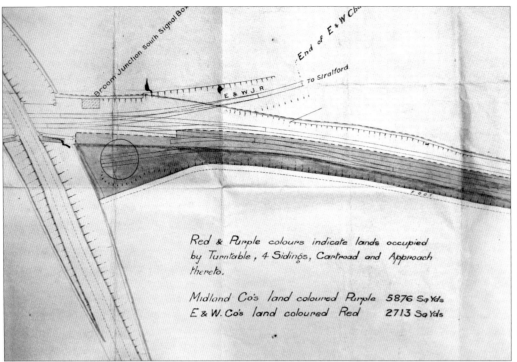

Red & Purple colours indicate lands occupied by Turntable, 4 Sidings, Cartroad and Approach thereto.

Midland Co's land coloured Purple   5876 Sq Yds
E & W. Co's land coloured Red   2713 Sq Yds

LEFT: The new regime at Stratford quickly took effect and one of their early achievements was to rectify some outstanding affairs with the Midland Railway company, primarily at Olney and Broom. Agreements were quickly made over the running costs of the junctions, stations and sidings, and this portion of a plan of Broom dated 1908 denotes the actual ownership of the turntable and surrounding sidings at the west end of the station. *Author's collection*

PAGE OPPOSITE: During the later part of the 19th century, Blisworth and Towcester were the focus of many abortive schemes for connections and extensions to both the N&BJR and the E&WJR. This set of plans illustrate some typical examples of these proposals; had any of them actually become reality the railway landscape at either location would have appeared very different indeed.

Putting the House in Order

In anticipation of the better times to come, the new management, in particular the chairman Harry Willmott and deputy chairman Sidney Herbert, grasped the opportunity of rationalising various aspects of the railways prior to the official date of amalgamation. The *Railway News* reported how considerable sums were being spent out of current revenue, financed by a reduction in '*useless labour and trains*', to increase efficiency and ensure that '*indoor and outdoor work was properly done and supervised*' whilst the Amalgamation Bill was passing through Parliament. In short, the unstructured and ramshackle operation of the previous individual companies, along with the ineffective control of the joint committee, had now been quickly replaced by a modern and professional management approach.

Another illustration of how the new management was now operating the company was the belated settlement of matters long outstanding with the Midland Railway, over the historical use of facilities at both ends of the joint committee system at Broom Junction and Olney. A new agreement was drawn up which provided for the Midland to pay one half of a sum representing 4% of the capital cost, backdated to 1st January 1892, of the four exchange sidings, land and turntable originally provided by the joint committee at Broom. The Midland were also to pay half the future cost of maintaining three of the same exchange sidings and the turntable, at a rate to be agreed by the respective engineers. The cost of the fourth siding and also the cart road alongside was to be shared '*according to user*'.

In return, the joint committee were to pay the MR, from the same date, one half of a sum representing 4% of the value of the land provided by the Midland on which the sidings and approach road were laid. The committee were also to bear the cost of maintaining and working their junction with the Midland, and to pay half the expenses of working and maintaining Broom station. In the case of Olney, the Midland were to accept £750 of an amount of £1,514 outstanding against the committee in respect

of siding charges up to 30th June 1906. From that date forward, they were then to pay the committee £40 per annum for the use of the sidings for marshalling purposes. A sum of £200 was also to be paid by the Midland for past use of the engine shed, turntable and ballast sidings originally provided by the committee at Olney. Further agreements were made on mileage charges, and the usage of Midland wagons and wagon sheets on traffic between Broom and Olney, with effect from 1st January 1908.

The old joint committee, along with the vestiges of its three constituent companies, was finally officially dissolved on 21st April 1909, after the conclusion of the usual various legal formalities, with the Stratford-upon-Avon & Midland Junction Railway company taking over the operation of the line from 1st January of that year.

Some E&WJR Statistics

The seven miles of the E&WJR line from Kineton to Fenny Compton, opened during 1871, generated revenue of just £792 in that year, with roughly equal amounts being contributed by passenger and goods traffic, all of which was conveyed in mixed trains. The total number of passengers carried was 11,472, whilst goods traffic amounted to just over 5,000 tons, most of which was coal and coke. Operating expenses for the year were £1,054 in excess of the total revenue.

The full opening of the line from Green's Norton to Stratford in 1873 failed to bring about any great improvement in fortunes, although in 1874 almost 90,000 passengers were carried and goods traffic increased to 65,000 tons. However, relatively little of the goods total consisted of the much anticipated carriage of iron ore. E&WJR trains ran a total mileage of over 160,000 miles during that year.

Unfortunately, however, operating costs continued to greatly exceed traffic receipts and the deficiency over the five years up to 1877 then averaged £5,750 per annum, a large sum for a small railway company. This contributed to the suspension

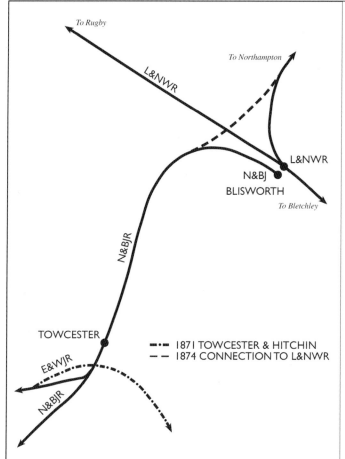

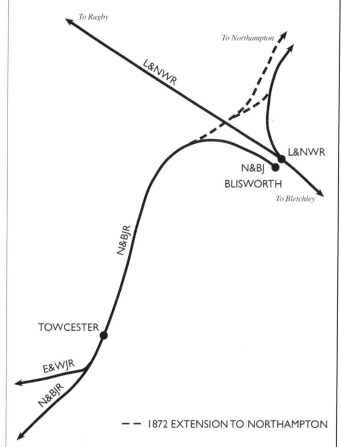

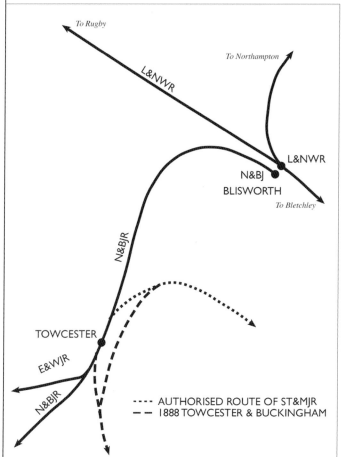

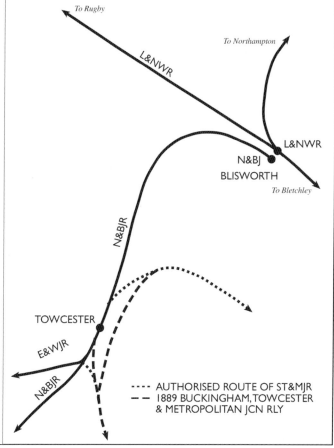

of passenger traffic in that year, further reducing the revenue, although the unlikely opening to passengers of the extension to Broom in 1879 did then bring 40,500 travellers onto that section of the E&WJR. Goods traffic remained at a reasonable level but, by 1879, the total train mileage operated by the E&WJR had fallen to just 27,000 per annum.

The resumption of passengers services on the main line in 1885 brought annual train mileages back to the levels of 1874, resulting in an increase in revenue of almost 50%, but the total for the year of £12,313 was still £3,700 below the cost of operating the line.

The early 1890s then saw a gradual improvement, with total revenue increasing to £19,000 in 1891 and, at last, the E&WJR were able to report a modest operating surplus of just £818. This continued to improve in subsequent years, reaching a peak of just over £5,000 in 1895. This was due to a healthy increase in goods traffic, brought about by the opening in 1891 of the

eastern extension to the Midland Railway at Ravenstone Wood Junction and also construction traffic for the new Great Central line at Woodford & Hinton.

However, by 1901, the line was again reporting an annual loss, and for the remainder of the decade results fluctuated between small deficits and surpluses, although 1906 saw the highest number of passengers ever carried by the E&WJR, a total of over 213,000. In its last year of independence, the E&WJR reported an operating shortfall of £1,613 for 1908, despite the changes in management which were already beginning to prepare the line for its new future as part of the S&MJR from 1st January 1909.

Overall, the East & West Junction Railway was hampered by the same underlying debts as its near neighbour, the N&BJR, and was also never able to pay any dividend to shareholders. However, amalgamation into the S&MJR at the end of 1908 would see a dramatic change in fortunes.

A deserted Stratford-upon-Avon E&WJR station, looking west from the Down platform circa 1905. The original Gloucester Railway Carriage & Wagon Company signal box, situated next to the main station building on the Up platform, was provided in 1879 for the opening of the extension to Broom Junction. The box and the early style of signal on the opposite platform would both be replaced some twenty years later, as part of a completely new installation provided by the Railway Signal Company of Fazakerley, Liverpool. Passenger facilities would also be progressively improved over the coming years, by the upgrading of the rather flimsy canopy attached to the main building and the similarly frugal shelter on the Down side, which backs onto the locomotive yard and engine shed. The unusually wide space between the two platforms was once the location of a siding in the earliest days of the line, which had been removed certainly by the early 1880s but was probably taken out when the extension to Broom was built. The area was then used to accommodate locomotive watering facilities at each end of the station and the somewhat unusual provision of a loading gauge on the Down line. The siding connection to the Great Western line curves away to the right in the distance beyond the platform ends, whilst the continuation of the Broom line is obscured by the far end of the Down platform. *John Alsop collection*

Chapter 1.4
THE LOCOMOTIVES AND ROLLING STOCK OF THE EAST & WEST JUNCTION RAILWAY

The locomotive and rolling stock history of the earliest years of the E&WJR is rather more clearly defined than that of its neighbour, the N&BJR. However, during the period immediately after the relinquishment of the new Beyer, Peacock engines in 1875, the situation becomes much less clear, with various hirings and temporary purchases of secondhand and often unusual locomotives being necessary to keep the trains running. Passenger services were withdrawn in 1877 but their resumption in 1885 brought further new engines to the line and, thereafter, the E&WJR locomotive history is relatively well recorded, with many of the subsequently purchased engines surviving through into the hands of the S&MJR after 1909.

Contractor's Locomotives

Construction of the East & West Junction Railway was commenced by Crampton, Peto & Betts in 1865. The first locomotive to appear was a Manning, Wardle 0-6-0 saddle tank, Works No. 177 of 1865. This was first steamed on 8th November of that year and arrived at the Kineton work site a few days later bearing the appropriate name of *Shakespear* [sic].

A sister engine, No. 178 of 1866, was also delivered to Fenny Compton shortly afterwards but little progress was being made and following the national financial hiatus of 1866, Crampton was declared bankrupt in July 1867. It appears that both locomotives were then disposed of and work did not recommence until after Crampton had been discharged from bankruptcy in 1870. The first short section of line between Fenny Compton and Kineton was eventually opened to traffic on 5th June 1871. The inaugural

train was headed by Manning, Wardle No. 178 which had obviously returned to the area and had been named *Kineton*.

Construction continued on the remaining sections and the completed through route from Green's Norton Junction, near Towcester, to Stratford-upon-Avon was finally opened on 1st July 1873. Crampton used an assortment of other small saddle tank locomotives on this later construction, including two outside cylinder Neilson 0-4-0s. The first of these to arrive, new in August 1871, was Works No. 1633 and this should have been followed by No. 1654. However, this engine appears to have been diverted elsewhere, with No. 1703 of 1871 instead arriving in early January 1872. The same month also saw the arrival of another Manning, Wardle, named *Byfield*, which commenced work at Towcester.

In addition, an unidentified 'Hawthorn & Co' four-coupled saddle tank locomotive appeared in the sale of surplus equipment following the opening of the line, so is presumed to have also been used during the construction.

The First Train

The first passenger train on the E&WJR ran between Fenny Compton and Kineton on Monday 5th June 1871. An apparent photograph of the event suggests that this was composed of the entire passenger stock of the line at that time, some three or possibly four vehicles, and was hauled by one of the Manning, Wardle 0-6-0 saddle tanks owned by Crampton, it not being unusual for the contractor to assist in the operation of a new railway in its early days. The chosen engine was Manning,

This well-known photograph is often claimed to be of the inaugural train over the first section of the E&WJR to be opened, between Fenny Compton and Kineton on Monday 5th June 1871. The rather small group of onlookers perhaps make this questionable but nevertheless it is certainly a very early view. The train is seen arriving at Kineton hauled by the Manning, Wardle 0-6-0ST *Kineton*, provided by the contractor Crampton & Co. The locomotive is still without an overall cab, has both dumb and standard types of buffers and also has a crude stovepipe extension to the chimney, no doubt to carry the exhaust away from the train and the locomotive crew. The carriage stock appears to consist of three, or possibly four vehicles; the latter would be in keeping with Sidney Smith's report of a trip on the line just two weeks later. The early arrangement of two signal arms on one post is also noteworthy; at this date they may have been used to merely signal the train into and out of the platform. *The Locomotive Magazine*

Wardle No. 178, which had by then been renamed *Kineton*, possibly to coincide with the opening of the line.

It is unclear as to whether this locomotive was borrowed, hired or purchased from Crampton but the latter seems more likely, as Board of Trade returns indicate that the E&WJR reported ownership of one locomotive until a date during 1873, when reinforcements arrived for the full opening from Blisworth to Stratford. At a later date, the small Manning, Wardle was certainly retired to a more suitable life elsewhere and it has been recorded that this was at a gravel pit in the Woodford area, owned by Crampton. However, the locomotive would return again to E&WJR stock a few years later.

Full Opening and New Locomotives

More suitable motive power was required for the full opening of the line in July 1873 and to operate the increased passenger and goods services. Accordingly, the railway purchased six locomotives and a selection of rolling stock through the offices of the '*Birmingham Waggon Company*', actually the Midland Waggon Company of Saltley, Birmingham. Finance was arranged on the basis of regular payments spread over a ten year period, after completion of which the stock was to become the property of the E&WJR. The six locomotives were provided by Beyer, Peacock & Co. Ltd and consisted of three of that maker's standard 0-6-0 tender design and three 2-4-0 side tank passenger engines.

The three tender 0-6-0s were Works No's 1235 to 1237, completed in February 1873 at a cost of £2,019 each and based on a design previously supplied to the Swedish Government Railway. The locomotives had inside frames, 4ft 6in driving wheels and 16in. x 24in. cylinders, a working pressure of 120lbs per square inch and were fitted with Stephenson link motion. They did not, however, have any braking system on the engine, a handbrake only being fitted on the tender. It has been suggested that these were numbered 1 to 3 by the E&WJR but this must assume that the old Manning, Wardle engine was not considered as the line's No. 1, although it was undoubtedly included in the total of seven locomotives in the return made to the Board of Trade at the end of 1873.

The new tender engines were immediately put to work on goods traffic over the line but their stay was to be short lived, with the railway running into financial difficulties almost immediately. As a result, they were reclaimed by the financiers in default of payment and were returned to Beyer, Peacock. A sale was then arranged to the Lancashire & Yorkshire Railway, who took delivery in May 1875 and numbered them 520 to 522. They remained at work on the L&YR for some years, with No. 522 reportedly being later rebuilt as a saddle tank and not being withdrawn until June 1903. No. 520 lasted until 1899, whilst No. 521 was scrapped by 1890.

The three tank engines, costing £1,684 each, were of standard Beyer, Peacock inside framed design and bore Works No's

ABOVE: The fledgling E&WJR ordered six locomotives from Beyer, Peacock for the full opening of their line from Green's Norton to Stratford-upon-Avon in 1873, three of which were standard inside framed 0-6-0 tender goods engines. After working on the E&WJR for around two years, the locomotives were reclaimed by the '*Birmingham Waggon Company*', who had financed their purchase. Eventually they were resold in 1875 to the L&YR, who photographed their No. 522 prior to its later rebuilding as a saddle tank. *Author's collection*

LEFT: The other three locomotives ordered by the E&WJR for their full opening in 1873 were standard Beyer, Peacock 2-4-0 side tank engines, based on a design previously supplied to a Swedish Railway, an example of which is posed here for an official works photograph. *Author's collection*

ABOVE, RIGHT & BELOW RIGHT: The three Beyer, Peacock 2-4-0 tanks met the same fate as their tender engine counterparts, being reclaimed by their suppliers and again sold on to the L&YR. One of them, renumbered as L&YR No. 518, was converted at Horwich Works to a carry a bunker-mounted 3-ton capacity crane in 1891 and was the kept there as a works engine. These three studies of the 2-4-0T show it at Horwich, above and below right, and in an official photograph probably taken when newly converted, right. Note its L&YR number was only carried on the rear of the bunker. *All author's collection*

1238-1240 of January 1873. They were again derived from an 1866 design for a Swedish company, on this occasion Bolderman & Son. The locomotives were supplied without cabs, and were fitted with straight link motion and screw hand brakes; driving wheels were 5ft in diameter, and the inside cylinders 15in. x 20in. They operated the through passenger services between Stratford and Blisworth for the next two years or so but, as with their 0-6-0 counterparts, they were summarily removed from the line in 1875 and returned to Beyer, Peacock. Once again a sale was arranged to the L&YR in May 1875 and the engines became No's 517 to 519 on that line, then having long subsequent careers in the north of England.

No. 517 was placed on the L&YR duplicate list as No. 517A and withdrawn in November 1909. Sister locomotive No. 518 was reconstructed as a crane tank in 1891 and was used thereafter at Horwich Works until September 1922, whilst No. 519 was withdrawn as No. 519A in 1902.

The Years From 1875 to 1885

Statistics provided to the Board of Trade show that the E&WJR owned six locomotives at the end of 1874 but the new Beyer, Peacock engines were to be returned to and subsequently sold by their makers in May of 1875. It must be assumed, therefore, that hired engines immediately took their place and this is to some extent confirmed in the Minutes of Evidence presented by the company in May 1875, in support of their application for an extension to Northampton. Here it was stated, under examination as to the cost of '*renting*' locomotives, that they had use of six but from differing sources, suggesting hiring from more than one supplier, almost certainly including Isaac Watt Boulton.

The loss of the Beyer, Peacock engines obviously lead to a motive power crisis on the E&WJR and traffic was temporarily suspended whilst alternative arrangements were made. Initially, it seems that the L&NWR may have provided some short term assistance but, by the end of 1875, Board of Trade returns indicated that the E&WJR were operating just three locomotives, all of which were hired.

A wide variety of locomotives are known to have been used by the E&WJR during the subsequent ten years but identification of just when and how they were acquired and replaced has been a somewhat complex and inconclusive process. Although the above mentioned annual returns do provide a statistical indication of the situation at year ends, the movements of individual engines within the intervening periods is often difficult to define.

The French Engines

It is known that, of the three locomotives on hire to the E&WJR at the end of 1875, two were tender engines. These were almost certainly two French locomotives that were obtained through Thomas Brassey, the well-known railway contractor.

These two outside cylinder engines, one a 2-4-0, and the other an 0-6-0, were reputedly used by Brassey on contracts in France but quite how they then came to be in the United Kingdom, let alone at Stratford-upon-Avon, is not at all clear. However, some sources have indicated the involvement of a certain William Barber Buddicom in the transaction and his links with Brassey and his activities with French railways are well recorded.

Hitherto, detailed information about these two apocryphal locomotives and their careers on the E&WJR, has been limited to a few handed down records, some of which conflict with each other. However, recent research has fortunately provided a few more details, and a somewhat clearer picture is now available.

La Savoie

This locomotive has been recorded as being an outside cylinder 0-6-0 tender engine, with 4ft 9in. driving wheels and 18in. x 24in. cylinders. A more precise identification has until recently been extremely difficult, although it has previously been described as a 'Bourbonnais' type product of Andre Koechlin, sold to Brassey from the *Chemin de Fer de Rhone et Loire* in around 1858. Its use by Brassey on contracts in the Savoy region of France were thought to have resulted in the name of *La Savoie* being applied to the engine.

However, the fortunate discovery of a newspaper account of a court case of early 1876 has now allowed a much more precise identification of the locomotive to be made. During May 1875, the engine was claimed to have emitted sparks whilst working a goods train to Blisworth, which set fire to a lineside hovel near Byfield and the report of the subsequent court hearing does provide significant details.

An independent engineer examined the locomotive, which was known locally as '*Savoy*', and reported that it was one of only two owned by the E&WJR at the time, that it had been constructed by '*Buddicombe of Rouen*' and was originally a '*six wheeled goods engine, but was now running with two*'.

This report conveniently confirms several previously elusive details. Firstly, it does clarify *La Savoie* as being in use on the E&WJR by at least May 1875 and still in use there in March 1876. It also seems to indicate that the engine was still named whilst running on the E&WJR, although it is possible that the anglicisation of its name to '*Savoy*' in the newspaper report could perhaps indicate some conveyed knowledge of a previous name, rather than one which it still carried. Significantly, it also does confirm the locomotive as actually being built by Buddicom in his works at Chartreux, Rouen, rather than him having been just the agent in its transfer to the E&WJR. In all probability the

No illustration has been found to date of the E&WJR's French Buddicom 0-6-0 *La Savoie*. However, this photograph of Nord No. 299 is representative of the type and at least serves to convey an impression of what must have been to local eyes a rather strange machine, hauling short goods trains on the line between Blisworth and Stratford. *From* La Machine Locomotive En France

engine carried the usual builder's plate indicating this origin.

Various sources have been consulted in an attempt to even more closely identify the engine and to find an illustration if possible. This lead to a French publication of 1986 entitled *La Machine Locomotive en France*. Although a precise candidate could not be found, the Buddicom long-boiler type 0-6-0s of around 1848 seemed to exhibit all of the necessary characteristics and this may therefore be as close as it is possible to get to the actual appearance of *La Savoie*.

Also significant is the knowledge that several of these early French Buddicom 0-6-0 classes were quite quickly modified to the 0-4-2 wheel arrangement by the removal of the coupling rods from the rear pair of wheels, to give greater flexibility of the wheelbase. This may also be reflected in the fact that *La Savoie* was reported as '*running with two*' on the E&WJR, which can either be interpreted as running with just two wheels coupled, or perhaps even as a single-driver.

The locomotive appears to have been used on the E&WJR for up to ten years and eventually found its way to the Bute Trustees at Cardiff, again through the hands of Brassey from whom it was presumably being hired. According to the *Locomotive Magazine*, it arrived at Cardiff in 1885 as a six-coupled saddle tank. Lists in the Stephenson Locomotive Society's archive also record it as an 0-6-0 saddle tank whilst on the E&WJR, so it is possible that it was rebuilt before leaving Stratford-upon-Avon.

It subsequently carried Cardiff Railway No's 25 and then 32, was further rebuilt at Tyndall Street in 1888, and seems to have survived in use until around 1907, when it was laid aside and then broken up after remaining derelict for a number of years.

The French 2-4-0

The other locomotive obtained from Brassey, and another Buddicom product, was a 2-4-0 tender engine, with outside cylinders and 5ft 6in. driving wheels. This has always been recorded as bearing the name *Ceres* whilst with the E&WJR but the discovery of a newspaper report of 23rd October 1875 does cast some doubt on this appellation. The report actually concerns the recent appearance of a new '*Fairlie*' locomotive on the E&WJR but mentions that the newcomer had been obtained due to '*the "Gers" of Rouen and brave "Wellington" proving inadequate for the traffic of the line …*'.

Newspaper reports cannot always be assumed to be factually correct but this use of '*Gers*' does correlate with *La Savoie* as both are *Départements* of France, and it is quite plausible that the two engine names could have been drawn from that same source. It also confirms the locomotive as another Buddicom product from Rouen. However, unlike *La Savoie*, a more precise identification of '*Gers*' has proved difficult, although there are several illustrations of early Buddicom 2-4-0 passenger engines to provide a general impression of the appearance of the locomotive.

It has been stated that the engine was used on the first of the reintroduced passenger services from Stratford to Blisworth in 1885 and so, along with its French stablemate, can be reasonably assumed to have stayed on the E&WJR for at least ten years. In its last years, it appears to have been used intermittently on ballast trains and was withdrawn as worn out shortly afterwards.

The other French locomotive used on the E&WJR is known to have been a Buddicom 2-4-0 tender engine, which with 5ft 6in. driving wheels was more suited to passenger work. Again no illustration of the actual locomotive has to date come to light but this early 20th century French postcard of a Ouest 2-4-0, built at Rouen in 1844, is probably a reasonable likeness. *Author's collection*

The E&WJR, along with its neighbour the N&BJR, had many dealings with Isaac Watt Boulton of Ashton-under-Lyne, who specialised in supplying old engines on hire to impecunious small railways. A contemporary newspaper report mentions 'brave "Wellington"' as being employed on E&WJR goods trains during 1875 and this can be identified as one of a trio of saddle tanks converted by Boulton from long-boiler type tender 0-6-0s. *Wellington* does not appear to have been itself captured by the camera but fellow conversion *Hercules* here provides a glimpse of the type. The rustic nature of Boulton's work is apparent, with the cab side panels being formed from parts of old tenders. *Author's collection*

Wellington – the Third Engine of 1875

The 'brave Wellington', which had also been noted as being inadequate in the newspaper report of 23 October 1875, was a small 0-6-0 saddle tank locomotive, on hire from Isaac Watt Boulton, the renowned dealer in secondhand and converted locomotives. Alfred Rosling Bennett, in his book *The Chronicles of Boulton's Sidings*, relates how an 0-6-0 long boiler type saddle tank was on hire to the E&WJR around 1875 and this can now be confirmed as *Wellington*.

This was originally a Thwaites & Carbutt (of Vulcan Works, Bradford) or possibly Stephenson tender locomotive, purchased by Boulton in Cardiff in 1866. After being used in its original form for a few years, it was later rather drastically converted into a saddle tank with 3ft 6in. wheels.

At some point in time, the impecunious E&WJR not unusually defaulted on payments to some of its creditors, and it is rumoured that an attempt was made to seize *Wellington* as recompense but this was thwarted when it was seen that the engine bore a plate indicating ownership by Boulton. However, it does seem that its stay on the E&WJR was terminated by the arrival of the new Fairlie locomotive late in 1875, as the end of year Board of Trade statistics do confirm that the line again had only three locomotives at that point in time.

The First Fairlie

As indicated by the aforementioned newspaper report of 23rd October 1875, the E&WJR had somehow managed to obtain, on hire or demonstration, a massive 0-6-6-0 Fairlie's Patent tank locomotive to enhance their obviously over-stretched motive power. The report lauded the newcomer as '*a magnificent new engine, a four cylinder double action Fairlie's Patent, weight 60 tons and complement 20 tons, capable of rushing away with a train of 1,000 tons on the level or 600 or 700 tons over the Morton Pinkney gradient*'. At this time it was would have been one of the largest locomotives in use in the United Kingdom and also the first to feature Walschaert's valve gear.

It seems that the Yorkshire Engine Company had on their hands ten large 0-6-6-0 Fairlie locomotives that had been originally constructed in 1874, under their Works No's 219 to 228. These double-ended locomotives, hugely proportioned by everyday standards, had twelve wheels of 3ft 9in. diameter, four cylinders of 17in. diameter by 22in. stroke and a weight of 77 tons in full working trim. The first five were modified to suit 5ft gauge track to fulfil an order placed by the Poti & Tiflis Railway of Georgia, although it is thought that only four eventually appeared on that system, with one believed to have been lost in transit at sea.

The other five locomotives, however, lingered unsold for some considerable time, despite being advertised for sale in various journals, such as *The Engineer* of 16th August 1878. Eventually, in 1881, a buyer was found in the shape of the Nitrate Railways of Peru but, before the locomotives were despatched to their new owner a year later, they were first modified by the addition of a Bissel truck at either end, thus converting them into a 2-6-6-2 configuration. It is known that, during 1881, Robert Fairlie himself paid a visit to the Yorkshire Engine Co's works and inspected these locomotives during their alteration. According to correspondence in the company files, one of them was apparently being stripped down for detailed examination, suggesting that it may have already been put to some use during the intervening years.

It therefore seems highly likely that this was the locomotive that had been used by the E&WJR in late 1875, probably whilst being hawked around by the manufacturers in an attempt to find a buyer. Doubtless the E&WJR would have been only too pleased to agree to a trial period over their line, seeing this as a way of cheaply obtaining, if only for a short time, some modern and reliable motive power.

A photograph contained in an article on the E&WJR in the *Locomotive Magazine* in 1911 supports this theory and shows that, with the exception of alterations to the chimneys, cab and footsteps, the Fairlie locomotive in question was indeed identical to the others of the batch. The photograph also appears to show an 'E&WJR' plate on one of the tank sides, the other bearing a plate indicating 'Fairlie's Patent'.

The Fairlie appears to have been in daily use on freight traffic

Some strange sights appeared on the E&WJR during the troubled years between 1875 and 1885 but by far the most exotic locomotive was this Fairlie's Patent 0-6-6-0T, which arrived in late 1875 and stayed for around a year. Although arousing some discontent, and possibly also jealousy, from the nearby N&BJR, whose tracks were shared from Towcester to Blisworth, the engine seems to have handled the increasing tonnages of iron ore carried by the E&WJR without difficulty. However, the giant locomotive, which was probably only ever on hire or demonstration from the makers, was soon returned home and eventually left for a more suitable life in Peru. The two plates on the tank sides bore the legends 'E&WJR' and 'Fairlies Patent'. *The Locomotive Magazine*

on the E&WJR from around October 1875 but it was not long before their neighbours, the N&BJR, took exception to the use of what they obviously considered to be an unacceptably large locomotive over their line from Towcester to Blisworth. Although some of the protestations were based on the safety of the locomotive in certain locations, there must also have been more than just a tinge of local rivalry involved in the decision to challenge the use of the engine over the line. The two neighbouring railways failed to reach an amicable agreement and the matter was therefore brought before the Railway Commissioners for arbitration on 14th February 1876.

Expert witnesses were produced by both parties, with one Mr Jacomb, the chief resident engineer of the London & South Western Railway, claiming on behalf of the N&BJR that the '*Towcester Road bridge of 40 foot span*' was liable to be overstrained by the Fairlie locomotive when the whole weight of the engine was on it. The E&WJR countered by pointing out that, when the engine was placed centrally on the bridge, due to its unusual length certain parts of it were not on the span at all and therefore the effective weight was no more than that of a normal engine. The fact that the Fairlie had run over the bridge almost daily since September 1875, without any problem, was also deemed to indicate that there should be no objection raised against its use on the line.

The N&BJR then claimed that there were certain points on their line where the Fairlie's unusual width made the engine unsafe, specifically in the goods yard at Blisworth, the passenger platforms there and at Towcester, and on two other bridges. The engine actually measured 8ft 7in. wide for a length of 6ft at either end and 9ft wide for the remainder of its length. In addition, there was a ledge or footplate extension of a further 6 inches on either side of the widest portions, making a total width of 10ft at a point 4ft 6in. from the ground. However, the E&WJR again countered that the width of the Fairlie engine was actually very little greater than that of an ordinary engine and in any case, it

had in fact already been reduced by 3 inches on either side. It was again pointed out that it had thus far caused no inconvenience or damage whatsoever to the N&BJR.

The E&WJR concluded their defence by stating that the objections made were '*frivolous and were not put forth bona fide*' and were merely intended to obstruct the operation of their trains, pointedly remarking that the N&BJR already had a comfortable arrangement with the L&NWR to provide a competing route for iron ore traffic.

The Commissioners, after visiting the various locations involved and having thoroughly examined both the locomotive and the claims of the two companies, duly delivered their findings on 2nd March 1876. They reported that the width of the Fairlie locomotive meant that a minimum space of only 1ft 4in. was available between the edge of the footplate and any structure on the lines in question. Board of Trade regulations did require that this should be at least one foot greater but the regulations referred to actually only applied to the distance from the sides of passenger carriages and so were considered to have no bearing on the case.

In addition, they commented that all of the bridges on the N&BJR line had been constructed to accommodate double track but thus far only a single line of rails had been laid. They therefore considered that as long as the N&BJR cautioned their staff to only stand on the unused portion of the trackbed when trains passed, they could not deem the locomotive to be unfit to work on the line. They did, however, recommend that the engine should be required to slacken speed before crossing bridges and should not exceed 10mph when on the bridges themselves. The Commissioners also felt that the 6 inch extension on part of the Fairlie's footplate should not be a problem at Blisworth and Towcester stations, as part of any potential overlapping was in fact due to the irregular shape of the platform edges, which had been allowed to bulge out from their original line of construction.

However, the sidings at Blisworth were thought to be a

different matter. In most cases there existed at least the usual 6ft space between tracks but at the point of exchange between the N&BJR and L&NWR, the space was more restricted. The Commissioners therefore decreed that the Fairlie, although suitable for shunting in the other sidings, should not be allowed to work where the clearance was less than 6ft, stating: '*We decide therefore that the engine is not unfit to be used on the line of the Northampton and Banbury Company over which the East and West Junction have running powers under their Act, distinctly at the same time not approving of its being taken upon sidings at the Blisworth terminus where the free space on either side is under six feet. We make no order about costs*'.

The locomotive does seem to have been regarded as a success on the E&WJR and they found that it had '*answered exceedingly well the purpose for which it had been procured*' and at the same time '*effected a great economy of labour in the conveyance of loads of iron ore*'. An additional reference to the use of the Fairlie over the E&WJR was also made in a report in the *Cambridge Independent Press* of 12th February 1876 on the then recent Abbot's Ripton accident. The subject of locomotive power on heavy goods trains was discussed and mention made of '*the Fairlie engine lately placed on the Junction Railway between Blisworth and Stratford, where the heavy traffic formerly required three or four trains per day … the new engine has taken the whole in one journey, its maximum load not yet having been provided*'.

There is unfortunately no record of the exact length of time that the Fairlie remained with the E&WJR, although some accounts do refer to it having been used on the line for around one year, thus giving a departure date of late 1876, or perhaps early 1877. It has also been stated that, after being returned to the Yorkshire Engine Co., the Fairlie was offered, presumably again on loan, to the London, Chatham & Dover Railway, although this opportunity was apparently declined. The successful sale to Peru must then have hastened the refurbishment of the locomotive for a more suitable life hauling heavy trains across the Andes.

Another Fairlie

Somewhat unbelievably, yet another Fairlie type is also recorded to have been used on the E&WJR during this period of random hiring and borrowing of locomotives. There have been several published references to the use of a smaller, single boilered, 0-4-4 tank version on the line, although no clear contemporary evidence of this has been discovered so far. This rather elusive engine was built by R.&W. Hawthorn as their Works No. 1699 in 1877, to the order of the Fairlie Engine & Rolling Stock Company, and was very much a passenger locomotive, with 5ft 6in. coupled wheels and 16in. x 24in. cylinders.

It seems that this Fairlie was used on the E&WJR for up to one year and although its precise dates of arrival and departure are unknown, it cannot have been on the line earlier than its building date during 1877 and must then have left to be refurbished in time for its presentation at the Paris Exhibition of June 1878, where it bore the name *Robert Fairlie*. Here the locomotive design was heavily criticised, with problems being anticipated with the flexible steam pipes and the complicated linkages for the brake system and valve gear.

It is also improbable that that the locomotive would have remained with the E&WJR after their passenger services were suspended from 23rd July 1877, so its visit to the line was presumably quite a short one and this would seem to be confirmed by the end of year Board of Trade statistics, which suggest that this second Fairlie must have arrived and departed within the same year.

It is therefore unlikely, although not impossible, that its time on the E&WJR coincided with the visit of the larger 0-6-6-0 Fairlie. It is perhaps more likely that the line benefited from consecutive trial or demonstration visits of these two locomotives. After its appearance at the Paris exhibition, the Fairlie was put up for sale but failed to find any takers until 1882 when, after a trial, it was purchased by the Swindon, Marlborough & Andover Railway. The locomotive was finally taken out of use in 1892.

Remarkably a second Fairlie's Patent locomotive appeared on the E&WJR in 1877 but on this occasion it was a perhaps far more suitable 0-4-4 passenger tank type. Soon after construction by R.& W. Hawthorn, the engine was used on the E&WJR for a short time before being refurbished and presented at the Paris Exhibition of June 1878, where it did not receive universal acclaim. The locomotive was eventually acquired in 1882 by the Swindon, Marlborough & Andover Railway, becoming No. 4 on that line, where it was photographed, close to the end of its days, some ten years later. *Author's collection*

Other Boulton Engines

The Board of Trade return at the close of 1875 indicates that the E&WJR then had three locomotives in use, two of which were tender engines. This total can be accounted for by the two French engines and the large Fairlie, which it can be assumed had now replaced *Wellington*.

The E&WJR's own half year report of 30th June 1876 then refers to four locomotives, two of them having tenders, which would indicate *La Savoie* and *Gers*. One of the other two would still have been the large Fairlie but the fourth engine, another tank locomotive, is more difficult to identify. It seems certain that 'brave *Wellington*' had by then gone back to Boulton, whilst the second Fairlie may not yet have appeared on the scene. There are, however, unconfirmed reports of other Boulton owned locomotives appearing on the E&WJR during this period.

The *Chronicles of Boulton's Sidings* suggests that *Nelson*, apparently a very similar tank locomotive to *Wellington*, was also hired, although a letter published in the *Locomotive Magazine* of June 15th 1922, from a J. Bradshaw, the son of the early locomotive superintendent of the E&WJR, suggests otherwise. The correspondent states that, in addition to personally recalling the 1873 batch of Beyer, Peacock locomotives that were returned to the makers, he could also confirm the tank engine named *Wellington* as being the only one hired from Boulton. In fact, he recalls that *Wellington*'s driver, a John Whitehead, was also provided with the locomotive.

However, a further engine must have arrived by the end of the year, as the Board of Trade return of December

Sir,—Referring to your article of April 15th, 1922, on the old East and West Junction Railway, there was an engine hired from the late Mr. Isaac Boulton, a tank engine named Wellington. The driver, who came with her, was a John Whitehead, who has long since been dead.

There was also an engine from the Somerset and Dorset Railway which only ran one trip, and to the best of my recollection, this was a six-wheeled coupled goods engine, with outside frames and built by Messrs. Fox, Walker & Co., Bristol.

After this engine ran one trip, and while shunting in Stratford-on-Avon goods yard, the leading tyre came off. It was then sent back. No other engine was supplied to this company beyond the one already mentioned from Mr. Isaac Boulton.

I do not remember reading the article which appeared in your magazine some years back, but I have a good recollection of the first lot of engines which were delivered by Messrs. Beyer, Peacock & Co. in 1873, at which time my father was in charge of the locomotive department there.—Yours truly,

J. BRADSHAW,

Douglas.   Loco. Supt., Isle of Man Ry.

1876 then shows five locomotives on the E&WJR, although unfortunately no analysis between tank and tender types is available.

To add to the intrigue, in his above mentioned letter, Bradshaw mentions other references to a Somerset & Dorset Railway 2-4-0 engine having been on hire from Boulton's around this time but he suggests that they were erroneous. This locomotive is referred to in an earlier article on the E&WJR in the *Locomotive Magazine* and also receives mention in *The Chronicles*, although Bennett states therein that there are no records of Boulton ever actually owning such an engine. However, Bradshaw instead suggests that, to the best of his recollection, it was an S&DJR outside framed, six-coupled goods engine built by Fox, Walker & Co. that was tried at Stratford-upon-Avon but that this was returned immediately after losing a driving wheel tyre on its first trip. However, this in itself seems unlikely to be accurate as neither the S&DJR, nor any of its constituents, had owned a suitable double framed 0-6-0.

The early 2-4-0 engines on the S&DJR were not outside framed and were actually supplied by George England and not Fox, Walker, although it does seem that some of these did actually find their way to the latter company in Bristol, as part payment for newly built 0-6-0 saddle tanks delivered in 1874. Yet more confusingly, Bertram Baxter, in Volume 4 of his *British Locomotive Catalogue 1825-1923*, has listed two of these SDJR 2-4-0s, No's 3 and 4, as being hired to the E&WJR as early as November 1874. However, this date seems a little unlikely, as the E&WJR probably still had their full complement of Beyer, Peacock locomotives at the time.

After the loss of the Beyer, Peacock locomotives, the E&WJR line was graced by a random selection of hired and borrowed motive power for several years. Amongst these was an engine from the Somerset & Dorset Railway, and although reports differ on a precise identification, the balance of probability suggests that it was a George England built 2-4-0 tender type. Several of these had been displaced from their home line by the purchase of new locomotives from Fox, Walker of Bristol, who took the old engines in part exchange. One apparently arrived at Stratford but lost a driving wheel tyre after making just one trip and was quickly returned whence it came. The type is illustrated here by S&DJR No. 2 in original condition. *Author's collection*

A rear three-quarters view of S&DR No. 3, in as built condition, at an unknown location in Somerset. These were the first locomotives ordered by the S&DR and they were built by George England at his Hatcham Ironworks at New Cross, in London, the order being placed in February 1861, with delivery being made almost exactly a year later. The photograph is believed to have been taken in 1862, probably not long after it had arrived on the line. Baxter notes two of these engines as being hired to the E&WJR, No's 3 and 4, for which there is as yet no proof. However, that raises the possibility that it was the locomotive illustrated here which arrived on the line in late 1874. *Neil Parkhouse collection*

The balance of probability therefore suggests that, as partly confirmed by Bradshaw, there was indeed an S&DJR engine at Stratford-upon-Avon around this time but its precise identity or source remains uncertain. It is perhaps most likely to have been a George England 2-4-0 from the batch received by Fox Walker.

The Return of the Manning, Wardle

Whatever the composition of the E&WJR locomotive fleet at the end of 1876, by the close of the following year, the company was down to just three engines again. Two of these can reasonably be presumed to have still been the French engines but with the complete withdrawal of passengers services on the line during 1877, it is probably unlikely that the third was a hired engine. It is known, however, that the Manning Wardle 0-6-0ST that had worked the first train back in 1871 did return to E&WJR stock around 1877. This is therefore likely to be the third engine listed at the end of that year, presumably being kept at Stratford for shunting purposes, whilst *La Savoie* and *Gers* managed the few goods trains left on the line.

A further, as yet unidentified, locomotive was then acquired during 1878, as the total for the end of that year had increased to four. Unfortunately, there are no obvious candidates for the identity of this engine, although a further hiring from Boulton, or another source, is the likely answer.

A New Engine at Last – the Beyer, Peacock 0-6-0ST

Despite their obvious lack of funds, the E&WJR had harboured plans since 1873 to extend their system to the

west and finally, on Whit Monday 2nd June 1879, the first train ran on the Evesham, Redditch & Stratford Junction Railway. Although nominally an independent company, the line had been sponsored by the E&WJR, who rather incongruously operated a passenger service on the route whilst their own main line trains were still suspended. The new line extended the existing E&WJR route westwards from Stratford to Broom Junction, where the Midland Railway's Evesham to Redditch line was joined, this providing an alternative through route.

This expansion required additional motive power, with the E&WJR by then only having the use of the two increasingly

No photograph has yet been located of the Beyer, Peacock 0-6-0ST ordered in 1879. Based on a design previously supplied to the Crewe Iron Co., this official view of *Crewe* would undoubtedly be representative of the E&WJR locomotive. *Author's collection*

decrepit French engines and two others, one of which was the probably unsuitable small Manning, Wardle. Somehow funds were made available to purchase, on the usual quarterly terms, a brand new Beyer, Peacock 0-6-0 saddle tank engine, of a proven design previously supplied to the Crewe Iron Company. The new locomotive, Works No. 1830 of 1879, had 4ft driving wheels, 16in. x 22in. cylinders, and a capacity of 1 ton of coal and just 700 gallons of water, a specification which would later lead to its early departure from the E&WJR.

The new arrival obviously displaced one of the other, probably hired, locomotives on the E&WJR, as at the year end the total number of engines remained at four.

More Beyer, Peacocks – No's 2, 3 and 4

The year of 1880 then saw a continuation of the relationship with the locomotive builders Beyer, Peacock, following the delivery of a new 0-6-0 tender locomotive, Works No. 1919, which became E&WJR No. 2. This was a relatively small, double framed engine, with 4ft 6½in. driving wheels, 17in. x 24in. cylinders and an operating pressure of 160 lbs per square inch. This increased the total of E&WJR locomotives to five at the end of that year but

twelve months later, this figure was still maintained, despite the acquisition of another tender engine similar to No. 2 in 1881 – probably indicating the loss of either *La Savoie* or *Gers*. The new engine, Beyer, Peacock Works No. 2049 of 1881, was of slightly different dimensions to its predecessor, with 5ft 1in. driving wheels, a slightly smaller boiler and was only fitted with an engine brake; the newcomer became No. 3 in the E&WJR fleet.

The next variation in E&WJR motive power occurred during 1884, with at the end of the year, the company reporting only four locomotives as being in use. However, 1885 saw the reintroduction of passenger services on the Blisworth to Stratford section, which by then had been suspended for eight long years. The shortfall in motive power was more than compensated for by the purchase of no less than three engines during that year. First to arrive, early in the year, was yet another tender 0-6-0 from Beyer, Peacock, of almost identical specification to No. 3, which logically became No. 4 on the line. Unlike No. 3, this latest engine was supplied from new with Westinghouse brake equipment.

However, the need to efficiently operate the new passenger services required something rather different to the lightweight six-coupled goods engines

ABOVE: The first of a long line of Beyer, Peacock outside framed goods 0-6-0s appeared on the E&WJR in 1880. This was allocated E&WJR No. 2 and is seen here in original condition alongside the coal stack at Stratford engine shed. The locomotive appears to carry lining on its tender, cabsides and sandboxes only, and was fitted with a shorter, wider chimney than the two engines which followed from Beyer, Peacock. *Author's collection*

RIGHT: In early 1881, a further Beyer, Peacock 0-6-0 joined the E&WJR fleet; No. 3 was very similar to its predecessor but had larger driving wheels and a boiler of slightly smaller dimensions. It is pictured here in official 'works grey' livery prior to delivery. The light grey paint scheme was applied for photographic purposes, because it showed up the details of locomotives and, in particular, the proposed lining arrangement. *Author's collection*

RIGHT: This early E&WJR era photograph of Beyer, Peacock 0-6-0 No. 3, standing on the Stratford turntable, appears to show it in a plain largely unlined livery. There is just a trace of lining visible on the front sandbox but nothing on the boiler or cabside, or on the tender side. *Author's collection*

BELOW: Another early view of No. 3, alongside the Up platform at Stratford, circa 1900. The locomotive is in immaculate condition, with much polished metalwork, including a gleaming dome and burnished connecting rods. Footplatemen and shed staff clearly took a pride in their engines. Lining can also now be seen on the tender and cab sides but not on the boiler. No compnay insignia is visible but presumably there was a cast iron 'E&W' plate on the tender which is just out of picture in both of these views. Note the driver is holding the handbrake. *Author's collection*

BELOW: A later view of No. 3, posed in front of the coal stack at Stratford, with the shed foreman standing alongside and resting a proprietorial hand on her footplate. The 'gent' on the footplate does not appear to be a railwayman. Note that the locomotive has been rebuilt since the earlier pictures, this taking place in 1898, No. 3 being fitted with a new Belpaire boiler, firebox and shorter chimney. There is no sign, however, of the vacuum brakes fitted in 1904, so the photograph would seem to date from between those years. With the new boiler not banded as previously, lining had been applied to it, whilst lining is also now visible on the frames and bufferbeam. The 'E&W' plate on the tender is also to be seen here. *John Alsop collection*

ABOVE & BELOW: E&WJR No. 4 followed from Beyer, Peacock in 1885 and was similar to its predecessors. However, it was fitted from new with the Westinghouse brake system, the pump for which can be seen prominently mounted on the side of the boiler, below, whilst its two predecessors only had hand-operated braking. In both of these views lining can be made out on the cab sides and sandboxes only, and note that the engine also sports different chimneys in each picture, with that above being the original; a new boiler was fitted in 1898, so presumably the view below post-dates that. As was usually the case, both of these photographs were taken at Stratford-upon-Avon, with relatively few E&WJR locomotive portraits being at other locations. *Both Author's collection*

Despite the arrival of the Beyer, Peacock 0-6-0s, the E&WJR still needed more suitable motive power for their newly reintroduced passenger services and, in 1885, two smart little 2-4-0 passenger tank engines were obtained from the same source, becoming No's 5 and 6. These had in fact been part of an order placed by the Swindon, Marlborough & Andover Railway in 1883 but they were unable to complete the purchase and the E&WJR was quick to benefit from the availability of the locomotives. No. 5 is here seen with its footplate crew posing for the photographer on the turntable at Woodford & Hinton, in a splendid study which picks out every detail of the locomotive's construction and lining. The engine is not, however, in original condition, having been fitted with a new boiler in 1907, which had been supplied by Beyer, Peacock. As such, it now has boiler lining and had also been equipped with a different design of dome. *John Alsop collection*

The Beyer, Peacock 2-4-0 Tanks – No's 5 & 6

The E&WJR did not have too much time to look around for suitable motive power for the reintroduction of their passenger services between Blisworth and Stratford, and fortunately Beyer, Peacock were again in a position to help. In 1883, the Swindon, Marlborough & Andover Railway had placed an order for three conventional inside cylinder tank engines to a proven design. The first of these was delivered as SM&AR No. 8 in 1884, whilst the remaining two were ready for delivery when the order was cancelled. In fact the third engine, SM&AR No. 10, was actually photographed in that guise by Beyer Peacock.

The E&WJR was therefore able to take advantage of the situation and the two locomotives, Beyer, Peacock Works No's 2466 and 2467, were quickly in their hands. They were placed in use on the new passenger services as E&WJR No's 5 and 6. Although recognisably a Beyer, Peacock product, they were of different appearance to the other engines on the E&WJR, with outside frames to the 4ft 6in. leading wheels but inside frames for the 5ft 6in. driving wheels.

It seems, however, that the design was not found totally satisfactory, as the engines tended to be unstable when running bunker first at speed and a restriction was soon put on this mode of operation, with it being totally prohibited between Broom and Stratford. Beyer, Peacock were in fact approached as early as 1894 to convert the engines to a 2-4-2 configuration to resolve this problem but nothing was done at the time or when the idea was again revived in 1906.

In addition to all of the above mentioned locomotives, it is also known that the E&WJR did hire *'locomotives, stock, and other materials'* from Thomas Russell Crampton during the early 1880s. In 1893, when the Manchester, Sheffield & Lincolnshire Railway purchased holdings in the E&WJR and the ER&SJR, they also inherited a certificate of indebtedness for some £9,385 from the former, which related to the hire of the above items from Crampton between 1881 and 1883.

ABOVE & LEFT: Two early photographs of No. 6 at Stratford, with the engine's side tanks in the process of being topped up with water in the view above, alongside the Up platform. Like No. 5, it too was fitted with a new boiler from Beyer, Peacock in 1907 but these pictures pre-date that, so No. 6 here displays the original type of dome that was fitted to both engines. There is also no lining visible on the boiler or the bufferbeam. Whilst the pictures were taken on different occasions, they are useful in depicting both sides of the locomotive at a similar period. The picture left shows the engine at the Down platform. *Both author's collection*

The Beyer, Peacock 0-6-0ST acquired in 1879 had been found wanting on E&WJR trains, with its water capacity in particular causing problems. A decision was therefore made in 1888 to purchase a replacement engine for the Broom line services and the E&WJR obtained via the sale of assets of the defunct Potteries, Shrewsbury & North Wales Railway a Yorkshire Engine Company 2-4-0T originally built in 1872, carrying the name *Hope*. This engine was destined to only have a short stay with the E&WJR but was at least photographed alongside one of the Beyer, Peacock 2-4-0Ts when both were undergoing some maintenance at Stratford shed. The original position of the nameplate on the tank side can be clearly seen. The date of the photograph is difficult to ascertain; it may have been taken on arrival at Stratford in 1888 or possibly whilst the locomotive was being readied for sale in 1895. *Author's collection*

Hope – Another No. 1

The E&WJR locomotive fleet stood at seven locomotives at the close of 1885. However, it is unclear as to which engine was either numbered or at least considered to be the railway's No. 1. The Beyer, Peacock saddle tank was perhaps the obvious candidate but the older Manning, Wardle 0-6-0 saddle tank inherited from Crampton was also still in use, although it is possible that this was being hired from him rather than owned by the E&WJR.

The seven locomotives reported to the Board of Trade were completed by the three tender 0-6-0s and the two new 2-4-0 tanks but the numbering sequence of the E&WJR fleet apparently only ran as far as No. 6. Whatever the answer to that conundrum, this total of seven engines was then to endure until the end of 1891 but, along the way, there was to be one further change, during the year of 1888.

The Beyer, Peacock 0-6-0 saddle tank had apparently been found rather less than satisfactory, particularly in terms of its water capacity, which restricted it to local journeys. Although it seems to have been used quite successfully to operate the Broom passenger service, it is also possible that the wider use of what was essentially a shunting locomotive had become something of a problem. A decision was therefore taken to sell the engine and it appears that it was probably set aside for disposal during 1888, pending the arrival of another engine. This, on arrival, then also had a claim to be another No. 1 of the E&WJR.

The newcomer was a secondhand engine from the sale of assets of the moribund Potteries, Shrewsbury & North Wales Railway, which had once been part of a wider and rather grand proposal to connect the Midlands with Holyhead. However, in an unfortunate parallel with the existence of the E&WJR, in 1880, the only small section of line that had been completed (between Shrewsbury and Lanymynech) was ordered to be closed by the Board of Trade owing to the poor condition of the track. The company then fell into receivership and the assets were sold where they stood, at various locations on the line, on 24th August 1888. The E&WJR, looking for a replacement for the aforementioned Beyer, Peacock saddle tank, took the opportunity of obtaining a

Yorkshire Engine Company 2-4-0 side tank engine, Works No. 185 of 1872 and bearing the name *Hope*, that had belonged to the PS&NWR

This was perhaps a more suitable passenger locomotive, having 5ft driving wheels, 15in. x 22in. cylinders and a coal capacity of one ton, although surprisingly, the tanks only held 600 gallons of water. In view of the stated reasons for the disposal of the Beyer, Peacock engine, *Hope* was therefore a somewhat strange replacement, unless the bargain was considered too good to refuse.

However, also relevant is the fact that a surviving E&WJR minute book of 1892 reveals that the company were then engaged in '*purchase hire instalments*' every six months with a B.P. Blockley, for a '*loco engine vide agreement with the E&WJR d/d 2 Feb 1890*'. Benjamin Pollard Blockley was an iron merchant of Bloxwich, later becoming founder of the Hawkesbury & Bedworth Brick & Tile Co. Ltd and it is recorded that when *Hope* later left the E&WJR around 1895, it was sent to Blockley and not directly to its new owner. This evidence strongly suggests that the E&WJR did not in fact purchase the engine from the sale of the PS&NWR, but obtained it through a dealer and returned it thence at the end of its useful life on the line.

The locomotive had arrived at Stratford in plain black livery and, after some refurbishment, took the place of the Beyer, Peacock engine, which appears to have been removed from the register of E&WJR assets at the same time, as the return to the Board of Trade at the end of 1888 did not show any increase in numbers. It is also possible that the displaced engine may also originally have been acquired on a hire-purchase arrangement and could have been relinquished on the arrival of the newcomer.

An early photograph showing *Hope* at Stratford reveals, under magnification, that the nameplate had been removed and directly in its place the lettering 'E&WJR' had apparently been substituted. It therefore seems likely that the name was not perpetuated during the locomotive's service with the E&WJR.

Whatever the statistical connotations, it does seem that the Beyer, Peacock 0-6-0ST did not arrive with its subsequent owners, the Rothervale Colliery Company, until April 1890,

The Beyer, Peacock 0-6-0ST, purchased new in 1879, had a relatively short life of around ten years with the E&WJR and was then sold to the Rothervale Colliery Company near Sheffield. It arrived with its new owners in April 1890 and was soon fitted with large *Rothervale No. 1* cast name/numberplates attached to the tank sides. Although no photograph exists of the locomotive in E&WJR ownership it is nevertheless tempting to suggest that this photograph, which was probably taken to celebrate its arrival at Rothervale Colliery, does still show the old E&WJR livery; the numeral on the cabside is very much in the E&WJR style of the period. The engine later became *Rothervale No. 0*, after a new No. 1 arrived at Rothervale in 1929, the cast '1' being ground off and replaced by a screwed on '0'. Scrapped in 1959, a *Rothervale No. 0* plate survives in the Chasewater Railway Museum. *Author's collection*

when it became No. 1 in their fleet. Photographic evidence shows the engine, probably on arrival at its new home, bearing not only a large tank-side cast name/numberplate reading *Rothervale No. 1* but also the number '1' on a fully lined cabside, all of which appears to be very much in the style of the E&WJR.

However, *Hope* was clearly not totally satisfactory either, or had possibly always just been seen as a stopgap as, after leaving

the line in 1895, it had also made its way to the industrial scene, being acquired by the Cannock & Rugeley Colliery Company in 1905, via B.P. Blockley of Bloxwich. Once again, the locomotive seems to have left the E&WJR running stock at a somewhat earlier date, as the Board of Trade statistics for the close of 1893 show only nine engines, despite the purchase of three more locomotives in the previous year.

Hope, having also soon found to be less than satisfactory by the E&WJR, had moved on to new owners in the form of the Cannock & Rugeley Colliery by 1905. Photographed on that company's system around 1910, the engine had been given a new guise as C&RC No. 8 *Harrison*. It had also been fitted with a new boiler and overall cab probably soon after arrival here. In later years it would receive a much more substantial rebuild, at the colliery's own workshops, as an 0-6-0 tank engine, thus losing much of its former appearance. Industrial life obviously suited these E&WJR veterans, as this survivor also had a long life, lasting into the mid 1950s. *Author's collection*

L&NWR Engines

In 1891, the long awaited eastern extension of the E&WJR from Towcester to Ravenstone Wood Junction was finally opened, which allowed the through running of Midland Railway goods trains from London to the West of England. Initially, these were operated by MR locomotives over the E&WJR line but after just a few months of operation, a derailment at Kineton prompted a reappraisal of this policy and the Midland withdrew from the agreement to use their own engines.

This gave the E&WJR an immediate problem, as they did not possess enough suitable locomotives to continue to work the Midland traffic and a quick solution was necessary. It might have been expected that the E&WJR would have turned to their usual supplier, Beyer, Peacock, but it is probable that they could not provide engines at short notice and the E&WJR therefore cast around for suitable motive power from other quarters.

A solution was found in the form of three elderly L&NWR 'DX' Class goods engines built in 1863 and 1866, and these arrived on the E&WJR in December 1891. Although all three were to a standard and proven L&NWR design, they presented various detail differences. The first engine, which became E&WJR No. 7, was originally Crewe Works No. 652 of September 1863, becoming L&NWR No. 648 in service and then No. 1891 on the duplicate list. It arrived at Stratford fitted with the vacuum brake. The other two 'DX' Class were originally Crewe Works No's 657 of 1863 and 894 of 1866, being L&NWR No's 809 and 825 respectively but had become No's 1945 and 1966 on the duplicate

list by the time of their sale. These two engines were only fitted with a hand operated engine brake. All three presented a rather antiquated appearance, with their original slope fronted smokeboxes and horizontally hinged flap-type smokebox doors.

An entry in the surviving E&WJR corporate journal of 1892 (a ledger of receipts and expenditures) poses an intriguing question about the purchase of these three L&NWR veterans. This refers to the '*hire of three locomotives 1st June to 30th June at £25 per engine per month, in accordance with a request of undertaking from the Stratford Company, and of an agreement with the Towcester Works & Wagon Co. dated 16th December 1891 - £450*'. A corresponding entry was also made in the journal for the period from 1st July to 30th December of the same year. Unfortunately, these are the only relevant E&WJR documents that have survived and so it is not possible to state whether these payments extended over a longer period.

The '*Stratford Company*' was the term then used to indicate the Stratford-upon-Avon, Towcester & Midland Junction Railway Company, who had then recently constructed the new line from Towcester to Ravenstone Wood. Under the terms of their Act, they were also empowered to repair the existing E&WJR line and, more relevantly, to provide any additional locomotives and rolling stock required to operate the upgraded lines. The rather shadowy '*Towcester Works & Wagon Company*' was a short lived concern which went into voluntary liquidation in 1897. Significantly, a major shareholder was one Saul Isaac, who also financed and constructed the ST&MJR line. It therefore seems highly likely that the three L&NWR locomotives were obtained and financed by Isaac and the Towcester Works & Wagon Company for the E&WJR line, and that a form of hire purchase by instalments had been arranged.

References in the same E&WJR journal also reveal that at some time during the latter part of 1892, an engine had been on hire from the Midland Railway for a period of twenty-seven days at a cost of £2 per day, and that the L&NWR also similarly provided a locomotive for an unspecified period. Unfortunately, the records are incomplete and it is not possible to ascertain for how long this assistance was required but, clearly, the E&WJR were having some difficulties in operating their traffic at that time.

ABOVE: With the line desperately in need of heavy goods engines in late 1891, three elderly L&NWR 'DX' Class 0-6-0s were purchased and allocated No's 7, 8 and 9 in the E&WJR fleet. Only one illustration showing No. 9 has so far been found. In this poor quality view, it is just identifiable behind classmate No. 8 as they stand together in the engine sidings at Stratford shed. No. 8 was withdrawn in 1908, having been fitted with the wheels from No. 9 when it was scrapped by the E&WJR in 1903. *Author's collection*

RIGHT: No. 7 also at Stratford in E&WJR days, when still in original condition. It was to be the only one of the three 'DX' Class to pass to the S&MJR in 1909, who rebuilt it with a more modern boiler and smokebox, and fitted a new set of wheels obtained secondhand from the L&NWR. Note the warning bell high up on the cabside, which was connected to the carriage communication cord. *Author's collection*

A fine study of No. 8, the second of the ex-L&NWR 'DX' Class 0-6-0s in the small E&WJR locomotive fleet, pictured alongside the coaling stage at Stratford-upon-Avon. Although it has long been thought that these engines carried their original L&NWR plain black livery throughout their E&WJR ownership, close study of this image does just reveal traces of lining, particularly on the tender side but also on the cab side and the sandbox, so it is possible they may have been re-liveried. The riveted panelling of the L&NWR tender meant that the E&WJR ownership plate had to be placed off-centre, resulting in a rather unbalanced appearance. The distinctive backward sloping smokebox door is apparent in all of these views; note the horizontal hinge, with the door opening upwards, whilst there is a short length of chain dangling down which was hooked on to the door to hold it open. The obligatory re-railing jack sits on the footplate just ahead of the cab and there is a better view at the rear of the engine of the 4-wheeled rail-mounted crane used for coaling. *John Alsop collection*

Back to Beyer, Peacock – No's 10, 11 and 12

The three ex-L&NWR locomotives held the fort for the E&WJR for the next few years until more modern replacements could be found. The first of these to arrive was another standard Beyer, Peacock tender 0-6-0 of similar dimensions to the existing No. 4. Although it bore Beyer, Peacock Works No. 3613 of 1894, it was not delivered to the E&WJR until April 1895, being allocated No. 10. Two years later, another similar engine, Beyer, Peacock Works No. 3812 of 1896, arrived at Stratford, becoming E&WJR No. 11, and then, in the first year of the 20th century Beyer, Peacock Works No. 4126 of 1900 appeared as No. 12.

All three of the latest engines were to a common design and although basically similar to the earlier Beyer, Peacock 0-6-0s, they had a slightly different boiler specification. All were delivered with both air and vacuum brake equipment. These new locomotives, together with the old L&NWR engines, kept the E&WJR going for the next two years but a major change to the locomotive policy was to occur in 1903.

RIGHT: Early views of the insides of locomotive cabs are rare but, fortunately, this unidentified E&WJR Beyer, Peacock 0-6-0 presented itself to the photographer, perfectly positioned without its tender, under the sheer-legs at Stratford shed. Taken in the early years of the 20th century, one of the E&WJR 2-4-0Ts can just be seen in the left background. *Author's collection*

LEFT: In 1894, the E&WJR returned once more to Beyer, Peacock for their next locomotive. No. 10 was another standard double-framed 0-6-0, almost identical in specification to its immediate predecessor No. 4. It was photographed on the track leading to the engine shed at Stratford, with the roof of the signal box and the station chimneys just peeping over the wall behind. *Author's collection*

ABOVE: The next 0-6-0 to arrive from the Beyer, Peacock stable was No. 11, which was delivered to Stratford-upon-Avon in early 1897. The locomotive is posed here in the traditional spot in front of the coal stacks at Stratford shed almost certainly when brand new, as there is not a mark or blemish to be seen upon it and the metalwork is all burnished to perfection. The low angle of the view coupled with some helpful lighting has enabled the photographer to capture all of the details of the E&WJR livery and lining. *Author's collection*

RIGHT: Another very similar engine was not long in following from Beyer, Peacock, with No. 12 appearing on the E&WJR in the first year of the 20th century. Once again the new arrival was captured on film on the coal road at Stratford shed, when still quite new. *Author's collection*

An Express Passenger Locomotive – No. 13

The inauguration of through services to Stratford from the newly opened Great Central line at Woodford & Hinton lead to the acquisition of what might be termed the E&WJR's only express passenger engine. Once again, Beyer, Peacock was the supplier but on this occasion the choice was a 2-4-0 tender locomotive, based on a design previously supplied to the Hull & Barnsley Railway.

E&WJR No. 13, which arrived at Stratford in July 1903, was a compact inside framed 2-4-0, with large 6ft 1in. driving wheels and 17in. x 24in. cylinders. The locomotive also introduced the Belpaire boiler to the E&WJR and notable too was the use of Stephenson link motion, in place of the Allan gear fitted to the line's previous Beyer, Peacock engines. Air and vacuum brake equipment were both fitted, and the new acquisition appeared in every way very suitable for what it was intended – handling the prestige services carrying American tourists from the capital to Shakespeare's birthplace.

E&WJR passenger 2-4-0 No. 13 was photographed, in traditional 'works grey' livery before its departure from the Beyer, Peacock works in May 1903. *Author's collection*

Much interest was aroused, both locally and nationally, by the arrival in July 1903 of the E&WJR's first and only true passenger locomotive. Beyer, Peacock were again the providers of a 2-4-0 tender engine which became E&WJR No. 13. The pride of the company's fleet is paraded for the camera on the old turntable at Stratford shed in May 1905. There is a good view of the slotted post Down starter signals behind. *Author's collection*

Another view of the new passenger engine, standing in the Up platform at Stratford-upon-Avon station, looking every bit the modern express engine, although in reality the 2-4-0 wheel arrangement was by now becoming rather outdated nationally by the introduction of 4-4-0 types on many lines. The E&WJR did consider having another 2-4-0 but were persuaded to go instead for a more powerful version of the standard Beyer, Peacock 0-6-0, which was considered to be more versatile. The locomotive is fully lined but the lining does not show up particularly well in this view. *Author's collection*

LEFT: In 1903, yet another 0-6-0 arrived from Beyer, Peacock. No. 14 appeared on the line during September but is seen here in works grey livery before departure to its new owners. However, the new locomotive differed somewhat from the earlier examples of its type, with smaller 4ft 9in. driving wheels and a straight footplate. *Author's collection*

BELOW: The arrival of newer Beyer, Peacock 0-6-0s made the future of the old L&NWR 'DX' engines somewhat questionable but, of the three, No. 7 was thought worthy of further investment. It received a new boiler and firebox, afterwards presenting a far more modern appearance in line with many of its former companions that were still in active service on the L&NWR. *Author's collection*

More 0-6-0s – Nos. 14, 15 and 16

September of the same year then saw the arrival of another goods 0-6-0 from Beyer, Peacock but this also represented something of a break with tradition, as No. 14 had, at 4ft 9in., somewhat smaller driving wheels than its immediate predecessors. The new engine did, however, share the same higher pressured Belpaire boiler, cylinders and motion with No. 13 but was not fitted with the Westinghouse brake and also differed externally from others by having a straight running plate.

A casualty of its arrival was one of the old L&NWR engines, No. 9, which was taken out of use in the same year, although it does appear that it was not scrapped immediately and certain parts, particularly the driving wheels, were used to keep the

other 'DX' 0-6-0s going. The future of sister engine No. 8 was also under consideration at the time, as a proposal to fit it with '*power brakes*' was rejected; this was because it was felt that the wooden tender underframe was not strong enough to bear the additional weight of the equipment. In the event, the locomotive soldiered on as it was for a few more years. The outlook was better for the remaining ex-L&NWR engine, No. 7, which received a new boiler and firebox, with the sale of the scrap materials recovered from the old fittings returning the sum of £145 5s 2d to the E&WJR coffers.

In addition, other improvements were made to the other older engines. Vacuum brakes were fitted to No's 2 and 3 in 1903, after a tendering process involving Beyer, Peacock, Peckett

RIGHT: Although now looking rather sorry for itself in this early 1920s photograph at Stratford, old Beyer, Peacock No. 2 had benefitted from a new Belpaire boiler and altered cab front in 1903, which at least brought the locomotive up to a more modern standard. *Author's collection*

BELOW: In 1904, classmate No. 3 was similarly rebuilt and was photographed at Stratford in immaculate condition, the picture almost certainly being taken to show the work that had been carried out. The engine was finished in the fully lined E&WJR livery, with cast brass number and ownership plates on the engine and tender respectively. *Author's collection*

and Avonside; the latter's offer of £101 was accepted. No. 2 also benefitted from a new boiler, whilst its typically Beyer, Peacock appearance was a little modified with the cab front spectacles being changed from square to a round profile. Sister engine No. 3 had to wait a further year before receiving a new Belpaire boiler from Beyer, Peacock at a cost of £933 17s 6d.

Around the same time, the distinctive shape of the original tall, copper capped, Beyer, Peacock chimneys also began to

disappear from the E&WJR locomotives, with a plainer and more modern straight sided type taking their place.

The purchase of more new engines was again considered early in 1904 and quotations were sought for 0-6-0 goods engines from both Beyer, Peacock and Robert Stephenson & Company. In the event, the former's estimate of £2,580 each was accepted, being some £400 less than their competitor. Quite whether the E&WJR had actually considered changing suppliers is not clear

The purchase of further 0-6-0 goods engines was considered during 1904 and quotations were obtained from both Beyer, Peacock and Robert Stephenson & Co. In the event, the E&WJR decided to stay with the proven Beyer, Peacock design and ordered two further examples similar to No. 14. The first, No. 15 arrived later that year, and was photographed outside the engine shed at Stratford probably not long afterwards. The elaborate lining scheme shows up well in this view and note the Beyer, Peacock works plate on the frames above the centre axle. *Author's collection*

Beyer, Peacock delivered No. 16 in 1906, the engine being photographed on Stratford turntable. Note the cast 'Nº 16' numerals that were fixed to the bufferbeam of the engine. *Author's collection*

but the obtaining of the two quotations may have just been a commercial manoeuvre. As a result, No. 15 joined the E&WJR fleet later in the year and was followed by a similar engine, No. 16, in 1906, both being identical to No. 14.

In the same year a proposal was made to purchase another 2-4-0 to the same design as No. 13. However, after some consideration, it was decided that the newer 0-6-0s were probably versatile enough to operate passenger trains to the required schedules and would allow for a more flexible locomotive fleet. Also, having again decided against the conversion of the two Beyer, Peacock tanks to a 2-4-2 wheel arrangement in 1906, the E&WJR did at least arrange for the fitting of new boilers to both in the following year, somewhat changing their external appearance.

Following the addition to stock of the three new goods 0-6-0s, the annual return to the Board of Trade then showed a total of fifteen locomotives in the ownership of the E&WJR, the highest number that would be reached. However, it would be reduced soon afterwards.

The Last Engines – No's 17 and 18

By the end of 1908, the E&WJR locomotive fleet had been reduced from fifteen to ten, with one reduction being accounted for by the withdrawal from service of the old L&NWR engine No. 8. Its L&NWR contemporary, No. 7, had also been placed on a duplicate list by the company, together with the Manning, Wardle saddle tank and the two oldest 0-6-0s, No's 2 and 3, these four engines no longer being considered as part of the working stock.

Somewhat confusingly, the E&WJR Board also stated in the same year that they were trying to sell engines No's 1, 3, 4 and 6. The probable reason for these accounting adjustments was that the company had been negotiating with Beyer, Peacock for two more powerful 0-6-0 goods engines, fitted with larger 18in. x 24in. cylinders, bigger boilers and the 'improved Manning, Wardle valve gear', also known as Isaacson's gear, which was intended to reduce coal consumption. Beyer, Peacock offered a price of £3,035 per locomotive, payable as usual by quarterly instalments over four years. The E&WJR Board resolved to order two but also to try and persuade the supplier to reduce the cost, owing to the falling price of copper.

An order was placed but financial pressures obviously forced a reassessment of the situation. A letter from Beyer, Peacock of 16th July 1908 suggested that they might be able to assist by postponing delivery for as long as possible, if the manufacturer were otherwise unable to dispose of the two locomotives that were then on order with them. However, the new E&WJR management regime was quickly taking hold of the situation prior to the full amalgamation into the S&MJR and, eventually, the two locomotives were delivered to Stratford in the last few days of 1908, although they were not added to running stock until the early part of 1909. The new engines became No's 17 and 18, and would prove to be the last locomotives to be purchased by the E&WJR, appearing on the line just as the new regime of the S&MJR was taking over operations. Immediately prior to the official amalgamation, the E&WJR renumbered their four duplicate list locomotives as 01, 02, 03 and 07.

ABOVE & RIGHT: After first considering the purchase of further tender 2-4-0s, the E&WJR management decided that a slightly more powerful version of their traditional Beyer, Peacock 0-6-0 design would be more useful. No's 17 and 18 arrived at Stratford in late December 1908, with the die already cast in terms of the line's amalgamation into the Stratford-upon-Avon & Midland Junction Railway. Although ordered by the E&WJR therefore, the two new locomotives never appeared in that livery and were added to the stock of the new S&MJR company in January 1909. *Both author's collection*

BELOW: One of the last acts of the E&WJR in 1908 was to place four of the older engines on to a duplicate list, adding a '0' in front of their numbers. The remaining L&NWR 'DX' thus became No. 07 and is seen at Stratford along with an old 4-wheeled brake coach, which had similary been placed on the rolling stock duplicate list as No. 05. It was latterly used as a breakdown tool van. *Author's collection*

E&WJR Locomotive Survivors

Most of the locomotives purchased after the resumption of E&WJR passenger services in 1885, plus the old Manning, Wardle saddle tank, passed into the ownership of the Stratford-upon-Avon & Midland Junction Railway on 1st January 1909. The exceptions were two of the ex-L&NWR 'DX' Class goods 0-6-0s which had been acquired in 1891 and the two short-lived tank engines which operated the ER&SJR service to Broom in the first few years. This pair, the Beyer, Peacock 0-6-0ST and the Yorkshire Engine Company 2-4-0T *Hope* were sold out of service but remarkably lived on in use at collieries far longer than any of the other E&WJR locomotives.

The longest lived and perhaps most celebrated of these survivals was that of the 1879-built Beyer, Peacock 0-6-0 saddle tank, which had only lasted on the E&WJR for nine years before being displaced from its duties in 1888. A sale was recorded to the Rothervale Colliery Company of Sheffield in April 1890, so it

appears that the locomotive had either lingered at Stratford unsold for two years or had possibly been released earlier to a third party. The engine was put to work at Treeton Colliery, where it remained in service for a remarkable sixty-nine years, seeing very little change, apart from routine maintenance and a renumbering from the initial *Rothervale No. 1* to an unusual *Rothervale No. 0* in 1929. It is thought that this might have been the result of a mistake by the Yorkshire Engine Co. who, when delivering a new engine to follow the colliery company's previous No. 9, numbered it as No. 1 instead of No. 10. Rothervale then ground off the number '1' from the plate on the older engine and replaced it with a cast brass number '0' which was screwed on in its place. When *Rothervale No. 0* was scrapped in October 1959, by then in the ownership of the National Coal Board, it was the very last survivor from the E&WJR's fleet of locomotives. Both of the plates survived the engine's scrapping and one of them is today on display in the Chasewater Railway Museum in Staffordshire.

RIGHT: A fine action study of the old E&WJR Beyer, Peacock 0-6-0ST hard at work during the 1930s, moving a rake of coal wagons at its long term home, Treeton Colliery, near Sheffield. In a similar manner some fifty years earlier during the 1880s, this tiny locomotive would have been heading off from Broom Junction with a rake of 4- and 6-wheeled coaches. *Author's collection*

BELOW: The locomotive was repainted in the 1930s but, apart from the change of number from '1' to '0' little else had changed since its days at Stratford-upon-Avon. It subsequently led quite a celebrated life at Treeton Colliery and upon surviving into the 1950s, was much sought out and photographed by enthusiasts. It was usually kept in sparkling condition, as in this view taken during March 1952, when it was still in regular use. *Author's collection*

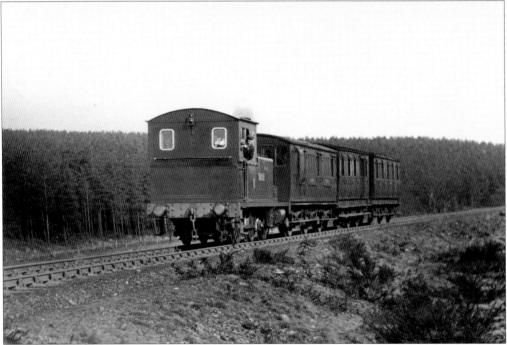

ABOVE & LEFT: After a rather drastic rebuilding into a 0-6-0T in 1916, the Yorkshire Engine Company 0-6-0ST *Hope* was hardly recognisable as the locomotive that had left Stratford way back in 1895. However, as Cannock & Rugeley Collieries No. 8 *Harrison*, it had a long and industrious life, and these two views from the 1950s show it, above, in typical colliery surroundings and, left, operating the daily 'Paddy train', a passenger service operated on the system by the colliery company conveying miners to and from work. Hauling this train of assorted ancient 6-wheeled stock along a single track line must have felt quite familiar to old *Hope*, which spent most of its time on the E&WJR working similar services between Stratford and Broom. *Author's collection*

By coincidence, the locomotive that had replaced the Beyer, Peacock saddle tank at Stratford in 1888 also had a lengthy afterlife at a colliery site. The Yorkshire Engine Company 1872-built 2-4-0 tank *Hope*, which had come via a locomotive dealer from the bankrupt Potteries, Shrewsbury & North Wales Railway, was also only to last a few years at Stratford, being displaced around 1893. The engine had found its way to a new owner, the Cannock & Rugeley Collieries, by 1895, where it was renamed and renumbered, to appear as No. 8 *Harrison* in the colliery fleet. However, unlike its Beyer, Peacock predecessor, after some early cosmetic alterations, it then underwent a far more drastic rebuilding by the colliery company into a rather utilitarian 0-6-0 side tank in 1916, which totally altered its appearance. Nevertheless, it was obviously a useful engine, as it was also destined to last into the National Coal Board era, finally being withdrawn in 1955.

The Carriage and Wagon Stock of the E&WJR – The Early Years

Fortunately far more is known about the carriage and wagon stock of the E&WJR than is the case for the N&BJR, although the record is still far from complete. Once again, the annual Board of Trade statistical returns provide a basic picture of the rolling stock in use on the line. The return for the close of 1871 states that the first section of the E&WJR opened with two carriages and a third vehicle categorised as '*other vehicles attached to passenger traffic*', which was presumably a brake.

Conversely, however, Sidney Smith's description of an early journey on the new line mentions that the train consisted of three vehicles and a brake, whilst the rather indistinct early photograph at Kineton, first published in the *Locomotive Magazine* (see page 161) could support either statement. The railway also possessed six coal wagons at the end of 1871.

The opening of the line throughout from Blisworth to Stratford on 1st July 1873 then brought an immediate need for more rolling stock in addition to the six new locomotives. This was obtained through the '*Birmingham Waggon Company*' on the same annual hire purchase basis spread over ten years. However, it is not clear whether this new rolling stock was actually constructed by that company, or whether they merely arranged the finance and sourced the vehicles from elsewhere, as was the case with the locomotives.

Whatever their origins, by the close of 1874, the rolling stock on the E&WJR had increased dramatically to thirteen carriages, nine other passenger train vehicles and no less than one hundred goods wagons of all types. The apparently large number of wagons may well have been in anticipation of the high volume of iron ore traffic that was expected to be carried by the new railway in its early years.

Contraction in 1875

As has already been related, the financial problems of 1875 resulted in the locomotives, along with most of the other rolling stock, being reclaimed by their financiers, with the result that, at the end of that year, the E&WJR were left with just four carriages and twelve wagons. It is known that these four remaining carriages, two Composites and two Thirds, were actually owned by the E&WJR, so quite possibly included some with which they had started operations back in 1871. All of the goods rolling stock was, however, being hired.

The E&WJR was in the doldrums for the next few years and so few changes occurred in the numbers of rolling stock reported to the Board of Trade at year ends. The passenger carriage stock remained at four until 1879 when, presumably due to the opening of the Broom line, a further three vehicles were added. However, the total then reduced to four again by the end of the following year and remained unaltered through to 1885.

Something is known of the history of one of these carriages, as some years later an old vehicle stood at Stratford, with wheels removed, bearing an inscription: '*SMJ Railway Co. old LN&WRly coach No. 273 built 1850 and worked between Euston and Birmingham from 1850 to 1870. Purchased in 1880 by East & West Junction Rly and used by them until 1908*'. Another old London & Birmingham Railway First Class 4-wheeled coach that had been used on the line in earlier days was later kept by

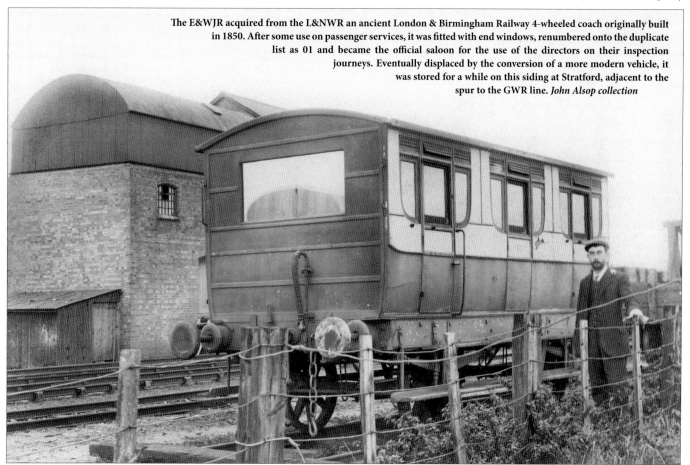

The E&WJR acquired from the L&NWR an ancient London & Birmingham Railway 4-wheeled coach originally built in 1850. After some use on passenger services, it was fitted with end windows, renumbered onto the duplicate list as 01 and became the official saloon for the use of the directors on their inspection journeys. Eventually displaced by the conversion of a more modern vehicle, it was stored for a while on this siding at Stratford, adjacent to the spur to the GWR line. *John Alsop collection*

the E&WJR as their Director's Saloon and at one time was No. 01 on their duplicate list.

The E&WJR goods stock had increased to twenty-two vehicles from the low point of twelve in 1875 and apart from a few fluctuations, was maintained at around this level until 1883, when a reduction was suddenly made to twelve again.

Expansion After 1885

The renovation of the line during 1884, as part of the agreement with the Stratford, Towcester & Midland Junction Railway, heralded a welcome revival in the fortunes of the E&WJR and also saw a reintroduction of passenger services between Blisworth and Stratford, from 22nd March 1885. New rolling stock was again needed and a batch of eleven new air-braked, 4-wheeled coaches was obtained from the Birmingham Railway Carriage & Wagon Company. These consisted of four First and Second Class Composite coaches, numbered 6 to 9 by the E&WJR, four Thirds numbered 10 to 13 and three Third Brakes numbered 14 to 16. These have been described as 'internally cramped' but were no doubt a definite improvement over the selection of stock that had carried the line through the difficult years to 1885.

Three other unspecified vehicles for use on passenger trains must also have been obtained during the year, as at the close of 1885, the statistical returns indicated the ownership of these in addition to the fifteen passenger vehicles. It is possible that they were horse boxes.

The goods stock had also been greatly enhanced, with the company now owning a total of forty-seven vehicles of all types. This set the pattern for the next ten years, with no variation being seen in the numbers of either passenger or goods stock until 1895, apart from a few small annual fluctuations of miscellaneous goods wagons.

The introduction of passenger services in 1892 over the newly opened line from Towcester to Ravenstone Wood did not necessitate the purchase of any additional stock, as the required carriages were hired from the Midland Railway. This was perhaps just as well, as the service only operated for a matter of three months.

The Joint Committee Years

The E&WJR belatedly joined with the ST&MJR and the ER&SJR in the formation of a Joint Committee, as originally provide for under the Act of 1883, although the three companies in many ways continued to act independently. Neither of the other two companies reported any ownership of rolling stock to the Board of Trade, with all vehicles continuing to be stated as being owned by the E&WJR.

The ST&MJR opened their line from Towcester to Ravenstone Wood Junction, on the MR's Bedford to Northampton line, in 1891. Several contractor's locomotives are known to have been used on the construction of the line, including a Black, Hawthorn 0-6-0 saddle tank named *Gavin* (Works No. 471/1881), and two Manning, Wardle 0-4-0 saddle tanks, *Hesketh* (Works No. 634/1877) and the other un-named but Works No. 900 of 1884.

One of the Beyer, Peacock 2-4-0Ts stands at Stratford-upon-Avon station Up platform, with a Blisworth train comprised of a horse box and three of the 4-wheeled carriages purchased from the Birmingham Railway Carriage & Wagon Company in 1885, for the reinstatement of passenger services in that year. The carriage livery would appear to be cream or white upper panels, with lake or, as described in some accounts, chocolate below the waistline. However, contemporary newspaper reports speak of these carriages being 'light brown' when first delivered, so they may possibly have been repainted in this full E&WJR livery in subsequent years. *Author's collection*

LEFT: The 0-6-0 *Carlisle*, which had a long career with various railway contractors, may have been used on the construction of the ST&MJR line. A letter from one E.C.B. Ashford in the *Railway Magazine* for October 1941 states that, after use on the Aston widening contract, *Carlisle* was then working in the Blisworth area, probably on the new line from Towcester to the MR at Ravenstone Wood Junction. *Minor Railways of England and Their Locomotives* notes it being used on the construction of 'certain lines that later became part of the S&MJR'. Built by Kitson & Co. in 1867, it is pictured here in later life on the Bishop's Castle Railway. *Author's collection*

BELOW: The first of a selection of the few known photographs of E&WJR rolling stock, after they had passed on into the ownership of the S&MJR on 1st January 1909. This ex-E&WJR brake van became SMJ No. 36. *Author's collection*

BOTTOM: SMJ No. 26 was an ex-E&WJR 8-ton horse box. Horse traffic was an important source of revenue for the line. *Author's collection*

These engines were apparently first used by Watson, Smith & Watson but when that company went into receivership in 1885, they passed to the new sub-contractor Baldry & Yerburgh. The latter company are also thought to have used an ex-L&NWR locomotive on the same contract but details are unclear.

One other notable engine which may have been used on the construction of the line was the Kitson tender 0-6-0 *Carlisle* (Works No. 1421/1868) which later performed on the Bishop's Castle Railway but was noted as having being employed at one time on 'certain lines which later became part of the S&MJR'.

A few significant variations in the totals of E&WJR rolling stock did occur in the final years through to amalgamation into the S&MJR, although the number of passenger carriages remained static at twelve until 1908.

Four more horse boxes were obtained from the Birmingham RC&W Co. in 1898, reflecting the growing importance of this traffic to the line. Other goods stock was slowly added until a total of seventy-five wagons were owned in 1903 but, in the next year, there was a sudden increase to 150 vehicles. These arrived on the line in November and were seventy-five 10-ton goods wagons, once again obtained from the Birmingham RC&W Co. at a cost of £65 10s each.

The need for these additional vehicles is difficult to attribute but it is noticeable that the increase is reflected by a similarly dramatic upturn in the tonnage of mineral traffic carried by the line, which escalated from around 64,000 tons in 1903, to 109,000 in the following year. As the additional traffic had presumably originated on the E&WJR system, it seems likely that it was due to increased production

The return to the Board of Trade for the end of December 1908, the last year of the existence of the E&WJR, shows the following rolling stock available for handover to the S&MJR:

Passenger carriages.. 8
Other vehicles for attachment to passenger traffic.............. 8
Goods wagons of all kinds... 147
Other carriages and wagons not included in the above 1

LEFT: An E&WJR cattle wagon, carrying SMJ No. 62. *Author's collection*

BELOW: SMJ No. 31 was another brake van. All of the ex-E&WJR carriages and goods wagons were added in to the S&MJR fleet and so were given new numbers. *Author's collection*

BOTTOM: Another ex-E&WJR horse box, which became SMJ No. 20. Note the horse boxes had solid passenger vehicle wheels, not the spoked type used on goods wagons. *Author's collection*

of iron ore, some of which was now originating from the quarries in the Easton Neston area and being carried by the newly united lines of the joint committee.

An additional five coal wagons and fifteen open wagons were also hired from the same source at the same time, whilst quotations were requested for the supply of more horse boxes, timber wagons, goods brake vans and box wagons. In the event, the E&WJR took delivery during 1905 of four further horse boxes, four cattle wagons, eight bolster trucks for timber and two goods brake vans; all were arranged on the usual deferred terms.

The year of 1908 saw a surprising reduction in the number of passenger carriages in use on the line, with only eight then being in use. There was a corresponding small reduction in the numbers of goods wagons and other passenger type vehicles, which may well have been due to early rationalisation by the new management. Nevertheless, two more brake vans had been ordered, this time 6-wheeled versions from Harrison & Camm, at £253 each and ten ballast wagons were also taken on hire at £9 2s per annum, in lieu of outright purchase. The reason for this slight reduction is perhaps explained by a letter received early in 1908 from the Birmingham RC&W Co., agreeing to a deferment of the hire purchase instalments due in June and September, upon payment of an additional 4% annual interest.

Towards the end of that year and probably in readiness for the official amalgamation into the S&MJR, the E&WJR renumbered their duplicate stock vehicles as follows:

Composite carriage 01
Van... 05
Third Class & Brake carriages........................... 014, 015, 016
Horse boxes 017
Goods wagons.. 01 to 07, 09, 010
Cattle wagons... 044, 045

The East & West Junction Railway Liveries

More is also known about the liveries applied to E&WJR locomotives and rolling stock than that of its near neighbour, the N&BJR, although there are still some conflicting statements. Although numerous photographs were taken which do show much useful information in terms of detail, they

The Manning, Wardle 0-6-0ST obtained from the contractors Crampton & Company, seen here posed outside Stratford-upon-Avon engine shed in fully lined E&WJR livery but bearing no corporate identity or numbering. The base livery colour of this engine has been described as 'chocolate brown' but this may well be a subjective reference to dark lake, which is also recorded as being applied to early E&WJR locomotives. The combination of smoke gently issuing from the tank engine's chimney and the proximity of another, larger locomotive behind has led to a slightly odd looking 'ghosting' effect on the latter's chimney. It is clear from many of these photographs that the engine crews and shed staff took a real pride in looking after the locomotive's in the E&WJR's small fleet. Note the lock on the tool box mounted on the footplate just behind the front bufferbeam. *Author's collection*

RIGHT: This poor quality but very early view of Beyer, Peacock 0-6-0 No. 3 at Stratford shows a part lined livery style but no sign of ownership and only a painted numeral on the cabside. *Author's collection*

BELOW: Another view of the early E&WJR locomotive livery is provided by Westinghouse brake fitted No. 4 at Stratford on an Up passenger train, reportedly in 1892. Once again, no company identification is visible, whilst the engine number appears to be simply painted onto the cabside and there is no sign of a number on the bufferbeam. At this period, the lining seems to have extended only to the tender and cab sides, and the sandboxes. Frames and bufferbeams were not lined, and the boiler bands appear polished rather than lined. *Author's collection*

BELOW: A further and possibly unique variation on the E&WJR locomotive livery is provided by 0-6-0 No. 10. Most unusually, ownership is announced on both tender and cabside, the latter on a brass plate combined with the engine number. No other photographic evidence has been seen to date showing this variation on another of the E&WJR's engines. It would also appear from careful study of the scan under heavy magnification that No. 10 is in a plain unlined version of the E&WJR livery. *Author's collection*

unfortunately cannot provide absolute confirmation of the base livery colours that were used.

The earliest locomotive livery seems to have been crimson lake, with black lining edged on both sides by yellow. Photographic evidence also shows burnished brass domes, chimney caps and other brightwork. However, some authorities state that this early livery was in fact brown and the Manning, Wardle 0-6-0 saddle tank is certainly recorded as having appeared in this colour at one time. It is of course possible that both claims are correct and that the earliest E&WJR livery was a dark crimson lake, which could easily have been considered to be brownish in hue in certain circumstances, particularly when the weathering of paint is taken into account.

Engine numbers were carried on the cab sides, initially as small painted numerals and then later on cast metal number plates with scalloped corners. The engine number was also to be found on the bufferbeam, in the form of polished raised numerals. Ownership was indicated by a larger but similarly shaped cast plate, bearing the initials 'E&W' and fixed to the tender or tank sides.

A variation was, however, found on engine No. 10, which carried a larger combined plate on its cabside, with the initials 'E&W' above the number but also had the usual ownership plate on the tender side. The Manning, Wardle 0-6-0 saddle tank also varied in having painted 'E&W' initials on its tank sides at one time but was also photographed without any form of company identity. It also appears to have only carried the number '1' on the bufferbeam.

The theory has long held that the trio of ex-L&NWR 'DX' Class goods locomotives remained in the standard unlined black livery of their former owners after their arrival on the E&WJR, although they did receive the usual cast cab and tender plates. However, the photograph of No. 8 at Stratford shed clearly shows traces of lining on the locomotive and tender, so it now appears the case that the E&WJR may well have painted all three in their own livery.

These two views of the Manning, Wardle 0-6-0ST provide a glimpse of a later livery style from 1904, with the engine still bearing the fully-lined chocolate or perhaps lake livery. The initials 'E & W' were now painted on the tank side and 'No. 1' was in cast numerals on the bufferbeam; however, no number is shown on the cabside. The clerestory roofed bogie carriage is a Great Central Railway vehicle. *Both author's collection*

A change appears to have been made to the locomotive livery in the early years of the 20th century. A contemporary article by T.R. Perkins on the Railways of Warwickshire, in the usually reliable *Railway Magazine* in November 1902, states that the locomotives of the E&WJR *'have bright brass dome covers and are painted black, with broad green lines edged with yellow'*. A further variation has also been suggested, with the 2-4-0 passenger engine No. 13 said to have arrived on the line in 1903 in a lined dark blue livery, with the next five 0-6-0s, No's 14 to 18, also following suit. This is impossible to verify from photographic evidence and these engines may also have been black.

There is little more certainty about the E&WJR coaching stock livery. Initially this seems to have been crimson lake, with the narrow waist panels picked out in cream or white. However, some accounts again state that the main colour was actually chocolate brown. Photographs also appear to show E&WJR carriages with the lower panels in what was probably crimson or possibly chocolate livery, with the upper half of the sides in cream or white. Intriguingly however, a newspaper report covering the reinstatement of E&WJR passenger services in 1885 speaks of *'new light brown carriages'* that were now running on the line. This may refer to the varnished teak style that was used on some railways and it is possible that the carriages were supplied from the manufacturer's stock in a standard livery to avoid delay.

Few detailed photographs or records exist to confirm the ownership style carried by coaching stock but a circular armorial device, consisting of a buckled belt containing the legend 'East & West Junction Railway', is known to have existed.

Only one clear photograph of a goods wagon in E&WJR livery has so far been located, an official view of a new 4-wheeled timber bolster. The base livery appears to be a mid-grey colour, with black ironwork and the legend 'E.& W.J.R.' in unshaded white, spaced along the full length of the body side. A small cast plate on the solebar carried 'E&WJR No. 102'.

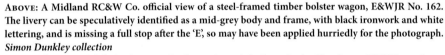
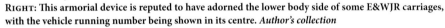

ABOVE: A Midland RC&W Co. official view of a steel-framed timber bolster wagon, E&WJR No. 162. The livery can be speculatively identified as a mid-grey body and frame, with black ironwork and white lettering, and is missing a full stop after the 'E', so may have been applied hurriedly for the photograph. *Simon Dunkley collection*

RIGHT: This armorial device is reputed to have adorned the lower body side of some E&WJR carriages, with the vehicle running number being shown in its centre. *Author's collection*

ANALYSIS OF E&WJR LOCOMOTIVES AND ROLLING STOCK 1871-1908

From yearly returns to the Board of Trade

As at Dec 31st:	1871	1872	1873	1874	1875	1876	1877	1878	1879	1880	1881	1882	1883
Engines / Tenders	1 / 0	1 / 0	7 / 3	6 / 3	3 / 2	4 / 1	3 / 0	4 / 2	4 / 2	5 / 3	5 / 3	5 / 2	5 / 2
Carriages	2	2	20	13	4	4	4	4	7	4	4	4	4
Other pass vehicles	1	1	11	9	0	0	1	0	0	0	0	0	
Wagons all types	6	6	93	100	12	22	20	11	22	22	22	20	12
Other rolling stock	0	0	0	0	0	0	2	1	0	0	0	2	

As at Dec 31st:	1884	1885	1886	1887	1888	1889	1890	1891	1892	1893	1894	1895	1896
Engines / Tenders	4 / 2	7 / 4	7 / 4	7 / 4	7 / 4	7 / 4	7 / 4	7 / 4	10 / 7	9 / 6	9 / 6	10 / 7	11 / 8
Carriages	4	15	15	15	15	15	15	15	15	15	12	12	12
Other pass vehicles		3	3	3	3	3	3	3	3	3	3	3	3
Wagons all types	12	46	46	42	42	42	42	45	42	42	41	41	43
Other rolling stock		1	1	5	5	5	5	1	4	4	4	6	7

As at Dec 31st:	1897	1898	1899	1900	1901	1902	1903	1904	1905	1906	1907	1908	
Engines / Tenders	11 / 8	11 / 8	11 / 8	12 / 9	12 / 9	12 / 9	13 / 10	14 / 11	14 / 11	15 / 12	15 / 12	10 / 8	
Carriages	12	12	12	12	12	12	12	12	12	12	12	8	
Other pass vehicles	3	7	7	7	7	7	7	7	11	11	11	8	
Wagons all types	63	67	67	67	75	75	75	150	159	159	156	147	
Other rolling stock	7	9	9	9	1	1	1	1	1	1	1	1	

Volume 2

The story of the Stratford-upon-Avon & Midland Junction Railway will be continued in Volume 2. This will cover the short period of independent ownership by the S&MJR from 1909 to 1923, during which the Northampton & Banbury Railway company was absorbed. After this, it will look at the years under London, Midland & Scottish Railway ownership between 1923 and 1948 and, finally, life under the nationalised British Railways regime, through to closure of the line in the 1960s. In addition, the route and features of the S&MJR will be fully described by way of a journey along the line and the present day remains of the railway will also be examined. The full contents for Volume 2 are given below.

CONTENTS TO VOL. 2

Appendix 1.1
OPENING AND CLOSURE DATES OF LINES

Section		BoT inspection date	Opened passengers	Opened goods	Closed passengers	Closed goods	Notes
Blisworth-Towcester	N&BJR	16/4/1866	1/5/1866	1/5/1866	7/4/1952	3/2/1964	A, G
Fenny Compton-Kineton	E&WJR	3/6/1871	5/6/1871	5/6/1871	7/4/1952	15/3/1965	B, G
Towcester-Cockley Brake Jct	N&BJR	29/5/1871	1/6/1872	Early1871	2/7/1951	29/10/1951	
Green's Norton Jct-Fenny Compton	E&WJR	26-27/6/1873	1/7/1873	1/7/1873	7/4/1952	3/2/1964	E, G
Kineton-Stratford-upon-Avon	E&WJR	26-27/6/1873	1/7/1873	1/7/1873	7/4/1952	15/3/1965	G
Stratford spur to GWR	E&WJR	4/8/1873	Not used	-/8/1873	Not used	15/3/1965	
Stratford-on-Avon station -Broom Junction	ER&SJR	23/9/1878	2/6/1879	2/6/1879	16/6/1947	13/6/1960	C
Towcester-Ravenstone Wood Jct	ST&MJR	17/5/1890	1/12/1892	13/4/1891	30/3/1893	30/6/1958	D, F
Roade spur to L&NWR	ST&MJR	17/9/1890	Not used	13/4/1891	Not used	24/5/1917	
Woodford West Jct-Woodford & Hinton	GCR		15/3/1899	15/3/1899	31/5/1948	15/3/1965	E
Woodford West Jct-Woodford South Jct	GCR		15/3/1899	15/3/1899	22/10/1900	22/10/1900	
Broom new curve	LM&SR		n/a	29/9/1942	n/a	13/6/1960	
Fenny Compton new conn WR to SMJ line	BR		n/a	7/3/1960	n/a	open	
Stratford-on-Avon new conn SMJ line to WR	BR		n/a	13/6/1960	n/a	15/3/1965	

The above closure dates to passengers are the officially used 'on and from' dates, with last trains actually running on the previous normal operating day.

A – Section from Blisworth station to RT&B Ironstone at Gayton remained open until 30/9/1967

B – Section from Fenny Compton to Kineton WD depot taken over by the Army from 28/7/1971 – remains open; closure date above refers to line beyond that point to Stratford

C – Stratford to Broom passenger services suspended as from 16/6/1947, permanent withdrawal from 23/5/1949

D – Line closed temporarily 30/6/1958 for motorway construction – not reopened as through route. Severed at Roade 1960 then used as two sidings for stock storage until 1964

E – The section from Woodford West Junction to Byfield remained open until 1/6/1965 to allow removals from Byfield Ironstone Siding

F – Opened to local goods traffic 13/4/1891 and through goods traffic from 2/7/1891

G – Passenger traffic suspended between Blisworth and Stratford from 23/7/1875, and reinstated 22/3/1885

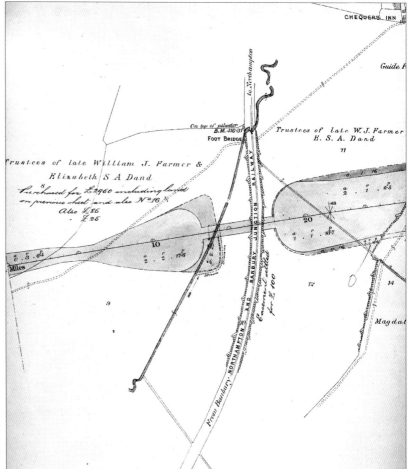

An early 1890s plan graphically illustrating how the massive embankment and viaduct of the MS&LR extension carved through the countryside near Helmdon and across the existing route of the N&BJR. *Author's collection*

Appendix 1.2
A CHECKLIST OF STATIONS AND SIDINGS

LOCATION	COMPANY	TYPE	OPENED PASS	OPENED GOODS	CLOSED PASS	CLOSED GOODS	NOTES
Blisworth	N&BJR	Station	1/5/1866	1/5/1866	7/4/1952	3/2/1964	A, B
Blisworth exchange sidings	N&BJR/L&NWR	Siding	n/a	1/5/1866	n/a	30/9/1967	
Blisworth RT&B siding	LM&SR	Siding		(i) 20/12/1941		(i) 1943	
				(ii) 1954		(ii) 30/9/1967	
Blisworth engine shed	N&BJR	MPD	Op 1/5/1866		Cl 1929		
Wheldon's siding (various locations)	N&BJR	Siding		By 1878		-/5/1927	
Tiffield	N&BJR	Station	-/10/1869	n/a	-/2/1871	n/a	C
Lloyd's siding	N&BJR	Siding	n/a	1/9/1873	n/a	By 1883	
Towcester East Junction	N&BJR/S&TJR	Junction	1/12/1892	13/4/1891	30/3/1893	30/6/1958	
Towcester	N&BJR	Station	1/5/1866	1/5/1866	7/4/1952	3/2/1964	
Towcester engine shed	N&BJR	MPD					D
Towcester junction	S&MJR	Junction	13/6/1910	13/6/1910	7/4/1952	3/2/1964	
Green's Norton Junction	N&BJR/E&WJR	Junction	1/7/1873	1/7/1873	13/6/1910	13/6/1910	
Kingthorn Wood	E&WJR	Station					O
Blakesley	E&WJR	Station	1/7/1873	1/7/1873	7/4/1952	3/2/1964	
Morton Pinkney	E&WJR	Station	1/7/1873	1/7/1873	7/4/1952	3/2/1964	
Woodford West Junction	E&WJR/GCR	Junction	15/3/1899	15/3/1899	7/4/1952	3/2/1964	
Woodford North curve	E&WJR/GCR	Connection	15/3/1899	15/3/1899	31/5/1948	3/2/1964	
Woodford South Curve	E&WJR/GCR	Connection	9/3/1899	9/3/1899	22/10/1900	22/10/1900	
Byfield	E&WJR	Station	1/7/1873	1/7/1873	7/4/1952	15/3/1965	
Byfield Ironstone siding	E&WJR	Siding	n/a	-/5/1915	n/a	1/6/1965	F
Aston-le-Walls siding	E&WJR	Siding	n/a	1910	n/a	5/1/1953	
Fenny Compton	E&WJR	Station	5/6/1871	5/6/1871	7/4/1952		
Fenny Compton exchange siding	E&WJR/GWR	Siding	n/a	5/6/1871	n/a		
North End	E&WJR	Station	-/8/1872	n/a	-/8/1877		G, O
Fenny Compton connection	BR	Connection		7/3/1960		Still in use	
Warwick Road	E&WJR	Station	-/12/1871	n/a	-/6/1873	n/a	H, O
Burton Dassett siding	E&WJR	Siding	n/a	c. 1873	n/a	11/11/1963	I
EHLR junction	E&WJR/EHLR	Junction	n/a	1/3/1922	n/a	27/1/1925	
West End sidings & Junction	LMS/WD	Sdgs/Junc	n/a	c. 1940	n/a	Still in use	J
Kineton	E&WJR	Station	5/6/1871	5/6/1871	7/4/1952	15/3/1965	
Ettington	E&WJR	Station	1/7/1873	1/7/1873	7/4/1952	15/3/1965	
Ettington limestone siding	E&WJR	Siding	n/a	By 1907	n/a	By 1916	
Clifford Sidings	E&WJR	Siding	n/a	By 1885	n/a	4/11/1963	K
Stratford-upon-Avon	E&WJR	Station	1/7/1873	1/7/1873	7/4/1952	15/3/1965	
Stratford-upon-Avon engine shed	E&WJR	MPD					
Stratford north curve	E&WJR/GWR	Connection	n/a	-/8/1873	n/a	15/3/1965	
Stratford south curve	BR	Connection		13/6/1960		15/3/1965	
Binton	ER&SJR	Station	2/6/1879	2/6/1879	16/6/1947	13/6/1960	
Bidford (Canada) brick siding	ER&SJR	Siding	n/a	8/11/1879	n/a	13/6/1960	
Bidford	ER&SJR	Station	1881	After 1916	16/6/1947		
Bidford station siding	ER&SJR	Siding		After 1916		After 1921	L
Broom East Junction	LM&SR	Junction		17/5/1942	16/6/1947	13/6/1960	
Broom West Junction	LM&SR	Junction	n/a	29/9/1942	n/a	13/6/1960	
Broom (North) Junction	E&WJR/MR	Junction	2/6/1879	2/6/1879	16/6/1947	13/6/1960	
Broom Junction	ER&SJR	Station	2/6/1879	2/6/1879	16/6/1947	13/6/1960	M, N
Bradden bridge	N&BJR	Goods station	n/a	1866	n/a	Early 1871	E
Wappenham	N&BJR	Station	1/6/1872	Early1871	2/7/1951	29/10/1951	
Helmdon	N&BJR	Station	1/6/1872	Early1871	2/7/1951	29/10/1951	
Helmdon connections	N&BJR/GCR	Connection	n/a	18/11/1895	n/a	By 1897	
Cockley Brake Junction	N&BJR/LNWR	Junction	1/6/1872	1/6/1872	2/7/1951	29/10/1951	
Ravenstone Wood Junction	ST&MJR/MR	Junction	1/12/1892	13/4/1891	30/3/1893	30/6/1958	
Salcey Forest	ST&MJR	Station	1/12/1892	13/4/1891	30/3/1893	1908	

Location	Company	Type	Opened pass	Opened goods	Closed pass	Closed goods	Notes
Roade Junction	ST&MJR/LNWR	Junction	n/a	13/4/1891	n/a	24/5/1917	
Sturgess siding	ST&MJR	Siding	n/a	27/9/1909	n/a	19/2/1957	
Stoke Bruerne	ST&MJR	Station	1/12/1892	13/4/1891	30/3/1893	1/4/1951	
Showsley siding	ST&MJR	Siding	n/a	27/9/1909	n/a	-/6/1918	
Easton Neston siding	ST&MJR	Siding	n/a	13/4/1891	n/a	22/6/1934	

A – Blisworth N&BJR platforms were refurbished and used as a temporary parcels sorting depot during the early 1960s

B – Joint station building N&BJR / L&NWR opened 1871

C – Dates shown for Tiffield station are those of first and last entries in *Bradshaw's Time Tables*

D – Towcester engine shed is presumed to have opened with the line in 1866. The date of closure is not known but was possibly on the opening of the extension to Banbury in 1872

E – Bradden Bridge was the terminus of the original section of the N&BJR, although passenger services only operated to Towcester. It is known that Bradden was used as a temporary goods depot until the line was extended as far as Helmdon in 1871

F – Byfield Ironstone siding – last traffic handled 12/12/1965 but remained open until 1/6/1965 for clearance of equipment

G – Dates shown for North End station are those of first and last entries in *Bradshaw's Time Tables* – it may also have been a goods siding

H – Dates shown for Warwick Road station are those of first and last entries in *Bradshaw's Time Tables*

I – An unadvertised platform existed at Burton Dassett and was in use intermittently between 1909 and 1946

J – The sidings and access to the Kineton WD depot were in use from 1940 – various alterations were made to the loops and junctions throughout the period to 1968. After 1971 the line from Fenny Compton was owned and operated by the Army

K – Clifford sidings were remodelled during WW2 and a double track section opened to Stratford. A new signal box was opened 27/9/1943

L – A short single siding existed behind the platform at Bidford station but opening and closure dates are not known. It did not appear in *WTT* up to 1916, although photographic evidence suggests that it was in use c1921

M – Broom Junction station opened with the line from Stratford on 2nd June 1879 but only as an exchange platform for the Evesham line. It became a public station from 1st November 1880

N – Passenger services from Stratford to Broom Junction were temporarily withdrawn from 16/6/1947 and permanently from 23/5/1949. The station remained open for Redditch-Evesham line passenger trains until 1/10/1962, when the line south of Redditch to Evesham was closed because of the state of the track. Proper closure procedures were deemed not to have been followed, however, and BR were then forced to operate a substitute bus service between Redditch and Evesham, calling at all of the stations until this requirement had been satisfied. Official closure finally took place on 17/6/1963

O – The E&WJR proposed the use of 'Pick up platforms' for passengers at various points along its route during the early years of operation. North End and Warwick Road stations may have been two of these, as they were included in *Bradshaw's Time Tables* for a number of years. Another was certainly proposed at Kingthorn Wood near Green's Norton but it is not known whether this, or any others, were actually brought into use

Towcester could be described as at the hub of the combined E&WJR and N&BJR systems, with lines radiating off in four directions. This view is another in the series of early postcards of the station during N&BJR days, looking eastwards from the Down platform towards the junction of the Blisworth and Ravenstone Wood lines. The scene is similar to that shown on page 20; coaching stock is again evident in the siding at the end of the Up platform and there is a much clearer view of the wooden structure that is thought to have once been the engine shed. Of most interest, however, is the 3–wheeled self-propelled trolley standing on the Up line, which is known to have been used by Edmund Stanton, the N&BJR traffic manager, for his regular inspection trips. He joined the N&BJR during its very earliest days and served the company loyally until 1910, when he retired upon its amalgamation into the S&MJR. *Author's collection*

INFORMATION SOURCES AND SUGGESTIONS FOR FURTHER READING

PRIMARY SOURCES
The National Archives, Kew
Comparatively few documents have survived from the N&BJR and the E&WJR periods and, with one exception, sadly the essential corporate Minute Books are not amongst them. However, there is still much of use and interest within the files, which mainly consist of Board of Trade reports and correspondence. Most are to be found within the following series:

MT6 – Board of Trade documents and plans, inspection reports and associated correspondence.

MT29 – Collated annual bound volumes of Board of Trade reports.

RAIL – Director's and Shareholder's minute books and journals, plans, correspondence, running power agreements, annual Board of Trade returns and accident reports, *Bradshaw's Time Tables* and guides, private siding agreements, general ephemera and miscellanea.

The Northamptonshire Record Office, Wootton Hall, Northampton
Deposited Parliamentary plans of proposed railway schemes.
General files and references to local railways.
'Unprofitable railway companies in England and Wales 1845 to 1923, with special reference to the south Midlands' – an unpublished thesis by N.M. Mason, University of London, 1982.

The British Newspaper Archive
This modern on-line resource has been of great assistance in filling gaps in the available archived information, and has also provided an essential chronology of the construction and operation of the various railway companies.
The pages of the *Banbury Guardian*, *Leamington Spa Advertiser* and *Northampton Mercury* have been particularly useful in this respect, and many miscellaneous references are to be found in various other regional and national newspapers.

SECONDARY SOURCES
Books
A History of the Railways of Northamptonshire, P. Butler, Silver Link Publishing, 2006
A History of the Stratford-upon-Avon & Midland Junction Railway, R.C. Riley & B. Simpson, Lamplight Publications, 1999
An Account of the Signalling of the S.M.J., M. Christensen, privately published, c1975
An Illustrated History of the Ashchurch to Barnt Green Line, R.J. Essery, Oxford Publishing Company, 2002
Branch Lines Around Towcester, V. Mitchell & K. Smith, Middleton Press, 2008
Great Central, Vols 2 & 3, George Dow, Locomotive Publishing Company/Ian Allan, 1962 & 1965
Industrial Locomotives of Buckinghamshire, Bedfordshire & Northamptonshire, Robin Waywell, Industrial Railway Society, 2001
LMS Engine Sheds Vol. 4, The Smaller English Constituents, Chris Hawkins & George Reeve, Wild Swan, 1984
Shakespeare's Railways, J. Boynton, Mid England Books, 1994
The Banbury to Verney Junction Branch, B. Simpson, Oxford Publishing Company, 1978
The Branch Lines of Warwickshire, C.G. Maggs, Sutton Publishing, 1994
The Chronicles of Boulton's Sidings, A.R. Bennett, Locomotive Publishing Company, 1927
The Fairlie Locomotive, R.S. Abbott, David & Charles, 1970

The Ironstone Quarries of the Midlands: Part II Oxfordshire, E.S. Tonks, Runpast Publishing, 1988
The Ironstone Quarries of the Midlands: Part III Northamptonshire, E.S. Tonks, Runpast Publishing, 1989
Minor Railways of England and Their Locomotives, G. Woodcock, Goose, 1970
The Northampton & Banbury Junction Railway, S.C. Jenkins, Oakwood Press, 1989
The Railways of Buckinghamshire from the 1830s: An account of those that were built as well as those which were not, F.G. Cockman, Buckinghamshire Archaeological Society, 2006
The Railways of Northamptonshire, D. Blagrove, Wharfside Publications 2005
The Redditch & Evesham Line, Bob Yate, Oakwood Press, 2014
The Stratford-upon-Avon & Midland Junction Railway, J.M. Dunn, Oakwood Press 1952, and fully revised and extended edition J.W.P. Rowledge, 1977
The Stratford-upon-Avon & Midland Junction Railway: The Shakespeare Route, A. Jordan, Oxford Publishing Company, 1982
Track Layout Diagrams of the Great Western Railway & B.R. Western Region: Section 29. S&MJR, R.A.Cooke, 2017
Woodford Halse: A Railway Community, R. Irons & S.C. Jenkins, Oakwood Press, 1999

Magazine Articles
Banbury Merton Street, *British Railway Journal* No. 70
Broom Junction, *British Railway Journal LMS Special*, 1988
Towcester, *British Railway Journal* No. 76
Locomotives Illustrated No. 161, April-June 2006
The Locomotive Magazine, notably April, May 1902, October 1911, February 1907,
The Railway Magazine, 1902, April 1910, 1912,

Railway Modellers Should Also See:
Model Railway Constructor June 1960 – Plans of L&YR 2-4-0 crane tank No. 518, ex-E&WJR
Model Railway News August 1961 – plans of S&MJR (ex-E&WJR) wagon and van
Model Railway News March 1963 – Byfield and Stratford signal boxes
Model Railway News January 1964 – Ettington station and goods shed
Model Railway News September 1970 – Plans of E&WJR Manning, Wardle 0-6-0ST
Model Railway News (unknown date) – Plans of M&SWJR Beyer, Peacock 2-4-0T (identical to E&WJR No's 5 & 6)
Railway Modeller March & July 1968 – Blakesley station
The Historical Model Railway Society archive also includes plans of S&MJR goods wagons, vans, coaches and a horse box.

In addition, the pages of a multitude of other magazines and journals, both society and commercially produced, have also provided many references, anecdotes and photographs relating to the S&MJR. The publications of the Railway Correspondence & Travel Society, the Stephenson Locomotive Society, the Industrial Locomotive Society, the Industrial Railway Society and the Historical Model Railway Society have been particularly informative in this respect.

Mention should also be made of the 'Unofficial SMJ Society' website (thesmjr.ning.com), which contains a wide variety of information and photographs of the line.

INDEX TO VOLUME 1

N&BJR trains ended their journeys from Blisworth and Towcester in the L&NWR terminus at Banbury Merton Street; once again running powers were necessary, on this occasion over the latter railway's Bletchley Branch from the remote location of Cockley Brake Junction. This view, taken from an elevated position at the end of the single island platform, looks southwards towards the station signal box and L&NWR locomotive shed, with Banbury gasworks dominant on the right. The GWR main line and station are also off camera to the right beyond the gas holder, and a goods siding was provided through that area for the exchange of traffic between the two railways. Also notable is the interesting array of vents and lamps on the roof of the ex-L&NWR passenger brake van in the foreground. In the distance it can just be discerned that trains are signalled into both the L&NWR and GWR stations. *C.L. Mowat*

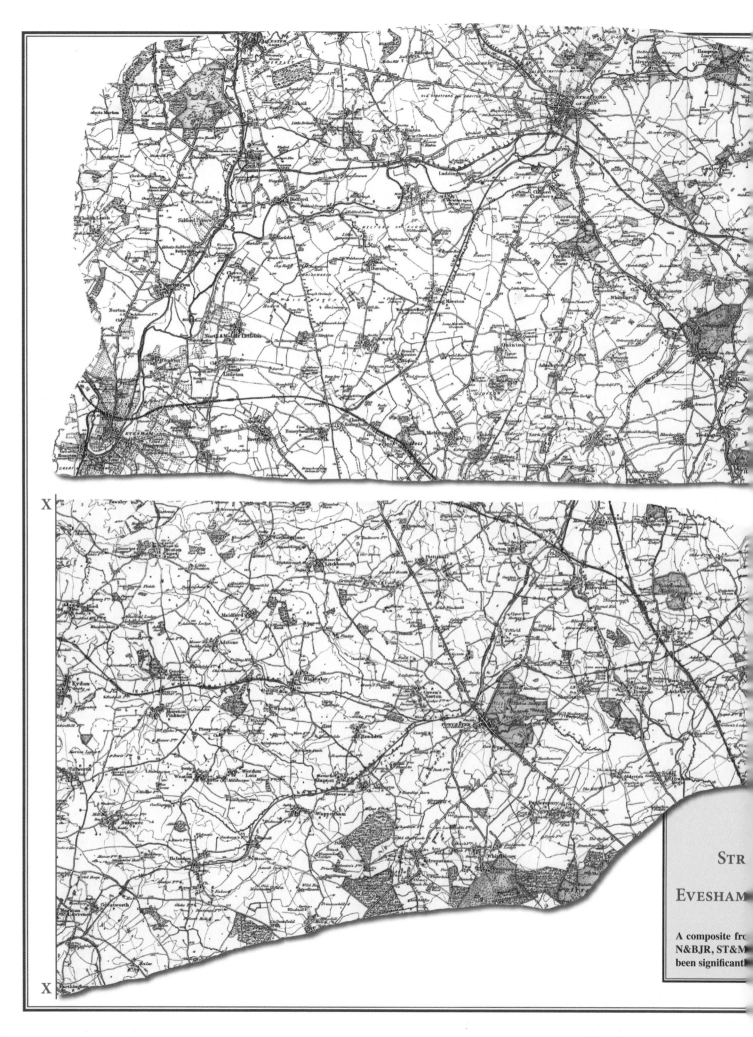

X

X

STR

EVESHAM

A composite fro
N&BJR, ST&M
been significantl